D0915067

The Friars Club
Encyclopedia of
JOKES

The Friars Club
Encyclopedia of
JOKES

Over 2,000 One-Liners, Straight Lines, Stories, Gags, Roasts, Ribs, and Put-Downs

*Compiled by Barry Dougherty
and H. Aaron Cohl*

Tess Press

PUBLISHED BY

Black Dog & Leventhal Publishers, Inc.
151 West 19th Street
New York, NY 10011

DISTRIBUTED BY

Workman Publishing Company
225 Varick Street
New York, NY 10014

Interior Design by Liz Trovato

Manufactured in the United States of America

ISBN-13: 978-1-60376-299-1

h g f e d c b

Library of Congress Cataloging-in-Publication Data available upon request

A Little Credit

The Friars Club has been the bastion of laughter longer than anyone can remember. They started in 1904 and while a few people around here may think they can recall those early days—trust me, they can't even recall the ham on rye they had an hour ago.

This private club that is home to actors, singers, dancers, musicians—and yes, even doctors, lawyers, and dentists—has been lucky to have among them the top comedians of all time. The Friars know a lot about comedy and their legendary roasts have been talked about, copied, trespassed, appalled, revered, scorned, applauded, and just plain loved for quite some time.

When the Friars first started there were no comedy clubs, no TV, no Internet—if you wanted to hear a joke you had to rely on your unfunny co-worker or annoying brother-in-law. And, if you wanted to tell one, you had to remember the countless jokes floating around the atmosphere. Thankfully today, with one-stop shopping, all you have to do is pick up *The Friars Club Encyclopedia of Jokes*, find a joke, any joke, and viola! Instant laughs.

But while you're telling those jokes, or listening to them, or just reading them to yourself, try to remember the men and women behind the funny. If it weren't for these comedians and other amusing sorts it would be a very quiet read. The Friars Club is proud of its roster of jokesters who will keep the laughs intact for the next hundred or so years until they need to upgrade the yuks. It's these brave souls who stand naked on a stage and throw caution to the wind hoping (and maybe a little praying) that when they finish talking the room will be noisy as hell from laughter.

To Ben Barto and Caleb Larson who worked their magic to research the laughs, I say—the book is out now, go buy it. To Howard Cohl, who started the ball rolling on the Friars book journey, don't just sit there—start thinking up more ideas! To the Friars Executive Director Michael Gyure and Executive Director Emeritus Jean-Pierre Trebot who love a good guffaw—forget the Club Managers Handbook, THIS is how you run a club—with laughs.

To Freddie Roman, the Dean of the Friars Club and master joker, thank you for inspiring so many young comics to ply their trade at the Friars. The Club has opened doors and introduced recent headliners and television superstars to the general public—apologies for those with no sense of humor that don't get the monumental significance of that. And to all of you who love a good laugh…enjoy the read.

—Barry Dougherty

Contents

Introduction

All the Friars Club ever did for me is put me on national television and tell everyone who would listen how many men I've had sex with. Not to mention all the times I've done it wearing a dress and how unfunny I am. Oh, and according to the Friars, I didn't deserve any of my money.

Old hat, really.

The Friars Club has been roasting celebrities since 1950. You know all those Dean Martin and Comedy Central roasts? The Friars Club did it first, and does it better. Mine happened to be the first one they ever broadcast on television (dirty words and all), so a record Comedy Central audience got to hear about my appalling sexual habits and lack of talent.

So that's what the Friars are known for. Roasting people.

What you probably don't know is what most people do at the Friars Club. They sit around and tell jokes. Some drink, some don't. Sometimes there's a little dinner. But they all tell jokes to one another. And jokes at the Friars Club are like hundred dollar bills at a casino. The more good ones you have the more people like you.

You are now holding in your hands the latest edition of the best of these jokes. It's like...oh I don't know...one of those stupid emails that one friend of yours always sends you with all the jokes in it. But in a book.

And I'm writing the foreword to this Big Book of Stolen Jokes because the night the Friars roasted me was one of the greatest nights in my life. All the jokes about my little dick and how fat I am...I loved them. The tales of my tremendously gay oral skills and overly hospitable anal cavity were like big hugs. And the more cross-dressing they said I did, the more I wanted to lay down my life for them.

But that other stuff? Up yours, Friars. I AM funny, and I deserve every dollar I've ever made.

Love,
Drew Carey
October 2008

A

Actors and Acting

How many actors does it take to change a lightbulb?

One hundred. One to change the bulb, and ninety-nine to say, "I could have done that."

—NORM CROSBY

I'm walking to work, up Sixth Avenue, and it's a lovely spring day and I see one of those mime performers. So the mime is doing that famous routine where he's pretending to be trapped in a box. So I stand there and watch the mime pretend to be trapped in a box. And he finishes up, and, thank God, he wasn't really trapped in a box. And I see on the sidewalk there he's got a little hat for money—change, tips, donations, contributions. So I went over and I pretended to put a dollar bill in his hat.

—DAVID LETTERMAN

The great actor was known for his many romances coast to coast, and over the years he was faced with many paternity suits. One day a young man came into his dressing room and introduced himself. "I'm your son," he said.

The Great One looked intently at the youth, then exclaimed, "So you are!" He turned to his valet and said, "Give the boy a pass."

—JOEY ADAMS

Playing Shakespeare is so tiring. You never get a chance to sit down unless you're a king.

—JOSEPHINE HULL

John Barrymore once said, "One of my chief regrets is that I can't sit in the audience and watch me."

—Joey Adams

The bum chose matinee time, when the streets of the theater district were crowded with people hurrying to get to the show, to do his panhandling. Sizing up a well-dressed gentleman, he lurched over and asked politely, "Sir, may I borrow a quarter?"

The well-heeled man looked over the top of his glasses at the bum, cleared his throat, and quoted, " 'Neither a borrower nor a lender be,' William Shakespeare."

The bum looked back at him and retorted, " 'Up yours, asshole,' David Mamet."

Danny Kaye noted the difference between comedy and tragedy in Russian drama. In both, everybody dies; but in the comedy, they die happy.

Did you hear that Jack Lemmon beat off a mugger with a 4-iron? How many strokes?

A number of years after he had worked on a film with a glamorous movie star, a certain cinematographer was asked to work with her again. The diva was not at all pleased with the results. "In the first film we did together I looked radiantly beautiful, and this time I look like a hag," she complained bitterly.

"Perhaps, Madame," suggested the cinematographer tactfully, "it has something to do with the fact that I was eight years younger then."

An actor's a guy who, if you ain't talking about him, he ain't listening.

—Marlon Brando

My uncle was thrown out of a mime show for having a seizure. They thought he was heckling.

—Jeff Shaw

Advertising

I saw a commercial on late-night TV. It said, "Forget everything you know about slipcovers." So I did. And it was a load off my mind. Then the commercial tried to sell me slipcovers, and I didn't know what the hell they were.

—Mitch Hedberg

A wealthy computer business mogul sees an advertisement on the Internet for the world's fastest and most expensive car, the Tri-Turbo Convertible Fantasy. It sells for $1 million. The executive decides he must have it, so he has eight of his most trusted assistants assigned to tracking down the vehicle. After months of searching, the car is located, bought, and delivered. Eager to play with his new toy, the executive takes it out for a spin.

At the first stoplight, an old man, looking about eighty-five years old, rides up to the Fantasy on an old Vespa. The old man sticks his head inside without waiting for an invitation, and says, "Quite a ride you got here, sonny. How fast will she go?"

"About 270," the executive responds.

"Come on," says the old man.

Just then, the light turns green and the executive decides to show the old man what the car can do. He floors it, and within seconds the car is doing 270. But suddenly, he notices in his rear-view mirror a dot that seems to be getting closer and closer, and so he comes to a stop. Then, whoooooooosh, "the thing" goes flying by! "What in the heck was that?" says the executive. "What can go faster than my Fantasy?"

Suddenly, "the thing" comes racing back towards him, and whooooosh, passes right by. This time the executive got a better look, and so help him, it looked like the old man on the Vespa. "That just couldn't be," he says to himself. Then, through his rear-view mirror, he sees it again. All of the sudden, WHAM! It smashes into the back end of the car.

The executive jumps out, and sure enough, it's the old man on the Vespa that crashed into him. "Are you OK?" asks the executive. "Is there anything I can do for you?"

"Yes," replies the old man, "unhook my suspenders from your side-view mirror, please."

Did you hear that Anheuser-Busch has taken over the Red Cross's public relations?

Their new slogan is "This Blood's for You."

Agents

Shakespeare said, "Kill all the lawyers." That's before there were agents.

—ROBIN WILLIAMS

The slovenly, obese Hollywood agent got up from his seat at the comedy club to go to the bathroom. Returning with Perrier and popcorn in hand, he inquired of a young woman, "Did I step on your foot a few minutes ago?"

"As a matter of fact you did," she replied tartly.

"Great! Then that's my table."

When I first got into the business, they told me I needed a press agent. So I hired one, a hundred dollars a week. The first week, no press at all. I called my agent, said, "What's happening?"

He said, "They're talkin' about ya, baby, they're talkin' about ya."

Two more weeks go by, two hundred bucks more, and no press. I'm pretty mad. I called my agent, said, "Hey, what's happening here?"

He said, "They're talkin' about ya, baby, they're talkin' about ya."

Five weeks go by. Five hundred bucks down the drain and not

a thing to show for it. I was so mortified and angry that I went down to his office, barged right in, and said, "What's happening? What've I got to show for my five hundred bucks?"

He said, "They're talkin' about ya, baby, they're talkin' about ya."

I said, "Oh yeah? So what're they saying?"

He said, "They're saying, 'Whatever happened to Will Jordan?' "

—Will Jordan

A small-time crook spent years planning the heist of the century: robbing the main vault of the bank. It went without a hitch, except that he forgot to disable one of the security cameras, and when he got home that night to count his cash, he found his face plastered all over the newspapers and television news.

He laid low, but it was pretty obvious that it was only a matter of days until he would be apprehended. Then he was struck by a brilliant idea. He pulled his hat down low, jumped into his car, and drove to the William Morris Agency, where he forced them at gunpoint to sign him to a five-year contract.

He was not seen or heard from again.

—Jimmy Myers

Aging

In certain parts of Miami, if everyone happens to be smiling at once, it's automatically declared Halloween.

It's hard for me to get used to these changing times. I can remember when the air was clean and sex was dirty.

—George Burns

You know you're getting old when you pick up the phone and a woman asks, "Do you know who this is?" and you say no and hang up.

—Franklin P. Adams

"I'm doing what I can," the doctor explained, "but I can't make you any younger, you know."

"The hell with that," said the patient. "I'm not interested in getting younger, I just don't want to get older."

—Joey Adams

A bunch of old guys would sit around playing chess in the park all day. One day a new guy showed up. He was pretty wrinkled and had white hair and he got in a game with one of the old guys. After looking at the new guy for a while, the other guy said, "You know, I just noticed. You're not wearing glasses, you got your real teeth, you got no hearing aid, you're in pretty good shape."

The new guy said, "Well, when I was a kid my parents took me to the doctor and the doctor said that if I wanted to stay in shape I should make love with a woman four times a day. And that's what I've been doing up to this very day."

"Really? How old are you?"

"Twenty-four."

—Jan Murray

The four stages of man are infancy, childhood, adolescence, and obsolescence.

—Art Linkletter

I've got everything I had twenty years ago—except now it's all lower.

—Gypsy Rose Lee

Nowadays there's a pill for everything—to keep your nose from running, to keep you regular, to keep your heart beating, to keep your hair from falling out. . . . Why, thanks to advances in medical science, every day people are dying who never looked better.

When an actress told Bob Hope she was "approaching forty," he couldn't help wondering from what direction.

"I'm only eighty, but I can have sex only about once a month or so," complained George Burns to Doc Meylackson, treasurer of the Friars Club.

"That's natural," said Doc.

"Yeah," Burns complained, "but Groucho Marx is eighty-five and he says he has sex twice a week."

"Okay," said Doc, "you say the same thing."

At his annual checkup, Bernie was given an excellent bill of health. "It must run in your family," commented the doctor. "How old was your dad when he died?"

"What makes you think he's dead?" asked Bernie. "He's ninety and still going strong."

"Aha! And how long did your grandfather live?"

"What makes you think he's dead, Doc? He's a hundred and six, and getting married to a twenty-two-year-old next week," Bernie informed him.

"At his age!" exclaimed the doctor. "Why does he want to marry such a young woman?"

"And what makes you think he wants to?"

—Henny Youngman

Naps are wonderful, aren't they? Sometimes I have to take a nap to get ready for bed.

—Marsha Warfield

I've reached an age when I look just as good standing on my head as I do right side up.

—Frank Sullivan

There are three ages of man: youth, middle age, and "Gee, you look good."

—Red Skelton

My wife never lies about her age. She just tells everyone she's as old as I am. Then she lies about my age.

I was born in 1962. True. And the room next to me was 1963 . . .

—JOAN RIVERS

My doctor has a great stress test. It's called "The Bill."

—JOEY ADAMS

My, my—sixty-five! I guess this marks the first day of the rest of our life savings.

—H. MARTIN

Paul Putney had planned a trip to Paris for a very long time, and the day after his retirement, he was on a plane. When he returned, his old friend Herb met him at the airport, and asked, "Well, Paul, how was Paris?"

"Oh, it was fine," replied the weary traveler, "but I wish I'd gone twenty years ago."

"When Paris was really Paris, eh?" said Herb, sympathetically.

"No," he admitted, "when Paul Putney was really Paul Putney."

I know a guy who looks forty years younger than he is. When he's not working, his wife must put a slipcover over him.

Animals

All creatures must learn to coexist. That's why the brown bear and the field mouse can share their lives and live in harmony. Of course, they can't mate, or the mice would explode.

—BETTY WHITE

What did one Hawaiian shark say to the other?

"Oh, no—not airplane food again."

A little old lady is starved for companionship, so she buys a couple of monkeys. The years go by and she becomes very attached to them. As happens, both monkeys die one day. Not wanting to part with them, she takes the dead monkeys to a taxidermist. The taxidermist asks her, "Would you like them mounted?"

The old woman replies, "No, just holding hands."

—Gregory Peck

Did you hear about the veterinarian and the taxidermist who went into business together?

Their slogan was, "Either Way, You Get Your Pet Back."

Eagles may soar, but weasels don't get sucked into jet engines.

—Steven Wright

Shirley had always wanted to see Australia, so she saved her money and went off on a two-week tour. She'd only been there three days when she fell head over heels in love with a kangaroo. So she blithely disregarded the advice of her tour guide and companions, had an aboriginal priest perform a wedding ceremony, and brought her new husband back to her house in the Midwest.

But she found that the course of new love was not without its problems, and in a few months she decided to consult a marriage counselor.

"Frankly, in your case it's not hard to put my finger on the heart of the problem," said the counselor almost immediately. "Besides the obvious ethnic and cultural differences between you and your husband, it's clearly going to be impossible to establish genuine lines of communication with a kangaroo."

"Oh, that's not it at all," Shirley broke in. "My husband and I communicate perfectly—except in bed. There it's nothing but hop on, hop off, hop on, hop off. . . ."

The first grade class gathered around the teacher for a game of "Guess the Animal." The first picture the teacher held up was of a

cat. "Okay, boys and girls," she said brightly, "can anyone tell me what this is?"

"I know, I know, it's a cat!" yelled a little boy.

"Very good, Eddie. Now, who knows what this animal is called?"

"That's a dog!" piped up the same little boy.

"Right again. And what about this animal?" she asked, holding up a picture of a deer.

Silence fell over the class. After a minute or two, the teacher said, "I'll give you a hint, children . . . it's something your mother calls your father."

"I know, I know," screamed Eddie. "It's a horny bastard!"

How many of those dead animals you see on the highway are suicides?

—Dennis Miller

Warren worked for a small mining operation, so he was used to the desolate little towns of the Southwest. But when he was sent to Dry Gulch for a couple of months, something seemed strange from the very beginning. One night when he was in the local saloon, he realized what it was.

"Say," he said to the bartender, "aren't there any women in this town?"

"Nope," admitted the bartender. "The men here had so little to offer that all the women packed up and left years ago."

Warren's face fell. "That's pretty grim. What do the guys do on a Saturday night?"

"They do it with pigs," was the bartender's cool reply.

"Yecch!" Warren retched and left in disgust. But after a few weeks of total boredom, he found himself back in the saloon, and casually inquired as to where the pigs in question were to be found.

The bartender was free with the information. "Just behind the farmhouse at the top of the hill."

One look at the pigs slopping around in the muddy pen was

almost enough to send Warren back down the hill. But just as he was turning away, he spotted the cutest pig you could ever hope to see, with big brown eyes, a bow on the top of her head, and not a bit of mud on her little pink trotters. Quite smitten, he led her out of the sty, down the hill, and into the saloon for a drink. But to Warren's surprise his arrival caused quite a commotion, and all the seedy types backed away from him into the far corners of the bar. "Hey, what's up?" asked Warren angrily of the bartender. "You told me everyone in the place goes out with pigs."

"True enough," admitted the bartender, "but we weren't expecting you to take the *sheriff's* girl."

My brother had a hamster. He took it to the vet—it's like bringing a disposable lighter in for repairs.

—WAYNE COTTER

The bitter Anatolian winter was almost over when one Armenian shepherd turned to the other and confessed that he could hardly wait until it was time to shear their flocks.

The other shepherd nodded, rubbing his hands together in anticipation. "It's great selling the wool in the market and spending some of the money on raki and women, eh?"

"That's not it," said his companion. "I just can't wait to see them naked."

This guy went to the zoo one day. While he was standing in front of the gorilla's enclosure, a gust of wind blew some grit into his eye. As he pulled his eyelid down to dislodge the particle, the gorilla went crazy, bent open the bars, and beat the hapless fellow senseless. When the guy came to, the zookeeper was anxiously bending over him, and as soon as he was able to talk he explained what had happened. The zookeeper nodded sagely and explained that in gorilla language, pulling down your eyelid meant "fuck you."

The explanation didn't make the gorilla's victim feel any better, and he vowed revenge. The next day he bought two large knives, two party hats, two party horns, and a large sausage. Putting the sausage in his pants, he hurried to the zoo and over to the gorilla's cage, into which he tossed a hat, a knife, and a party horn. Knowing that the big apes were natural mimics, he put on a party hat. The gorilla looked at him, looked at the hat, and put it on. Next he picked up his horn and blew on it. The gorilla picked up his horn and did the same. Then the man picked up his knife, whipped the sausage out of his pants, and sliced it neatly in two.

The gorilla looked at the knife in his cage, looked at his own crotch, and solemnly pulled down his eyelid.

What do you get when you cross a porcupine with a tapeworm?
   About ten feet of barbed wire.

Fernandez had made a lot of money in show business as a ventriloquist and decided to retire as a gentleman farmer. He found a farm he liked, but he thought it was somewhat overpriced, so he decided to have some fun with the farmer as they toured the outbuildings.

"How's the barn holding up?" he asked, turning toward the swaybacked horse in a corner stall.

"The roof leaks and the tractor's thirty-five years old," replied the horse. The farmer, not realizing it was Fernandez throwing his voice, turned pale.

"Mooo," said the cow in answer to the ventriloquist's next question. "My stall's falling apart and the feed's all moldy."

The farmer started to quake.

Next were the chickens. "Need a new coop, holes in the wire," they cackled.

"Just a dang minute," interrupted the farmer, grabbing his prospective buyer by the shoulders. "Don't talk to the sheep—they lie."

What's the best way to stop a runaway horse?
   Bet on it.

As a merchant in the caravan business, Ahmed was well aware that a neutered camel can go longer and further without water than one which has not been neutered. But although he knew he was losing money, he couldn't bear the thought of inflicting such pain on his lead camel, which was really more of a pet than a beast of burden.

Walking through the bazaar one day, he found the solution to his dilemma: a sign that read "Camels Gelded Without Pain." Making inquiries of the stall's proprietor, he was assured that the operation was quick and absolutely painless. There would be no suffering. A price was negotiated and the merchant returned the next day with his favorite camel in tow. The camel gelder picked up two bricks, approached the camel from the rear, took aim, and smashed the bricks together with a sound like a thunderclap. With a bellow of agony, the camel collapsed to its knees.

The merchant was horrified. "You promised it would be painless!" he cried, cradling his camel's head.

"Why it is," explained the gelder, "as long as you don't get your thumbs caught between the bricks."

Would somebody please explain to me those signs that say, "No animals allowed except for Seeing Eye dogs?" Who is that sign for? Is it for the dog, or the blind person?

—Jerry Seinfeld

Did you hear about the lion who consulted an eminent Beverly Hills psychiatrist?

The king of the beasts complained that every time he roared, he had to sit though a two-hour movie.

Recently the director of a local municipal zoo, having acquired a rare Indonesian ape named Oscar, was quite displeased to find that the large aggressive animal had broken free from his cage and was roaming throughout the city. The matter was serious because the members of the staff of the zoo, while expert at caring for animals, had had no experience in capturing them.

The zoo director appealed to the office of the mayor for help, and the secretary to the mayor asked, "Have you looked in the Yellow Pages?"

The director said he hadn't, but would, immediately. To his surprise, under "Animal Capturing Service" he found a listing for the A-1 Ape Apprehenders. He called them and within twenty minutes a truck arrived at the administration office of the zoo.

A small man emerged and rushed to the director, who was waiting at the door.

"Is there a wooded area in the vicinity?" the little man asked.

The director said there was, about a half mile away.

"Hop in the truck," the little man said.

The director did and they drove off. Minutes later they arrived at a small grove and immediately spotted Oscar in a tree on a branch about twenty-five feet above the ground.

The two men got out, went to the back of the truck, and the little man opened the door. An excited little dog jumped out and began running around in circles.

The little man reached into the truck and took out a suitcase, which he opened. In the suitcase were a pair of handcuffs, which he handed to the zoo director, a sawed-off shotgun, which he leaned against the trunk of the tree, and a baseball bat.

"Now," the little man said, "I'm going up into the tree with the baseball bat, and I'm going to knock the ape out of the tree. The instant the ape hits the ground, the dog will grab the ape by the crotch. The ape, instantly and instinctively, will grab at his crotch with both hands. You snap the handcuffs on and we've got him."

The zoo director, pointing to the shotgun leaning against the tree, said, "I'm not too sure about this. What's the gun for?"

The little man said, "Look, I'm an expert. I know what I'm doing and things will go just fine. After all, I have the baseball bat. I know my job and it'll never happen, but if the ape should, by any chance, knock me out of the tree, *shoot the dog!*"

The Easterner had always dreamed of owning his own cattle ranch, and finally made enough money to buy himself the spread of his dreams in Wyoming.

"So what did you name the ranch?" asked his best friend when he flew out to visit.

"We had a hell of a time," admitted the new cowboy. "Couldn't agree on anything. We finally settled on the Double R Lazy L Triple Horseshoe Bar-7 Lucky Diamond Ranch."

"Wow!" His friend was impressed. "So where are all the cows?"

"None of 'em survived the branding."

What do you give an elephant with diarrhea?
Lots of room.

Ever notice when you blow in a dog's face he gets mad at you, but when you take him in a car he sticks his head out the window?

—George Carlin

A woman needs only four animals in her life: a mink on her back, a jaguar in her garage, a tiger in her bed, and a jackass to pay for it all.

What's the biggest drawback of the jungle?
An elephant's foreskin.

A panda walks into a pub and sits down for a drink. While he's downing his pint, he looks across and sees this fine woman at the end of the bar, so he pulls up a stool next to her. He chats her up and the next thing he knows they are getting on like a house on fire.

Then the panda says: "God, I could do with a bite to eat," and in reply the woman asks him around to her place for a meal. Being the randy panda that he is, he readily accepts.

Back at her place, after a fulfilling meal, one thing leads to another and the panda ends up having sex with the woman.

In the morning as the panda is about to leave, the woman says to him, "Hey, wait a sec, I'm a prostitute." Seeing the baffled expression on the panda's face she tells him to look it up in the dictionary.

So the panda looks up "prostitute" and the definition says: "Takes money for sex."

After reading this the panda relaxes and says, "That's all right because I'm a panda."

The woman, confused, looks up "panda" in the dictionary and reads the definition: "Eats shoots and leaves."

A monkey sitting in a tree in Africa sees a huge lion sleeping on the ground below, with his tail going up in the air every five seconds. He thinks to himself, "That's a big lion, if I fuck this lion up the ass, I'll be the king of the jungle." When the lion's tail goes up again, the monkey jumps down and fucks the lion up the ass. The lion wakes up and chases the monkey through the jungle, the monkey dives through a row of trees and lands in the lobby of a big hotel. He picks up a newspaper and covers his face as if to read it. The lion comes through, roaring, "Did anybody see a monkey come in here?" From behind the paper the monkey yells, "The one that fucked the lion up the ass?" The lion roars back, "Holy shit! It's in the paper already?"

—Jeff Pirrami

When I woke up this morning, I could feel tension mounting. Tension is my dog.

—Tom Cotter

A sloth was walking through the jungle one day when he was set upon by a gang of vicious snails.

The snails left him bleeding and confused at the bottom of a tree. Several hours later he summoned the strength to go to the police station and report the assault. He was asked by the desk sergeant to describe his attackers.

He replied, "I don't know what they looked like, it all happened so fast."

A horse wanders into a bar and orders a tall one.
    The bartender says, "Hey, fella, why the long face?"

Birds

Ever let your parakeet out of its cage? My parakeet will fly across the room, right into the mirror. . . . He will hit that mirror: *Bang!* And he will fly off in some other direction trying to get it together. He's so stupid. Even if he thought the mirror was another room, you'd think he'd try to avoid hitting the other parakeet!

—JERRY SEINFELD

Some months ago I saw a man breaking a loaf of whole-wheat bread and tossing the pieces at pigeons. I was curious, and I asked him, "Why whole-wheat bread?"
    He answered very seriously, "Everybody gives them white bread or cake. This way they'll remember me."

A man suspects his wife of cheating on him, so he goes to the pet store to shop for a parrot. He sees quite an assortment of parrots for sale for five hundred to a thousand dollars, but that's a bit more than he wants to spend, so he's delighted to come across one in the corner for sale for thirty dollars. "How come that one's so cheap?" he asks the clerk.
    "To tell ya the truth, his dick's oversized and embarrasses the customers," is the explanation. The husband buys the bird anyway, and installs it on a perch right over the bed.
    The next day the first thing he does after coming home from work is to rush upstairs. "Well, what happened today?" he asks the bird.
    "Well, the milkman came, and . . . your wife told him to come

into the bedroom, and . . . they took off their clothes, and . . . got into bed."

"So what happened next?" screams the irate husband.

"I don't know," says the parrot. "I got hard and fell off my perch."

A nine-year-old shoeshine boy in Boston sees all these pigeons flying around and is getting quite annoyed. "Fuck off, fuck off," he says to the pigeons.

An old lady comes up to the little boy and says, "Little boy, the pigeons are here because they are hungry and want some of your sandwich. If you don't want them around say, 'Shoo, shoo.' Then they'll fuck off."

—BUDDY HACKETT

What do you do with a bird with no wings?
   Take it for a spin.

My parakeet died. We were playing badminton.

—DANNY CURTIS

Myron's mother was very hard to please, but one year he thought hard and finally came up with a truly inspired birthday present: a gorgeous parrot that spoke six languages. He paid an exorbitant price and arranged to have the bird, in an ornate antique cage, delivered to her apartment on the appointed day.

That evening he came by for the birthday dinner. "So, Mom, did you get my present?" he asked casually.

"Yes, Myron, I did. And I must say it's cooked up very nicely."

"You didn't cook it!" gasped Myron. "Mom, that bird cost me fifteen hundred dollars. And it spoke English, Portuguese, Mandarin, Urdu, Arabic, and Russian!"

"Now, Myron," the old woman chided, "if it really spoke all those languages, why didn't it say something?"

This is a story about a guy who has a horny parrot. It's terrible. Every time he reaches into the cage, the bird humps his arm. He invites his mother to tea, the bird keeps saying foul things. . . . Finally he takes the parrot to a vet.

The vet examines the bird extensively, says, "Well, you have a horny parrot. I have a sweet young female bird, and for fifteen dollars your bird can go in the cage with mine."

The guy's parrot is listening and he says, "Come on! Come on! What the hell!"

Finally, the guy says all right, hands over the fifteen dollars.

The vet takes the parrot, puts him in the cage with the female bird, closes the curtain. . . . Suddenly, *"Kwah! Kwah! Kwah!"* Feathers come flying out.

The vet says, "Holy gee," runs across the room, and opens the curtain. The male bird has the female bird down on the bottom of the cage with one claw. With the other claw he's pulling out all her feathers. He's saying, "For fifteen bucks, I want you naked. *Naked!*"

—Orson Bean

What do you call a missing parrot?
A polygon.

What do you call a parrot wearing a raincoat?
Polly unsaturated.

This young lady walks into a pet store to buy a parrot. The guy behind the counter says that he only has one and that it's a real "smart-ass" with a vulgar vocabulary and rude temperament.

The woman says, "That's okay, I know how to handle smart-asses like that. I want the parrot anyhow."

So the woman gets the bird home, puts it in her room, and starts to get ready for bed. Just as she gets her slacks off the parrot says: "Awk . . . nice legs, baby!"

Well, the woman isn't gonna take such abuse, so she takes the bird out of the cage and puts it in the freezer for three minutes.

While the parrot's in the freezer, he becomes real sure that this was the wrong thing to say, and is making a large mental note about saying that again.

The next night, again the woman is getting ready for bed. This time the parrot knows not to say anything about her legs, but after she removes her blouse, and then her bra, the parrot just can't resist any longer. He blurts out, "Awk . . . great tits, baby, let's see ya shake um."

Once again the woman gets upset and she decides that instead of three minutes in the freezer, she is going to keep the parrot in for five minutes. This time the parrot has lots of time to think. Remorse gives way to desperation, and finally to anger.

Finally, the woman opens the freezer door, takes out the near frozen parrot and says, "Well, have you learned your lesson?"

The parrot, still shivering and barely able to speak, says, "Awk, yea, yea, sure, sure, but I have just one question."

The woman says, "Yes?"

The parrot says, "Awk . . . what did the turkey do, ask for a blow job?"

The old rooster could never get enough. He screwed every chicken in the barnyard and wore them all out, so the farmer put him in with the ducks. Pretty soon all the ducks were begging for a rest, so the farmer tethered the rooster out in a cornfield. After a while the farmer looked out his window and saw that the bird was lying on the ground and looked dead as a doornail. Going out to check, he found the rooster lying down all right, but with its eyes wide open. "What's the matter?" he asked.

"Shhhhhhhh," hissed the rooster, motioning upward with the tip of a wing. "Turkey vultures!"

Why did the pervert cross the road?
Because he was looking for a chicken.

Cats

I gave my cat a bath the other day. . . . He sat there, he enjoyed it, it
was fun for me. The fur would stick to my tongue, but other than
that . . .

—STEVE MARTIN

**We have two cats. They're my wife's cats, Mischa and Alex. . . .
Women always choose sensitive names: Muffy, Fluffy, Buffy. Guys
name cats things like Tuna Breath, Fur Face, Meow Head.
They're nice cats. They've been neutered and they've been de-
clawed, so they're like pillows that eat.**

—LARRY REEB

Human milk is better than cow's milk. It's cheaper, keeps over the
weekend, and the cat can't get at it.

—DONALD MCGILL

**I found out why cats drink out of the toilet. My mother told me
it's because it's cold in there. And I'm like: *How* did my mother
know *that*?**

—WENDY LIEBMAN

A famous art collector is walking through Greenwich Village when he
notices a mangy cat lapping milk from a saucer in the doorway of a
store, and he does a double take. He knows the saucer is very old and
valuable, so he saunters casually into the store and offers to buy the
cat for two dollars.

But the store owner says, "I'm sorry, but the cat isn't for sale."

The collector says, "Please, I need a hungry old tomcat around the
house to catch mice. I'll give you ten dollars for him."

And the owner says, "Sold," and hands over the cat.

Then the collector says, "Listen, for the ten bucks I wonder if you'd throw in that old saucer. The cat's used to it and it'll save me buying a dish."

And the owner says, "Sorry, buddy, but that's my lucky saucer. So far this week I've sold sixty-eight cats."

—Soupy Sales

I don't like cats. I prefer dogs, because dogs don't care. If a dog can do it, you can watch. You don't say that about cats. You only get to hear cats.

—Jim Stafford

I'm used to dogs. When you leave them in the morning they stick their noses in the door crack and stand there like a portrait until you return eight hours later. A cat would never put up with that kind of rejection. When you returned, she'd stalk you until you dozed off and then suck the air out of your body.

—Erma Bombeck

What do you do if a cat spits at you?
Turn the grill down.

Dogs

I've got a sheep dog. He doesn't have fleas—he's got moths.

—Joey Adams

Why do dogs lick their balls?
Because they can.
So why do they stick their noses in women's crotches?
Same reason.

Two guys were walking down the street when they came across a dog sitting on the sidewalk studiously licking his balls.

"Would I ever like to do that," sighed one man enviously.

"Go right ahead," encouraged his friend. "But if I were you, I'd pat him first."

I sold my dog for one hundred thousand dollars. I got two fifty-thousand-dollar cats for him.

—JOEY ADAMS

A guy walks into a bar with a dog under his arm, puts the dog on the bar, and announces that the dog can talk and that he has a hundred dollars he's willing to bet anyone who says he can't. The bartender quickly takes the bet and the owner looks at the dog and asks, "What's the thing on top of this building, which keeps the rain from coming inside?"

The dog answers, "ROOF."

The bartender says, "Who are you kidding? I'm not paying." The dog's owner says, "How about double or nothing and I'll ask him something else."

The bartender agrees and the owner turns to the dog and asks, "Who was the greatest ballplayer of all time?" The dog answers with a muffled "RUTH."

With that the bartender picks them both up and throws them out the door. As they bounce on the sidewalk, the dog looks at his owner and says, "DiMaggio?"

Why are dogs better than kids?
When you get sick of your dog, you can put it to sleep.

I have a great dog. She's half Labrador, half pit bull. It's a good combination. Sure, she might bite off my leg, but she'll bring it back to me.

—JIMI CELESTE

I have a dachshund. It curses when it barks.
Why?
You would too if you were draggin' your balls on the sidewalk.

—BILLY CONNOLLY

They say a dog is man's best friend, but I don't buy it. How many of your friends have you neutered?

—LARRY REEB

My neighbor told me, "My dog was my only friend. I told my wife that a man needs at least two friends, so she went out and bought me another dog."

—JOEY ADAMS

What's the difference between a poodle humping your leg and a pit bull humping your leg?

You let the pit bull finish.

Hearing a noise behind him, a street corner violinist turned around to see two dogs screwing in the alley. "Don't just stand there," growled one of them, "play 'Bolero.'"

"Now cheer up, Paul," soothed his buddy Bill over a couple of beers. "You and Louise seem to be doing just fine. And frankly, it seems a little silly for you to be jealous of a German shepherd. After all, you work all day and you live out in the sticks. That dog's good company for Louise."

"Good company!" snorted Paul, nearly spilling his beer. "Hey, the other night I caught her douching with Gravy Train."

My dog can bark like a congressman, fetch like an aide, beg like a press secretary, and play dead like a receptionist when the phone rings.

—GERALD P. SOLOMON

I went to an exclusive kennel club. It was very exclusive. There was a sign out front: "No Dogs Allowed."

—PHIL FOSTER

Dogs laugh, but they laugh with their tails. . . . What puts man in a higher state of evolution is that he's got his laugh on the right end.

—Max Eastman

My neighbor has two dogs. One of them says to the other, "Woof!"

The other replies, "Moo!"

The first dog is perplexed. He says, "Moo? Why did you say, 'Moo?'"

The other dog answers, "I'm trying to learn a foreign language."

—Morey Amsterdam

Two ladies are at the vet's office. One has a poodle and the other a Great Dane. The lady with the Great Dane asks the poodle lady, "Why are you here?"

"Oh," the woman says, "my dog keeps scratching himself, so I'm here to get some flea spray. What about you?"

The Great Dane lady says, "I'm here because my dog is over-sexed. If I bend over to wash the floor or pick up anything, he wraps his paws around me and starts to hump me."

"So you're here to get him neutered?"

"No," says the other woman, "I'm here to get his nails clipped."

—Norm Crosby

They say barking dogs never bite. I know it, and you know it, but does the dog know it?

—Joey Adams

A dog teaches a boy fidelity, perseverance, and to turn around three times before lying down.

—Robert Benchley

I've got a Chihuahua. They're good. If you lose one, just empty out your purse.

—JEAN CARROLL

Anybody who doesn't know what soap tastes like never washed a dog.

—FRANKLIN P. JONES

The other day I saw two dogs walk over to a parking meter. One of them says to the other, "How do you like that? Pay toilets!"

—DAVE STARR

Little old lady to dog owner: "Is that your German shepherd outside?"
"Yeah, so what?"
"Well, my cat just killed it."
"Ha, how could your cat kill my dog?"
"It got stuck in his throat!"

I got my grandmother a Seeing Eye dog, but he's a little sadistic. He does impressions of cars screeching to a halt.

—LARRY AMOROS

They have dog food for constipated dogs. If your dog is constipated, why screw up a good thing? Stay indoors and let 'im bloat!

—DAVID LETTERMAN

Hear about the new breed that's half pit bull and half collie?
    After it mauls you, it goes for help.

Insects

At their annual football game, the big animals are really trouncing the little animals with a tremendous offensive game. At half time the score is 33 to 0, and it's only with considerable effort that the little animals manage to stop the opposition's kickoff return on the twenty-two yard line. On the first down, the big animals send the hippopotamus around the right end, but as soon as he gets to the line of scrimmage—*Bang!*—he's stopped cold.

Back in the huddle, the squirrel, the captain of the little animals, says, "Say, that was great! Who stopped the hippo, anyway?"

"Me," says the centipede.

On the second down, the rhino charges around the left end, but he, too, is stopped cold at the line of scrimmage.

"Terrific," cheers the squirrel. "Who did it this time?"

"Me," says the centipede.

On the third down the big animals send the elephant right up the middle, but he doesn't get one yard before he's knocked flat on his back.

"Was that you again?" asks the squirrel of the bug.

"Yup," says the centipede modestly.

"Well, where the hell were you during the first half?" demands the squirrel.

"Taping my ankles."

I bought an ant farm. I don't know where I'm gonna find a tractor that small.

—Steven Wright

Ants can carry twenty times their own body weight, which is useful information if you're moving and you need help carrying a potato chip across town.

—Ron Darian

What did the worm say to the caterpillar?

"What'd you do to get that fur coat?"

As of yet there have been no deaths attributed to the killer bees in Texas. However, we caught two bees this week planning a murder.

—Dennis Miller

Two ants met in this woman's belly button and decided to explore the rest of her body. Agreeing to meet back in the same place in a week, one ant headed north while the other went south.

Seven days later, they returned to the belly button. "I had a great time," reported the ant who had ventured north. "There were these two big hills, and every day I went skiing, and at night I slept in this nice warm valley."

"I had a hell of a time," sighed the other ant. "First I had to walk through this thick jungle, then I fell down this huge hole, and by the time I climbed out I was so tired that I fell asleep in this smelly cave. But that wasn't the worst of it: every night, this giant worm came in and threw up in my face."

Look at that ugly little bee. Makes honey. I'm a nice-looking person, and all I can do is make a little wax with my ears.

—Milt Kamen

The Armed Forces

There's the stealth plane, the invisible plane. What good is an invisible airplane gonna do? The enemy looks down on their radar and says, "Well, there's no aircraft here. But there's two little guys in a sitting position at forty thousand feet!"

—Will Durst

How many U.S. Marines does it take to screw in a lightbulb?

Fifty. One to screw it in and the other forty-nine to guard him.

They're gonna cut back on the troops in Europe by one hundred thousand. Can you imagine what a loser you gotta feel like when you get laid off by the army?

—Jack Cohen

Two drill sergeants were standing outside the PX, bitching about the long hours. "This job works me so damn hard," complained Meade, "that even making love to my wife is getting to feel like a chore."

"No way could that be considered work," objected Daly. They argued the point back and forth and finally agreed to turn the question over to the next person to come out of the PX. This happened to be Perkins, a private in Daly's platoon.

"Tell me, soldier," began Meade, "if you got up every day at five A.M., worked your ass off for eighteen hours, went home, prepared your gear for the next day, and fell into bed, would making love be a pleasure or hard work?"

Perkins scratched his head. "I'd have to say it would be a pleasure, sir," he finally replied.

"And why is that?"

"Because if it were work, Sergeant Daly would have me doing it already."

How can you identify a Rumanian jet fighter in a snowstorm?

It's the one with chains on the propellers.

The general issued a rousing battle cry: "Onward to victory!"

Half an hour later, an urgent message reached him. "Need further instructions. Victory not on our maps."

New recruit: Colonel Santer always says, "Never take a drink when you feel as if you need one," and old Nettelfield says, "Never take a drink except when you need one." Now, how on earth do I know what to do so I don't get in trouble?

Seasoned soldier: Follow both rules, and you'll be all right.

The sergeant put his troops through a fancy drill, at the end of which they lined up three rows deep. Walking down the line, the sergeant stopped in front of each soldier, whacked him on the chest with his baton, and barked, "Did that hurt, soldier?"

"No, *sir!*" each replied.

"Why not?" yelled the sergeant.

"Because I'm a United States Marine, *sir!*" came the reply.

Continuing on, the sergeant saw a huge penis sticking out of the line and proceeded to whack it with his baton. "Did that hurt, soldier?" he boomed.

"No, *sir,*" answered the private.

"And why not?"

"Because it belongs to the guy behind me, *sir!*"

We had a colonel named Fat Ass Johnson. That wasn't his real name . . . but they called him Fat Ass Johnson. No one ever called him Fat Ass Johnson to his face, but I once called him that on the phone. You see, I was working in the motor pool. That's where they keep trucks and jeeps and vehicles like that.

The phone rings. The sign said, "Recruits, do not answer phone." I didn't know what's a recruit, so I said hello.

A voice said, "Soldier, what vehicles have you got available?"

I said, "Six trucks, seven jeeps, an MA armored car, a half-track, and Fat Ass Johnson's command car."

He said, "Have you any idea who you're talking to?"

I said, "No, sir."

He said, "This is Colonel Johnson."

I said, "Colonel, do you have any idea who you're talking to?"

He said, *"No."*

I said, "Bye-bye, Fat Ass!"

You have to have a physical before you get into the army. A doctor looks in one ear, another doctor looks in the other, and if they can't see each other, you're in. If they can see each other, you become an MP.

—Joe E. Brown

Did you know the Republic of Ireland is hard at work on a new airborne weapon?

They're calling it the Spud missile.

There's this to recommend army life: You never have to decide what to wear.

Art and Artists

The penniless artist was cornered by her landlord, who demanded several months back rent.

"Just think," the artist pleaded, "some day tourists will be pointing at this building and saying, 'The great abstract painter Susan Krechevsky used to live here.'"

The landlord shrugged. "And if you don't pay up, they can come by tomorrow and say that."

Joey Frisco bought a painting of the Last Supper at an actor's charity function. Later, after a few bad days at the track, he took the painting to a pawn shop. The pawnbroker looked at it and said he didn't know much about Last Supper paintings, and asked what Joey thought it was worth.

"Well," said Joey, "at least t-t-ten dollars a p-p-p-plate."

—RED BUTTONS, ABOUT JOEY FRISCO

I saw some things at the auction labeled "Art Objects." Considering what they looked like, I'd object, too.

You go to the ballet and you see girls dancing on their tiptoes. Why don't they just get taller girls?

—GREG RAY

I went by the museum the other day and saw something disturbing. They replaced that statue *The Thinker*—with a computer.

Often they hang the painting when they should hang the artist instead.

I may not know anything about art, but I know what's suitable for framing.

How many surrealists does it take to change a lightbulb?
Two, one to hold the giraffe, and the other to fill the bathtub with brightly colored machine tools.

Atheism

Not only is there no God, but try getting a plumber on weekends.

—Woody Allen

An atheist is a guy who watches a Notre Dame—SMU football game and doesn't care who wins.

—Dwight D. Eisenhower

What do you get when you cross an insomniac, an agnostic, and a dyslexic?
Someone who lies awake all night wondering if there really is a Dog.

They have Dial-a-Prayer for atheists now. You can call up and it rings and rings, but nobody answers.

—Tommy Blaze

I used to be an agnostic, but now I'm not so sure.

Did you hear about the new Cabbage Patch Dolls for atheists' kids? They're stuffed with catnip and dressed as early Christians.

I once wanted to become an atheist, but I gave up—they have no holidays.

—Henny Youngman

What's the worst thing about being an atheist?
   You have no one to call to when you're having an orgasm.

What do you get when you cross a Jehovah's Witness with an atheist? Someone who rings your doorbell for no reason.

As long as there are algebra exams, there will be prayer in the schools.

I guess I began to doubt the existence of God after I had been married about three years.

—Brian Savage

Most people past college age are not atheists because, for one thing, you don't get any days off. And if you're an agnostic, you don't know whether you get them off or not.

—Mort Sahl

B

Babies

The baby is great. My wife and I have just started potty training. Which I think is important because when we want to potty train the baby, we should set an example.

—Howie Mandel

A little boy asks his mother, "Where do babies come from?" Mom says, "The stork," and the boy says, "Who's fucking the stork?"

—Jeff Pirrami

Gracie: My sister had a baby.

George: Boy or girl?

Gracie: I don't know, and I can't wait to find out if I'm an uncle or an aunt.

—George Burns and Gracie Allen

Looking at their new baby, the mother said, "Those tiny arms, he'll never be a boxer. Those tiny legs, he'll never be a runner."
The father said, "He'll never be a porn star either."

—Bob Hope

I remember a lot of things from before I was even born. I remember going to a picnic with my father and coming home with my mother.

—Foster Brooks

A young woman was sitting on the bus, cooing to her baby, when a drunk staggered aboard and down the aisle. Stopping in front of

her, he looked down and pronounced, "Lady, that is the ugliest baby I have ever seen."

The woman burst into tears and there was such an outcry of sympathy among the other passengers that they kicked the drunk off. But the woman kept on sobbing and wailing, so loudly that finally the driver pulled the bus over to the side of the road.

"Look, I don't know what that bum said to you," the driver told his inconsolable passenger, "but to help calm you down I'm going to get you a cup of tea." And off he went, coming back shortly with a cup of tea from the corner deli.

"Now, calm down, lady," soothed the driver, "everything's going to be okay. See, I brought you a cup of nice hot tea, and I even got a banana for your pet monkey."

Bachelors

I'm single because I was born that way.

—Mae West

Being a bachelor is great. You get home-cooked meals, along with a variety of cooks.

Why do married men gain weight and bachelors don't?

Bachelors go to the refrigerator, see nothing they want, then go to bed.

Married guys go to the bed, see nothing they want, then go to the refrigerator.

Every man has it in his power to make one woman happy . . . by remaining a bachelor.

I think—therefore I'm single.

—Lizz Winstead

At the conclusion of the physical exam, the doctor summoned his patient into his office with a very grave look on his face. "I hate to be the one to break it to you, Fred," he said, "but I'm afraid you've got six months to live."

"Oh my God," gasped Fred, turning white. When the news had sunk in, he said, "Listen, Doc, you've known me a long time. Do you have any suggestions as to how I could make the most of my remaining months?"

"Have you ever married?" asked the doctor.

Fred explained that he'd been a bachelor all his life.

"You might think about taking a wife," the doctor proposed. "After all, you'll need someone to look after you during the final illness."

"That's a good point, Doc," mused Fred. "And with only six months to live I'd better make the most of my time."

"May I make one more suggestion?" asked the doctor. When Fred nodded, he said, "Marry a Jewish girl."

"A Jewish girl—how come?" asked Fred.

"It'll seem longer."

Baldness

A fool and his money are soon parted, but nobody can part a two-dollar toupee.

—FRED ALLEN

My hair is my own. I paid for it, I own it.

—CARL REINER

Why did the bald man cut a hole in his pocket?

He wanted to run his fingers through his hair.

How you lose or keep your hair depends on how wisely you choose your parents.

—Edward R. Nida

The way not to freeze up in an awkward or embarrassing situation is to pay a compliment. You will lessen the tension. I remembered that. I was talking to this guy I didn't know very well, and his toupee blew onto the sidewalk. Very embarrassing. So I said, "Gee, I like your hair like that."

—George Miller

One old lady turns to another: "Ooh, who did your hair? Who did your hair? My God, your hair looks like a wig!"
The other old lady says, "It *is* a wig."
The first one says, "Is that so? You could never tell."

—Larry Best

Banks

A record number of savings-and-loan failures left America with a nationwide shortage of flimsy toaster ovens, cheap pocket calculators, and ugly dinnerware.

—P. J. O'Rourke

Gracie: Where do you keep your money?
George: In the bank.
Gracie: What interest do you get?
George: Four percent.
Gracie: Ha! I get eight.
George: You get eight?
Gracie: I keep it in two banks.

—George Burns and Gracie Allen

I went to the bank and reviewed my savings. I found out I have all the money I'll ever need. If I die tomorrow.

—HENNY YOUNGMAN

What did the Jewish bank teller say to her customers?
"You never write, you never call, you only visit when you need money."

A little girl in tears came running to her father.
"What's the matter?" asked her father.
"You gave me some bad financial advice," she said.
"I did? What did I do?" asked the astonished father.
"You told me to put my money in that big bank, and now that big bank is in trouble."
"What are you taking about, that's one of the largest banks in the world," he said, "surely there must be some mistake."
"I don't think so," said the girl, "they just returned one of my checks with a note saying 'No Funds'."

Sign above bank teller's station: "To err is human, to forgive is not bank policy."

Rothschild, the famous banker, was strolling down a crowded street in Vienna when he was jostled by a pickpocket. "Watch out!" warned his companion. "That fellow's trying to steal your silk handkerchief."
"So what?" said Rothschild with a shrug. "We all started small."

The banks have a new image. Now you have "a friend." Your friendly banker. If the banks are so friendly, how come they chain down the pens?

—ALAN KING

I bank at a women's bank. Three or four days a month it's closed due to cramps.

—JUDY CARTER

I went to the bank the other day. . . . I asked the banker to check my balance. . . . So he pushed me!

Did you hear about the moron who tried to rob a bank?
  He tied up the safe and blew the guard.

A rather scruffy-looking man came into a bank. Reaching the head of the line, he said to the teller, "I wanna open a fucking checking account."
  "Certainly, sir," answered the teller, "but there's no need to use that kind of language."
  "Couldja move it along lady? I just wanna open a fucking checking account," growled the would-be customer.
  "I'll be glad to be of service, sir," said the teller, flushing slightly, "but I would appreciate not being spoken to in that way."
  "Just lemme open a fucking checking account, okay?"
  "I'm afraid I'm going to have to speak to the branch manager," said the flustered teller, slipping off her stool and returning shortly with a dapper middle-aged man, who asked how he could be of service.
  "I just won the ten-million-dollar lottery," snarled the man, "and all I wanna do is open a fucking checking account."
  "I see," said the manager sympathetically. "And this bitch is giving you trouble?"

Beauty

I don't have anything against face-lifts, but I think it's time to stop when you look permanently frightened.
  —Susan Forfleet

Oh my God—look at you. Anybody else hurt in the accident?
  —Don Rickles to Ernest Borgnine

Adam was the perfect figure of a man, and Eve was indescribably beautiful . . . so where did all the ugly people come from?

Here's my morning ritual: I open a sleepy eye, take one horrified look at my reflection in the mirror, and then repeat, with conviction . . . "I'm me and I'm beautiful, because God doesn't make junk."

—ERMA BOMBECK

I read in *Cosmopolitan* that women like to have whipped cream sprayed over their breasts. Unfortunately, my girlfriend has silicone implants. So I use nondairy topping.

—JEFF SHAW

He took my glasses off and said, "Without your glasses, why, you're beautiful."
I said, "Without my glasses, you're not half bad either."

—KIT HOLLERBACH

Her hair has more body than I do.

Showgirl Carol Gale filed a malpractice suit after a plastic surgeon accidentally injected her with Silly Putty instead of silicone. Carol claimed that overnight she went from a 34B to a 42 long.

—DICK MARTIN

I'm tired of all this nonsense about beauty being only skin-deep. That's deep enough. What do you want, an adorable pancreas?

—JEAN KERR

"I've had it with my husband. He's such a clean freak," a disgruntled woman complained to her friend. "Every night he makes me wash and scrub my face."
"What's wrong with that?" her friend asked.
"Then he wants to iron it."

Sometimes I just go to the beauty parlor for an estimate.

—Phyllis Diller

The most common error made in matters of appearance is the belief that one should disdain the superficial and let the true beauty of one's soul shine through. If there are places on your body where this is a possibility, you are not attractive. You are leaking.

—Fran Lebowitz

A Peeping Tom called me and asked me to lower my shade.

—Jim Baily, impersonating Phyllis Diller

Birth

In the natural childbirth classes my wife and I took, the birthing process was represented by a hand puppet being pushed through a sock. So at the actual birth I was shocked to see all this blood. The thing I had prepared myself for was a lot of lint.

—Steve Scrovan

I want to have children, but my friends scare me. One of them told me she was in labor for thirty-six hours. I don't even want to do anything that feels good for thirty-six hours.

—Rita Rudner

They call us "coaches." The job is to remind your wife to breathe. Think about that for a second. You realize exactly how worthless I am in this thing? When was the last time you had to be reminded to breathe? It's like saying, "Digest!"

—Robert Klein

In this day and age, women can have kids for other women, through surrogate motherhood. Is that the ultimate favor or what? I think I'm a good friend. I'll help you move. Okay. But whatever comes out of me after nine months, I'm keeping. I don't care if it's a shoe.

—SUE KOLINSKY

After going through Lamaze, Leboyer, and La Leche classes with his expectant wife, the proud new father remained by his wife's bedside throughout labor and the delivery. Wanting to be as sympathetic as possible, he took his wife's hand afterward and said emotionally, "Tell me how it was, darling, how it actually felt to give birth."

"Okay, honey," his wife replied. "Smile as hard as you can."

Beaming down beatifically at his wife and newborn child, the man followed her instructions. "That's not so hard."

She continued, "Now stick a finger in each corner of your mouth."

He obeyed, smiling broadly.

"Now stretch your lips as far as they'll go," she went on.

"Still not too tough," he remarked.

"Right," she snapped. "Now pull them over your head."

Beverly Hills is so exclusive that, when a woman gives birth, she breaks Perrier.

—FREDDIE ROMAN

A guy calls the hospital. He says, "You gotta send help! My wife's going into labor!"

The nurse says, "Calm down. Is this her first child?"

He says, "No! This is her husband!"

This guy came into work one day with a fistful of cigars and started passing them out left and right to celebrate the birth of his son.

"Congratulations, Eric," said his boss. "How much did the baby weigh?"

"Four and a half pounds," reported the father proudly.

"Gee, that's kind of small."

What did you expect?" retorted Eric indignantly. "We've only been married three months."

I told my mother I was going to have natural childbirth. She said to me, "Linda, you've been taking drugs all your life. Why stop now?"

—LINDA MALDONADO

We delivered our child by natural childbirth, the procedure invented by a man named Lamaze, the Marquis de Lamaze, a disciple of Dr. Josef Mengele, who concluded that women could counteract the incredible pain of childbirth by breathing. I think we can all agree that breathing is not a reasonable substitute for anesthesia. That's like asking a man to tolerate a vasectomy by hyperventilating.

—DENNIS WOLFBERG

I was born by C-section. This was the last time I had my mother's complete attention.

—RICHARD JENI

Doctor to parents of ugly baby: "I charge five dollars if it's a boy and five dollars if it's a girl. Let's just say this one's on the house."

—BOB HOPE

You have this myth you're sharing the birth experience. Unless you're passing a bowling ball, I don't think so. Unless you're circumcising yourself with a chain saw, I don't think so. Unless you're opening an umbrella up your ass, I don't think so!

—ROBIN WILLIAMS

A woman entered the hospital to deliver her tenth child.

"Congratulations," said the nurse, "but don't you think this is enough?" The woman replied, "Are you kidding? This is the only vacation I get each year."

Birth Control

If men got pregnant . . . women would rule the world.

I asked my doctor if I should have a vasectomy. He said, let a sleeping dog lie. The last time I had sex, my self-winding watch stopped.

—LENNY RUSH

An idealistic young doctor volunteered for two years' service with the Peace Corps. He was put in charge of a population-control program in a remote Nepalese hill town. It turned out to be impossible for the women to keep track of birth control pills, so the doctor decided to concentrate on the use of condoms.

His first patient was a man whose wife had given birth to six children in as many years, and neither wanted more. The doctor explained to the man how the sheaths worked, and said that if he wore one conscientiously, his wife would not get pregnant. So he was surprised when the fellow's wife came in a month later and he found she was pregnant again.

"What happened?" he scolded. "All your husband had to do was keep the condom on—is that so difficult?"

"He try, he try very hard," stammered the poor woman, "but after three days, he have to pee so bad he cut the end off."

Hear about the woman who loved to have sex, but refused to take birth control pills?

Her boyfriend charged her with practicing license without a medicine.

The young Irish bride made her first appointment with a gynecologist and told him that she and her husband wished to start a

family. "We've been trying for months now, Doctor Keith, and I don't seem to be able to get pregnant," she confessed miserably.

"I'm sure we'll solve the problem," the doctor reassured her. "If you'll just take off your underpants and get up on the examining table . . ."

"Well, all right, Doctor," agreed the young woman, blushing, "but I'd rather have my husband's baby."

I'm Catholic. . . . My mother and I were unpacking and she found my diaphragm. I had to tell her it was a bathing cap for my cat.

Two little girls from a tough neighborhood were walking down the block to school and one said to the other, "Hey, know what I found on the patio the other day? A condom."

"Oh, yea," said her friend. "What's a patio?"

An attractive saleswoman was driving her car through Montana when she ran out of gas. Getting out of her car, she saw nothing in the barren countryside except a single rundown shack and, on closer inspection, two dim-looking country boys sitting on the front porch.

"Hey there, where's the nearest gas station?" asked the woman.

"Oh, 'bout twenty-five miles west as the crow flies," was the answer.

It was getting dark, so the woman decided to take her chances and ask for a room for the night.

"Fine with us . . . 'cept we only got one bed," said the second man with an evil leer.

"Okay," said the woman reluctantly. But when they were getting ready for bed, she added, "I can't help it if you two take advantage of me, but please wear these condoms."

Looking as though they'd never seen rubbers before, the country boys put them on.

The next morning they gave the woman a gallon of gas and she went on her way. Three months later the guys were sitting on their porch and one says to the other, "Hey, Luke?"

"Yeah?"

"Do you really care if that lady gets pregnant?"

"Naw, not really."

"Then you think we can take these things off now?"

After the birth of his third child, Warner decided to have a vasec-tomy. During the operation, one of his testicles accidentally fell on the floor, and before the nurse could scoop it back up, the doctor had stepped on it. Unfazed, the doctor simply asked the nurse for a small onion, which he proceeded to suture inside the scrotum.

Two weeks later Warner was back for his post-op checkup.

"How's it going?" asked the doctor.

"I gotta tell you, I'm having some problems," admitted the patient.

"Such as?"

"Well, Doc, every time I take a leak, my eyes water, every time I cum, I get heartburn, and every time I pass a Burger King, I get a hard-on!"

I was involved in an extremely good example of oral contraception two weeks ago. I asked a girl to go to bed with me and she said no.

—Woody Allen

A woman with eight children happened to run across a childhood friend of hers on the street corner. "Myrna," she asked, "how come you got no kids?"

"I practice preventive measures," was the answer.

"Preventive measures? What's that?" asked Evelyn.

"I use two saucers and a box. My husband's a lot taller than I am and we like to screw standing up. When he gets a hard-on I pull up my dress, spread my legs, and put the two saucers on the table. He stands up on the box so he can get all the way inside me and starts jumping up and down."

"So where does all this get you?" asked Evelyn, confused.

"That's when I got to watch him very closely. When his eyes get as big as those two saucers, I kick the box out from under him."

One of the best things people could do for their descendants would be to sharply limit the number of them.

—OLIN MILLER

The newlyweds stopped at a farmhouse and asked if they could rent a room for the night. By noon the next day they were still not up and about, so the farmer yelled up that it was last call for breakfast.

"Don't worry about us," called the groom, "we're living on the fruits of love."

"Okay," screamed the farmer, "but quit throwing the damned skins out the window—they're choking the ducks."

Heard anything about the "morning after" pill for men? It works by changing your blood type.

They've got a new birth control pill for men now. I think that's fair. It makes a lot more sense to take the bullets out of the gun than to wear a bulletproof vest.

—GREG TRAVIS

A handsome fellow was traveling across the country and was out in the middle of the Iowa cornfields when night started to fall. Coming up to a farmhouse, he asked the farmer if he could put him up for the night. The farmer explained that he didn't want the guy sleeping under the same roof as his lovely daughter, but gave him permission to sleep in the barn. As the traveler headed for the barn, the farmer shouted after him that he was putting a barricade of eggs around his daughter's room just in case he should get any ideas. "If a single egg's broken in the morning," he yelled, "I'll shoot you in the back."

The fellow bedded down comfortably enough in the hay, but all night he was tossing and turning, thinking of the farmer's daughter. Finally, he couldn't take it anymore. He ran inside, through the wall of eggs and into the girl's room, where she showed him a very good time until it was almost dawn. Then, in something of a panic, he left the room and began frantically gluing all the eggs back together.

The last one had just been set in place when the farmer came out of his room. "Boy have you got will power," he commented, looking admiringly at his guest. "Not a single egg broken. Just for that, you get breakfast on the house." Taking five eggs off the pile, the farmer took them into the kitchen and cracked the first one against the edge of a bowl. Nothing came out. He cracked the second egg and still nothing came out. And the third, fourth, and fifth. Of course, they were all empty.

"Goddamn rooster's been using a rubber again!" groaned the farmer.

The phrase itself—birth control—doesn't make sense. It's nine months earlier that you need the control.

When Liam decided it was time for his friend Brendan to part with his virginity, he accompanied him to the local brothel and explained Brendan's condition to the madam.

"Don't worry, my boy, we'll get a nice lass to take care of ye," she promised. "You just do your part and make sure ye wear one of these."

And the madam took a condom out of her drawer and rolled it down over her thumb by way of instruction.

Brendan parted eagerly with his money and bounded up the stairs to Room Twelve, where a cheerful farm girl soon showed him the ropes.

After he'd cum, a frown passed over her face. "The rubber must have torn," she muttered. "I'm wet as the sea inside."

"Oh no, it didn't, Miss," Brendan cheerfully reassured her, holding up his thumb as evidence. "It's good as new."

"Mom, I'm pregnant," announced the sixteen-year-old one morning in a belligerent tone of voice.

Her mother paled.

"And it's all your fault," continued the girl.

"My fault?" gasped her mother, startled. "I bought you books, showed you pictures. I told you all about the facts of life."

"Yeah, yeah—but you never taught me how to give a decent blow job, did you?"

Birthdays

I think it's wonderful that you could all be here for the forty-third anniversary of my thirty-ninth birthday. We decided not to light the candles this year—we were afraid Pan Am would mistake it for a runway.

—Bob Hope

What greeting card is on sale only in Kentucky?
    "Happy Birthday, Uncle Dad."

It's an awful thing to grow old alone. My wife hasn't had a birthday in six years.

You know you're getting old when, by the time you've lit the last candle on the birthday cake, the first one has burned out.

You know you're getting old when the heat from the candles on the birthday cake keeps you from getting close enough to blow them out.

Books and Writing

First guy: Hey, did you hear Joe's writing a book?
    Second guy: Why doesn't he just buy one? It's faster.

I have a new book coming out. It's one of those self-help deals, it's called *How to Get Along with Everyone*. I wrote it with this other asshole.

—Steve Martin

Do you realize what would happen if Moses were alive today? He'd come down from Mount Sinai with the Ten Commandments and spend the next five years trying to get them published.

I went to a bookstore and asked the woman behind the counter where the self-help section was. She said, "If I told you, that would defeat the whole purpose."

—Brian Kiley

From the moment I picked it [a book] up until I laid it down, I was convulsed with laughter. Some day I intend reading it.

—Groucho Marx (attributed)

He writes so well, he makes me feel like putting the quill back in the goose.

—Fred Allen

A famous literary critic got drunk and confused at a cocktail party, and ended up in his host's pantry, reading the phone book. After about seventy-five pages, he looked up and murmured, "Plenty of characters, but the plot's weak."

I love being a writer. What I can't stand is the paperwork.

—Peter De Vries

I just heard about the greatest book club. You send in fifteen dollars a month for a year—and they leave you completely alone!

I never think at all when I write. Nobody can do two things at the same time and do them both well.

—Don Marquis

Getting a phone message from one of her authors, the editor called back. "What can I do for you, Tom?" she asked cordially.

"It's about my manuscript," said the writer. "The one I sent you a couple of months ago?"

"Uh, yes . . . yes. Can't wait to read it," stammered the editor, scratching her head, unable to summon up the slightest memory of the manuscript. "But remind me, Tom, is it a historical novel?"

"No," replied the writer dryly, "or at least, it wasn't when I sent it in."

I just got out of the hospital. I was in a speed-reading contest. I hit a bookmark.

—STEVEN WRIGHT

Why pay a dollar for a bookmark? Use the dollar as a bookmark.

—FRED STOLLER

Looking down sternly from the bench, the judge asked the defendant why, after a blameless six decades, she had turned to a life of crime.

"Your Honor, I began working on my memoirs," she explained, "and they were just too damn boring."

Boredom

"Now that you've made it to the top, Mike, what's the best thing about it?" asked the executive VP.

After a thoughtful pause, the new CEO replied, "These days, when I bore people, they think it's their fault, not mine."

She has the reputation of being outspoken—by no one.

—JACK PAAR

No one really listens to anyone else, and if you try it for a while, you'll see why.

—MIGNON MCLAUGHLIN

If you can't stand solitude, maybe you bore others, too.

—Bob Gordon

Bosses

The irritable director of a big agency had just concluded a presentation to a major client. Sensing it hadn't gone too well, he turned furiously on his hapless secretary and snarled, "Where the hell's my pen?"

"Why, behind your ear, Mr. Montclair," she stammered.

"Goddamit Brenda, you know how busy I am," he howled back. "Which ear?"

Definition of a power struggle: When your boss has the power and you have the struggle.

A man had been walking across a street, when all of a sudden he was clobbered by a hit-and-run driver. He died and was welcomed into Heaven by St. Peter.

"Life here is very similar to life down there," the saint said, pointing down to earth. "You can still get hurt up here, but it's offset by the fact that nothing is illegal and everything is free. Just be careful, and enjoy yourself."

Amazed and somewhat bewildered, the man started to take in the sights. Not watching where he was going, he stepped off the curb and was almost run over by an Oldsmobile Cutlass. "Wow, who the heck was that?" the man wondered aloud.

"That was Mr. Olds," said St. Peter. "He's a driving maniac, but you've got to be careful if you're going to stay here."

The newcomer nodded and continued on. A minute later, as he was carefully crossing over to a striptease joint, a speeding Cadillac nearly ran him over.

"Goddamn it! Who the hell was that asshole?" he screamed at St. Peter, who was still keeping an eye on him.

"None other than Mr. Ford. As you can see, the idiot enjoys driving fast," replied St. Peter. "I know it's difficult, but do try to be careful."

The man made extra sure before he attempted a third crossing, but just as he was about to reach the other side successfully, a Maserati driven by some long-haired freak appeared out of nowhere and bumped him back across the street.

"Okay, who the fuck was *that*?" he screamed as he lay sprawled at the saint's feet.

"Keep your voice down," St. Peter hissed. "That's the boss's son."

The boss, Ms. Bennett, always scheduled the weekly staff meetings for four thirty on Friday afternoons. When one of the employees finally got up the nerve to ask why, she explained, "I'll tell you why— I've learned that's the only time of the week when none of you seem to want to argue with me."

After the annual office Christmas party, Dawkins woke up with a pounding headache, cotton-mouthed, and utterly unable to recall the events of the preceding evening. After a trip to the bathroom, he was able to make his way downstairs, where his wife put some coffee in front of him.

"Louise," he moaned, "tell me what went on last night. Was it as bad as I think?"

"Even worse," she assured him, her voice dripping with scorn. "You made a complete ass of yourself, succeeded in antagonizing the entire board of directors, and insulted the president of the company to his face."

"He's an asshole—piss on him."

"You did," Louise informed him. "And he fired you."

"Well fuck him," retorted Dawkins feebly.

"I did. You're back at work on Monday."

A man was working at a construction site where each day the boss left at 11:00 A.M. and was gone for two hours. This became such a regular occurrence that the rest of the workers decided to spend the two hours in the bar across the street. The man, however, decided to head home for some extra nookie with his wife. When he got home, he found his boss busy banging his wife in the bedroom! Well, he walked right out and headed back to the job.

The following day, the man was working his ass off when everyone headed across to the bar. "Hey, aren't you coming?" asked one of them.

"Hell no," said the man. "I almost got caught yesterday!"

The orderly's duties included bringing his new boss a cup of coffee at six o'clock every morning, and every morning the boss was enraged because the coffee cup arrived two-thirds full. None of his insults and fits of rage produced a full cup of coffee, until he threatened the fellow with a one-third cut in pay.

The next morning he was greeted with a cup of coffee full to the brim, and the morning after that, and the morning after that. Finally, the boss couldn't resist smugly complimenting the orderly on his mastery of the new technique.

"Oh, there's nothing much to it, sir," admitted the fellow cheerfully. "I take some coffee in my mouth right outside the mess hall, and spit it back in outside your door."

The two old coots were both only a year short of retirement from the assembly line but, one Monday morning, that didn't keep Joe from boasting to Manny about his sexual endurance.

"Three times," gasped Manny admiringly. "How'd you do it?"

"It was easy." Joe looked down modestly. "I made love to my wife, and then I rolled over and took a ten-minute nap. When I woke up, I made love to her again and took another ten-minute nap. And then I put it to her again. Can you believe it! I woke up this morning feeling like a bull, I'll tell you."

"I gotta try it," said Manny. "Lorraine won't believe it's happening."

So that night he made love to his wife, took a ten-minute nap, made love to her again, took another nap, woke up and made love to her a third time, then rolled over and fell sound asleep.

He woke up feeling like a million bucks, pulled on his clothes, and ran to the factory, where he found his boss waiting outside for him.

"What's up, Boss?" he asked. "I've been working for you for twenty years and never been late once. You aren't going to hold these twenty minutes against me now, are you?"

"What twenty minutes?" growled the boss. "Where were you Tuesday? Where were you Wednesday?"

The slave driver of the Roman galleon leered down at his galley slaves and bellowed, "I've got some good news and some bad news. The good news is that you'll be getting double rations tonight."

The murmuring of the surprised slaves was interrupted by the bellow of the slave driver. "The bad news is that the commander's son wants to water ski."

Business

Sign in a corporate boardroom: "Thank heavens this is a free country where you can do exactly as the government pleases."

"My boy decided to go into business on a shoestring," said George. "He's tripled his investment, but he's still not satisfied, can you believe it?"

"Why not?" asked his friend.

"He can't think of anything to do with three shoestrings."

Two shoe salespeople were dispatched to a remote African country. In just a few days, their employer received telegrams from each.

One read: "Get me out of here—no one wears shoes." The other read: "Send more inventory—no one here owns shoes."

One New York shoe store ordered a large consignment of shoes from a manufacturer in Buffalo. A week later the store manager

received a letter saying, "Sorry, we cannot fill your order until full payment is made on the last one."

The manager wrote back, "Please cancel the new order. I can't wait that long."

—Joey Adams

First entrepreneur: I've got a great idea. I'm going to open up a bar and grill in the middle of the Sahara Desert.

Second entrepreneur: That's a ridiculous idea. You'll be lucky to get more than one customer a month.

First entrepreneur: Okay, but just think how thirsty he'll be!

Deciding it was time for a history review, the teacher asked the class, "Who can tell me what historical figure said, 'I have not yet begun to fight'?"

The little Japanese girl in the front row raised her hand and answered, "John Paul Jones."

"Very good, Miako. Now, who can tell me who said, 'I regret that I have but one life to give for my country'?"

Again the little Japanese girl was the only one to raise her hand, and piped up, "That was Nathan Hale."

The teacher said to the class, "What's going on? So far, Miako is the only one to answer any of my questions."

Suddenly a voice was heard from the back of the room. "Aw, fuck the Japanese!"

"Who said that?" asked the teacher sharply.

Miako's hand shot up. "Lee Iacocca!" she said brightly.

—Wayland and Madam

Don't trust a computer you can't throw out a window.

—Steve Wozniak

Three guys went into business for themselves. Said the first, "I put up sixty-five percent of the capital, so I'm the president and chairman of the board."

"I put up thirty percent of the money," said the second, "so I'm appointing myself vice president, secretary, and treasurer."

"Well I put up five percent," pointed out the third partner. "What's that make me?"

The chairman said, "I'm appointing you vice president of sex and music."

"That sounds mighty fine," said the third man, "but what does it mean?"

"It means that when I want your fucking advice, I'll whistle."

"How'd you get this big executive job?" asked the secretary. "You've only been here three months."

The young man shrugged modestly and explained, "I ran into my father and he took a liking to me."

—JOEY ADAMS

Struthers was assigned to show an important stockholder around the rubber-goods factory. The woman nodded approvingly when shown the giant machine that spit out an endless stream of rubber nipples.

"One of our steady sellers, lotsa babies being born these days," Struthers explained.

Not much later the stockholder inquired as to the function of another huge machine spitting out little rubber discs. "Condoms," Struthers informed her. "Big sellers, too."

"Understandably," she commented. "But why's that needle coming down and punching a little hole in each one?"

"Hey," he whispered conspiratorially, "we can't let the nipple business go downhill now, can we?"

Loeb and Weinstein were discussing the affairs of a fellow textile merchant. "Did you hear about Schwartz?" asked Loeb.

"Hear what? How's business for him?"

"Finished. Over the weekend his warehouse burned to the ground."

"Such a nice guy, Schwartz," responded Weinstein. "And finally he gets the good luck he deserves."

The bum rang the doorbell of a Beverly Hills mansion, and rang and rang, undissuaded by the fact that it was the middle of the night.

Finally, ten minutes later, the disheveled homeowner came to the door, pulling his silk dressing gown around him.

"What are you doing leaning on my doorbell at this hour?" he asked.

"Can I have two dollars?" asked the bum.

"Why did you have to wake me out of a sound sleep for two goddamn dollars?" the millionaire raged.

"I don't tell you how to run your business," was the cool response, "so don't tell me how to run mine."

An elderly real estate businessman and his young protégé are standing on top of a ridge overlooking a vast valley of undeveloped land. The businessman says, "Stick with me, kid, and someday that will all be mine."

You don't want another Enron? Here's your law: If a company can't explain *in one sentence* what it does, it's illegal.

—LEWIS BLACK

The businessman decided it was time to give his daughter, a recent business school graduate, a little lecture. "In business, ethics are very important," he began. "Say, for instance, that a client comes in and settles his account with a hundred-dollar bill. After he leaves, you notice a second hundred dollar bill stuck to the first one. Immediately you are presented with an ethical dilemma. . . ." The businessman paused for dramatic effect. "Should you tell your partner?"

You may recall that not too long ago the state of Kentucky enticed Toyota to build a plant near the city of Georgetown, after offering

the company a very sweet deal. Well, one day Martha Layne Collins, the Governor of Kentucky, was scheduled to meet with both the Pope and the president of Toyota. Very upset, her secretary rushed into her office with the confession that she had scheduled both appointments for the same time, and that both distinguished visitors were on their way.

"Which do you want to see first?" she asked the governor.

"I'll see the Pope first," Collins answered. "I only have to kiss his *ring*."

Weiss and Stein went into business together and opened a wholesale men's clothing outlet. Things went well for a year or so, but then the recession came along and they found themselves sitting on ten thousand plaid jackets, which they couldn't sell to save their souls. Just as they were discussing bankruptcy, a fellow came in and introduced himself as a buyer for a big menswear chain in Australia. "Wouldn't happen to have any plaid jackets would you?" he asked. "They're selling like crazy down under."

Weiss looked at Stein. "Maybe we can work something out, if the price is right," he said coolly to the Aussie.

After some tough negotiating, a price was agreed on and the papers were signed. But as he was leaving, their big prospect said, "Just one thing, mates. I've got to get authorization from the home office for a deal this big. Today's Monday. If you don't get a cable from me by Friday, the deal's final."

For the next four days, Stein and Weiss paced miserably back and forth, sweating blood and wincing every time they heard footsteps outside their door. On Friday the hours crept by, but by four o'clock they figured they were home free—until there was a loud knock on the door. "Western Union!" a voice called out.

As Stein collapsed, white-faced, behind his desk, Weiss dashed to the door. A minute later, he rushed back into the office waving a telegram. "Great news, Stein," he cried jubilantly, "great news! Your mother's dead!"

C

California

California is a fine place to live—if you happen to be an orange.

—FRED ALLEN

The only difference between California and yogurt is that yogurt has active culture.

—WOODY ALLEN

I just heard about the Mercedes back-to-school sale in Beverly Hills.

—RED BUTTONS

So you call this California, the land of golden sunshine, do you? Well, let me tell you something. Every day of every year, the sun shines on New York three hours before it shines on you, so all California gets is New York's secondhand sunshine. Think that one over.

—JAMES THORNTON

Everybody in Los Angeles is in therapy. It's a good thing they don't have parking spaces for the emotionally handicapped. There'd be no place to park.

—JACKSON PERDUE

They know only one word of more than one syllable here, and that is fillum.

—LOUIS SHERWIN

An intellectual in Hollywood is anyone who can read freeway signs without moving his lips.

You can take all the sincerity in Hollywood, place it in the navel of a fruit fly, and still have room enough for three caraway seeds and a producer's heart.

—FRED ALLEN

When I first came to Hollywood, Joe greeted me at the Friars and said, "This is the only t-town in the country wh-wh-where you wake up in the m-m-m-morning and listen to the birds coughing."

—MILTON BERLE, ABOUT JOEY FRISCO

Los Angeles is a great place. Where else can you smell the air and see it coming at you at the same time? You want to see blue water, you have to look in the toilet bowl.

—JACKIE GAYLE

Living in California adds ten years to a man's life. And those extra ten years I'd like to spend in New York.

—HARRY RUBY

There are two million interesting people in New York and only seventy-eight in Los Angeles.

—NEIL SIMON

How many Californians does it take to change a lightbulb?

Six. One to turn the bulb, one for support, and four to relate to the experience.

Good news: Adolf Hitler has been found, alive! And he'll be tried for murder.

Bad news: He'll be tried in California.

Cars and Driving

Have you noticed? Anyone driving faster than you is an idiot, and anyone driving slower than you is a moron.

—GEORGE CARLIN

What a horrible car accident. I had the right of way, but the other guy had the truck.

How come you have to pay someone to rotate your tires? Isn't that the basic idea behind the wheel? Don't they rotate on their own?

—JERRY SEINFELD

I was in a cab the other day, and—you'll find this hard to believe— it was actually driven by an American citizen.

—STEVE ALLEN

What did it say on the redneck's bumper sticker?
I Know Jack Shit.

Signs on the freeway are funny. They have a sign that says, "Orange Cones Mean Men at Work." What else could orange cones mean? Psychedelic witches embedded in asphalt?

—KAREN BABBIT

I like driving around with my two dogs, especially on the freeway. I make them wear little hats so I can use the car pool lanes.

—MONICA PIPER

A hundred years ago we were much smarter. Then you lived until you died, and not until you were just run over.

—WILL ROGERS

Everything is drive-through. In California they even have a burial service called Jump-in-the-Box.

—WIL SHRINER

The wheel was man's greatest invention until he got behind it.

—BILL IRELAND

A lot of friction is caused by half the drivers trying to go fast enough to thrill their girlfriends and the other half trying to go slow enough to placate their wives.

—BILL VAUGHAN

A man was driving along in his beat-up old Dodge, when suddenly it broke down. He was parked on the side of the road, trying fix it, when a Jaguar pulled up in front of him and offered to help.

After a few minutes the two men obviously weren't going to get the old car going again, so the Jaguar driver offered to tow the Dodge to the nearest garage.

A few minutes later the two had hitched up the old Dodge to the Jaguar, and they agreed that if the Jaguar driver was going too fast, the man should blow his horn and flash his lights to get him to slow down. With that, the two men got into their cars and the Jaguar driver started to pull away, with the Dodge behind it.

At the first traffic light, a Ferrari pulled up beside the Jaguar and started to rev his engine provocatively. As soon as the light turned green, the Ferrari and Jaguar drivers hit their accelerators and took off. Before long the cars were racing at over 120 mph.

As the cars sped along, they passed through a police speed trap. The officer couldn't believe his eyes when he saw the three cars go by, and he decided that he couldn't catch them all by himself, so he decided to radio for help: "You won't believe what I just saw! I saw a Ferrari and a Jaguar doing 120 mph side by side, and a beat-up old Dodge behind them flashing his lights and blowing his horn trying to get by!"

I think all cars should have car phones in them and their license plates should be their phone numbers. So you can call 'em up and tell 'em to get the hell out of the way. Old people would have eight-hundred numbers.

—JOHN MENDOZA

Why do they call it rush hour when nothing moves?

—ROBIN WILLIAMS

Nothing depreciates your car so fast as a new model in your neighbor's garage.

The gas-station attendant looks at the car and says, "You got a flat tire."

I say, "No, the other three just swelled up."

—WILL ENGVALL

Some guy came running up to me the other night and said, "Somebody stole my car!"

I said, "Did you see him?"

—BILL BARNER

What does it take to get a cab driver's license? I think all you need is a face. This seems to be their big qualification. And a name with eight consonants in a row. Have you ever checked out some of the names on the license? The *o* with the line through it? What planet is *that* from? You need a chart of the elements just to report the guy: "Yes, Officer, his name was Amal—and then the symbol for boron!"

—JERRY SEINFELD

I was stopped once for going fifty-three in a thirty-five-mile-per-hour zone, but I got off. I told them I had dyslexia.

—SPANKY (STEVE McFARLIN)

The guy was such a bad driver, the police gave him a season ticket. . . .

Kermit: Fozzie, where did you learn to drive?
　　Fozzie: I took a correspondence course.

　　　　　　　　　　　　—Jerry Juhl and Jack Burns

My car insurance is with one of those companies that questions everything. I think I've got the One-Hundred-Dollar Debatable.

My license plate says PMS. Nobody cuts me off.

　　　　　　　　　　　　—Wendy Liebman

Why do women have such trouble parking cars?
　　Because all their lives they've been told that this [hold hands a few inches apart] is eight inches.

Americans are broad-minded people. They'll accept the fact that a person can be a dope fiend, a wife beater, and even a newspaperman, but if a man doesn't drive, there's something wrong with him.

　　　　　　　　　　　　—Art Buchwald

I like doing things to help people. People don't wear their seat belts anymore. I figure, I'll make fuzzy clothes and make seats out of Velcro.

　　　　　　　　　　　　—Andy Andrews

Anybody abuse rental cars? If I'm really bored, I'll take one to Earl Scheib and have it painted for $29.95. This really messes up their paperwork for months and months. The thing that bothers me is when you have to return one with a full tank of gas. It makes everybody mad. They say bring it back full. You know what I do now? I just top it off with a garden hose.

　　　　　　　　　　　　—Wil Shriner

Television sets are becoming very popular in automobiles these days. My uncle has a television set in his automobile, but it led to a little trouble. You see, he was sitting in the car, watching television, while his wife was driving on the highway at sixty miles per hour. Then the commercial came on, and he stepped out to go to the bathroom.

—JACKIE CLARK

What is happening when you hear varoom . . . screech, varoom . . . screech, varoom . . . screech?

A moron is trying to drive through an intersection with a flashing red light.

A man walked up to the counter of an auto-parts store. "Excuse me," he said, "I'd like to get a new gas cap for my Yugo."

"Sure," the clerk replied. "Sounds like a fair exchange to me."

What does a moron say when you ask her if her blinker is on?

It's on. It's off. It's on. It's off. It's on. It's off.

Liz: I get so nervous and frightened during driving tests!

Doctor: Never mind, you'll pass eventually.

Liz: But I'm the examiner!

If you don't like the way women drive, get off the sidewalk.

What do you call the owner of an American-made car?

A pedestrian.

Celebrities

Michael Jackson

A salesman was in Dallas, Texas, for the first time. He wandered into a bar and proceeded to down a pretty fair number of straight Jack Daniels in a couple of hours, becoming quite sloshed.

Suddenly, he noticed Michael Jackson on a news program on the bar's TV. "There's the biggest horse's ass who ever walked on earth," he exclaimed.

With that, the cowboy sitting next to him stood, punched him in the jaw, and sat back down on the bar stool.

"Whew," said the salesman, climbing back up on his bar stool. "I better be careful what I say. I had no idea I was in Michael Jackson country."

"You aren't in Michael Jackson country, you idiot," replied the bartender, "you're in *horse* country!"

The Kennedys

Why did Maria Shriver marry Arnold Schwarzenegger?

So they could breed a bulletproof Kennedy.

G. Gordon Liddy, Oliver North, and Ted Kennedy are captured by the enemy and sentenced to fifty lashes for spying. The colonel was in a kindly mood, and allowed them a choice of something to put on their backs.

"What do you want on your back, Liddy?" the colonel barked.

"Nuthin," huffed Liddy. He received his lashes without a sound.

"What do you want on your back, North?"

"Suntan oil please," answered North. As the whip descended time after time, North screamed in pain.

"What do you want on your back, Teddy?" the colonel asked for the third time.

"Liddy," answered Kennedy.

Jack Lemmon

What does a caddie say to Jack Lemmon, who, when lying tenth and facing a thirty-five-foot putt, asks him for advice on how a putt will break?

Who cares?

Willie Nelson

What has a 175 legs and 5 teeth?

The front row of a Willie Nelson concert.

Richard Nixon

Did you hear they're building an archive for the Nixon papers?

No admission charge—but you have to break in.

Miscellaneous Celebrities

Ed Sullivan and a friend were at a huge gathering, and his friend was amazed at all the people whom Ed knew. "Actually, I think I know every important person in the world," said Ed, "and then some."

"Come on," said his friend, "that's impossible."

"Well, pick someone and I'll tell you if I know him," said Sullivan.

"OK, how about the Pope?"

"Of course I know the Pope."

"Prove it," said his friend.

So, eager to prove the point, Ed and his friend traveled to Vatican City. When they arrived, hundreds of thousands of people were milling about St. Peter's Square, waiting to hear the Pope. Standing way in the back, Ed said to his friend, "You wait here, and in twenty minutes you'll see me on the balcony talking to the Pope. And just so that you know it's me, I'll wear this bright orange jacket."

An hour goes by, and there is no sign of Ed on the balcony with the Pope. The friend, thinking Ed had duped him all along, starts looking around at the crowd. Suddenly, an elderly Italian man taps the friend on the shoulder and says, "Hey, sonny, who's that guy up there with Mr. Sullivan?"

Hubert Humphrey was asked to be an adviser on a university student's dissertation. A request he accepted with delight. All proceeded well, and on the date the paper was due, the student delivered a nicely bound copy. Two months went by and the student hadn't heard a word. So, he went to Mr. Humphrey's office and asked him what he thought of the paper. "Well," said Mr. Humphrey, "I think it needs to be redone."

Although dejected, the student decided to take another crack at the project.

And two months later, the student delivered the new version to Mr. Humphrey, and another month went by without hearing a word.

So, again, the student went to see Mr. Humphrey, and again, Mr. Humphrey told him it had to be redone.

Totally beside himself, the student went back to the drawing board and rewrote the paper for a third time. Two months later he returned to Mr. Humphrey's office with the new term paper in hand, and said to him, "I've re-researched and rewritten to the extent that I've left no stone unturned and no thought unanalyzed. There is just nothing more I can do."

"OK," said Mr. Humphrey, "I guess I read this one."

O. J. Simpson went off and joined the French Foreign Legion. Stationed at a desert in Northern Africa, he asked the regimental sergeant major:

"What do you men do for sex out here?"

"Well, there's this camel out back," replied the sergeant major.

"How disgusting. I'd never consider such an outrageous thing," said O.J.

After six months, O.J. once again went to see the sergeant major.

"Take me to that damn camel, but make sure none of the other men know anything about it."

"Yes, sir."

It was really terrible, and when he was through, O.J. was thoroughly disgusted with himself.

"Do the men really use the camel this way?" O.J. asked the sergeant major.

"Oh, no, they ride it down the path to a nearby whorehouse."

What do Pete Rose and the Mafia have in common?

More than three thousand hits.

Charity

"Billy, this morning I was inspired to see on the news that before coming here you were at the opening of Tempura House, the new shelter for lightly battered women."

—ROGER EBERT, ABOUT BILLY CRYSTAL

Young Mrs. Townsend wanted very much to participate in the correct charities, and when the annual Junior League Easter Charity Ball came around, she volunteered to head the committee. It took a lot of organizing, but the party went off without a hitch, and she dined and danced into the wee hours.

When the festivities ended, she was dismayed to observe a bag lady bundled on the sidewalk next to her Saab Turbo. Hearing the rustle of Mrs. Townsend's taffeta skirts, the old woman extended a grimy palm and asked the socialite if she could spare any change.

"Oooh," gasped Mrs. Townsend, "the nerve, and after I spent all night slaving to help people like you! Aren't you *ever* satisfied?"

Remember the poor—it costs nothing.

—Josh Billings

'Tis always more blessed to give than to receive; for example, wedding presents.

—H. L. Mencken

Hear about the great bank robbery in Israel? They got ten thousand dollars in cash and more than sixty million dollars in anonymous pledges.

—Gene Baylos

He'll be remembered best by the good he did for people. I have to tell you about the benefit I did with Bob Hope when Ed [Sullivan] insisted we join him at St. Albans Hospital to bring a little cheer to the veterans coming home from Vietnam.

"One thing they don't want is sympathy," Bob explained. "When I walk into a ward filled with kids who can't get out of bed and are harnessed to contraptions, I usually say, 'That's okay, fellas, you don't have to get up for me.'"

—Joey Adams, about Bob Hope

I never thought God would hold someone accountable for not raising money.

—Pat Robertson, on Oral Robert's warning that God might "call him back" if contributions were inadequate

When in doubt about a contribution, make it money. It's the easiest gift to exchange.

We do not quite forgive a giver. The hand that feeds us is in some danger of being bitten.

—Ralph Waldo Emerson

Mrs. Rossdale was on her way to meet a friend, when a bum came up to her with his hand out. "Lady, can you help me? I haven't eaten in three days."

"So force yourself," she snapped, and walked on.

A large part of altruism, even when it is perfectly honest, is grounded upon the fact that it is uncomfortable to have unhappy people about.

—H. L. Mencken

A clergyman famous for his abilities to get the collection plate filled turned his talents to a Sunday school audience. Drawing an elaborate analogy between his role as the pastor of a congregation to that of a shepherd to his flock of sheep, he paused dramatically, then turned to the children.

"And who can tell me what a shepherd does for the sheep?"

A little hand shot up. "I know, Reverend—shears them!"

Did you hear about the frustrated wealthy golfer who donated a set of fourteen golf clubs to a local charity? All but one had a swimming pool with it.

The businessman was rather put off when the bum approached him with a request for five dollars to buy a cup of coffee.

"You can buy coffee for sixty cents," he responded tartly.

"Right you are," conceded the bum cheerfully, "but I like to leave a big tip."

The pig complained to the cow, saying, "I know you give milk, leather, and beef, but I give pork, pigskin, and even my bristles are used for brushes. Why are you loved so much more?"

"Maybe," the cow said sweetly, "it's because I give while I'm still alive."

You can't take it with you. You never see a U-Haul following a hearse.

—Ellen Glasgow

A good deed never goes unpunished.

—Gore Vidal

At the Harvest Festival in church, the area behind the pulpit was piled high with tins of fruit for the old-age pensioners. We had collected the tinned fruit from door to door. Most of it came from old-age pensioners.

—Clive James

Without warning, a hurricane blew across the Caribbean. The luxurious yacht soon foundered in the huge waves and sank without a trace. Only two survivors, the boat's owner and its steward, managed to swim to the closest island. Observing that it was utterly uninhabited, the steward burst into tears, wringing his hands and moaning that they'd never be heard of again. Meanwhile, his companion leaned back against a palm tree and relaxed.

"Dr. Karpman, how can you be so calm?" moaned the distraught steward. "We're going to die on this godforsaken island. They're never going to find us."

"Let me tell you something, Mitchell," began Karpman with a smile. "Four years ago I gave five hundred thousand dollars to the United Way, and five hundred thousand dollars to the United Jewish Appeal. Three years ago I did very well in the stock market, so I contributed eight hundred and fifty thousand to each.

Last year business was good, so both charities got a million dollars."

"So?" screamed the wretched steward.

"It's time for their annual fund drives," the yachtsman
pointed out, "and I know they're going to find me."

This year alone Georgie Jessel personally supported more than a million Jews in Israel—and 325 chorus girls in the United States.

—JACK BENNY

A woman was chatting with her next-door neighbor. "I feel real
good today. I started out this morning with an act of unselfish
generosity. I gave a five-dollar bill to a bum."

"You mean you gave a bum five dollars? That's a lot of money
to give away like that. What did your husband say about it?"

"Oh, he thought it was the thing to do. He said, 'Thanks.' "

Children

I was asking my friend, who has children, "What if I have a baby and I
dedicate my life to it and it grows up to hate me? And it blames
everything wrong with its life on me?" And she said, "What do you
mean, 'If'?"

—RITA RUDNER

Insanity is hereditary—you get it from your children.

—SAM LEVENSON

Children are stupid. That's why they're in school. I'd lecture for an
hour about percentages and interest rates and at the end I'd ask one
simple question: You put ten grand in the bank for one year at five
and a half percent and what do you get?

Some kid would always yell out, "A toaster!"

—JEFFREY JENA

**Little Mortie got a real surprise when he barged into his parents'
room one night. "And you slap me for sucking my *thumb*?" he
screamed.**

The wealthy old man looked around the table at his sons and daughters and their spouses gathered for a family reunion. "Not a single
grandchild," he said with a sigh. "Why, I'll give a million dollars to
the first kid who presents me with a little one to bounce on my knee.
Now, let's say grace."

When the old man lifted his eyes again, his wife was the only
other person at the table.

**As a kid I used to have a lemonade stand. The sign said, "All you
can drink for a dime." So some kid would come up, plunk down
the dime, drink a glass, and then say, "Refill it."**

I'd say, "That'll be another dime."

"How come? Your sign says—"

"Well, you had a glass, didn't you?"

"Yeah."

"Well, that's all you can drink for a dime."

—Flip Wilson

If a kid asks where rain comes from, I think a cute thing to tell him
is, "God is crying." And if he asks why God is crying, another cute
thing to tell him is, "Probably because of something you did."

—Jack Handey

**Children are a great comfort in your old age—and they help you to
reach it faster, too.**

—Lionel M. Kauffman

I tell you one thing that's great about children. They don't need a
show to have fun. What do they need? A book of matches, some oily
rags, a little brother . . . that's all they need.

—Dave Attell

A child develops individuality long before he develops taste. I have seen my kid straggle into the kitchen in the morning with outfits that need only one accessory—an empty gin bottle.

—ERMA BOMBECK

Ask your child what he wants for dinner only if he's buying.

—FRAN LEBOWITZ

Once upon a time a four-year-old boy was visiting his aunt and uncle. He was a very outspoken little boy and often had to be censured to say the right thing at the right time. One day at lunch, when the aunt had company, the little boy said, "Auntie, I want to tinkle." Auntie took the little boy aside and said, "Never say that, sonny. If you want to tinkle, say, 'I want to whisper.'" And the incident was forgotten.

That night when Uncle and Auntie were soundly sleeping, the little boy climbed into bed with them. He tugged at his uncle's shoulder and said, "Uncle, I want to whisper."

Uncle said, "All right, sonny, don't wake Auntie up. Whisper in my ear."

The little boy was sent back to his parents the next day.

—GEORGE JESSEL

In America there are two classes of travel: first class, and with children.

—ROBERT BENCHLEY

Any kid'll run an errand for you if you ask at bedtime.

—RED SKELTON

I've got nothing against kids. I just follow the advice on every bottle in my medicine cabinet: "Keep away from children."

The pretty teacher was concerned about one of her eleven-year-old students. Taking him aside after class one day, she asked, "George, why has your schoolwork been so poor lately?"

"I'm in love," the boy replied.

Holding back an urge to smile, she asked, "With whom?"

"With you," he said.

"But, George," she said gently, "don't you see how silly that is? It's true that I would like a husband of my own some day. But I don't want a child."

"Oh, don't worry," the boy said reassuringly, "I'll use a rubber."

Late one night, little Johnny woke up to some loud noises coming from his parents' bedroom. He got out of bed and walked down the hall toward their room. Before he got to the end of the hall, the noises had stopped and the bathroom light had gone on. Little Johnny walked into the bathroom and saw his father removing a used condom.

"Daddy, what are you doing?" asked little Johnny.

His father looked around nervously, wondering what he could tell his son. "I, um, I'm just checking out the bathroom for mice," replied his father.

Johnny looked at his father with a gaze of confusion and said, "Well, what are you doing? Screwing them?"

It seems that a little girl and a little boy are arguing about differences between the sexes, he arguing that boys are inherently better and she that girls are. The subject, of course, spills over into the personal realm, so that the real issue is which of the two children is superior. Finally, the boy drops his pants and says, "Here's something I have that you'll never have!"

The little girl is pretty upset by this, since it is quite clearly true. She turns and runs home.

A while later, she comes running back with a smile on her face.

She drops her pants, and says, "My mommy says that with one of these, I can have as many of those as I want!"

Hanging out with a baby is like hanging out with a really, really small . . . really, really hammered person all the time. That's really all a baby is. Just the smallest drunkest person that you've ever seen in your life. I found myself talking to my sister's baby the same way I do a buddy at the end of a Saturday night. It's the same conversation. It's just me standing over him going, "What's wrong dude? Why you crying?"

—Nick Swardson

Two Iraqi fathers meet on the street and ask each other how they've been. One replies, "Terrible. With this war, I've lost my house and business. How have you been? And the boys, how are they? My two sons became suicide bombers." The other man says, "These kids blow up so fast these days."

—Jeff Pirrami

When you talk to a kid on the phone, you gotta remember the conversation could go in any direction. You just gotta get ready. There's no segues in the conversation. "Dad, are you coming home tomorrow?" "No, I'm not." "I have one thousand pennies."

—Ray Romano

Alligators have the right idea. They eat their young.

—Eve Arden

The rotten kid next door isn't completely useless—at least ten parents use him as a bad example.

I don't have any kids. Well, at least none that I know about. I'd like to have kids one day, though. I want to be called Mommy by someone other than Spanish guys in the street.

—Carol Leifer

Circumcision

Two men were standing at adjacent urinals when one said to the other, "I'll bet you were born in Newark, Ohio."

"Why, that's right," said the second man in surprise.

"And I'll bet you were circumcised when you were three days old."

"Right again. But how'd you—"

"And I'll bet it was done by old Doc Steadman."

"Well, yes, but how did you know?" asked the second man in amazement.

"Well, old Doc always cut them at a sixty-degree angle," explained the first guy, "and you're pissing on my shoe."

An old Jew was retiring from the string and twine business. "Herschel," he implored his best friend, "I got one last load of string. Buy me out so I can retire with an empty shop and a clear heart."

Herschel had no interest in purchasing a load of string, but his old friend's impassioned pleading finally wore him down. "Myron, all right, all right," he finally conceded. "I'll buy some of your string—enough to reach from the tip of your nose to the tip of your dick."

To Herschel's surprise, his friend embraced him warmly and left without another word. He was even more surprised when a truck arrived the next morning loaded with a massive roll of string. "Myron, what is this?!" he screamed at his friend over the phone.

"My nose is in Palm Beach," explained Myron happily, "but the tip of my dick is buried somewhere outside Minsk."

I am not a rich man, but whatever I have is profit. I began with nothing—not only that, but after I was a few days old, they took something away from me.

—George Jessel

A small-town doctor routinely performed circumcisions, and got in the habit of saving the foreskins in a jar of formaldehyde. Many years went by, it came time to retire, and the doctor was cleaning out his office when he came across the jar, now completely full. "Why throw it out?" he reasoned. So he took it to the tailor's shop downstairs with instructions to make whatever he saw fit.

Two weeks later the tailor presented him with a beautiful little wallet. "A wallet! That's all I get after a lifetime of work?" exclaimed the doctor. "There were hundreds and hundreds of foreskins in that jar!"

"Relax, Doc, just relax," said the tailor soothingly. "Rub it for a minute or two and it turns into a suitcase."

An adult man was converting and becoming a Jew. When asked if he minded being circumcised, he replied, "Why not, it's no skin off my nose."

—RED BUTTONS

What is the proper medical term for the circumcision of a rabbit?

A hare cut.

Vaudeville, radio, and television entertainer Eddie Cantor sent this telegram to producer Irving Thalberg after the birth of Thalberg's first son: "Congratulations on your latest production— I'm sure it will look better after it's been cut."

—JOEY BISHOP

Anybody here know what you call the man who performs the ritual of the bris? You know what it is? That's right. A moyel. A moyel. I want to tell you about a man who was walking along the street in New York.

He passed by a jewelry shop, walked inside, and said to the owner, "Could you repair my watch?"

He said, "I'm sorry, I don't repair watches."

"You don't repair watches? What do you do?"

"I'm a moyel."

"You're a moyel? Then why do you put all those watches in the window?" asked the man.

He says, "Well, what would you put in the window?"

—Dr. Murray Banks

College

College is the best time of your life. When else are your parents going to spend thousands of dollars a year just for you to go to a strange town and get drunk every night?

—David Wood

I have a daughter who goes to SMU. She could've gone to UCLA here in California, but it's one more letter she'd have to remember.

—Shecky Greene

I was thrown out of NYU. On the metaphysics final I looked within the soul of the boy sitting next to me.

—Woody Allen

If you've never met a student from the University of Chicago, I'll describe him to you. If you give him a glass of water, he says, "This is a glass of water. But is it a glass of water? And if it is a glass of water, why is it a glass of water? And eventually he dies of thirst."

—Shelley Berman

How many Harvard grads does it take to screw in a lightbulb?

Just one. He grabs the bulb and waits for the world to revolve around him.

I went to college, majored in philosophy. My father said, "Why don't you minor in communications so you can wonder out loud?"

So I did. I got out of school, landed a job as a morning DJ on an all-philosophy radio station, WYMI. "Good morning, it's 8:05 on YMI. For those of you just waking up, what's the point, really?"

—MIKE DUGAN

A graduate with a science degree asks, "Why does it work?"

The graduate with an engineering degree asks, "How does it work?"

The graduate with an accounting degree asks, "How much will it cost?"

The graduate with a liberal arts degree asks, "Do you want fries with that?"

I couldn't get a date the entire freshman year of college. The whole year I spent . . . well, they call it "stalking" now. But I call it "getting to know you."

—DAVID ALAN GRIER

Comedians

When the iceman cometh, I hope he cometh all over you.

—RED BUTTONS, ABOUT JOEY BISHOP

You know, you can be only thirty-five years old, but if your first joke doesn't get a laugh, you get to be eighty in a hurry. And if you're eighty and you get laughs in a hurry, then you get to be thirty. Jack will always be thirty.

—GEORGE BURNS, ABOUT JACK BENNY

Joey Adams received an honorary law degree from a Chinese university. I am told that a horse once graduated with an honorary degree from this institution. It was the first time in history a college gave an honorary degree to an entire *horse*.

—BOB HOPE

What a wonderful thing to be conscious. I wonder what the people in New Jersey do?

—Woody Allen

Take Bob Hope, for example. Take away his class, his dignity, his charm, and what have you got? Milton Berle!

—Al Bernie

I've known all of you, Bill. And the truth is, you do taste like chicken. I love you, man!

—Robin Williams, about Billy Crystal

The Friars hosted a night in honor of Gene Baylos. Gene did a good bit of Joe E.'s routine that night, and right before, Joe was introduced to say something nice about Baylos.
   "I like Gene," he said. "He's got very witty ears."

—Joey Adams, about Joe. E. Lewis

Sammy was brought up in a poor colored family—and grew up in a rich Jewish home.

—Red Buttons, about Sammy Davis, Jr.

He's so popular, when he was in Vietnam they were shooting at him from both sides.

—Don Rickles, about Bob Hope

I'd like to introduce Henny Youngman, the king of the one-liners— that's because the schmuck can't remember two. This man is the only comic in town that can tell four jokes in a minute, because he's never interrupted by laughs. I love him—I have no taste, but I love him.

—Milton Berle, about Henny Youngman

Jerry is the only man to get a Dear John letter from Typhoid Mary—they caught him selling Portnoy coloring books on Sesame Street.

—MILTON BERLE, ABOUT JERRY LEWIS

In France, Jerry Lewis is hailed as a genius. That's the same country that burned Joan of Arc.

—CHARLIE CALLAS, ABOUT JERRY LEWIS

This [bleeping bleep] is Man of the Year? I wouldn't vote him Jew of the Block.

—JAN MURRAY, ABOUT JERRY LEWIS

What pisses me off, here's a man, says one fucking word, "Marvelous!" Everybody's marvelous. You're fucking marvelous. You're marvelous. He gets the fucking Oscar.

—PAT COOPER, ABOUT BILLY CRYSTAL

Conscience

A guilty conscience is the mother of invention.

—CAROLYN WELLS

Conscience is the inner voice that warns us that someone may be looking.

—H. L. MENCKEN

Conscience is the one thing that hurts when everything else feels great.

Confession is good for the soul only in the sense that a tweed coat is good for dandruff.

—PETER DE VRIES

A Sunday school teacher was having a hard time getting her young charges to grasp the message of the Good Samaritan. Finally, she pointed at one of the least attentive children and asked, "Alison, suppose on the way to church you passed a vacant lot and saw a man in ragged clothes lying on the ground, so badly beaten up that he was covered in blood . . . What would you do?"

The eight-year-old's response: "I'd throw up!"

Christ died for our sins. Dare we make his martyrdom meaningless by not committing them?

—JULES FEIFFER

Conservation and Ecology

I didn't realize how bad the smog was getting until they started making freeway signs in Braille.

Pollution is so bad that when I put air in my tires, two of them died.

—LEE TULLY

The giant panda lives in bamboo thickets and feeds on bamboo shoots. There are only thirty-six giant pandas left. The reason there are only thirty-six giant pandas left is the shortage of bamboo shoots, which the natives eat in great quantities, especially with baked giant panda.

—JACK DOUGLAS

It's not that our rivers aren't fit to drink . . . but where else can you see the fish coughing?

Help beautify our city dumps—throw something pretty away today!

The other day I bought a wastebasket and brought it home in a paper bag. And when I got home I put the paper bag in the wastebasket.

—LILY TOMLIN

I just found out where all that chemical fertilizer comes from: plastic horses.

A new report from the government says raw eggs may have salmonella and may be unsafe. In fact, the latest government report says it wasn't the fall that killed Humpty Dumpty—he was dead before he hit the ground.

—JAY LENO

What about all those detergents that are going out into our rivers and the ocean? If this keeps up, it's going to leave a ring around the country.

—JOHN BYNER

Pollution is so bad in New York that I saw the Statue of Liberty holdin' her nose.

—MOMS MABLEY

Save Water—Shower with a Friend

Two tall trees are growing in the woods. A small tree begins to grow between them.

One tall tree says to the other, "Is that a son of a beech or a son of a birch?" The other tall tree says it cannot tell. Then one day a woodpecker lands on the small tree.

One tall tree says, "Woodpecker, you are a tree expert. Can you tell if that is a son of a beech or a son of a birch?"

The woodpecker takes a taste of the small tree. He replies, "It is neither a son of a beech nor a son of a birch. That, gentlemen, is the best piece of ash I have ever had my pecker in!"

Cooking

I can't cook. I use a smoke alarm as a timer.

—Carol Siskind

My wife's not the worst cook in the world, but she keeps burning the coffee. You would, too, if you kept pouring it through the toaster all the time.

—Jack E. Leonard

Did you hear about the guy who went ice fishing and brought home a hundred pounds of ice?
   His wife died trying to cook it.

My husband says I treat him like he's a god; every meal is a burnt offering.

—Rhonda Hansome

When microwave ovens didn't exist . . . did people sit around [in an emotional vacuum] saying, "Heat is so boring. I wish I could bombard a potato with mutant intergalactic energy?"

—Colin McEnroe

When Marilyn Monroe was married to Arthur Miller, his mother always made matzo ball soup. After the tenth time, Marilyn said, "Gee, Arthur, these matzo balls are pretty nice, but isn't there any other part of the matzo you can eat?"

Eating her cooking is like playing Russian roulette. I never know which meal is going to kill me.

—Harvey Stone

Courage

This guy was so brave, he went down to the Russian embassy and sang "Look for the Union Label" in Polish.

—RED BUTTONS

The Texan was trying to impress on the New Englander the valor of the heroes of the Alamo. "I bet they were braver than any man from your part of the country," he declared.

"I suppose you've never heard of Paul Revere?" countered the New Englander.

"Sounds familiar," said the Texan. "Isn't he the guy who ran for help?"

The new employee had only been with the firm for a few months when she went in to ask for a raise.

"So soon!" The boss was taken aback. "Certainly not. In this company you have to work yourself up."

"I have!" she insisted. "Look at me—I'm trembling all over."

"In the center ring," cries the ringmaster, "we have Nero, the boldest and bravest animal trainer in the world. Watch, ladies and gentlemen, as he puts his head between the jaws of our man-eating lion!" The crowd roars as Nero pulls out his head unscathed.

"Now, folks, watch this!" shouts the announcer, as Nero unzips his pants and puts his prick between the giant teeth. "Don't do it!" shrieks the audience as the lion's jaws clamp shut. But without flinching Nero pulls them open and removes his unharmed penis. Wild cheers fill the arena.

When the noise dies down, the ringmaster steps forward and announces, "Ladies and gentlemen, a prize of five thousand, yes, five thousand dollars, to any man in the audience who'll try that trick." His jaw drops as a small, effeminate-looking man steps right up to the ringside. "You're going to repeat that trick with our man-eating lion in front of all these people?" the ringmaster asks incredulously.

"Certainly," says the man, "but I must tell you something first. I don't think I can open my mouth as wide as the lion did."

A young man was so proud of his new red Cadillac that he just had to show it off, so he cruised through the bad part of town. At a stoplight a giant older man hauled him out of the driver's seat, drew a circle around him in the road, and told him not to step out of the circle unless he wanted to get the shit beat out of him.

The older man started to demolish the Caddie, beginning with the headlights and windows, when he heard the young man laughing. He moved on to the body and engine, but in between crashes he couldn't help hearing the young man's hysterical giggles. Finally, the older man came over with his crowbar and said, "What in hell you laughin' at? Your fancy car's never gonna run again."

Snickering, the young man replied, "So? Ever since you've been tearing up my car, I've been stepping in and out of this circle."

Crime

Did you hear about the practical joker who sent an anonymous telegram to the town's ten leading citizens? It read: "All has been found out. Flee before dawn."

Seven of the ten did.

If you had a penny and you were on top of the Empire State Building, and you took that penny and threw if off the Empire State Building and it hit somebody in the head, it would kill him. Talk about getting your money's worth.

—HEYWOOD BANKS

The kindergarten class went on a field trip to the local police station, where a kindly patrolman showed them around. Stopping in front of a "Ten Most Wanted" poster, he explained how citizens often help bring about arrests.

"Are those pictures of the bad guys?" asked one six-year-old. The policeman soberly informed him they were indeed.

"Well," pursued the kid, "why didn't you hold on to him after you took his picture?"

Kowalski started working weekends and late into the nights on a secret project. Finally, after months of work, he went to his friend Rositzke's house to show him the fruits of his labor. "Check this out," he said. "I made it." And he proudly handed his buddy a seventeen-dollar bill.

"It's a beautiful counterfeit," said Rositzke admiringly, "but you're never going to get anywhere with a seventeen-dollar bill."

"Oh, yeah?" Kowalski was furious. "Just wait!" And he ran to the deli on the corner. A few minutes later he came back, beaming from ear to ear.

"Well?" asked Rositzke.

"Told you he'd give me change," declared Kowalski proudly. "And look! Two seven-dollar bills and a three."

I think crime pays. The hours are good, you travel a lot.

—WOODY ALLEN

This little old lady was held up by a rough character with a gun. She wasn't a bit scared. "You should be ashamed of yourself, robbing a poor little old lady like me," she protested. "A man your size should be robbing a bank."

—JOEY ADAMS

You think New York is bad? You ought to go to Detroit. You can go ten blocks and never leave the scene of the crime.

—RED SKELTON

The streets just aren't safe anymore. Yesterday I asked a cop how to get to Riverside Drive and he said, "First you go up to Seventy-ninth Street. If you get that far . . ."

I have six locks on my door, all in a row, and when I go out I only lock every other one. 'Cause I figure no matter how long somebody stands there and picks the locks, they're always locking three.

—Elayne Boosler

Did you hear about the juvenile delinquent from Beverly Hills?

He's too young to drive, so he only steals cars with chauffeurs in them.

Did you hear about the gay pickpocket?

He leaves the wallet, but takes out the owner.

—Red Buttons

How did the dumb guy rob the drive-through window at the bank?

He put his gun in the little basket along with a note that said, "This is a stickup."

When I was a kid, one cop could have taken care of the whole neighborhood. Now one cop wouldn't be safe in the neighborhood.

—Mike Royko

New Orleans is the only city in the world where you go in to buy a pair of nylon stockings and they want to know your head size.

—Billy Holliday

Did you hear about the deviant burglar who broke into a house and only stole the remote control?

Every night he drives past their window and changes the channel.

A jeweler called the police station to report a robbery. "You'll never believe what happened, Sergeant. A truck backed up to my store, the doors opened, and an elephant came out. He broke my plate glass window, stuck his trunk in, sucked up all the jewelry, and climbed back into the truck. The doors closed and the truck pulled away."

The desk sergeant said, "Could you tell me, for identification purposes, whether it was an Indian elephant or an African elephant?"

"What's the difference?" asked the jeweler.

"Well," said the sergeant, "an African elephant has great big ears and an Indian elephant has little ears."

"Come to think of it, I couldn't see his ears," said the jeweler. "He had a stocking over his head."

—Joey Adams

What's Kurt Waldheimer disease?

It's like Alzheimer's disease, except you only forget war crimes.

Just as the prisoner was being strapped into the electric chair, the priest said, "Son, is there anything I can do for you?"

The prisoner said, "Yeah, when they pull the switch, hold my hand."

—Dick Gregory

How many serial killers does it take to change a lightbulb?

Just one. But first he has to dismember the old one and masturbate in front of it.

I was in Atlantic City at a bar and a tough looking guy walked up to me and said, "Hey, buddy, you want to buy a ring?" I asked him what it looked like. He said, "Don't look now, but the guy next to you is wearing it."

—Gene Baylos

"Great news, Mr. Oscarson," the psychiatrist reported. "After eighteen months of therapy, I can pronounce you finally and

completely cured of your kleptomania. You'll never be trapped by such desires again."

"Gee, that's great, Doc," said the patient with a sigh of relief.

"And just to prove it, I want you to stop off at Sears on the way home and walk the length of the store. You'll see—you'll feel no temptation whatsoever to shoplift."

"Oh, Doctor, how can I ever thank you?"

"Well," suggested the doctor, "if you do have a relapse, I could use a microwave."

This guy in Texas is going to get the electric chair. He's borderline psycho, borderline retarded. He's like a singer/actress—can't do either one really well, but dabbles in both fields. All these guilty liberals are saying, "You can't kill crazy people, they're crazy. They don't know what they did."

Well, if they don't know what they did, then they don't know you're gonna kill 'em! Put 'em in the electric chair and tell 'em it's a ride.

—Bobby Slayton

You're not gonna believe this. I saw a murder. I got there five minutes after it happened. Apparently, from what I saw, the body fell onto a chalk line exactly the same shape.

—Howie Mandel

Did you know that in some countries the penalty for shoplifting is marriage?

Joe: Tomorrow I'm getting married for the fourth time.
    Jim: What happened to your first three wives?
    Joe: They all died, Jim.
    Jim: How did that happen?
    Joe: My first wife ate poison mushrooms.
    Jim: How terrible! And your second?
    Joe: She ate poison mushrooms.
    Jim: And your third ate poison mushrooms, too?

Joe: Oh, no. She died of a broken neck.

Jim: I see, an accident.

Joe: Not exactly. She wouldn't eat her mushrooms.

A burglar breaks into a house in the best area of town. He's sure that there's nobody home, but he sneaks in, doesn't turn on any lights, and heads for where he thinks the valuables are kept. Then he hears a voice say, "I can see you! Jesus can see you, too!"

He freezes in his tracks! He doesn't move a muscle! A couple of minutes go by. The voice repeats "I can see you! Jesus can see you, too!"

He slowly takes out his flashlight, switches it on, and looks around the room. He sees a bird cage with a parrot in it. "Did you say that?" he asks the parrot.

The parrot says again, "I can see you! Jesus can see you, too!"

"Hah! So what? You're just a parrot!" says the burglar.

"I may be just a parrot," replies the parrot. "But Jesus is a Doberman!"

A guy was in show business. He was a psychic. He knew the exact day he was going to die. The warden told him.

—Henny Youngman

I wonder if somewhere there's a gangster who's owned by a syndicate of singers?

Ladies and gentlemen of the jury, have you reached a verdict?

"We have, Your Honor. We find the man who robbed that bank not guilty."

Cynicism

No matter how cynical you become, it's never enough to keep up.

—Lily Tomlin

All modern men are descended from a wormlike creature, but it shows more on some people.

—WILL CUPPY

Over dinner with his hard-hearted friend, the incurable romantic sighed and declared, "Love is the last word."

The cynic shook his head and countered, "Only in a telegram."

A cynic is a man who, when he smells flowers, looks around for a coffin.

—H. L. MENCKEN (ATTRIBUTED)

I was going to buy a copy of *The Power of Positive Thinking,* and then I thought, What the hell good would that do?

—RONNIE SHAKES

A pessimist is a man who thinks all women are bad; an optimist hopes they are.

Reality is the only obstacle to happiness.

In April, if the glands still work properly, it is possible to see the world as it might be if only it were not the world.

—RUSSELL BAKER

I don't believe in astrology. But then I'm an Aquarius, and Aquarians don't believe in astrology.

An optimist is a parent who'll let his kid borrow the new car for a date.

A pessimist is one who won't.

A cynic is one who did.

There is one thing women can never take away from men. We die sooner.

—P. J. O'ROURKE

D

Dating

I'm dating a homeless woman. It was easier to talk her into staying over.

—Garry Shandling

Eve said to the serpent, "You know I could go for a bite to eat, but I don't know you from Adam."

—Red Buttons

I can't even find someone for a platonic relationship, much less the kind where someone wants to see me naked.

—Gilbert Gottfried

A date is a job interview that lasts all night. The only difference between a date and a job interview is that there are not many job interviews where there's a chance you'll end up naked at the end of it.

—Jerry Seinfeld

I have this eerie feeling that my imaginary friend is sleeping with my imaginary girlfriend.

—Tom Cotter

Jack the Ripper's mother said, "Why don't I ever see you with the same girl twice?"

—Red Buttons

I asked this guy if he had the time. He said he'd love to give it to me, but he wasn't sure he could make a commitment.

—Carol Siskind

These are very confusing times. For the first time in history, a woman is expected to combine intelligence with a sharp hairdo, a raised consciousness with high heels, and an open, nonsexist relationship with a tan guy who has a great bod.

—Lynda Barry

The matchmaker had been trying for years to find someone for young Seymour, but nobody met Mrs. Schwartz's standards. One day he showed up for his visit in an unusually good mood. "Have I got the girl for your Seymour," he announced, leaning over conspiratorially. "Nothing less than a princess, Princess Margaret Rose!" Ignoring the fact that Mrs. Schwartz had turned pale, the matchmaker went on. "She's a *lovely* girl. You know she has her own palace right on the Côte d'Azur, plus a chalet for the winter season in Gstaad, and of course, there's the penthouse in Manhattan if you should get lonely for your son—"

"But wait, she's a *shiksa*," interrupted Mrs. Schwartz. "That's totally unacceptable."

"Let me tell you a little about the palace. Sixty-five rooms, not counting the servants' quarters or the stables, and maybe you'd like to ice skate or take a dip in a nice indoor Olympic-sized pool? Rembrandts and Caravaggios everywhere, and on the grounds—"

"Moishe, listen to me," broke in Mrs. Schwartz. "A gentile girl, I don't care who she is, is absolutely out of the question."

"And maybe your Seymour likes a nice car?" The matchmaker went on, unperturbed. "In the garage is a Rolls Royce, a Ferrari, a Maserati, and the two Mercedes used for errands around town. And, of course, there's a couple of chauffeurs in case Seymour should get tired of driving . . ."

The ongoing inventory of Princess Margaret Rose's attractions, physical and material, failed to remove the frown from Mrs.

Schwartz's face. Finally, the matchmaker said, "Listen, let's give the boy a chance to hear all this for himself."

Reluctantly, Mrs. Schwartz agreed. To Seymour, sitting on the couch next to his mother, the matchmaker once again patiently catalogued the splendor of all that Princess Margaret Rose, *shiksa* or not, had to offer.

"Ma, I gotta say, it doesn't sound so bad," admitted Seymour.

It took another good hour or so, but finally the two men persuaded Mrs. Schwartz to go along with the arrangement, and with much handshaking and back-patting, the matchmaker was shown to the door.

"Well," he said as it closed behind him, "at least half my job is done."

I'm thirty-three, single. . . . Don't you think it's a generalization that you should be married by thirty-three? That's like looking at somebody who's seventy and saying, "Hey, when are you gonna break your hip? All your friends are breaking their hips—what are you waiting for?"

—SUE KOLINSKY

Infatuation is when you think that he's as sexy as Robert Redford, as smart as Henry Kissinger, as noble as Ralph Nader, as funny as Woody Allen, and as athletic as Jimmy Connors. Love is when you realize that he's as sexy as Woody Allen, as smart as Jimmy Connors, as funny as Ralph Nader, as athletic as Henry Kissinger, and nothing like Robert Redford—but you'll take him anyway.

—JUDITH VIORST

It's slim pickings out there. When you're first single, you're so optimistic. At the beginning you're like: I want to meet a guy who's really smart, really sweet, really good-looking, has a really great career. . . . Six months later you're like: Lord, any mammal with a day job.

—CAROL LEIFER

What do I think of computer dating? It's terrific if you're a computer.

—Rita Mae Brown

She was a lovely girl. Our courtship was fast and furious—I was fast and she was furious.

—Max Kauffmann

When I think of some of the men I've slept with—if they were women, I wouldn't have had lunch with them.

—Carol Siskind

Whoever called it necking was a poor judge of anatomy.

—Groucho Marx

I once went for a job at one of the airlines. The interviewer asked me why I wanted to be a stewardess, and I told her it would be a great chance to meet men. I was honest about it! She looked at me and said, "But you can meet men anywhere."

I said, "Strapped down?"

—Martha Raye

Why is it a mistake to date a necrophiliac?
He just wants you for your body.

Why are women wearing perfumes that smell like flowers? Men don't like flowers. I've been wearing a great scent. It's called New Car Interior.

—Rita Rudner

Two women met for lunch and the topic soon came around to their love lives. "Same old thing, you know," said the married one. "How about you, Pam?"

With a shy smile, Pam confessed that she'd been seeing a really attractive man. "He's gorgeous, honestly—really well built

and six feet two, with this thick blond hair—and he has his own computer consulting business, a beautiful apartment, a nice car, but the best thing about him is that he's totally honest and sincere and straightforward with me."

"Wow!" exclaimed her friend. "How come I haven't heard about this dreamboat until now?"

"There's one small snag," admitted Pam with a grimace. "Ted also makes all his own dresses."

A guy walks into a bar and goes right up to a beautiful redhead sitting alone in the corner. "Hey, wanna fuck?" he asks.

"Your place or mine?" she answers coyly.

"Well, if it's going to be a hassle. . . ."

How many of you ever started dating someone 'cause you were too lazy to commit suicide? This guy says, "I'm perfect for you, 'cause I'm a cross between a macho and a sensitive man." I said, "Oh, a gay trucker?"

—JUDY TENUTA

I wouldn't mind being the last man on earth—just to see if all of those girls were telling me the truth.

—RONNIE SHAKES

What's the advantage of being the last woman on earth?
You can be rotten and he'll still love you.

I've been on so many blind dates, I should get a free dog.

—WENDY LIEBMAN

A young couple were in a car parked on Lovers Lane and the young man turned admiringly to his pretty date and said, "Gee, you smell good. You wearing perfume or something?"

The girl blushed charmingly and confessed that she was wearing a new perfume that she'd bought especially with him in mind. "You smell good, too," she said. "What do you have on?"

"Well, I have a hard-on," blurted the young man, "but I didn't know you could smell it."

I'm kind of lazy. I'm dating a pregnant woman.

—RON RICHARDS

How do you qualify to be the girlfriend of a Hell's Angel?
You have to be able to suck start a Harley.

The horny college kid borrowed his roommate's car, scraped together every penny he could find, picked up his date at her parents' house, and took her to a nice restaurant for dinner. But he got more and more upset when she proceeded to order everything pricey on the menu: fancy mixed drinks, lobster, champagne—the works. Finally, he couldn't stay silent anymore—and blurted, "Does your mother feed you like this at home?"

"Nope," she replied with a demure smile, "but my mom's not trying to get laid either."

Parking in the driveway after their first date, Roger leaned over and gave Linda a passionate kiss. When she responded warmly, he unzipped his fly and pulled her hand to his penis. Furious, Linda opened the door and jumped out of the car.

"I've got just two words for you," she screamed. "Drop dead!"

"And I've got just two words for you," Roger screamed back. "Let go!"

A guy puts his hand down his wife's pants.

She says, "Would you take off your ring? It's hurting me."

He says, "That's not my ring. It's my wristwatch."

Death and Dying

It's not that I'm afraid to die. I just don't want to be there when it happens.

—Woody Allen

Ellen and Dan had been married for fifty-seven years when her health began to fail. Eventually she was hospitalized, and within a few weeks it became evident that she had only a few more days to live. "Dan, I have only one last request," she whispered to her husband with the last of her strength.

"Anything, dearest," her husband told her tenderly.

"In all these years, we never had oral sex, and I don't want to die without knowing what it feels like. Go down on me."

Dan was more than a little taken aback, but he figured he'd gotten off easy all those years and that she probably wouldn't last more than another day or two. So he closed the door and proceeded to comply with his wife's dying wish. He was even more startled to observe a distinct blush on her cheeks the next day at what he expected would be his final visit. To Dan's amazement and that of the whole hospital, Ellen was sitting up in bed the following day, and within a week she was well enough to be discharged.

Dan was in the room when the doctor told them the happy news, and Ellen was shocked to see her husband break down in tears. "Dan, what's wrong? What's wrong?" she implored.

"I was just realizing," sobbed Dan, "that I coulda' saved Eleanor Roosevelt."

Peter and James have been friends for more than sixty years. One day Peter says, "James, let's make a pact: whoever dies first will try to come back and tell the other what heaven's like."

They both agree, but none too soon, because the next day James is done in by a sudden heart attack.

Six months later, just when Peter is giving up any hope of

hearing from his friend, a voice wakes him up in the middle of the night.

"James, is that you?" Peter asks in amazement.

"You're right, you're not wrong," James answers.

"Well, tell me. What's it like?"

"You wouldn't believe it. All day long, all we do is eat and fuck. We get up in the morning, eat breakfast, and fuck, then we eat lunch and fuck until dinner. After dinner we fuck some more. We fuck until we pass out, then we wake up and fuck some more," James explains.

"Holy shit!" exclaims Peter. "If that's heaven, I can't wait to die!"

"Who said anything about heaven?" a perplexed James replies. "I'm in Nevada and I'm a rabbit."

Did you hear about the hillbilly who passed away and left his estate in trust for his bereaved widow?

She can't touch it until she's fourteen.

There are two things we're sure of: death and taxes. Now, if only we could get them in that order!

—Joey Adams

"Here lies the body of Harry Hershfield. If not, notify Ginsberg and Co., undertakers, at once."

—Harry Hershfield's suggestion for his own epitaph

When Irving retired, he and his wife, who was much younger, moved to Boca Raton. Once they'd settled in, he decided it was about time to make a will, so he made an appointment with a lawyer.

"It's nice and straightforward," he instructed the attorney. "Everything goes to Rachel—the house, the car, the pension, the life insurance—on condition that she remarry within the year."

"Fine, Mr. Patron," said the lawyer. "But do you mind my asking why the condition?"

"Simple: I want at least one person to be sorry I died."

I know a guy who saved all his life to buy a cemetery plot. Then he took a cruise and was lost at sea.

—NORM CROSBY

The obituary editor of a Boston newspaper was not one to admit his mistakes easily. One day he got a phone call from an irate subscriber who complained that his name had been printed in the obituary column.

"Really?" replied the editor calmly. "And where are you calling from?"

—JOEY ADAMS

Two old guys wonder if there's baseball in heaven, and promise each other that the first to die will somehow let the other one know. A week later, one of them dies. And a week after that, his friend recognizes his voice coming down from the clouds.

"Joe, I've got some good news and some bad news," the disembodied voice reports. "The good news is that there is a baseball team in heaven. The bad news is that you're pitching on Friday."

The phone rang in the Obituary Department of a Miami newspaper. "How much does it cost to have an obituary printed?" asked a woman.

"It's five dollars a word, ma'am," replied the clerk politely.

"Fine," said the woman after a brief pause. "Got a pencil?"

"Yes, ma'am."

"Got some paper?"

"Yes, ma'am."

"Okay, write this down: 'Cohen dead'."

"That's it?" asked the clerk disbelievingly.

"That's it."

"I'm sorry, I should have told you, ma'am—there's a five-word minimum."

"Yes, you should've, young man," snapped the woman. "Now let me think a minute. . . . All right, got a pencil?"

"Yes, ma'am."

"Got some paper?"

"Yes, ma'am."

"Okay, here goes: 'Cohen dead. Cadillac for Sale'."

My uncle Pat, he reads the obituaries in the paper every morning. And he can't understand how people always die in alphabetical order.

—HAL ROACH

The reports of my death are greatly exaggerated.

—MARK TWAIN

Eternity is a terrible thought. I mean, when's it going to end?

—TOM STOPPARD

For the four executives, the high point of the annual stockholders meeting was their Sunday afternoon golf game. They had just teed off on the twelfth hole when an assistant golf pro came tearing across the green, red-faced and out of breath. "Mr. Webster, Mr. Webster," he gasped, "I have terrible news. Your wife has just been killed in a car accident."

Webster turned to his companions and said, "Guys, I gotta warn you. Six more holes and you're gonna see a man crying his eyes out."

How can they tell?

—DOROTHY PARKER, ON BEING INFORMED OF
THE DEMISE OF PRESIDENT CALVIN COOLIDGE

The son was sitting at the bedside of his elderly father, who was dying. "Where do you want to be buried," asked the son, "Forest Lawn or New York City?"

The old man got up on his elbow and said, "Surprise me!"

—JOEY ADAMS

Death is nature's way of telling you to slow down.

For three days after death, hair and fingernails continue to grow, but phone calls taper off.

—JOHNNY CARSON

If Shaw and Einstein couldn't beat death, what chance have I got? Practically none.

—MEL BROOKS

A guy returns from a long trip to Europe, having left his beloved cat in his brother's care. The minute he clears customs, he calls his brother and inquires after his pet.

"The cat's dead," replies his brother bluntly.

The guy is devastated. "You don't know how much that cat meant to me," he sobs into the phone. "Couldn't you at least have given a little thought to a nicer way of breaking the news? For instance, couldn't you have said, 'Well, you know, the cat got out of the house one day and climbed up on the roof, and the fire department couldn't get her down, and finally she died of exposure . . . or starvation . . . or something'? Why are you always so thoughtless?"

"Look, I'm really, really sorry," says his brother. "I'll try to do better next time, I swear."

"Okay, let's just put it behind us. How are you, anyway? How's Mom?"

There was a long pause. "Uh," the brother finally stammers, "uh . . . Mom's on the roof."

The waiter dies and his wife is distraught. One day she meets someone who assures her that she can speak to her beloved husband
through a medium, and arranges a visit. At the séance the wife
presses both hands on the table and calls out, "Sam, Sam, speak to
me!"

A haunting, whistling noise follows, and then a faint voice cries,
"I can't—it's not my table!"

**I'm desperately trying to figure out why Kamikaze pilots wore
helmets.**

—George Carlin

When I die, I want to go like my grandfather . . . in his sleep. Not
screaming like the other passengers in his car.

**Some sad news from Australia . . . the inventor of the boomerang
grenade died today.**

—Johnny Carson

Having been informed after a regular medical examination that he
was virtually certain to die within twenty-four hours from a rare and
obscure disease, the doomed man rushed home, told his wife, and
proceeded to make love to her as often as he could manage until late
into the night. He finally fell asleep, but then awoke, began to fondle
his wife, and whispered in her ear, "I want to make love to you one
last time!"

"That's easy enough for you to say, Roy," was her exhausted,
yawned response. "You don't have to get up in the morning."

**A man called the undertaker one afternoon and sobbed: "Come
and bury my wife."**

**"But I buried your wife ten years ago," replied the under-
taker.**

"I got married again," the man sobbed.

"Oh," said the undertaker. "Congratulations."

I sometimes wonder if necrophiliacs are really into dead people or if they just enjoy the quiet.

—Doug Stanhope

If I ever commit suicide, I'm going to fling myself off the top of a skyscraper, but before I do, I'm going to stuff my pockets with candy and gum. That way when the onlookers walk up, they can go, "Oh man, he really must have been dep—hey, Snickers!"

—Patton Oswalt

Debts

Mr. Stone was in dire need of periodontal work, so Dr. Graves performed a series of operations over a three-month period. The patient, however, paid only the first third, ignoring all Dr. Graves's remittance notices and threats of collection agencies. Finally, the desperate dentist enclosed a snapshot of his three little children in a note reading, "Dear Mr. Stone—here's why I need the money you owe me."

Dr. Graves was thrilled when an envelope arrived from Stone the next week. Opening it up, he found a large photograph of a gorgeous woman. Scrawled on the bottom was a note from his errant patient: "Dear Dr. Graves—here's why I can't pay."

A manufacturer said to a storekeeper, "Thank you, Mr. Schwartz, for your patronage. I wish I had twenty customers like you."

"Gee, it's good to hear you talk like that, but I'm kind of surprised," admitted Schwartz. "You know that I protest every bill and never pay on time."

The manufacturer said, "I'd still like twenty customers like you. The problem is, I have two hundred."

—Joey Adams

Dieting

What do a fat girl and a moped have in common?

They're both fun to ride as long as nobody sees you.

A guy ate a dinner that was so big, when he asked what he could wash it down with, he was told, "Lake Erie."

—Henny Youngman

I have a great diet. You're allowed to eat anything you want, but you have to eat it with naked fat people.

—Ed Bluestone

Finally admitting he was grossly overweight, this man decided it was time to take advantage of a special introductory offer from a new weight-loss clinic in town. After handing over his payment, he was shown into an empty room, where he was soon joined by a gorgeous blond. "Hi," she said. "If you catch me, I'm yours."

It took a while, but after a prolonged chase, he succeeded—and was delighted to find he'd lost ten pounds in the process. After that, he gave up all ideas of dieting and managed to drop ten more pounds with a brunette and eight with a redhead. But he was still fifty pounds overweight, so he decided to sign up for the clinic's more drastic program. He was waiting eagerly in an empty room when the door opened and in came a three-hundred-pound gay guy, who grinned and said, "If I catch you, you're mine!"

A girl who is a picture of health usually has a nice frame.

The biggest seller is cookbooks and the second is diet books—how not to eat what you've just learned how to cook.

—Andy Rooney

The second day of a diet is always easier than the first. By the second day, you're off it.

—JACKIE GLEASON

She's so fat, she's my two best friends. She wears stretch caftans. She's got more chins than the Chinese telephone directory.

An overweight man went to his doctor and said, "I'm desperate, Doc, I'm desperate. I've gotta lose weight. Every diet I try, nothing works. Nothing works. You gotta give me something to help me lose weight."

The doctor says, "Don't worry, I got a great diet. It's going to sound a little odd, but it works. Just, whatever you eat, whatever food you put in your body, you have to put it up anally. It all goes up your ass."

The overweight guy said, "You sure of this—because I . . ."

"Trust me. Trust me. It works. You gotta try it."

"All right, I'll try." He goes away and three months later, he comes back and he's lost forty pounds. He says, "Doc! This is fabulous, this is great! Look at this diet! You did fabulous—I've lost all this weight!"

The doctor says, "I'm glad to hear that, but what are you doing? Why are you moving your ass back and forth?"

He says, "I'm chewing gum."

What's it mean to go on the Scarsdale Diet?

You shoot your doctor, then spend the rest of your life eating bread and water.

Another good reducing exercise consists of placing both hands against the table edge and pushing back.

—ROBERT QUILLEN

I just found out about a fabulous new diet. It has two parts. First, you can only eat bagels and lox, and second, you have to live in Syria.

I've been on the Valium diet for eight and a half years now. If you take enough Valium, it'll help you lose weight. It doesn't really curb your appetite, but most of your food falls on the floor.

—GEORGE MILLER

Is she fat? Her favorite food is seconds.

—JOAN RIVERS

You do not sew with a fork, and I see no reason why you should eat with knitting needles.

—MISS PIGGY, ON CHOPSTICKS

Let me put it this way: According to my girth, I should be a ninety-foot redwood.

—ERMA BOMBECK

In one of his pictures, Jimmy Cagney shoved a grapefruit into a girl's face, and it was considered shocking. Now it's considered a diet.

I went on a diet, swore off drinking and heavy eating, and in fourteen days, I lost two weeks.

—JOE E. LEWIS

There's someone at every party who eats all the celery.

—KIN HUBBARD

Divorce

If it weren't for divorce, where would coffee shops get their waitresses?

It's a sad fact that 50 percent of marriages in this country end in divorce. But, hey, the other half end in death. You could be one of the lucky ones!

—RICHARD JENI

This guy called up his lawyer to tell him he was suing for divorce, and the lawyer inquired as to his grounds for the suit.

"Can you believe my wife says I'm a lousy lover?" sputtered the husband.

"*That's* why you're suing?" asked the lawyer.

"Of course not. I'm suing because she knows the difference."

The workaholic husband was trying to appease his wife, who was infuriated by how little time he spent at home. "Tell me what you want, Louise," he begged. "Nothing's too good for you. How about a new Cuisinart?"

She shook her head.

"A mink? Floor length this time?"

Her pout deepened.

"A two-week Caribbean cruise?"

She shook her head more vehemently.

"A ski chalet? Or maybe a place at the beach?"

Still no. "So what *do* you want, Louise?" asked her frustrated mate.

"A divorce."

"Gee, I wasn't planning to spend *that* much," he admitted.

Alimony is like buying oats for a dead horse.

—Arthur (Bugs) Baer

The wages of sin is alimony.

—Carolyn Wells

God made man. God made women. And when God found that men could not get along with women, God made Mexico.

—Larry Storch

Divorce is painful. There's an easy way to save yourself a lot of trouble. Just find a woman you hate and buy her a house.

—Pat Paulsen

Shatzkin was used to the occasional late-night call, usually from a client who'd had an accident of some sort, but this night it was an agitated woman obviously in the middle of a violent argument with her husband.

"Tell me, Mr. Shatzkin," she yelled over the noise of her mate's ranting in the background, "if a husband leaves his wife, is she or is she not legally entitled to the house and its contents?"

"I can't give such advice over the phone, especially without knowing the particulars of the case," the lawyer reasonably pointed out. "Call my office in the morning and we'll set up an appointment."

The background roars had subsided, and the woman continued in a normal tone without skipping a beat. "She's also entitled to the time-share, both cars, and the joint savings account? Thank you very much." And she hung up with a triumphant smile.

A lonely divorcée was driving home from work one evening, when she saw a man trying to hitch a ride. She picked him up and they got to talking.

"What do you do?" she asked him.

"I recently escaped from prison, where I was serving a life sentence for killing my wife."

"Oh, does that mean you're available?"

Open marriage is nature's way of telling you you need a divorce.

—MARSHALL BRICKMAN

Many a man owes his success to his first wife. And his second wife to his success.

—JIM BACKUS

An explorer went into an undiscovered tomb for the first time, and in the center of the tomb there was a lamp. So he picked it up, and as he started to rub the dirt off it, a genie came out of the lamp and said, "I want to know the person you hate the most."

The explorer said, "That's gotta be my ex-wife. Why?"

"I am a cursed genie. I will grant you three wishes, but whatever you wish for, your ex-wife will get double the amount."

"Okay, I wish for a billion dollars."

"Granted, but your ex-wife gets two billion dollars."

"I wish for a mansion in California with a swimming pool, and tennis courts, everything."

"Granted, and your ex-wife gets two. Now make your final wish."

The explorer walked around for a few minutes, returned to the genie with a stick, and said, "You see this stick, I'd like you to beat me half to death."

Why do divorces cost so much?

Because they're worth it.

Doctors and Dentists

The thing that bothers me about doctors is they give you an appointment six weeks ahead, then they examine you, then they ask, "Why did you wait so long to see me?"

—Joey Adams

Did you hear about the resourceful proctologist?

He always used two fingers, in case his patients wanted a second opinion.

Once I was sick and I had to go to an ear, nose, and throat man to get well. There are ear doctors, nose doctors, throat doctors, gynecologists, proctologists—anyplace you've got a hole, there's a guy who specializes in your hole. They make an entire career out of that hole. And if the ear doctor, nose doctor, throat doctor, gynecologist, or proctologist can't help you, he sends you to a surgeon. Why? So he can make a new hole!

—Alan Prophet

"Yeah, Doc, what's the news?" answered Fred when his doctor called with his test results.

"I have some bad news and some really bad news," admitted the doctor. "The bad news is that you only have twenty-four hours to live."

"Oh my God," gasped Fred, sinking to his knees. "What could be worse news than that?"

"I couldn't get hold of you yesterday."

So my eye doctor told me, "Did you know you have one eye set higher than the other eye?"

"No."

"It's no big deal. It doesn't affect your vision or anything. I just thought you'd like to be self-conscious for the rest of your life."

—BRIAN REGAN

A woman calls the nurses' station and says, "I would like to know how Mrs. Goldberg is doing."

The nurse looks it up and says, "She's doing fine. May I tell Mrs. Goldberg who called?"

She says, "This is Mrs. Goldberg. I called you because my doctor wouldn't tell me anything."

—STEWIE STONE

I don't like going to the dentist. I don't like having any part of a man in my mouth, for that matter.

—MARTIN MULL

A team of Hollywood doctors were working furiously to revive a patient whose heart had stopped in the middle of a quadruple bypass operation. Unfortunately, their efforts were to no avail, and the patient expired on the table.

"Oh, Doctor," cried one of the attending nurses, "what a terrible shame."

"Hey, lighten up, Peggy," the head surgeon said reassuringly. "It's not as though we were making a movie."

Never go to a doctor whose office plants have died.

—ERMA BOMBECK

Casey came home from the doctor looking very worried. His wife said, "What's the problem?"

He said, "The doctor told me I have to take a pill every day for the rest of my life."

She said, "So what? Lots of people have to take a pill every day their whole lives."

He said, "I know, but he only gave me four pills."

—HAL ROACH

My doctor is wonderful. Once, in 1955, when I couldn't afford an operation, he touched up the X-rays.

—JOEY BISHOP

Medical science has made a lot of progress with new miracle drugs. No matter what illness you have, the doctor can keep you alive long enough for you to pay your bill.

—JOEY ADAMS

The doctor explained to the heart patient that he would be able to resume his romantic life as soon as he could climb two flights of stairs without becoming winded. The patient listened attentively and said, "What if I look for a woman who lives on the ground floor?"

—JOEY ADAMS

I'd like to be an obstetrician. Look at all the guys you have working for you all the time.

—BERT HENRY

I went to the doctor. I said, "Doc, my foot, I can't walk!"

He said, "You'll be walking before the day is out." He took my car.

—BUDDY HACKETT

A guy who has a stuttering problem goes in to his doctor. . . . "Ex-ex-ex-cu-cu-se m-m-me, D-D-oc, but but I-I have th-th-this st-st-stuttering problem and I-I-I was wo-wondering if you c-c-c-could help m-m-m-me.

"Well, take off your clothes and get into this gown and let me check you over."

The guy gets into the gown and the doctor begins his examination. Finally, the doctor, obviously surprised, says, "I see what the problem is. Your penis is so large that it's pulling on your abdominal muscles, which in turn is causing strain on your vocal chords."

"W-w-w-well, c-c-can you h-h-help m-m-me?"

"Sure I can, but we'll need to cut off about eight inches."

"G-g-go a-a-a-head, D-D-Doc, I-I-I-I can't t-t-t-take this an-anymore. D-d-do it."

Six months later, the guy goes back to the doctor. "Well, Doc," he says, "I must say, the operation was a great success, but my sex life really sucks and I would like my operation reversed. Please put back what you took off."

The doctor replies, "F-f-f-f-f-fuck off!"

A young lady is in the hospital for an operation. She says, "Doc, how long after my operation will I have to wait until I can have sex again?"

He says, "You know, Miss Kandol, you're the first person who ever asked me that before a tonsillectomy."

Sobel goes into the optometrist's office. He opens the door and says to the receptionist, "I think I need my eyes checked."

She says, "You're not kidding. This is the Ladies Room."

The doctor tells his patient, "Well I have good new and bad news. . . ."

The patient says, "Lay it on me, Doc. What's the bad news?"

"You have Alzheimer's disease."

"Good heavens! What's the good news?"

"You can go home and forget about it!"

Jimmy walks into a doctor's office and says, "Doc, you gotta help me. I've got a constant erection. At first it was fun, but then it became painful and embarrassing."

He takes down his pants, and his hard-on is sticking straight out.

The doctor whacks it with two fingers, a little bug jumps off, and it goes right down.

Jimmy says, "Gee, Doc, that's great. How much do I owe you?"

The doctor says, "If you help me find that bug, you don't owe me anything."

Harry answers the telephone, and it's an emergency room doctor.

The doctor says, "Your wife was in a serious car accident, and I have bad news and good news. The bad news is she has lost all use of both arms and both legs, and will need help eating and going to the bathroom for the rest of her life."

Harry says, "My God. What's the good news?"

The doctor says, "I'm kidding. She's dead."

Patient: Doctor, I think I swallowed a pillow.

Doctor: How do you feel?

Patient: A little down in the mouth.

Patient: How much to have this tooth pulled?

Dentist: Ninety dollars.

Patient: Ninety dollars for just a few minutes' work?

Dentist: I can extract it very slowly if you like.

Patient: I'm in a hospital!? Why am I in here?

Doctor: You've had an accident involving a train.

Patient: What happened?

Doctor: Well, I've got some good news and some bad news. Which would you like to hear first?

Patient: Well . . . the bad news first. . . .

Doctor: Your legs were injured so badly that we had to amputate both of them.

Patient: That's terrible! What's the good news?

Doctor: There's a guy in the next ward who made a very good offer on your shoes.

Doctor: I have some good news and I have some bad news, which shall I tell you first?

Patient: Do begin with the bad news, please.

Doctor: All right. Your son has drowned, your daughter is in a coma, your wife has divorced you, your house got blown away, and you have an incurable rare disease.

Patient: Good grief! What's the good news?

Doctor: The good news is that there is no more bad news.

Patient: Doctor, ya gotta help me. Every time I sneeze, I have an orgasm.

Doctor: Really! What are you taking for it?

Patient: Black pepper!

Doctor: Nurse, how is that little boy doing, the one who swallowed ten quarters?

Nurse: No change yet.

Why did the doctor fail as a kidnapper?

Because nobody could read the ransom notes.

What's worse than having your doctor tell you that you have VD?

Having your dentist tell you.

Nurse: Doctor, there is an invisible man in your waiting room.

Doctor: Tell him I can't see him now. Next.

Patient: Doctor, I think I need glasses.

Teller: You certainly do. This is a bank.

John: How can I lose twelve pounds of ugly fat?

Doctor: Cut your head off.

A doctor has come to see one of his patients in a hospital. The patient has had major surgery on both of his hands.

"Doctor," says the man, who excitedly and dramatically holds up his heavily bandaged hands. "Will I be able to play the piano when these bandages come off?"

"I don't see why not," replies the doctor.

'That's funny," says the man. "I wasn't able to play it before."

Tom: What's good for excessive wind, Doctor?

Doctor: A kite!

As the doctor completed an examination of the patient, he said, "I can't find a cause for your complaint. Frankly, I think it's due to drinking."

"In that case," said the patient, "I'll come back when you're sober."

A man walked into a crowded doctor's office. As he approached the desk, the receptionist asked, "Yes, sir, may we help you?"

"There's something wrong with my dick," he replied.

The receptionist became aggravated and said, "You shouldn't come into a crowded office and say something like that."

"Why not? You asked me what was wrong and I told you," he said.

"We do not use language like that here," she said. "Please go outside and come back in and say that there's something wrong with your ear or whatever."

The man walked out, waited several minutes, and reentered. The receptionist smiled smugly and asked, "Yes?"

"There's something wrong with my ear," he stated.

The receptionist nodded approvingly. "And what is wrong with your ear, sir?"

"I can't piss out of it," the man replied.

There was a horrible mistake at the hospital. A man who was scheduled for a vasectomy was instead given a sex change operation. The doctors gathered at his bed afterward to tell him the bad news.

"Ohhhh no!!!" the patient wailed, "I'll never be able to experience an erection again!"

"Of course you'll still be able to experience an erection," replied one surgeon, "only it will have to be someone else's."

A police officer had just pulled a car over. When the officer walked up to the car, a man rolled down the window and said, "What's the problem officer? By the way, I am a doctor." The officer responded, "I stopped you for running that red light behind you." Just then the doctor's wife leaned forward from the passenger seat and said, in an obnoxious voice, "I told him to stop at that light. But did he listen? No. He just kept right on going. Thinks because he's a doctor he can do what he wants." The doctor turns to his wife and yells, "Shut up!"

The officer then continued, "And just before the light, I clocked you going fifty in a thirty." The wife leans forward and again squawks, "I told him to slow down. But did he listen? No. He never listens to me." The doctor then looks at his wife and says, "Hey, didn't I just tell you to shut up?" The officer then looks at the wife and says, "Does he always talk to you this way?"

"Only when he's been drinking," she says.

A man went to his dentist because he felt something wrong in his mouth. The dentist examined him and said, "That new upper

plate that I put in six months ago is eroding. What have you been eating?"

The man replied, "All I can think of is that about four months ago, my wife made some asparagus and put some stuff on it that was delicious . . . hollandaise sauce. I loved it so much, I now put it on everything . . . meat, toast, fish, vegetables—everything."

"Well," said the dentist, "that's probably the problem. Hollandaise sauce is made with lots of lemon juice, which is highly corrosive. It's eating away at your upper plate. I'll make you a new plate, and this time I'll use chrome."

"Why chrome?" asked the patient.

The dentist replied, "It's simple. Everyone knows that there's no plate like chrome for the hollandaise!"

After the dentist finished examining the woman's teeth, he says, "I am sorry to tell you this, but I am going to have to drill a tooth."

The woman says, "Ooooohhhh, I'd rather have a baby!"

To which the dentist replies, "Make up your mind, I have to adjust the chair."

A woman who was seeing a doctor for a rare skin ailment was prescribed male hormones for her condition. She was a little worried about some of the side effects she was experiencing.

"Doctor," she said, "the hormones you've been giving me have really helped, but I'm afraid that you're giving me too much. I've started growing hair in places that I've never grown hair before."

The doctor reassured her. "A little hair growth is a perfectly normal side effect of testosterone. Just where has this hair appeared?"

"On my balls."

All my doctor does is send me to see other doctors.

I don't know if he's really a doctor or a booking agent.

Sam and John were out cutting wood, and John cut his arm off. Sam wrapped the arm in a plastic bag and took it and John to a surgeon.

The surgeon said, "You're in luck! I'm an expert at reattaching limbs! Come back in four hours." So Sam left, and when he returned in four hours, the surgeon said, "I got done faster than I expected. John is down at the local pub." Sam went to the pub, and there was John, throwing darts.

A few weeks later, Sam and John were cutting wood again, and John cut his leg off. Sam put the leg in a plastic bag and took it and John back to the surgeon.

The surgeon said, "Legs are a little tougher. Come back in six hours." Sam left, and when he returned in six hours, the surgeon said, "I finished early. John's down at the soccer field." Sam went to the soccer field, and there was John, kicking goals.

A few weeks later, John had a terrible accident and cut his head off. Sam put the head in a plastic bag and took it and the rest of John to the surgeon.

The surgeon said, "Gee, heads are really tough. Come back in twelve hours." So Sam left, and when he returned in twelve hours, the surgeon said, "I'm sorry, John died."

Sam said, "I understand—heads are tough."

The surgeon said, "Oh, no! The surgery went fine! John suffocated in that plastic bag."

A fellow was suffering from constipation, so his doctor prescribed suppositories.

A week later he was back at the doctor's, complaining that his constipation had gotten worse, not better.

The doctor asked, "Have you been taking the suppositories regularly?"

"What do you think I've been doing," said the fellow, "shoving them up my ass?"

The *New England Journal of Medicine* reports that nine out of ten doctors agree that one out of ten doctors is an idiot.

Drink and Drinking

Phil Harris sees a psychiatrist once a week to make him stop drinking—and it works. Every Wednesday, between five and six, he doesn't drink.

—Joe E. Lewis

The bartender was dumbfounded when a gorilla came in and asked for a martini, but he couldn't think of any reason not to serve the beast. And he was even more amazed to find the gorilla coolly holding out a ten-dollar bill when he returned with the drink.

As he walked over to the cash register, he decided to try something. He rang up the sale, headed back to the animal, and handed it a dollar in change. The gorilla didn't say anything, he just sat there sipping his martini.

Finally the bartender couldn't take it anymore. "You know," he offered, "we don't get too many *gorillas* in here."

And the gorilla replied, "At nine bucks a drink, I'm not surprised."

Alcohol is good for you. My grandfather proved it. He drank two quarts of booze every mature day of his life and lived to the age of one hundred and three. I was at the cremation—that fire would not go out.

—Dave Astor

Let's get out of these wet clothes and into a dry martini.

—Robert Benchley (also attributed to Alexander Woollcott)

A man is never drunk if he can lay on the floor without holding on.

—Joe E. Lewis

A man walks into a bar and orders a beer. After a few minutes he says to the bartender, "Hey, if I show you the most amazing thing you've ever seen, will you give me another beer on the house?" "We'll see," said the bartender. "I've had a lot of nuts come in here, and I've seen some pretty amazing things in my day."

So the man pulls a hamster and a tiny piano out of his brief-case, and puts them on the bar. Then the hamster begins to play Chopin.

"Not bad," said the bartender, "but I'll need to see more."

"Okay, hold on," says the man as he pulls a frog from his briefcase. Suddenly, the frog starts singing "My Way."

A patron nearby jumps up from his table and says, "That's amazing! I'll give you a thousand dollars right now for that frog."

"Sold!" says the man, who exchanges the frog for the cash.

The bartender then says to the man, "You know, its none of my business, but I think you just gave away a real fortune in that frog."

"Not really," says the man, "the hamster is also a ventriloquist."

One night Judge O'Brien tottered into his house very late and very drunk indeed, so bombed that he had managed to throw up all over himself. In the morning he sheepishly told his wife that a drunk sitting next to him on the train home had managed to vomit all over him.

The judge managed to make it into the courthouse, where it occurred to him that his story might not be truly convincing to his wife. Inspired, he called home and said, "Honey, you won't believe this, but I just had the drunk who threw up on me last night show up in court, and I gave him thirty days."

"Give him sixty days," said the judge's wife. "He shit in your pants, too."

One reason I don't drink is that I want to know when I'm having a good time.

—Nancy Astor

The owner of a bar is just locking up when there is a ring at the doorbell. He opens the door and there's a snail sitting there.

"What do you want?" asks the owner.

"I want a drink," says the snail.

"Go away, we're closed, and we don't serve snails!"

The snail begs and pleads for a drink. The owner, now fed up with the sniveling snail, kicks him and slams the door shut.

ONE YEAR LATER

The owner is locking up the bar when the doorbell rings. He opens the door, looks down, and sees the snail.

"What did you do that for?" asks the snail.

An alcoholic is someone you don't like, who drinks as much as you do.

—DYLAN THOMAS

Two drinking buddies made a night of it. As they closed the last bar in town, one admitted to the other, "God, I hate getting in at this hour. All I want to do is take my shoes off and crawl into bed, but Marge always wakes up and nags the shit out of me for what seems like hours."

"Sneaking's not the way to do it," said his buddy conspiratorially as they staggered arm in arm down the sidewalk. "Try slamming the front door, stomping upstairs, and yelling, 'Hey, baby, let's fuck.' My wife always pretends she's sound asleep."

I saw this wino—he was eating grapes. I was like, "Dude, you have to wait."

—MITCH HEDBERG

What contemptible scoundrel stole the cork from my lunch?

—W. C. FIELDS

What's the difference between an alcoholic and a drunk?
    A drunk doesn't have to go to meetings.

The whole world is about three drinks behind.

—Humphrey Bogart

How many drunks does it take to change a lightbulb?
   Two. One to hold the bulb and the other to drink until the room spins.

If you don't drink, when you wake up in the morning, that's the best you're gonna feel all day.

—Martin Mull

This guy's not an ordinary, garden-variety drunk. Far from it. Last year he donated his body to science, and he's preserving it in alcohol until they can use it.

Actually, it only takes one drink to get me loaded. Trouble is, I can't remember if it's the thirteenth or fourteenth.

—George Burns

Why do elephants drink?
   It helps them forget.

The Ten Stages of Drunkenness
   1. Witty and charming
   2. Rich and famous
   3. Benevolent
   4. Clairvoyant
   5. Fuck dinner
   6. Patriotic
   7. Crank up the Enola Gay
   8. Witty and charming, Part Two
   9. Invisible
   10. Bulletproof

Work is the curse of the drinking class.

—OSCAR WILDE

I am sparkling; you are unusually talkative; he is drunk.

I drink to forget I drink.

—JOE E. LEWIS

When you stop drinking, you have to deal with this marvelous personality that started you drinking in the first place.

—JIMMY BRESLIN

A woman drove me to drink and I never even had the courtesy to thank her.

—W. C. FIELDS

I once shook hands with Pat Boone and my whole right side sobered up.

—DEAN MARTIN

One night a man walks into a bar with a pig. The bartender, being the observant sort, noticed right off that the pig had a wooden leg. He goes over to the man and asks about it.

The man says, "For a beer I'll tell you all about this very special pig." The bartender figures it's got to be a good story, and so he gives the man a beer.

The man begins, "Let me tell you about this pig. He is one special pig. One night, about a year ago, my house caught fire. This pig broke out of his pen, came into the house, dragged my two littlest children out of the house, woke me and my wife, and then guided us out of the house. This pig saved my life and my family's lives."

The bartender, impressed but still wondering about the leg, says, "Well, that's great. But why does he have a wooden leg?"

The man says, "Well sir, with a pig this special you don't eat it all at once."

140

A fellow decides to take off early from work and go drinking. He stays in the bar until it closes at 2 A.M., at which time he is extremely drunk.

When he enters his house, he doesn't want to wake anyone, so he takes off his shoes and starts tiptoeing up the stairs. Halfway up the stairs, he falls over backwards and lands flat on his rear end. That wouldn't have been so bad, except that he had a couple of empty pint bottles in his back pockets, and they broke, and the broken glass carved up his buttocks terribly. But he was so drunk, he didn't know he was hurt.

A few minutes later, as he was undressing, he notices blood, so he checks himself out in the mirror, and, sure enough, his behind is cut up something terrible. Well, he repaired the damage as best he could under the circumstances, and he went to bed.

The next morning, his head was hurting, and his rear was hurting, and he was hunkering under the covers, trying to think up some good story, when his wife came into the bedroom.

"Well, you really tied one on last night," she said. "Where'd you go?"

"I worked late," he said, "and I stopped off for a couple of beers."

"A couple of beers? That's a laugh," she replied. "You got plastered last night. Where the heck did you go?"

"What makes you so sure I got drunk last night, anyway?"

"Well," she replied, "my first big clue was when I got up this morning and found a bunch of Band-Aids stuck to the mirror."

A guy rushes into a bar, orders four expensive thirty-year-old single malts, and has the bartender line them up in front of him. Then, without pausing, he downs each one.

"Whew," the bartender remarks, "you seem to be in a hurry."

"You would be, too, if you had what I have."

"What do you have?" the bartender sympathetically asks.

"Fifty cents."

I'd rather have a bottle in front of me than a frontal lobotomy.

A man in a nice suit goes into a bar. He says, "Bartender, give me a triple Jack Daniels."

He gives him a triple Jack Daniels, and he belts it down. He has five more in a row, belts them all down, passes out dead drunk, and someone kicks him in the ass.

The next night, he walks into the bar and says, "Bartender, give me a triple Jack Daniels."

He gives him a triple Jack Daniels, and he belts it down. He has five more in a row, belts them all down, passes out dead drunk, and someone in the bar kicks him in the ass.

The next night, he walks into the bar and says, "Bartender, give me a triple tequila."

He says, "I thought you drank Jack Daniels."

He says, "Not anymore. Jack Daniels makes my ass hurt."

There were two drunks waiting for the bus. One was holding a large bag.

The drunk next to him asked, "Hey, what have you got in that bag there?"

The other drunk replied, "Porcupines."

"How many porcupines have you got in that bag then?" the first drunk asked.

"I'm not telling you!" replied the other.

"I'll tell you what," said the first, "if I guess how many porcupines you have in that bag, will you give me one?"

"I'll tell you what," replied the other, "if you guess how many porcupines I have in this bag . . . I'll give you both of them!"

What is the difference between a dog and a fox?
About five drinks.

A patron is sitting at a bar, and from out of an old suitcase he takes out a tiny piano and a little man about a foot tall. The little man sits down at the piano and starts playing beautifully.

A fellow sitting next to the patron at the bar looks on in sheer amazement.

"That's unbelievable! Where on earth did you get him?" says the fellow.

"Well, I have this magic lamp here that was given to me by a genie."

"Could I try it?" asks the fellow.

"Sure, be my guest."

The fellow rubs the lamp, and out comes a handsome genie.

"For what do you wish?" asks the genie.

"I'd like a million bucks," says the fellow.

Suddenly, the room is filled with a million quacking ducks.

"I asked for a million *bucks*, not *ducks*," the fellow says to the patron.

"I know," said the patron. "The genie is a little hard of hearing. You don't really think I asked for a twelve-inch pianist, do you?"

A drunk was staggering home with a pint of booze in his back pocket, when he slipped and fell heavily. Struggling to his feet, he felt something wet running down his leg.

"Please, God," he implored, "let it be blood!"

A man with no arms walked up to a bar and asked for a beer.

The bartender shoved the foaming glass in front of him.

"Look," said the customer, "I have no arms—would you please hold the glass up to my mouth?"

"Sure," said the bartender, and he did.

"Now," said the customer, "I wonder if you'd be so kind as to get my handkerchief out of my pocket and wipe the foam off my mouth."

"Certainly." And it was done.

"If," said the armless man, "you'd reach in my right-hand pants pocket, you'll find the money for the beer."

The bartender got it.

"You've been very kind," said the customer. "Just one thing more. Where is the men's room?"

"Out the door," said the bartender, "turn left, walk two blocks, and there's one in a filling station on the corner."

How many brewers does it take to change a lightbulb?
About one-third less than for a regular bulb.

A heavily inebriated gentleman is going ice fishing. He starts to drill a hole with his auger when a loud booming voice says, "There's no fish down there!"

So he stops drilling and moves a little ways and starts to drill again. The same voice booms, "There's no fish down there!"

So he moves a little further and is about to drill again, but the voice immediately comes again, "There's no fish down there either!"

The drunk looks around and says, "Who are you anyways? God?"

"No, I'm the rink manager!"

Drugs

Now MTV is running that "Rock Against Drugs" campaign. Right. That's an awful lot like "Whores Against Sex."

—BOB HARRIS

Why did the moron take two hits of mescaline?
So he could go round-trip.

Now they're calling taking drugs an epidemic—that's 'cause white folks are doing it.

—RICHARD PRYOR

I took Benzedrine and got clairvoyance. With Benzedrine you can have a very wide view of the world—like you can decide the destiny of man and other pressing problems, such as, which is the left sock?

—MORT SAHL

A wonder drug is a medicine that makes you wonder whether you can afford it.

Reality is just a crutch for people who can't cope with drugs.

I'm not addicted to cocaine. I just like the way it smells.

—RICHARD PRYOR

Drugs may lead to nowhere, but at least it's the scenic route.

—STEVEN WRIGHT

If God dropped acid, would he see people?

—GEORGE CARLIN

Every four minutes on television you see a brand-new pharmaceutical commercial. A new drug comes out, they make a sixty-second spot. The first fifty seconds they tell you how wonderful this drug is. The last ten seconds you get a list of side effects far worse than any disease I can ever imagine. And I for one do not want menstrual cramps.

—FREDDIE ROMAN

E

Education

Never try to teach a pig to sing; it wastes your time and it annoys the pig.

—Paul Dickson

The night before her wedding, Maria pulled her mother aside for an intimate little chat. "Mom," she confided, "I want you to tell me how I can make my new husband happy."

The bride's mother took a deep breath. "Well, my child," she began, "when two people love, honor, and respect each other, love can be a very beautiful thing."

"I know how to fuck, Mom," interrupted the girl. "I want you to teach me how to make lasagna."

In real life, I assure you, there is no such thing as algebra.

—Fran Lebowitz

The government said Americans are all geographically illiterate and economically ignorant. It's true. How many times have you said to yourself, "Where did all my money go?"

—Alan Prophet

I had a terrible education. I attended a school for emotionally disturbed teachers.

—Woody Allen

My parents sent my brother through law school. He graduated. Now he's suing them for wasting seven years of his life.

—Mike Binder

I have never let my schooling interfere with my education.

—MARK TWAIN

A naive young fellow got engaged to a lovely girl, and when they went in for their blood tests, it quickly became apparent to the doctor that the husband-to-be had no idea what sexual intercourse consisted of. Taking pity on the bride, Dr. Jones explained about the birds and the bees and the coconut trees, but the vague smile on the young man's face was unconvincing. The doctor's second attempt to explain the ritual of the wedding night left the groom-to-be smiling and nodding, but clearly baffled. So the good doctor gave it one more try, to no avail.

Thoroughly frustrated, the doctor instructed the young woman to undress and lie down upon the examination table. She obeyed happily enough, and Dr. Jones, a humanitarian through and through, proceeded to demonstrate for the young man. For forty minutes he demonstrated. Finally, sweaty and exhausted, he hauled himself up on his elbows, turned to the fiancé, and said, "Now do you understand what I've been trying to tell you?"

At last a glimmer of comprehension came into the young man's blue eyes. "I've got it now, Doc," he cried happily.

"Good, good," said the doctor in relief, getting down from the table and pulling up his pants. "Do you have any further questions?"

"Just one," admitted the young man.

"Yes?" asked the doctor testily.

"All I need to know, Dr. Jones, is how often do I have to bring her in?"

If there is a hell, it was modeled after junior high school.

—LEWIS BLACK

I find that the three major administrative problems on a campus are sex for the students, athletics for the alumni, and parking for the faculty.

—CLARK KERR

If law school is so hard to get through, how come there are so many lawyers?

—CALVIN TRILLIN

I always try to avoid clichés like the plague!

Did you know that five out of three people have trouble with fractions?

Embarrassment

Man is the only animal that blushes. Or needs to.

—MARK TWAIN

What's the ultimate in embarrassment for a woman?
When her Ben-Wa balls set off the metal detector at the airport.

The bathroom scale manufacturer was very proud of the new model being introduced at the trade fair. "Listen to these features: it's calibrated to one one-hundredth of a pound; it can measure your height as well, in feet or meters; it gives you a readout via an LED or human-voice simulator; and that's not all . . ."

"Very impressive," interrupted a none-too-slender sales rep for a chain of home furnishings stores, "but before I place an order, I'll have to try it out.

"Be my guest," said the manufacturer graciously.

But no sooner had the sales rep taken his place on the scale than a loud, very human-sounding voice issued forth: "One at a time, please, one at a time!"

There was this guy who desperately wanted to have sex with his girlfriend. However, he was too embarrassed because of his extremely small penis. So one night he took her to a dark place where she couldn't see it, and after furiously making out with her, dropped his pants and put his penis in her hand.

"Sorry, I don't smoke," she whispered.

I think I embarrassed the lady next to me on the plane. It was one of those flights that you sleep on, and I sleep in the nude.

—Johnny Dark

Mike was touching up the paint in the bathroom one weekend when the brush slipped out of his hand, leaving a stripe across the toilet seat. So Mike painted the whole seat over, and went off to a ball game.

His wife happened to get home early, went upstairs to pee, and found herself firmly stuck to the toilet seat. At six o'clock Mike found her there, furious and embarrassed, but he was unable to dislodge her for fear of tearing the skin.

With considerable difficulty, Mike managed to get her into the backseat of the car and then into a wheelchair at the county hospital, where she was wheeled into a room and maneuvered, on her knees, onto an examining table. At this point the resident entered and surveyed the scene.

"What do you think, Doc?" asked the nervous husband.

"Nice, very nice," he commented, stroking his chin. "But why the cheap frame?"

Two very elegantly dressed people are dancing. During a waltz the woman's necklace comes undone and falls down into her evening gown. Still dancing, she tries to wriggle about to make the necklace fall to the floor, but it winds up caught on something inside the back of her dress. She asks her partner to get it for her.

"How do you propose I do that?" he asks her.

"Just put your hand down the back of my dress and pluck it out," she instructs him.

They dance around a bit more, all the other couples watching,

as he puts his hand down the back of her dress and fishes around. Embarrassed, he says, "I feel the perfect ass."

"Never mind the compliments," she says, "just find the necklace."

—CARY GRANT

An hour after checking into the motel, the traveling salesman stormed up to the front desk. "What kind of chickenshit joint are you running?" he demanded.

"What's the problem, sir?" stammered the confused desk clerk.

"I went up to my room, unlocked the door, and there was a man holding a gun," blustered the irate guest. "He told me to get on my knees and give him a blow job or he'd blast my brains all over the room."

"Oh my God," gasped the clerk, shocked and embarrassed. "What did you do?"

The salesman screamed, "Well, you didn't hear any shots, did you?"

A guy goes to see his grandmother and takes one of his friends with him. While he's talking to his grandmother, his friend starts eating the peanuts that are on the coffee table, and finishes them off.

As they're leaving, the friend says, "Thanks for the peanuts."

The grandmother says, "Yeah, since I lost my dentures I can only suck the chocolate off 'em."

Enemies

When my enemies stop hissing, I shall know I'm slipping.

—MARIA CALLAS

A man cannot be too careful in the choice of his enemies.

—OSCAR WILDE

I always cheer up immensely if an attack is particularly wounding, because I think, well, if they attack one personally, it means they have not a single political argument left.

—Margaret Thatcher

During the Indian Wars, a cavalry brigade led a charge against a tribe of Cheyenne warriors, completely decimating the Indians. At the end, the only one left alive was the Indian chief. "Since you fought so bravely," said the cavalry officer, "I'm going to spare your life."

Just as the chief was trying to find words to express his gratitude, over the hill came a mess of Indians, who completely wiped out the cavalry brigade. The only survivor was the officer, to whom the Indian said, "I'm not going to be as generous as you were—you're going to die. But you can have three wishes before I kill you."

The officer nodded, thought for a minute, and said, "I'd like to see my horse." The horse was brought around, the officer whispered in its ear, and the horse tore off, only to return in an hour or so with a luscious blond on its back.

"Please feel free to make use of my teepee," offered the chief tactfully. When the officer emerged some time later, the chief asked about his second wish.

"I'd like to see my horse." Again the horse received a whispered command and galloped off, this time returning with a lovely redhead. Again the chief gestured graciously toward his teepee, and again waited an appropriate amount of time before inquiring as to his prisoner's last wish.

"I'd like to see my horse." This time when the horse was led up to him, the officer grasped its bridle firmly, pinched its lips with his other hand, and whispered fiercely, "Watch my lips—I said *posse*."

Love your enemy—it'll drive him nuts.

He hasn't an enemy in the world—but all his friends hate him.

—Eddie Cantor

A Chinese man was having a quiet drink when a Jewish guy came over and slugged him so hard, he fell off the bar stool. "Wha . . . what the hell was that for?" asked the poor guy, pulling himself upright.

"That was for Pearl Harbor."

"But I'm not Japanese, I'm Chinese," he said.

"Japanese, Chinese, they're all the same to me," snorted the aggressor, and returned to his beer.

A few minutes later, the Chinese man went over and slammed the first guy headfirst into the bar. Watching him stagger to his feet, he explained calmly, "That was for the *Titanic*."

"The *Titanic*?" Dazed and bewildered, the Jew protested, "The *Titanic* was sunk by an iceberg."

"Iceberg, Goldberg, they're all the same to me," explained the Chinese man.

The American pilot finally downed the Messerschmidt, but was so impressed with the German's flying skill that he went to visit him in the field hospital. Finding the fellow in pretty bad shape, the American asked if he could do anything for him.

The soldier admitted that he did have a favor to ask. "The leg they amputated . . . on your next bombing run, could you drop it over the fatherland?"

"Sure, pal." It was a pretty weird request, but the pilot was happy to oblige and came back to tell him the mission had been carried out. The grateful German gasped his thanks, and another request. "The other leg got very bad—they had to cut it off. Could this, too, be dropped over my homeland? It would mean a great deal to me."

The American shrugged, but returned two days later with the news that the job was done. "Many thanks," whispered the

downed soldier, now ashen-faced and unable to lift his head from the pillow. "I have just one final request. Last night they had to amputate my right arm—"

"Now hang on just a darn minute," interrupted the American angrily. "Are you trying to escape?"

I never hated a man enough to give him his diamonds back.

—Zsa Zsa Gabor

I bring out the worst in my enemies and that's how I get them to defeat themselves.

—Roy Cohn

A man was walking down a narrow lane in Belfast, Northern Ireland, when a shadowy figure jumped out and blocked his way with a machine gun.

"Don't move!" he commanded. "Are you a Protestant or a Catholic?"

"Neither," gasped the fellow in relief. "I'm Jewish."

The gunman hit him with a burst of bullets, and smiled broadly as he said to himself, "I must be the luckiest Arab in Ireland tonight."

"Well," snarled the tough old sergeant to the bewildered private, "I suppose after you get discharged from the army, you'll be waiting for me to die so you can come and spit on my grave."

"Not me, Sarge!" the private replied. "After I get out of the army, I ain't never going to stand in line again!"

Ethics

The contractor wanted to give the government official a sports car. The official objected, saying, "Sir, common decency and my basic sense of honor would never permit me to accept a gift like that."

The contractor said, "I quite understand. Suppose we do this: I'll sell you the car for ten dollars."

The official thought for a moment and said, "In that case, I'll take two."

—JOEY ADAMS

It's said that George Bernard Shaw was seated at dinner one night next to an attractive woman. "Madam," he asked boldly, "would you go to bed with me for a thousand pounds?"

The woman blushed scarlet and shook her head sharply.

"For ten thousand pounds?" the eminent man pursued.

"I would not," she declared.

"Then how about the sum of fifty thousand pounds?"

The colossal sum gave the woman pause. After some reflection, she replied coyly, "Perhaps."

"And if I were to offer you five pounds?"

"Mr. Shaw!" The woman was shocked. "What do you take me for?"

"We have already determined what you are," he pointed out calmly. "Now we are merely haggling over the price."

With one look at his voluptuous new patient, all the gynecologist's professional ethics went right out the window. Instructing her to undress completely, he began to stroke the soft skin of her inner thigh. "Do you know what I'm doing?" he asked softly.

"Checking for any dermatological abnormalities, right?"

"Right," crooned the doctor, beginning to fondle her breasts and gently pinch her nipples. "And now?"

"Looking for any lumps that might be cancerous."

"Right you are," reassured the doctor, placing her feet in the stirrups, pulling out his cock, and entering her. "And do you know what I'm doing now?"

"Yup," she said, looking down. "Catching herpes."

A traveling vaudeville troupe visited a small town. While at their hotel, a man visited them and said he was the town's self-appointed morals keeper. He'd heard that the troupe used dirty jokes in their act. The troupe's manager assured him that they didn't. The man then said he'd be sitting in the first row with his wife, and if he heard any dirty language, he'd shut down the show.

That night, the star of the show came out with a co-star and they began their act. "Say, do you know what the best part of a woman is?" asked the star.

"No," replied the co-star, "what is the best part of a woman?"

The man in the first row leaped to his feet and declared firmly, "If he says 'cunt' I'm stopping the show."

—CHARLES COBURN

A key part of candidate Decker's reform program was the elimination of the X-rated video stores springing up on Main Street. As she stood before the crowd, her face grew red with anger at the very thought of this threat to public decency and morals. "I actually rented one of these filthy cassettes," she declared boldly, "and was disgusted to witness horrible acts of perversion: sodomy, oral sex, one man engaging in the sex act with three women, a woman accommodating four men, even sex with a dog! Vote for Lynn Decker, ladies and gentlemen, and I guarantee this blight on our community will be eliminated!" Catching her breath, she asked, "Any questions?"

Twelve hands shot up. "Where'd you get the tape?"

Ethnic Specials

A little Jewish guy is at a urinal in the men's room when a big black guy runs in, whips it out, and starts doing his business in the urinal next to him.

The black guy says, "Just made it."

The little guy says, "Can you make me one in white?"

—JAN MURRAY

What do Jewish women make for dinner?
Reservations.

A Russian, a Jamaican, an American, and a Mexican were on a rafting expedition together. Mid river, the Russian pulled out a huge bottle of Stolichnaya, took a swig, and threw it overboard.

"Hey, what the hell'd you do that for?" blurted out the American.

"We have so much vodka in Russia that we can afford to waste it," explained the Russian cheerfully.

A few miles downstream the Jamaican took out a huge bag full of marijuana, rolled a giant joint, took a few puffs, and tossed it overboard.

"Jesus, that stuff's expensive," bellowed the American. "What'd you do that for?"

"In Jamaica, weed grows everywhere, mon," said the Jamaican with a grin. "We can afford to waste it."

Thinking hard, the American suddenly smiled at the Mexican. "Don't even think about it," the Mexican said.

Three crews were competing for a contract with the telephone company. In order to select the most qualified, the phone company instructed each crew to go out and see how many telephone poles they could erect in one day.

At the end of the day the Jewish crew reported thirty-five poles to the phone company official, who was obviously impressed.

"Good, but not good enough," he told the Italians, who had installed thirty-two. "Well?" he asked, turning to the Iranian crew.

"Two," said the foreman proudly.

"So why are you so proud of yourself? Those guys did thirty-five and those did thirty-two," he said, pointing to the other crews.

"Yeah," said the Iranian foreman, "but look how much they left sticking out of the ground."

Definition of a WASP:
Someone who thinks Taco Bell is the Mexican phone company.

How can you tell where Amish people live in Appalachia?
They have a dead horse up on blocks in the front yard.

I was in the bar the other day and heard two guys speaking Iranian. I said to them, "Why are you speaking Iranian? You're in America now, speak Spanish."

—Milton Berle

Jewish foreplay is three hours of begging.
Italian foreplay is "Maria, I'm home."

—Milton Berle

Why do Polish names end in "ski"?
They don't know how to spell "toboggan."

Three guys were up on the roof of the apartment building on a hot summer day.
"Man, you should check this out," said one of the guys to the other, stepping up onto the parapet. "The wind really whips off the river around this building. Look." And he jumped off into space, plummeting for a few stories, then catching an updraft and floating gracefully to the sidewalk below like an autumn leaf.
Watching the maneuver in astonishment, one guy gasped in admiration. Then, crossing himself, he took a flying leap off the building, only to splatter onto the street a few seconds later.
Surveying the gruesome spectacle, the other guy ruefully shook his head. "That Clark Kent, give him a few drinks and he goes crazy."

How many Amish does it take to screw in a lightbulb?
The Amish don't have lightbulbs. They bake pies.

Did you hear about the Jewish good luck charm? It's a rabbi's foot.

—Milton Berle

A farmer on a kibbutz was talking to a Texan. The Texan says, "How big is your farm?"

"Well," he says, "it's two hundred feet by three hundred feet. How big is your ranch?"

The Texan says, "I could get in my car and drive from sunrise to sunset and never reach the end of my land."

The Israeli says, "I once had a car like that, too."

—Alan King

Why do Canadians like to do it doggie style?
So they can both keep watching the hockey game.

—Norm Crosby

An American, a Russian, an Iraqi, and an Israeli were walking down the street, when a man came up to them and said, "Excuse me. I'm with the Gallup Organization and we're conducting a public-opinion poll about the meat shortage—"

The Russian said, "What's meat?"

The American said, "What's a shortage?"

The Iraqi said, "What's public opinion?"

And the Israeli said, "What's excuse me?"

The Ecuadorian captain had grown increasingly anxious over rumors of an impending air strike from neighboring Peru. "Pedro,"
he ordered his aide-de-camp, "I want you to climb that mountain and report any signs of Peruvian military activity."

"Sí, Capitano," replied Pedro. He trudged up the mountain, and as soon as he crossed the ridge, he saw a squadron of planes heading their way. "There are many planes coming, Capitano," he promptly radioed back.

"Friends or enemies?" the Captain demanded urgently.

Pedro again lifted his binoculars to the sky. "They're flying very closely together, *Capitano*," he replied. "I think they must be friends."

The Italians and the Jews have a lot in common. It was an Italian who invented the toilet seat, but the Jew had brains enough to put a hole in it.

—MILTON BERLE

What do you get when you cross a WASP and a Mexican?
    A migrant stockbroker.

Do you know what the four shortest books in history are? *Famous Jewish Astronauts, Ten Thousand Years of German Humor, Irish Gourmet Cooking*, and *Negroes I Have Met While Yachting*.

—MILTON BERLE

Heard about the black and the Mexican who opened up a restaurant?
    It's called Nacho Mama.

The prostitute was quite impressed when her Chinese client took her up to his room in the swanky Hotel Crillon, where they screwed for quite a while, until he rolled off, gasping for breath. *"Pardonnez-moi, Mademoiselle, je suis fatigueé."* he explained, and went into the bathroom to freshen up.

When he returned, she was even more impressed by a second energetic round of sex. After a while, though, he lay back on the bed, sighing, *"Pardonnez-moi, Mademoiselle, je suis fatigueé."* Off he went to the bathroom again, and again returned revived and ready for another session of lovemaking.

After the sixth screw, the hooker was so tired, she excused herself for a bathroom break. What did she find when she pulled back the shower curtain? Five Chinese guys!

Why do Italians have such short necks? It's from standing in front of a grand jury and shrugging their shoulders and saying, "I don't know."

—MILTON BERLE

How many Teamsters does it take to change a lightbulb?
Ten. You gotta *problem* with that?

What do Japanese men do when they have erections?
Vote.

Hear about the new synagogue in Harlem?
It's called Temple Beth-You-Is-My-Woman-Now.

Hear about the guy who was half Jewish and half Japanese?
He was circumcised at Benihana's.

Fred was the manager for a construction project in downtown Rochester and his first job was to take bids from the local construction companies for the job. The first interview was with a representative from Zabriskie Brothers.

"You've seen the plans," said Fred. "How much'll you charge to get the job done?"

"Two hundred thousand dollars," said Zab.

"Reasonable," commented Fred. "What's the breakdown?"

"One hundred thousand for materials, one hundred thousand for labor."

"Okay," said Fred, jotting down the bid and showing him to the door, "I'll get back to you."

The next interview was with Gennaro Rossellini of Fratelli Rossellini, who came up with a four-hundred-thousand-dollar bid. "Half for labor, half for materials," he explained.

"That's a little high," admitted Fred, "but I'll get back to you."

The third bid came in from Ben Cohen of Cohen Construction. Calculating quickly, he offered, "Six hundred thousand dollars."

"Jesus, that's high," exclaimed Fred. " Could you break that down for me?"

"You bet. Two hundred grand for me, two hundred grand for you, and two hundred grand for Zab."

How can you tell when a female WASP is experiencing an orgasm?
She uncrosses her legs.

Mrs. Hildebrand instructed each of her second graders to use the word "choo-choo" in a sentence.

Little Jennifer said, "The choo-choo pulled into the station right on schedule."

Little Leroy said, "De choo-choo is goin' too fast."

Little José said, "You touch my Chevy an' I'll choo-choo."

What's furry and generates enough smoke to melt an iceberg?
An Eskimo in heat.

What do you call a skinny WASP?
A WISP.

It so happened that Myron and Vinnie came of age at the same time. From his father, Vinnie received a brand-new handgun, while at his bar mitzvah on the other side of town, Myron's father strapped a beautiful gold watch on his wrist. The next day after school, Vinnie was full of admiration for the watch, while Myron was consumed with envy after one glance at the pistol. So the two friends decided to trade gifts.

That night when Vinnie checked to see whether it was dinnertime, his father asked, "Where'd you get thatta watch?" And on hearing the story, he exploded. "Whatsa matter wid' yous? Here I am t'inkin' you gotta some brains in your head."

Vinnie looked frankly confused, so his father explained that some day Vinnie would probably get married. "An' somma day," he went on, "yous gonna find her in bed wit' another guy. An' whatta you gonna do then—look atta you watch and say, 'How long you gonna be?'"

Why did God create armadillos?
So Mexicans would have something to eat on the half shell.

What does a WASP do when his car breaks down?
Calls the nearest Chevrolet dealership.
What does a Mormon do when his car breaks down?
Calls the nearest Cadillac dealership.
And what does a Jew do when his car breaks down?
Puts a "For Sale" sign in the window and takes a cab to the nearest Hilton.

They have a new poster out to build Australian pride.
It says: "Australia—Land of Strong Men (and Nervous Sheep)."

Seen the Canadian bumper sticker?
It says, "I'd Rather Be Driving."

What do you call a Filipino contortionist?
A Manila folder.

Following a tragic shipwreck in the Mediterranean, the body of an attractive young woman washed up on the beach near St. Tropez. The *gendarme* who came across it during his rounds went off to contact the coroner's office, and when he came back, he was horrified to find his best friend on top of the corpse, going at it as hard as he could.
"Pierre, Pierre!" shouted the *gendarme*. "That woman . . . she is dead!"
"Dead!" howled Pierre, jumping up. "*Sacre bleu*—I took her for an American!"

During the war, I was hidden by an Italian couple in their basement. Of course, that was South Philly.

—NORM CROSBY

Did you hear about the guy who was half Polish and half Italian? He made himself an offer he couldn't understand.

Hear about the disadvantaged WASP?
     He grew up with a black-and-white TV.

What does the bride of a Russian man get on her wedding night that's long and hard? A new last name.

How many Italians does it take to screw in a lightbulb?
     Two. One to screw it in and one to shoot the witnesses.

What's a WASP's idea of mass transit? The ferry to Martha's Vineyard.

How do you get twenty Argentinians in a phone booth?
     Let them think they own it.

I know an Italian man who married an Irish woman. Their son wanted to commit a crime, but he couldn't because he was too drunk.

—NORM CROSBY

A young country Irish lad is at the local barn dance. He spies in the distance a fine-looking young lassie. After building up as much courage as he can, he saunters over to her and asks her if she would like to dance. She does, so they do. After a few slow dances, he looks her straight in the eye and says, "Can I smell your pussy?" to which she, not altogether unsurprisingly, replies, "You certainly can*not*!"

He nonchalantly turns to her and says, "Oh, it must be your feet then."

Why does an Englishman close his eyes when he has sex? Because he doesn't like to see a woman disappointed!

Why does an Australian man close his eyes when he has sex? Because he doesn't like to see a woman enjoy herself!

Hear about the Newfie who was killed while ice fishing? Got run over by the Zamboni!

A Newfie comes up to the bar and orders five shots of whiskey. As he sets them up, the bartender asks what he is celebrating.

The Newfie replies that he just got his first blow job.

"Hey, that's great," says the bartender. "Let me buy you one, too."

"No thanks," says the Newfie. "If five don't kill the taste, nothing will!"

What would be the definition of a European heaven?

A Europe where the Italians are the lovers, the French are the cooks, the British are the policemen, and the Germans are the engineers. [Every nation doing a job that they are good at.]

In that case, what would be the definition of a European hell?

A Europe where the Italians are the engineers, the French are the lovers, the British are the cooks, and the Germans are the policemen.

What would you call it when an Italian has one arm shorter than the other?

A speech impediment.

An Italian lady's husband needs an operation, and she can't afford it. They tell her, "Mrs. Rigatoni, we have a television show

called *Medic*. If you let us operate on your husband on television, you'll get the operation for free, plus we'll pay you."

She says, "But I got-a no clothes to wear on-a the TV." So they take her out and they buy her a few new dresses. On the big night, she gets made up and gets her hair done. She gets interviewed on the show before the operation, and after the show, they come backstage to see her.

One of the doctors says, "Mrs. Rigatoni, I'm very sorry, but your husband passed away during the operation."

She says, " 'Atsa show biz."

This guy wanted to marry a lady from the old country, but the old country had a law that you have to be from the old country to marry someone from there, so, in other words, he'd have to have 50 percent of his brain removed. He goes to his doctor and says, "I've just got to marry this woman, I love her so much. . . ."

So the doctor says, "Well, it's risky, but okay." So into the operating room they go for the brain removal procedure. Later, when the guy wakes up, the doctor comes in and says, "We are verrrryyyy sorry, but we accidentally removed seventy-five percent of your brain instead of fifty percent."

The guy looks up and says, "I object, Your Honor!"

Every time an Indian walks into the chief's teepee, he sees that the chief is masturbating. They finally realize this is a serious problem, so they fix him up with a nice woman, and she starts living with him in his teepee.

One day, one of the Indians walks in and there's the chief masturbating again. He says, "Chief, what you doing? We fix you up with beautiful woman."

The chief says, "Her arm get-um tired."

Horowitz and Shmolowitz are on a camel, traveling through the desert. They are dying of thirst, and finally they come to an oasis.

Horowitz and Shmolowitz drink at a water hole, but the camel refuses to take a drink.

Horowitz says, "I've got an idea. You hold the camel's head under water, and I'll suck on his rear end and try to draw some water up into his mouth."

Shmolowitz dunks the camel's head under the water and Horowitz starts sucking like mad.

After a few minutes, Horowitz yells, "Raise his head a little. All I'm getting is mud from the bottom."

What time did the Chinese man go to the dentist?
Tooth hurty.

What would you call an Amish guy with his arm up a horse's ass?
A mechanic.

How many WASPs does it take to change a lightbulb?
Two. One to call the electrician and one to mix the martinis.

What's the Irish version of a queer?
Someone who prefers women to liquor.

What are the two biggest lies in Poland?
"The check is in your mouth" and "I won't come in the mail."

I love how New York is so multicultural. I wish I was ethnic. 'Cause if you're Hispanic and you get angry, people are like, "He's got a Latin temper." But if you're a white guy and you get angry, people are like, "That guy's a jerk."

—Jim Gaffigan

Why can't we have racism that's ignorant but nice? You could have stereotypes about race that are positive. You could say, " 'Those Chinese people, they can fly!' 'You know about the Puerto Ricans . . . they're made of candy!' '"

—Louis C.K.

It is cold outside. The other night, I came home and my wife was sitting in front of the fire, curled up with an Afghan, so I grabbed his beard and started beating him with his sandals.

—Tom Cotter

How can you tell the Irish guy in the hospital ward?
He's the one blowing the foam off of his bed pan.

There were three guys traveling in Africa: a Frenchman, a Japanese, and an American. They are captured by a tribe of fierce headhunters.

The witch doctor says to them, "We are going to slaughter you, but you might take some comfort in the fact that we don't believe in waste here, and that therefore every part of your body will go to some use. We will weave baskets out of your hair, we will render your bones for glue, and we will tan your skin and stretch it over wooden frames for canoes. Now we are going to allow you an honorable death, so I will give you each a knife and allow you to say some last words before killing yourselves."

The Japanese guy yells, "*Banzai!*" and commits hara-kiri.

The French guy yells, "*Vive la France!*" and slits his throat.

Then the American guy takes the knife, pokes holes all over his body, and yells, "There's your fucking canoe!"

A black guy, a Jewish guy, and a redneck are working digging a
ditch. The black guy's shovel hits something, he picks it up, and
it's a lamp. He starts to rub the dirt off and a genie comes out.

The genie goes, "Arggh! I will give you each one wish."

The black guy says, "I want my own country, where the broth-
ers and sisters can live in peace and harmony in freedom for-
ever."

The genie says, "Done."

He says to the Jew, "What about you?"

The Jew says, "I want my own country, so the Jews can live in
peace and harmony with no persecution forever and ever."

The genie says, "Done."

Then the genie says to the redneck, "What about you?"

The redneck says, "Now let me get this straight. The blacks are all gonna live in their own country, and the Jews are all gonna live in their own country?"

The genie says, "That's right."

The redneck says, "Fuck it. I'll take a Diet Coke."

I was reading the *New York Times* and there was an article saying there is now proof that Jesus was Irish. The researcher, Dr. Melanie Leahy, said the proof was "indelible and unreproachable."

She said the facts are:

1. He lived with his parents until he was twenty-nine.

2. He went out drinking with the lads the night before he died.

3. He thought his mother was a virgin, and she, the good woman, God bless her, thought he was God.

Did you hear the latest about the fighting on the West Bank?
Italy surrendered.

Man: Let me have some grits and an RC.

Guy behind the counter: You must be from Georgia.

Man: What the hell kinda stereotypical remark is that? If I walked in here and asked for a sausage, would you think I was Polish?

Guy: No.

Man: If I walked in here and asked for some chow mein, would you think I was Chinese?

Guy: No.

Man: If I walked in here and asked for some pizza, would you think I was Italian?

Guy: No.

Man: Then why in the hell do you think I'm from Georgia?

Guy: Because this is a hardware store.

What's the Cuban national anthem?
"Row, Row, Row Your Boat."

What do you call four Mexicans in quicksand?
Cuatro Sink-o

How about the Mexican midget who committed suicide?
He hung himself from the rear-view mirror.

An Englishman, a Frenchman, and a Russian are stranded on a
desert island. One morning after a storm, they find an old sealed
bottle on the beach. They open it and a huge genie flies out and says,
"Oh, masters, thank you for letting me out of prison! I've been there
for far too long. Because I am so grateful, I will fulfill two wishes for
each of you!"

The Englishman says, "I want to be filthy rich and I want to go
home."

The genie grants his wishes and he is gone.

The Frenchman says, "I want to have lots of women who adore me
and I also want to go home."

The genie grants his wishes and he is gone.

The Russian grows very sad and says pensively, "Why, weren't
they good company! I wish for an unlimited supply of vodka and . . .
I want both of them back!"

The bus stops and two Italian men get on. They seat themselves
and engage in animated conversation. The lady sitting behind
them ignores their conversation at first, but her attention is gal-
vanized when she hears one of the men say: "Emma come first.
Den I come. Two asses, dey come together. I come again. Two
asses, dey come together again. I come again and pee twice. Den I
come one-a more."

"You foul-mouthed swine," retorted the lady indignantly. "In
this country we don't talk about our sex lives in public!"

"Hey, coola-downa, lady," said the man. "Imma justa teachin'
my fren' howa to spella Mississippi."

Did you hear about the summer camp in the Adirondacks for Native American kids?

It's called Camp Shapiro.

A little Italian grandfather comes up to customs. The customs official says, "Have you got anything to declare?" He thinks a second and he says, "It's a nice-a day!"

Experience

A man who carries a cat by the tail learns something he can learn in no other way.

—MARK TWAIN

We should be careful to get out of an experience only the wisdom that is in it—and stop there, lest we be like the cat that sits down on a hot stove lid. She will never sit down on a hot stove lid again—and that is well, but also she will never sit down on a cold one anymore.

—MARK TWAIN

Do you know the difference between education and experience?

Education is when you read the fine print; experience is what you get when you don't.

—PETE SEEGER

It's said that Tom Watson, head of IBM, was asked if he was going to fire an employee whose recent mistake had cost the company six hundred thousand dollars. Watson shook his head, and explained, "I just spent six hundred thousand dollars training him. Why would I want anyone else to hire his experience?"

Experience: a comb life gives you after you lose your hair.

—JUDITH STERN

What did one lab rat say to the other?

"I've got my scientist so well trained that every time I push the buzzer, he brings me a snack."

The personnel director was interviewing a job applicant. "Given that you have no experience whatsoever in this field, you're asking for an awfully high salary," she pointed out.

"I suppose so," replied the applicant, "but think how much harder the work's going to be if I don't know anything about it."

Farmer Bob was returning from town with his cow, Missy, and his dog, Rusty, in the pan of his truck. On a really slick section of hillside, with a steep drop of a couple of hundred feet, he lost control of his truck and plummeted over the side. As the truck rolled over several times, the dog and cow were thrown down the slope. All were alive, but the farmer, unfortunately, was beneath the truck and in severe pain with a broken leg, several cracked ribs, and a broken wrist and arm.

By and by, a state trooper came along. Treading his way carefully down the slope, he came upon the cow first. She had suffered a broken leg. Knowing how much pain she was in, the trooper took out his gun and put Missy out of her misery. He proceeded down the slope and came across Rusty, crawling along, dragging his two broken legs. He had been hit pretty hard. Again, the state trooper unholstered his gun and did the kindest thing.

He then continued on to Farmer Bob. The trooper stared down at him and said, "Are you in much pain, sir?"

To which Farmer Bob, eyeing the gun on the trooper's hip, replied instantaneously, "Never felt better, sir!"

In the days when tall wooden ships sailed the high seas, there was this one ship sailing during a war. That morning, the lookout shouted, "Enemy ship on the horizon."

The captain said to his ensign, "Get me my red shirt."

The ensign, rather bewildered by this odd request, did as his captain ordered.

Though the battle was a long one, the captain and his crew managed to fend off the enemy ship.

Later that day, the lookout shouted, "Two enemy ships on the horizon."

As before, the captain said to his ensign, "Get me my red shirt." And, as before, the ensign did as his captain asked. The battle took the rest of the day to fight, and again they managed to defeat the two enemy ships.

That evening, the ensign asked his captain, "Sir, why, before every battle, do you ask for your red shirt?"

The captain replied, "Well, if I am wounded in battle, the blood will not show and the crew will continue to fight."

The crew was listening, and they were impressed. They had a brave captain.

The next morning, the lookout shouted, "Ten enemy ships on the horizon."

The ensign looked at his captain, waiting for the usual orders. The captain said to his ensign, "Ensign, get me my brown pants."

F

Failure

Failure has gone to his head.

—WILSON MIZNER (ATTRIBUTED), ABOUT A BANKRUPT
BUSINESSMAN WHO REMAINED INCORRIGIBLY OPTIMISTIC

If at first you don't succeed, destroy all evidence that you tried.

—NEWT HEILSCHER

When Winston Churchill was defeated in his bid for reelection as prime minister, his wife consoled him with the thought that the defeat was a blessing in disguise. "If so," responded Churchill, "then it is very effectively disguised."

My friends all told me I'd never be anything but a failure at this business, so I decided to do something about it—I went out and made some new friends.

He's never been very successful. When opportunity knocks, he complains about the noise.

Faith

Old Mrs. Watkins awoke one spring morning to find that the river had flooded not only her basement but the entire first floor of her house. And, looking out her bedroom window, she saw that the water was still rising. Two men passing by in a rowboat shouted up an invitation to row to safety with them.

"No, thank you," replied Mrs. Watkins tartly. "The Lord will provide." The men shrugged and rowed on.

By evening the water level forced Mrs. Watkins to climb out on her roof, where she was spotted by a cheerful man in a motorboat. "Don't worry, lady," he called across the water. "I'll pick you right up."

"Please don't trouble yourself—the Lord will provide." Mrs. Watkins then turned her back on her would-be rescuer, who buzzed off downriver.

Pretty soon Mrs. Watkins was forced to take refuge atop her chimney, the only part of the house still above water. Fortunately, a Red Cross cutter came by on patrol. "Jump in, ma'am," urged a rescue worker.

Mrs. Watkins shook her head vehemently. "The Lord will provide." So the boat departed, the water rose, and the old woman drowned.

Dripping wet and thoroughly annoyed, she came through the pearly gates and demanded to speak to God.

"What happened?" she cried. "I thought the Lord would provide."

"For cryin' out loud, lady," said God wearily, "I sent three boats."

—RED SKELTON

Saintly Mrs. Ficalora came to morning mass as usual, kneeled down, and unburdened herself. "Dear God," she admitted, "sometimes I just don't understand the wisdom of your ways. My neighbor, that godless slut Angie D'Onofrio never sets foot in church, is on her fourth husband—which doesn't keep her from entertaining half the men in the parish—yet she has two fine houses, three cars, all the jewels a woman could want, and a closet full of furs. Why has she been so blessed and I not?"

"Because," God's voice boomed from behind the altar, "she doesn't bug me!"

Among many other attractions, the traveling circus featured
Wanda the Wondrous, a faith healer who claimed the ability to
heal any malady, slight or serious, real or imagined. She usually
drew a big crowd, from which she would select a few people on
whom to practice her healing skills. Among the unfortunate one
Friday night, were Cecily Sussman, on crutches due to a congeni-
tal spinal malformation, and Irving Bland, who had suffered
from a terrible lisp all his life. "Cecily and Irving," asked Wanda,
"do you wish to be healed?"

"Yeth, ma'am," said Irving, and Cecily nodded vigorously.

Wanda motioned them behind a purple velvet curtain and
proceeded to chant and pray, grinding powders together and
swaying before the audience. Finally she intoned, "Cecily, throw
out your left crutch."

A crutch came sailing over the curtain.

"Cecily, throw out your right crutch."

A second crutch clattered on the floor at the healer's feet.

"Now, Irving," asked Wanda solemnly, "say something to the
people."

Irving's voice came clearly from behind the purple curtain.
"Thethily Thuthman just fell on her ath."

The minister of an Oklahoma farming parish convened a prayer
meeting to pray for rain during a serious drought. Noting that on that
cloudless morning the church was full to overflowing, he came to the
pulpit and posed a single question to his flock. "You all know why
we're here," he said. "What I want to know is, why didn't any of you
bring umbrellas?"

One night little Johnny finished his prayers with "God bless
Grandma," and the very next day his grandmother kicked the
bucket. Johnny told his family about his prayer, but no one
seemed to give it too much thought. A week later he ended his
prayers with "God bless Grandpa," and the next day his grandfather died. The family was running a little scared by now, and

when Johnny finished his prayers one night with "God bless Daddy," his mother thought maybe she better warn her husband about it.

All that night Johnny's dad couldn't sleep for worrying, and the next day he came home from work early. "I had a terrible day worrying about all this," he confided to his wife.

"You think you had a bad day," she said. "The mailman came to the door and dropped dead."

Fame

The pope decided to visit America and was gratified to see a huge crowd waiting for him at JFK Airport. But it was disconcerting to hear them chanting, "Elvis! Elvis! Elvis!" as he stepped down from the plane. "Oh, my children, thank you," he said, bowing his head modestly. "But I am not Elvis."

No one seemed to hear him, and he was ushered into a white stretch limo with "Elvis" written in diamonds on the doors. "Bless you," he said to the sequined chauffeur, "but I am not Elvis."

When the limo pulled up to the Waldorf, it had to make its way through a huge crowd crammed behind police barricades. The crowd was chanting, "Elvis! Elvis! Elvis!"

Shaking his head, the pope followed his luggage to the most sumptuous suite in the hotel. As he was unpacking, the door behind him opened and in walked three lovely women clad in the scantiest of negligees. The pope looked them over for a moment or two, cleared his throat, and began to sing, "Well, it's one for the money, two for the show. . . ."

The story is told that Winston Churchill, scheduled to address the entire United Kingdom in an hour, hailed a cab in London's West End and told the cabbie to drive as fast as he could for the BBC.

"Sorry, sir," said the cabbie, shaking his head. "You'll have to find yourself another cab."

"And why is that?" asked the annoyed prime minister.

"Ordinarily it wouldn't be a problem, sir," explained the driver apologetically, "but Mr. Churchill's broadcasting at six o'clock and I want to get home in time to hear him."

Churchill was so gratified that he pulled a pound note out of his wallet and handed it over. The cabbie took one look at the bill and said, "Hop in, sir—the devil with Mr. Churchill."

I was walking down Madison Avenue and I saw a very good-looking tie in a shop window. So I went in, and before I could say anything, the manager said, "Oh, Tony Randall. In my store! Please, just a minute, I gotta call my wife, she'll never believe me!"

He calls her up and says to me, "Here, say hello, say anything, talk to my wife. Say anything!" He flattered me so much that I bought the tie, bought six shirts. I didn't have enough money. I said, "Will you take a check?"

He said, "Do you have any identification?"

November 16, 1916, was the Friars Frolic in honor of Enrico Caruso in the Great Hall of the Monastery. The Friars' abbot, George M. Cohan, was the toastmaster; Friars Victor Herbert and Charles Emerson Cook wrote a special song for the occasion; and Irving Berlin arranged the entertainment, which included Al Jolson, John Barrymore, and Enrico Caruso himself.

Into this setting ambled the young vaudevillian Joey Frisco. Every hotshot in town was waiting patiently backstage to get on. Big as they were, they each had a respect for Caruso that amounted to awe. The famous opera star stood in the wings, waiting his turn, but nobody actually had the courage to address the great man himself—that is, nobody but Frisco. "Hey C-C-Caruso," he nudged, "d-d-don't do 'D-D-Darktown Strutters' Ball.' That's my number, and I follow you."

—JOEY ADAMS, ABOUT JOEY FRISCO

I don't mind men who kiss and tell. I need all the publicity I can get.

—RUTH BUZZI

Three guys were sitting around talking about what being really, really famous would be like. The first guy defined it as being invited to the White House for a personal chat with the president.

"Nah," disagreed the second fellow. "Real fame would be being in there chatting when the hot line rings, and the president won't take the call." The third guy said they both had it wrong. "Fame," he declared, "is when you're in the Oval Office and the hot line rings, the president answers it, listens for a second, and then says, 'It's for you.'"

George Jessel could spend as much on a girl as Mike Todd could on a night of gin. A couple of years back he chartered a plane to take him from Cleveland to New York because he had a date and no commercial airline could get him in on time. Due to the low ceiling, we couldn't land, and kept circling for more than an hour. Tension mounted, and conversation in the plane ceased. "My luck," I murmured. "We'll get killed and you'll get top billing."

—JOEY ADAMS

When the brash young advertising executive arrived at La Coupole for his lunch appointment, he spotted Bill Gates at a corner table and went right over. "Excuse me for interrupting your meal, Mr. Gates," he began, "but I know how much you appreciate enterprise and initiative. I'm trying to win over a very important account today—it could really make or break my company—and the clients I'm meeting with would be incredibly impressed if you stopped by our table at some point and said, 'Hello, Mike.' It would be an incredible favor, Mr. Gates, and some day I'd make it up to you."

"Okay, okay," sighed Gates, and went back to his smoked pheasant. He finished and was putting on his coat when he remembered the young man's request. Obligingly, he went over to his table, tapped him on the shoulder, and said, "Hi, Mike."

"Not now, Bill," interrupted the young man. "Can't you see I'm eating?"

Eddie Cantor and Georgie Jessel were on the same bill on a vaudeville unit. When they arrived in town, Jessel saw the billing, which read: "Eddie Cantor with Georgie Jessel."

Georgie berated manager, Irving Mansfield. "What kind of conjunction is that—Eddie Cantor with Georgie Jessel?" Irving promised to fix it.

The next day the marquee read: "Eddie Cantor but Georgie Jessel."

—JOEY ADAMS

I don't have a photograph, but you can have my footprints. They're in my socks.

—GROUCHO MARX

A big-time celebrity was doing a benefit at a senior citizens home. He went up to one of the elderly ladies, sat down beside her, and said, "Do you know who I am?"

She said, "No, but go to the front desk. They'll tell you who you are."

—NORM CROSBY

Family

Happiness is having a large, loving, caring, close-knit family in another city.

—GEORGE BURNS

Nothing in life is "fun for the whole family."

—JERRY SEINFELD

George: This family of yours, did they all live together?

Gracie: Yes, my father, my uncle, my cousin, my brother, and my nephew used to sleep in one bed, and my—

George: I'm surprised your grandfather didn't sleep with them.

Gracie: He did. But he died and they made him get up.

—George Burns and Gracie Allen

After all, what is a pedestrian? He is a man who has two cars—one being driven by his wife, the other by one of his children.

—Robert Bradbury

The trouble with the average family is it has too much month left over at the end of the money.

—Bill Vaughan

My parents used to send me to spend summers with my grandparents. I hate cemeteries!

—Chris Fonseca

I worked some gigs in the Deep South . . . Alabama . . . you talk about Darwin's waiting room. There are guys in Alabama who are their own father.

—Dennis Miller

The middle-aged man walked into the bar with a shit-eating grin on his face and ordered a round for the house. "It's nice to see someone in such a good mood," commented the bartender. "Mind if I ask why?"

"This is the happiest day of my life—I'm finally taller than my brother Jim," explained the fellow, beaming from ear to ear.

The bartender studied his customer disbelievingly. "Are you trying to tell me that at your age you actually grew taller?"

"Of course not! See, Jim was in an accident on the interstate yesterday," he explained cheerfully, "and they had to amputate both his legs."

Hamlet is the tragedy of tackling a family problem too soon after college.

—Tom Mason

The reason grandparents and grandchildren get along so well is that they have a common enemy.

—Sam Levenson

My parents threw a great going-away party for me. According to the letter.

—Emo Philips

Fashion

A woman's dress should be like a barbed-wire fence: serving its purpose without obstructing the view.

—Sophia Loren

I went to a store and asked to see something cheap in a dress. The saleswoman said, "The mirror is to the left."

—Jim Baily, impersonating Phyllis Diller

One night, Fred came home from work and told his wife over dinner that he had just signed up to play with the company hockey team. Worried that he might hurt himself, his wife went out the next day to buy him a jock strap.

The effeminate salesclerk was only too happy to help her. "They come in colors, you know," he told her. "We have Virginal White, Ravishing Red, and Promiscuous Purple."

"I guess white will do just fine," she said.

"They come in different sizes, too, you know," said the clerk.

"Gee, I'm really not sure what Fred's size is," confessed his wife. So the clerk extended his pinkie.

"No, it's bigger than that."

The clerk extended a second finger.

"No, it's bigger than that," said the wife.

A third finger.

"Still bigger," she said.

When the clerk stuck out his thumb too, she said, "Yes, that's about right."

So the clerk put all five fingers in his mouth, pulled them out, and announced expertly, "That's a medium."

Never let a panty line show around your ankles.

—JOAN RIVERS

What counts is not how many animals were killed to make the fur, but how many animals the woman had to sleep with to get the fur.

—ANGELA LAGRECA

A lot of women are getting tattoos. Don't do it, that's sick. That butterfly looks great on your breast when you're twenty, thirty. When you get to be seventy, eighty, it stretches into a condor.

—BILLY ELMER

When Mr. Petrowski realized he was having trouble reading road signs, he knew it was time to visit the eye doctor and get his first pair of glasses. Seating him in front of the eye chart, the opthalmologist instructed his patient to cover one eye with his hand. But despite the doctor's repeated instructions, Mr. Petrowski seemed incapable of anything other than a saluting motion.

Finally the opthalmologist lost all patience. Fashioning a mask out of a brown paper bag and cutting out a hole for one eye, he put it over the man's head. "How does that feel, Mr. Petrowski?" he asked.

After a little pause, Petrowski answered, "The fit is fine, Doctor, but I confess I was hoping for something a little more stylish, maybe something in a tortoiseshell frame."

A well-endowed woman entered a chic Madison Avenue boutique and tried on every evening gown in the store. Finally setting eyes on a very sexy, low-cut dress hanging in the display window, she asked the exhausted salesclerk if she could try it on.

"Of course, madam," he muttered through clenched teeth, squeezed into the window, and began the painstaking task of taking the dummy apart to remove the gown. Eventually he succeeded and was able to hand it over to the demanding customer.

"How do I look?" she asked, emerging from the dressing room. "Does it show off my marvelous breasts to advantage?"

"Oh, absolutely," the clerk assured her, "but do hairy chests run in your family?"

My dad's pants kept creeping up on him. By sixty-five, he was just a pair of pants and a head.

—JEFF ALTMAN

I know a guy who loves wearing a dress so much that when he saw the movie *Some Like It Hot*, he thought it was a documentary.

I base my fashion taste on what doesn't itch.

—GILDA RADNER

A man and a woman walk into a very posh Rodeo Drive furrier. "Show the lady your finest mink!" the fellow exclaims.

The owner of the shop goes in back and comes out with an absolutely gorgeous full-length coat.

The lady tries it on, looks wonderful in it, and the man says, "It's yours."

The furrier sidles up to the guy and discreetly whispers, "Ah, sir, that particular fur goes for sixty-five thousand dollars."

"No problem! I'll write you a check!"

"Very good, sir," says the shop owner. "Today is Saturday. You may come by on Monday to pick the coat up after the check has cleared."

So the man writes a check, and he and the woman leave.

On Monday, the fellow returns. The store owner is outraged. "How dare you show your face in here," he exclaims. "There wasn't a single penny in your checking account!"

"I just had to come by," said the guy, grinning, "to thank you for the most wonderful weekend of my life!"

Where lipstick is concerned, the important thing is not the color, but to accept God's decision on where your lips end.

—Jerry Seinfeld

I just put on what the lady says. I've been married three times, so I've been well supervised.

—Upton Sinclair

Fathers

My uncle was always unhappy on Father's Day because he never had children to celebrate it with.

"Weren't you happy at home?" I asked him.

He said, "Oh, sure. My wife laughs at everything I do. That's the reason we don't have children."

—Joey Adams

What lazy S.O.B invented the Clapper? What do I have to invent so I don't have to get off my lazy butt and go over and flip that light switch. My father had a Clapper thirty years ago—me.

—George Wallace

My father never cheated on my mother. He used to cheat on me. He used to pick other kids up after school, take them to the zoo, take them to play ball. One day he came to me. He says, "Look, I got to level with you. I met another kid."

—Dom Irrera

My father and I have been butting heads since I was in the womb. He left a deep impression on me. It's more like a dent, and it's above my right ear.

—Tom Cotter

Female Anatomy

What's the difference between a woman and a volcano?
Volcanoes don't fake eruptions.

Hear about the woman who was so ugly that when she was born the doctor slapped her mother?

Who enjoys sex more, the man or the woman?
The woman.
How can I prove it? When your ear itches and you put your little finger in and wiggle it around and take it out again, what feels better, your finger or your ear?

My wife told me of a book about finding the G-spot. I went to a bookstore. I couldn't even find the book . . . my wife bought it for me. There were no pictures, maps, or diagrams. It just said it was about a third of the way in. Great. Compared to who?

—Robert Schimmel

Why's beauty more important than brains for a woman?
Because plenty of men are stupid, but not very many are blind.

A man and his wife are on a cruise. During bad weather she falls overboard and can't be found. A few weeks later the man gets a call. "We found your wife's body," he's told. "It was found washed up on a desert island and there's an oyster in her vagina. What should we do?"

The man thought about it and said, "Send me the pearl and reset the trap."

—Dick Capri

Why did they send so many women with PMS to the Gulf?
They fight like animals, and they retain water for four days.

When Ernie walked into the pharmacy and asked for rubbers, the girl behind the counter asked politely, "What size, please?"

"Gee, I don't know," answered Ernie, a little flustered, so she instructed him to use the fence out back to determine the correct size. And as he walked out the back door, she ran out a side door and behind the fence.

The fence had three holes in it.

Putting his penis in the first hole, Ernie felt capable hands gently stroking it. Reluctantly, he pulled it out and inserted it in the second hole, and within seconds, he felt a warm sensation, a level of sensation he never before felt. Groaning with pleasure, he managed to pull out and stick it through the third hole. There, expert lips and tongue gave him the blow job of his dreams. Jumping up, the salesgirl hurried back behind the counter and was standing there smiling when Ernie staggered back through the door.

"Your size, sir?" she asked politely.

"Forget the rubbers," he grunted. "Just gimme three yards of that fence."

I love the lines men use to get us into bed. Please, I'll only take a minute. What am I, a microwave?

—Beverly Mickins

If I ever write a sex manual, I'd call it *Ow, You're on My Hair.*

—Richard Lewis

Did you hear about the girl who had tits on her back?
She was ugly to look at, but a whole lot of fun to dance with.

Why is a clitoris like Antarctica?
Because men know it's down there, but how many really care?

Why do women have two sets of lips?
So they can piss and moan at the same time.

The newlyweds undressed and got into bed. "Sweetheart," asked the new wife, "could you please hand me that jar of Vaseline over there?"

"Baby, you aren't going to need any Vaseline," he growled amorously. But at her insistence, he handed it over, and she proceeded to smear it liberally all over her crotch.

After watching this procedure, the husband asked the wife a favor. "Remember that long string of pearls I gave you for an engagement present? Could you get them out of the bureau drawer for me?"

"Of course, lover," replied his bride, "but whatever do you want them for?"

"Well," he explained, looking down at the Vaseline smeared all over her, "if you think I'm going into a mess like that without chains, you're crazy!"

A soldier in Vietnam walked into a whorehouse in Saigon, went up to the madam, and asked, "Do Oriental women really have horizontal ones?"
"Why?" asked the madam. "Are you harmonica player?"

He just kept rushing through the lovemaking, which is the part I like, the beginning part. Most women are like that. We need time to warm up. Why is this hard for you guys to understand? You're the first people to tell us not to gun a cold engine. You want us to go from zero to sixty in 5.5. We're not built like that. We stall.

—ANITA WISE

Why's the new contraceptive sponge such a great idea?
Because after sex your wife can get up and wash the dishes.

It seems there was this woman who hated wearing underwear. One day she decided to go shopping for a new pair of shoes, and since she was wearing a skirt, the salesman was enjoying an excellent view. After the third or fourth pair of shoes, the guy couldn't stand it anymore. "Lady," he said, "that's some beautiful sight. I could eat that pussy full of ice cream."

Disgusted, the woman ran out of the store and went home. When her husband got home from work, she told him about the incident and asked him to go beat the shit out of the salesman. And when he flatly refused, she wanted to know why.

"Three reasons," said her husband. "Number one: you shouldn't have been out in a skirt with no underpants. Number two: you have enough shoes to last you ten more years. And number three: any son of a bitch who can eat that much ice cream I don't want to mess with in the first place."

What does a woman say after her third orgasm?
You mean you don't know?

"No, Jerzy," said Stella when her stupid friend asked her to go jogging. "I'm not feeling too well."

"Whaddaya mean, not feeling well?"

"You know," she explained, blushing a bit, "it's that time of the month."

"Whaddaya mean, that time of the month?"

"You know," she went on, "I have my period."

"Whaddaya mean, period?"

"You know, Jerzy," Stella blurted in exasperation. "I'm bleeding down there!" And she lifted her skirt to show him.

"No wonder," he screamed. "Someone's cut your pee-pee off!"

Two lesbians were having a drink at the bar when a good-looking woman waved at them from across the room.

"Nice," commented Brenda. "I'd like to get between her legs sometime soon."

"No you wouldn't," said her companion disparagingly. "She's hung like a doughnut."

Leonard desperately wanted to become a doctor and had really crammed for his medical boards, so he wasn't in the least fazed by the question: "Name the three advantages of breast milk."

Quickly he wrote, "1. It contains the optimum balance of nutrients for the newborn child." He added, "2. As it is contained within the mother's body, it is protected from germs and helps develop the child's immune system." Then Leonard was stumped. Sitting back and racking his brains until he'd broken into a sweat, he finally scribbled, "3. It comes in such nice containers."

The gynecologist stuck up his head after completing his examination. "I'm sorry, Miss," he said, "but removing that vibrator is going to involve a very lengthy and delicate operation."

"I'm not sure I can afford it," sighed the young woman on the examining table. "Why don't you just replace the batteries?"

Finances

"Henry Junior thinks money grows on trees," the overworked businessman complained to his secretary one day. "Tonight he's getting a talking-to that'll really get across the value of a dollar."

"How'd it go?" asked the secretary the next morning.

"Not so good," he admitted glumly. "Now he wants his allowance in Deutschmarks."

Americans are getting stronger. Twenty years ago it took two people to carry ten dollars' worth of groceries. Today, a five-year-old can do it.

—Henny Youngman

A millionaire and his wife had everything money could buy—until the fellow gambled on a few bad stock tips and lost everything. He came home that night with a heavy heart and explained their newly straitened circumstances to his wife.

"Since we need to start somewhere, Myrna," he went on, "you better learn to cook so we can let the kitchen staff go."

His wife thought it over for a few moments. Nodding, she suggested, "Okay, George, but you better learn to screw so we can fire the chauffeur."

There are several ways in which to apportion the family income, all of them unsatisfactory.

—Robert Benchley

Before going to Europe on business, a man drove his Rolls-Royce to a downtown New York City bank and went in to ask for an immediate loan of $5,000. The loan officer, taken aback, requested collateral and so the man said, "Well then, here are the keys to my Rolls-Royce." The loan officer promptly had the car driven into the bank's underground parking for safe keeping, and gave him $5,000.

Two weeks later, the man walked through the bank's doors and asked to settle up his loan and get his car back. "That will be five thousand dollars in principal, and fifteen dollars and forty cents in interest," the loan officer said. The man wrote out a check and started to walk away. "Wait, sir," the loan officer said. "While you were gone, I found out you are a millionaire. Why in the world would you need to borrow five thousand dollars?"

The man smiled. "Where else could I park my Rolls-Royce in Manhattan for two weeks and pay only fifteen dollars and forty cents?"

I'm living so far beyond my income that we may almost be said to be living apart.

—E. E. CUMMINGS

Just about the time you think you can make both ends meet, somebody moves the ends.

—PANSY PENNER

Fitness and Exercise

They say the best exercise takes place in the bedroom. I believe it, because that's where I get the most resistance.

—JEFF SHAW

You have to stay in shape. My grandmother, she started walking five miles a day when she was sixty. She's ninety-seven today, and we don't know where the hell she is.

—ELLEN DeGENERES

You just can't go to a public pool and splash around anymore. Everyone's swimming laps now. Some guy jumped in behind me and said, "How long you gonna be using this lane, dude?"
    "Until my bladder's empty, punk."

—TOMMY SLEDGE

Whenever I feel like exercising, I lie down until the feeling passes.

—ROBERT MAYNARD HUTCHINS

We work out entirely too much. We waste time. A friend of mine runs marathons. He always talks about this "runners' high," but he has to go twenty-six miles for it. That's why I smoke and drink. I get the same feeling from a flight of stairs.

—LARRY MILLER

My fitness goals are different from most people's. Most people want to lose enough weight so they look good in a bathing suit, or they want to lower their cholesterol. I just want to lose enough so my stomach doesn't jiggle when I brush my teeth.

—KEVIN JAMES

Mr. Universe: Don't forget, Mr. Johnson, your body is the only home you'll ever have.

Mr. Johnson: Yes, my home is pretty messy. But I have a woman who comes in once a week.

I like long walks, especially when they are taken by people who annoy me.

—FRED ALLEN

My doctor recently told me that jogging could add years to my life. I think he was right. I feel ten years older already.

—MILTON BERLE

For me, exercise just doesn't make sense—like a vegetarian going to a barbecue.

I tried Flintstones vitamins. I didn't feel any better, but I could stop the car with my feet.

—JOAN ST. ONGE

Flying

Why do WASPs fly so much?
 For the food.

Orville Wright said to his brother, Wilbur, "You were only in the air for twelve seconds. How could my luggage be in Cleveland?"

—RED BUTTONS

Brian Dwyer reminded us of the pilot who told the passengers he had some good news and some bad news. "The bad news is that we're doing seven hundred and fifty miles per hour at thirty-two thousand feet, but we're lost. The good news is that we're making very good time."

—JOEY ADAMS

I had the chance to go to London a couple of months back. Had kind of a weird flight over, though, 'cause one of the flight attendants got very angry with me. I didn't eat all of my dinner. She said, "Sir, you really shouldn't waste all that food. There are people starving on Air India."

—TIM CAVANAGH

I'm giving up flying. I was at the airport and I saw a sign: "Take Out Insurance." I thought, if the lobby's that dangerous, imagine what it's like in the plane.

—CORBETT MONICA

How do you know you're flying Vatican Airlines?

The emergency instructions are in Latin, so good Catholics can get out first.

I took an economy flight. There wasn't any movie, but they flew low over drive-ins.

—RED SKELTON

I said, "I believe ya can, Maynard, I've seen ya do a lot of wild things. I think you can fly." We went up to Willard's Bluff. . . . He Scotch-taped a hundred and forty-six pigeons to his arms. He said, "I know I can do it, I know I can."

I said, "Don't repeat yourself, just do it."

He was airborne for a good twenty seconds. Then some kid came from outta nowhere, threw a bag of popcorn in the stone quarry, and he bashed his brains out.

—JONATHAN WINTERS

The Concorde was great. It travels at twice the speed of sound. Which is fun except you can't hear the movie until two hours after you land.

—Howie Mandel

Fabio and Nunzio rent a private plane for the day and are doing fine until it's time for touchdown. Fabio is busy with all the instrument readings and finally gets the plane down, but has to screech to a stop. "Boy, that's a short runway," he says, wiping his forehead.

"Yes," agrees Nunzio, "but look how wide it is."

I think I agree with the old lady who said if God has intended us to fly, he would never have given us railroads.

—Michael Flanders

He was a little "off," I think is the term. . . . One day he said to me, "I'm gonna fly."

I love when the stewardess says, "Your seat cushion becomes a flotation device." Well, why doesn't the plane just become a boat?"

—Steve Shaffer

Flying? I've been to almost as many places as my luggage!

—Bob Hope

Flying doesn't thrill me. . . . We don't know how old the planes are, and there's really no way for us to tell, 'cause we're laymen. But I figure if the plane smells like your grandmother's house, get out. That's the bottom line.

—Garry Shandling

It was considered a great step forward in civil aviation when the first fully automated flight was ready for its maiden transcontinental journey. Bigwigs of every sort were shown to their seats

and served champagne cocktails by cyborg hostesses, while hundreds of airline employees waved from the runway. Suddenly, the engine snapped on and the plane made a perfect takeoff into the cloudless sky.

A silky, mechanical voice came over the speakers. "Welcome aboard this historic flight, ladies and gentlemen, and simply press the call button if you would like more champagne to be served by one of our robot attendants. Even those of you who may have been anxious about flying in the past can now relax in the knowledge that this flight is free from the possibility of human error. Every aspect—altitude, air pressure, course setting, weather conditions—is being continuously monitored by state-of-the-art computer circuitry, so virtually nothing can go wrong . . . go wrong . . . go wrong. . . ."

Mr. Rosenberg, a middle-aged man, is sitting in a window seat on a plane going to Israel. Just before takeoff, a huge Arab wearing a beautiful multicolored caftan walks down the aisle and sits beside him. A few minutes later, the plane takes off. All is well. For a while. But then, Mr. Rosenberg realizes that he has to go to the washroom. That wouldn't be a problem, but he looks over and sees that the Arab beside him is sound asleep, and Mr. Rosenberg, being a meek man, is afraid to disturb him. So he figures he'll hold it in until the Arab wakes up. As luck would have it, the Arab just keeps snoring away, and Mr. Rosenberg is feeling increasingly more uncomfortable.

After a while, he starts to feel nauseous as well. He tries and tries to hold it in, but then "Aaarrgghh!!"—he throws up all over the Arab and his beautiful garment. He thinks, Oh, no! Now he's gonna kill me! and sits there in nervous apprehension, waiting for the Arab to wake up.

Finally, the Arab wakes up and finds this vomit all over him. Mr. Rosenberg says to him, "Well, do you feel better now?"

Did you hear that Alitalia and El Al were merging to form a new airline?

It's going to be called Well I'll Tell Ya. . . .

Ever been frisked on a plane trip? They frisk you and then, on the
plane, everybody has a steak knife!

—SHELLEY BERMAN

**Frequent flier miles are the business traveler's equivalent of
combat pay.**

Too bad about the kamikaze pilots. They had to do all their bragging
ahead of time.

—TOMMY SLEDGE

Food

**Two elderly women are at a Catskills mountain resort and one of
them says, "Boy, the food at this place is really terrible." The
other one says, "Yeah, and such small portions."**

—ALVY, IN *ANNIE HALL*, SCREENPLAY BY
WOODY ALLEN AND MARSHALL BRICKMAN

**A hamburger walked into a bar, climbed up onto a bar stool,
looked at the bartender, and ordered a tall, cold beer. The bartender looked at the hamburger for a moment and replied, "I'm
sorry, sir, but I can't sell you that drink." The hamburger
thought about this for a second and said, "I'm over twenty-one.
Why can't you sell me a drink?" After looking at the hamburger
for another moment, the bartender replied, "I'm sorry, we don't
serve food in here."**

Food is an important part of a balanced diet.

—FRAN LEBOWITZ

We got so much food in America, we're allergic to food. Allergic to food! Hungry people ain't allergic to shit. You think anyone in Rwanda's got a fucking lactose intolerance?!

—Chris Rock

I think Pringles' initial intention was to make tennis balls. But on the day that the rubber was supposed to show up, a big truckload of potatoes arrived. But Pringles was a laid-back company. They said "Fuck it. Cut 'em up! We can play tennis later."

—Mitch Hedberg

I will not eat oysters. I want my food dead. Not sick, not wounded . . . dead.

—Woody Allen

In a store, I saw that peanut butter and jelly in the same jar stuff. What's the point to that? I'm lazy but . . . I want to meet the guy who needs that. "I could go for a sandwich, but I'm not gonna open two jars."

—Brian Regan

Foreign Countries

Canada

Canada is a country so square that even the female impersonators are women.

—Richard Benner

What's a WASP's idea of open-mindedness?
    Dating a Canadian.

What do you call a witty man in Canada?
    A tourist.

China

Why are the Chinese such bad drivers?
    No peripheral vision.

**When the president visited Beijing, the zoo was one of the high-
lights of his tour. The premier proudly showed him to the grand
cage housing a giant panda and a little lamb. "This is our peace-
ful coexistence exhibit," he explained proudly.**

**The president was most impressed. "It certainly seems to
work well," he commented politely.**

**"It does, it does," the premier assured him. "Of course, we
have to put in a new lamb every morning."**

What's the worst thing about massacring a thousand Chinese students? An hour later, you feel like massacring a thousand more.

England

**I say help the British! If it weren't for them, we'd be talking some
language we couldn't understand.**

—Bo Brown

The English think incompetence is the same thing as sincerity.

—Quentin Crisp

**There's an old song to the effect that the sun never sets on the
British Empire. Well, while we were there, it never even rose.**

—Ring Lardner

I'm married to an English guy. He's a typical English guy. He's very
reserved. In fact, it wasn't until after we were married that I actually
knew he wanted to go out with me.

—Kit Hollerbach

It's spring in England. I missed it last year. I was in the bathroom.

—MICHAEL FLANDERS

One afternoon the red phone on Prime Minister Thatcher's desk rang.

Gorbachev was on the line, asking an urgent favor. "The AIDS virus has reached the USSR, and we are suffering from an acute condom shortage. In fact," the premier confessed, "there are none at all to be had in the Moscow pharmacies. Would it be possible for you to ship me eight hundred and fifty thousand condoms— immediately—so that we can deal with this public health threat?"

"Why, certainly, Mikhail," replied Mrs. Thatcher graciously. "Will Friday do?"

"That would be wonderful," sighed the Russian in evident relief. "Oh, and Maggie, one specification: they must be five inches around and nine inches long."

"No problem at all," the prime minister assured him breezily. Hanging up, she had her secretary get the managing director of the largest condom manufacturer in Great Britain on the line. He informed her that a rush order to those specifications would be no problem for his assembly line.

"Excellent, excellent," chirped Thatcher. "Now just two more things . . ."

"Yes, Madam?"

"On the condoms must be printed, 'Made in Great Britain,'" Thatcher instructed.

"But of course," the industrialist assured her.

"And 'Medium.'"

The sun never sets on the British Empire because God doesn't trust the Brits in the dark.

What does an English woman say after sex?

"Feel better now, ducky?"

When I meet an Englishman and he speaks with that funny accent, I'd never say, "You're a liar." But . . . I believe that if you wake an Englishman in the middle of the night, he'll speak just like us.

—MILT KAMEN

Ireland

The problem with Ireland is that it's a country full of genius, but with absolutely no talent.

—HUGH LEONARD

What do you call a member of the Irish Republican Army who only carries a snubnosed thirty-eight and a switchblade?
   A pacifist.

What do the Irish say during foreplay?
   "Brace yourself, Bridget."

A leprechaun is an Irish fairy that grants you three wishes if you grant him one.

—MILTON BERLE

What's an Irishman's idea of a seven-course meal?
   A six pack and a potato.

France

The handsome American strode into a department store in Paris and headed straight for the lingerie counter. He was intently studying the array of lacy underthings when the salesclerk bustled over to him.
   "Do you have something in mind, *Monsieur*?" she asked.

"I certainly do, ma'am," the American emphatically replied. "That's why I want a nice gift."

An American couple is in Paris on a long-awaited trip, when suddenly the wife dies of a heart attack. The husband decides to have her buried there since they had looked forward to their visit to France for many years.

All arrangements are made, when he suddenly realizes that he doesn't have a black hat for the funeral. The hotel concierge tells him that what he wants is a *"chapeau noir."* So off he goes to find a store that is open late.

First he meets a *gendarme* and in his fractured French asks, *"M'sieur, ou pou-vais-je acheter un capeau noir?"*

The policeman is a bit surprised since the American has asked where he can buy a black condom, but, after thinking a bit, he gives our friend directions. The store—if that is what it is— looks a little seedy and rundown, but the man behind the counter looks friendly, so in goes the American and says, *"M'sieur, je veux acheter un capeau noir."*

"Mais, monsieur, j'ai des capeaux rouges, des capeaux blancs, et des capeaux marrons, mais pas des capeaux noire." After explaining that he has red, white, and brown condoms, but no black condoms, the man asks the American why he wants a black condom, *"Pourquoi avez vous besoin d'un capeau noir?"*

"Ma femme est morte."

After the American says that his wife is dead, the man exclaims, *"O, Monsieur! Quelle beau sentiment!*—What a beautiful sentiment!"

Two Frenchmen were strolling along a boulevard, when one of them gasped, *"Mon Dieu*—here come my wife and my mistress!"

"Sacre bleu!" exclaimed his friend. "I was about to say the same thing."

Germany

Did you hear about the German-Chinese restaurant?
An hour after you eat, you're hungry for power.

A German call girl—what a frightening thought. Like, when she calls, you listen!

What is the German word for constipation?
FarFromPoopen

Israel

What's the difference between an Israelite and an Israeli?
About thirty calories.

Is it true that if you get lost in the desert in Israel, you're rescued by a big dog carrying a keg of seltzer?

Abbreviations mean different things in different countries. A sign in front of an American motel saying "TV" means television. In Israel, it means "Tourists Velcome."

Heard about the Japanese-Jewish restaurant?
It's called So-Sue-Me.

How many WASPs does it take to plan a trip to Israel?
Two. One to ask where, and one to ask why.

Japan

If the Japanese are such technological giants, why do they still eat with sticks?

I just bought a rather unusual tree. Twenty-four feet high, cost a fortune. It's a bonsai sequoia.

A prosperous Japanese businessman visited England and had such a pleasant stay that he decided to return the following year. This time, however, it was his bad luck to hand over his two thousand yen to a particularly rude and harried clerk at the foreign exchange desk in the airport.

Counting the money the clerk had shoved through the grill, the Japanese protested in heavily accented English, "Last time I get two hundred British pounds. Now only one hundred and forty."

"Fluctuations," said the clerk tersely, motioning to the next customer.

The indignant Japanese drew himself up to his full five feet and snapped, "Fuck you British, too!"

If a Japanese man is late, he has to kill himself. It means he has a cheap watch.

Russia

A passerby watched the progress of two workmen on a Leningrad street. One stopped every twenty feet to dig a hole, the second filled it in as soon as he was done, and they moved on to the next site. Finally, overcome by curiosity, the observer asked what in heaven's name they were doing. "You certainly aren't accomplishing anything," she pointed out.

"You don't understand at all," protested one worker indignantly. "We are usually a team of three: I dig the hole, Sergei plants the tree, and Vladimir packs the dirt back in. Today Sergei is home with the flu, but that doesn't mean Vladimir and I get to stop working, does it?"

First Russian: Hear the terrible news? The coach of our Olympic skiing team died after they lost the gold medal to the Americans.

Second Russian: *Nyet!* When did he die?

First Russian: Tomorrow.

I have read about those Russian tractor factories where vodka-sodden workers fulfill their monthly quota in a frantic last-minute push that can succeed only if they attach the transmission with Scotch tape. Why have I always taken it for granted that those goofballs would be so good at annihilating continents?

—CALVIN TRILLIN

At the Congress of Nations, a dispute broke out about the nationality of Adam and Eve.

"They were English," stated the British delegate, "because only an Englishman would have been such a gentleman as to give his own rib to make a woman."

"*Mais non!*" protested the French delegate. "Look at Adam's elegance, even nude. He was a Frenchman."

The Israeli delegate demurred, pointing out that the Bible clearly stated that the Creation occurred in the Holy Land. "So Adam and Eve were of the Chosen People; they were Jews."

The Rumanian shook his head. "Adam and Eve could only have been Russian," he maintained, "because only a Russian could eat so poorly, dress so badly, and still call it Paradise."

A Russian official came up to a factory worker and said, "If you drank a shot of vodka, could you still work?"

The worker said, "I think I could."

Then the Russian official said, "If you drank five shots of vodka, could you work?"

And the worker said, "Well, I'm here, aren't I?"

—YAKOV SMIRNOFF

Mrs. Gorbachev is the only wife of a Russian leader to weigh less than he does.

—MARK RUSSELL

How many Russian leaders does it take to change a lightbulb?
Nobody knows. Russian leaders don't last as long as light-bulbs.

Stalin was giving a speech in a small auditorium. During a pause, someone in the audience sneezed.

Looking up from his notes, Stalin asked, "Who sneezed?"

No one answered. Stalin ordered the guards to escort the last three rows of people outside, where they are executed.

Stalin then asked, "Now, who sneezed?"

Again, no one answered. Again, Stalin ordered the guards to escort the people in the last three rows outside. Shots are heard.

Again, Stalin asked, "Now! Who sneezed?"

A small, bespectacled man in the second row raised his hand and said, "Um, I did, Comrade."

To which Stalin replied, "Bless you."

Friendship

Nothing screams, "Welcome for one night," like the inflatable mattress. "Hey, I threw a sheet on a pool raft. Hope you like it."

—GREG FITZSIMMONS

Little old lady: Why are you sitting here all by yourself, little boy? Haven't you anyone to play with?

Little boy: Yes, I have one friend—but I hate him.

Benjamin Franklin said, "Fish and visitors smell in three days,"
but old friends from college usually smell already.

—P. J. O'ROURKE

Poor Hackley—half his friends deserted him the day he lost his money. The rest left as soon as they found out.

Luigi and Marco had been friends since kindergarten, and remained inseparable throughout their childhood. And when Luigi finally decided to get married, the old friends decided to make a night of it.

At the reception the booze flowed like water, the band played on, and it was well past midnight when Luigi realized he hadn't seen his wife or Marco for quite some time. Staggering around, he finally found his bride and his best friend energetically screwing on a couch upstairs.

The groom gazed at the oblivious couple for a few moments, and then burst into laughter so hysterical that the noise brought several members of his family running.

Taking in the scene, his father asked, "What the hell's so goddamn funny?"

"That Marco," said Luigi, wiping the tears of laughter off his cheek, "he's so drunk he thinks he's me."

He's really a wonderful guy. Why, if I asked him to, he'd give me the shirt off his back. After all, it's mine.

Funerals

Two Scotsmen were avid golfers and had played together every Thursday for many years. The sixth tee was near the road that led to the local cemetery.

One day, as they reached that particular tee, a funeral passed by, and old Hamish turned and raised his club in salute.

"Mon," exclaimed Hector, "in all these years we've been a-playing this course, and that's the first time I've seen ye paying any respect for the dead."

"Aye, weel," explained Hamish, "when you have been married to a woman for forty years, she's entitled to a wee bit of respect."

My uncle invented the solar-powered funeral home. He's got basic solar technology, big solar panels on the roof; the sun beats down, it heats up the panels. Trouble is, he can't cremate, he can only poach.

—HEYWOOD BANKS

An anthropologist had been studying an obscure Thai hill tribe when he contracted a particularly virulent case of jungle rot and was dead in a week. His heartbroken widow accompanied the casket back to Milwaukee, where she invited his three best friends to attend an intimate funeral. When the brief service was over, she asked each of the friends to place an offering in the casket, as had been the custom of the tribe he had been living with. "It would mean a great deal to Herbie," she said, then broke down into racking sobs.

Moved to tears himself, the first friend, a doctor, gently deposited a hundred dollars in the coffin.

Dabbing his cheeks, the second friend, a stockbroker, laid one hundred and fifty dollars on the deceased Herbie's pillow.

The third friend, a lawyer, wrote a check for four hundred and fifty dollars, put it in the casket, and pocketed the cash.

The businesswoman ordered a fancy floral arrangement for the grand opening of her new outlet, and she was furious when it arrived adorned with a ribbon that read, "May You Rest in Peace."

Apologizing profusely, the florist finally got her to calm down with the reminder that in some funeral home stood an arrangement bearing the words "Good Luck in Your New Location."

You give the people what they want, they'll turn out.

—A RIVAL PRODUCER, OBSERVING THE CROWD
AT LOUIS B. MAYER'S FUNERAL

If you don't go to people's funerals, they won't come to yours.

A friend of mine willed her body to science, but science is contesting the will.

—Joey Adams

When old Mr. O'Leary died, an elaborate wake was planned. In preparation, Mrs. O'Leary called the undertaker aside for a private little talk. "Please be sure to secure his toupee to his head very securely. No one but I knew he was bald," she confided, "and he'd never rest in peace if anyone found out at this point. But our friends from the old country are sure to hold his hands and touch his head before they're through paying their last respects."

"Rest assured, Mrs. O'Leary," comforted the undertaker. "I'll fix it so that toupee will never come off."

Sure enough, the day of the wake, the old-timers were giving O'Leary's ancient corpse quite a going-over, but the toupee stayed firmly in place. At the end of the day, a delighted Mrs. O'Leary offered the undertaker an extra hundred dollars for handling the matter so professionally.

"Oh, I couldn't possibly accept your money," protested the undertaker. "What's a few nails?"

There's a funeral procession with two hearses, and behind the two hearses is a guy with a vicious dog and behind him about a hundred guys. As they're all passing through town, a guy steps off the curb and asks the guy with the dog what's going on.

"My dog killed my wife and my mother-in-law," was the answer.

"Can I borrow the dog?" the guy asks.

"Get in line."

—Henny Youngman

G

Gambling

Mrs. Fisher, the sixth-grade teacher, tells the class that today they're going to have a spelling bee. Instructing the first kid to stand up, she asks, "Robert, what does your father do for a living? Say it nice and clearly, and then spell it out."

"My father's a baker," answers Robert. "B-A-K-E-R-R."

"That's not quite right, Robert. Try again," chides Mrs. Fisher gently.

"B-A . . ." says Robert, thinking hard, "K-E-R."

"Very good. Now, Cecily?"

"Doctor. D-O-C-T-O-R," Cecily says smugly and sits down.

"Very good. Herbie?"

Herbie stands up and says, "Shipbuilder. S-H-I-T—"

"No, Herbie," interrupts Mrs. Fisher. "Try again."

"Ship . . . builder. S-H-I-T—"

"No, no, no. Go to the blackboard and write it out and you'll see your mistake."

As Herbie heads toward the front of the class, Mrs. Fisher turns to the next child, Lenny, who jumps up and says, "My father's a bookie. That's B-double O-K-I-E, and I'll lay you six to one that that dope puts 'shit' on the board."

If there was no action around, he would play solitaire—and bet against himself.

—Groucho Marx, about his brother Chico (attributed)

We spend $48 million in lottery tickets. You can't trust us with our money. "How you planning for your retirement?"

"Powerball."

—Wanda Sykes

Gambling is a sure way of getting nothing for something.

—Nick the Greek

Barry used to supplement his income by gambling at poker, joining games wherever he happened to find himself. And he thought he'd seen it all, until he happened into a game in a little town in Tennessee and found himself seated next to a German shepherd. A few hands later, the dog drew a straight flush and collected the jackpot.

"Unbelievable," exclaimed Barry. "I've played plenty of poker in my day but I never imagined I'd see a dog win at poker."

"Ah, we usually wipe him out," said an old geezer at the table with a dismissive snort. "Every time he gets a good hand, he wags his tail."

Las Vegas is the only town in the country where you can have a good time without enjoying yourself.

—Joe E. Lewis, according to Robert Merrill

Bernice used to nag her husband constantly because he just sat around the house all weekend watching television, checking out the ball games, and drinking beer. "Sunday's the only day of the week you could actually spend a little quality time with your daughter, Lloyd, and instead she just watches a couch potato in action," she complained week after week. So Bernice was astonished to come home one Saturday at dinnertime and hear little Amy chirp happily, "Mommy, guess what? Daddy took me to the zoo today, and we saw lots of animals!"

"No kidding?"

"And guess what?" continued the kid enthusiastically. "One of them paid ten to one!"

The compulsive gambler walked into a gay bar, ordered a drink, and struck up a conversation with a fellow at the bar. When his companion went to take a leak, the gambler turned to the guy on

the other side of him and said boldly, "I bet you fifty dollars you've got terrible hemorrhoids."

Knowing this wasn't the case, the man readily agreed to the bet, stood up, and pulled down his pants. The gambler looked and looked, didn't find a single hemorrhoid, promptly handed over the fifty dollars, and headed for the men's room. The winner sat back down on his bar stool and delightedly recounted the story to his friend on his return.

To his surprise, his friend paled. "That son-of-a-bitch!" he cried. "Just ten minutes ago he bet me a hundred dollars he'd have you drop your pants in the middle of the bar!"

A racing tout was complaining to Joe that he hadn't won a single race either with or for a wealthy sucker. "He gives me a thousand dollars a race to bet for him," he cried, "and I've given him twenty-three straight losers."

"G-g-g-get away from that b-bum!" snarled Frisco. "H-he's unlucky for you."

—Joey Frisco, as told to Goodman Ace

Did you hear about the moron who lost fifty dollars on the football game?

Twenty-five dollars on the game, and twenty-five dollars on the instant replay.

Harry walks into work one Monday morning with a huge grin on his face.

One of his co-workers says, "Why are you so happy?"

Harry says, "I went to Bingo for the first time in my life this weekend and I won a thousand bucks."

A week later, Harry walks into work on Monday morning and he's skipping down the hall, high-fiving everyone.

One of his co-workers says, "You win at Bingo again?"

Harry says, "No, no, it's better than that. I bought my first lottery ticket this weekend and I won ten grand. I'm feeling so damn lucky that I think I'm going to ask that new Indian girl in Accounting out on a date."

The next Monday morning Harry is doing cartwheels down the hall.

One of the co-workers says, "Did you win another lottery?"

Harry says, "No, no, it's better than that. You know that Indian girl from Accounting I asked out? Well, we had a great time at dinner, so I invited her up to my apartment for drinks, we wind up in bed, and the next thing I know, she's giving me the best blow job I ever had."

One of his co-workers says, "Man, are you frigging lucky."

Harry says, "No, no, it's better than that. She's blowing me, I look down, and you know that red dot on her forehead? I scratched it . . . and I won another ten grand."

Growing Up

I'm on a plane and it hits me: when did it become a federal regulation that you have to have at least seven crying babies on every flight? I just want to know—Where are they going? Why are they on planes? They have no appointments, they were born just days ago. Our times are so hectic that babies are born and go, "I just popped out of the womb, I gotta dry up, learn to breathe—I'll be on the two o'clock, it's the best I can do."

—Paul Reiser

An old woman is making dinner. In comes her fifteen-year-old grandson. "So, Sidney, what did you learn in school today?" she asks.

"Today was sex education," he replies.

"Sex education. What's that?" she asks.

"We learn things like premature ejaculation, and all about penises and vaginas and—"

She cuts him off, screaming, "Stop! I don't ever want to hear that kind of language coming out of you! Now go up to your room. You'll get no dinner tonight."

Thirty minutes later the kid's mother comes home and asks, "Where's Sidney?"

"I sent him up to his room," the old woman answers. "I asked him what he learned in school today and he said 'sex education' and I asked what that was and he started saying the filthiest words you ever heard. I can't even repeat them."

"Ma, that's what they teach the kids these days. You asked him a simple question and he gave you an honest answer."

The old woman feels bad now. "I didn't realize," she says. "I'll go upstairs and get him and bring him down to dinner myself." So she goes up to his room. When she opens his door, she sees him in the corner masturbating.

"Sidney," she says, "when you're finished with your homework. . . ."

—NORM CROSBY

The Peace Corps is a sort of Howard Johnson on the main drag into maturity.

—PAUL THEROUX

I worry about my kid dating these days. Kids go out and they have to worry about things like herpes and AIDS. I want my son to meet an old-fashioned girl—one with gonorrhea.

—NORM CROSBY

Gullibility

A couple and a single man were shipwrecked on a desert island. It didn't take long for the single guy to get pretty horny, and finally he comes up with an idea for getting into the wife's pants. Climbing way up a tall palm tree, he hollers back down to the couple, "Hey, y'all, quit fucking down there!" The husband looks

over at his wife—who's standing ten feet away—and says, "What the hell's he talking about?"

This goes on for several hours, until the married man is overcome with curiosity and decides to climb up the palm to see for himself what the other guy's problem is. As he's going up, the horny fellow jumps down to the beach, grabs the wife, and proceeds to screw her like crazy.

The man finally reaches the top where the single guy had been, looks down, and says, "Goddamn if he wasn't right—it does look like they're fucking down there!"

Miss DeAngelo was a none-too-bright girl who had moved to Hollywood with dreams of becoming a star. She didn't find fame or glory, but she did encounter plenty of men willing to enjoy her plentiful charms, and eventually she found herself named in a divorce case.

When it was her turn on the stand, the prosecutor came forward. "Miss DeAngelo, the wife of the defendant has identified you as the 'other woman' in her husband's life. Now, do you admit that you went to the PriceRite Motel with this Mr. Evans?"

"Well, yes," acknowledged Miss DeAngelo with a sniff, "but I couldn't help it."

"Couldn't help it?" asked the lawyer derisively. "How's that?"

"Mr. Evans deceived me."

"Exactly what do you mean?"

"See, when we signed in," she explained, "he told the motel clerk I was his wife."

When the moron walked into the corner bar late one night, he was obviously steaming mad. He downed three shots before a friend came over and asked what was wrong.

"It's my wife, I can't believe it. When I got home tonight she was lying in bed all hot and bothered, and it made me suspicious. So I looked around, and sure enough, there was a naked guy hiding behind the shower curtain. Can you beat it?"

"Jesus. No wonder you're so pissed off," said his friend sympathetically.

"Yeah, but that's not all," the furious man went on. "That son of a bitch in the shower, he lied his way out of it."

"I tell you, sir, America is a great country and I praise God that I came over," the foreigner was expounding to a new acquaintance. "Where else, I ask you, could it happen that you could do a hard day's work, then find yourself outside the gates, standing in the rain, waiting for the bus—"

"You call that great?" queried the man next to him at the bar.

"Ah, but wait now. A big black limousine pulls up and the boss opens the back door and says, 'It's a hell of a night to be out in the rain. Why don't you come in here and warm up?' And when you're inside, he says, 'That coat's awfully wet—let me buy you a new one, all right?' And after he's bought you a coat, he asks where you live and says, 'That's a long drive on a night like this, why not come to my house?' So he takes you to his big mansion and gives you a big meal and a few drinks and a warm bed for the night and a hot breakfast and a ride back to work. I tell you, this is a great country. It would never happen to me in my country."

"And it happened to you here?" asked his acquaintance skeptically.

"No. But it happened to my sister."

It was just before a critical offensive, and the troops were being issued their weapons. Lenski was last in line, and they handed out the last rifle to the man in front of him. Furious, Lenski shouted, "Hey, what about my gun?"

"Listen, bud," advised the munitions officer, "just keep your hands out in front of you as though you were holding one, and yell, 'Bang! Bang!'"

"You gotta be joking," blustered Lenski. "You must be trying to get me killed!"

'Trust me," said the officer, sending Lenski out into the field with a reassuring pat on the shoulder.

Pretty soon Lenski found himself in the thick of battle with a Russian infantryman advancing on him. Having little choice, he raised his hands, pointed at the soldier, and yelled, "Bang! Bang!" The Russian fell over, stone dead. This worked on about twenty Russians. Fired with confidence, Lenski returned to the munitions officer and asked about a bayonet.

"Oh, we're all out," said the officer apologetically, "but if you just point with your index finger and scream, 'Stab! Stab!' you'll get excellent results."

Out went Lenski into battle again, and soon he was surrounded by heaps of dead Russian soldiers. In fact, he thought he had wiped out the whole platoon and was just taking a breather when he saw a giant Russian coming toward him. Strutting forward, Lenski shouted, "Bang! Bang!"

The Russian kept on coming.

"Stab! Stab!" cried Lenski.

The Russian kept on coming, right over Lenski, crushing him to a pulp.

The last thing the unfortunate infantryman heard was the Russian muttering, "Tank, tank, tank. . . ."

Guns

We need guns. . . . Suppose a man comes home early and finds another man with his wife. What's he supposed to do, poison him? How about suicide? Can you imagine trying to beat yourself to death with a stick?

Let's be objective about this. Guns are not the real problem. The real problem is bullets.

—PAT PAULSEN

Ditsey Baummortal went duck hunting with old Uncle George Terwilliger. A flock of ducks flew over head and Uncle George took a potshot at them and one fell down on the beach, dead.

Ditsey walked over and looked at it. "Hey, Uncle George," he said, "that was a waste of ammunition to shoot that duck. The fall alone would have killed it."

—"Senator" Ed Ford

Two strangers met on a golf course and the conversation came around to their occupations. The first man said he was in real estate; in fact, he owned a condominium complex that was just visible in the distance.

The second man said he was a professional assassin. His new acquaintance was skeptical until the man took some pipes out of his golf bag and assembled them into a rifle.

"I'll be damned," said the first guy.

"The best part of this rifle is the high-power scope," confided the assassin, handing him the gun.

"You're right," said the first man. "I can see into my apartment with it. There's my wife . . . and she's in there with another man!" Furious, he turned to the assassin and asked how much he charged for his services, to which the reply was, "A thousand dollars a bullet."

The man said, "I want to buy two bullets. I want you to kill my wife with the first one and blow the guy's balls off with the second."

Agreeing to the offer, the assassin looked through his scope and took aim. Then he lifted his head and said, "If you'll hang on a minute, I can save you a thousand dollars."

Why do I need a gun license? It's only for use around the house.

—Charles Addams

A cowboy sauntered into a saloon and swaggered toward the bar. Before reaching the bar, he pulled out his six shooter, quickly aimed at a hat laying on the bar, and fired, causing the hat to jump ten feet into the air. With incredible precision, the cowboy fired five more shots, each one sending the hat flying in a different direction. With a final twirl, the cowboy put his pistol back into the holster.

Obviously impressed, the barman paused from cleaning a glass and said, "Mighty fine shootin', pardner." The cowboy smiled and gently tapped his gun.

"Now if I was you," continued the barman, "I'd file down the foresight and the trigger, and coat the body of the gun with ketchup."

"Oh?" said the cowboy, "Will that make me shoot better?"

"Nope," said the barman, "but that hat belongs to Mad Dog Johnson, and as soon as he gets back from the John, he is going to shove that pistol right down your throat."

The NRA is attempting to lift the ban on machine-gun sales. Well, as an avid hunting enthusiast, I've been hoping to buy a fully automatic Uzi. One thing about a machine gun, it really takes the guesswork out of duck hunting.

—Mark Russell

Handicaps

If blind people wear sunglasses, why don't deaf people wear ear-muffs?

—SPANKY (STEVE MCFARLIN)

A husband reading a newspaper says to his wife, "You know, honey, I think there might be some real merit to what this article says, that the intelligence of a father often proves a stumbling block to the son."

"Well, thank heaven," said the wife, "at least our James has nothing standing in his way."

A guy at a bar sees another guy fall off his stool three times. He asks him where he lives and takes him home. When he gets there, he says, "Mrs. Phillips, I have your husband here."

She says, "Where's his wheelchair?"

—HENNY YOUNGMAN

The personnel director was interviewing people for the position of account executive. One candidate offered excellent references and experience, and he was well-dressed and well-spoken. The only catch was a disconcerting mannerism: the fellow couldn't seem to stop winking.

So the personnel director decided to be frank. "You've got all the qualifications for the job, and I'd really like to hire you, but I have to be honest. I'm afraid that facial tic of yours might put clients off."

"I'm glad you brought that up, sir," said the candidate, "because

all I need to make that annoying wink go away is a couple of aspirins. See for yourself. I've got some on me." And he began emptying his pockets onto the desk. The prospective employer was startled to see dozens of packages of condoms piling up—ribbed ones, lubricated ones, multicolored ones, every variety imaginable.

"Aha," cried the young man happily, "here they are." He brandished two aspirin tablets, swallowed them, and sure enough the wink went away in less than a minute.

"So much for the wink," said the personnel manager sternly, gesturing at the mountain of rubbers, "but what about all this stuff here? I don't want the company to be represented by some wild womanizer."

"No fear. I'm a happily married man."

"So how can you account for the contents of your pockets?"

"It's quite simple, sir," the fellow assured him earnestly. "Did you ever go into a drugstore, winking like crazy, and ask for a box of aspirin?"

Know why the Siamese twins moved to London?
    So the other one could drive.

Heard about the new nonprofit institution called AMD?
    It's "Mothers Against Dyslexia."

Did you hear about the dyslexic who tried to commit suicide?
    He threw himself behind an oncoming train.

Years ago, Phil Silvers had a crush on Olivia De Havilland. She went out with him several times, but when he asked her to the Academy Awards dinner, social high mark of the season, she said, "I'll go with you on one condition—that you don't wear those silly glasses."

Phil promised to do without them and kept his word. He arrived at her door that evening in white tie and tails, with a corsage of orchids and a Seeing Eye dog.

—PHIL SILVERS, ACCORDING TO JOEY BISHOP

Dyslexics of the world, *untie*!

Did you hear about the blind gynecologist?
   He could read lips.

When Georgie Jessel read, he used a monocle. "I'd rather be called eccentric than use a Seeing Eye dog," he said. "I'm too old to see without glasses. At the Friars' one afternoon, monocle and all, our Harlem Disraeli was scanning the menu.

   "What's the matter, Georgie?" inquired Fred Allen. "Doesn't the other eye eat?"

   —Fred Allen, according to Joey Allen

A deaf man and a deaf woman got married. On their wedding night, the woman got into bed, then the man turned off the light and joined her. Quickly, she jumped up and turned the light back on.

   "Wait," she signed, "how will I know if you want to have sex or not?"

   "I know," he said, "if I want to have sex with you, I'll reach over and squeeze your breast once. If I don't want to have sex, I'll reach over and squeeze your breast twice."

   "Okay," she said, and got back in bed. Ten seconds later she was up again with the light on.

   "Wait," she signed, "how will you know if I want to have sex or not?"

   "Well," he said, "if you want to have sex, reach over and grab my dick once. If you don't want to have sex, reach over and grab my dick a hundred times."

The bell rings at the brothel. A girl answers the door, and there in a wheelchair is a guy with no arms and no legs.

   She says, "What do you think you're gonna do here?" He winks and says, "I rang the bell, didn't I?"

What song did the mermaid sing to the sailors?
"I Can't Give You Anything but Head, Baby."

One day on a busy street corner, a huge man walks up to a police officer and says, "Thcuse me offither, can you tell me where thidee thid, and thacramento ith?"

The police officer doesn't reply.

The large man asks his question again, but still no reply.

Finally the frustrated man walks away. An onlooker then walks up to the officer and asks, "Officer, why didn't you tell that man where thirty-third and Sacramento is?"

The police officer replies, "Thure and dit the thit ticked out of me!"

Health

Sergeant Mack had a fine time during his stay in Hong Kong, but paid for it when he came down with a strange type of Oriental venereal disease. So he made the rounds of every American doctor in the community. To his horror he discovered that not only were they unable to cure him, but they all informed him that the only course of treatment was to have his penis amputated.

Desperate, Sergeant Mack made an appointment with a leading Chinese doctor, figuring that he might know more about an Eastern malady. "Do you think, Doctor Cheung, that I need to have my dick amputated?" he asked anxiously.

"No, no, no," said the Chinese doctor testily.

A huge smile broke out over the serviceman's face. "Boy, that's *great*, Doc. Every one of those American medics said they'd have to cut it off."

"Those Western doctors—all they ever want to do is cut, cut, cut," explained Dr. Cheung exasperatedly. "You just wait two weeks. Penis fall off all by itself."

I'd collapse—but I'm too weak.

—Harry Hershfield

Which doesn't fit with the rest: AIDS, herpes, gonorrhea, condominiums.
  Gonorrhea. You can get rid of gonorrhea.

My sister's got asthma. In the middle of an attack, she got an obscene phone call. The guy said, "Did I call you or did you call me?"

—John Mendoza

Hypochondria is the only disease I haven't got.

My allergy tests suggest that I may have been intended for life on some other planet.

Anybody who can swallow an aspirin at a drinking fountain deserves to get well.

There are people who strictly deprive themselves of each and every eatable, drinkable, and smokable that has in any way acquired a shady reputation. They pay this price for health, and health is all they get for it.

—Mark Twain

Three addicts went into a favorite back alley to shoot up. The first addict sterilized his needle, swabbed it with alcohol, and shot up. Then he passed it to the next fellow, who swabbed the needle with alcohol and shot up. Then he passed it to the third addict, who stuck the needle right into his arm.
  "Are you crazy, man?" screamed the first two. "Haven't you heard of AIDS? You could get sick, man, you could *die*."
  "Don't be ridiculous," said the third guy in a lofty tone. "I'm wearing a condom."

If penicillin is such a wonder drug, how come it can't cure bread mold?

—RON SMITH

They just tested the tap water in Los Angeles and found traces of estrogen and antidepressants. So it's nice to know my son's going to grow up and have huge breasts but it's not going to bother him that much.

—GREG FITZSIMMONS

I don't do much. I'm too lazy. That's my problem. Hang around my couch, watching the TV. Just too lazy. I realized this the other day: I get hit by a truck tomorrow—a big truck could hit me, paralyze me from the neck down. Wouldn't affect my lifestyle a bit really.

—NORM MACDONALD

If exercise is so good for you, why do athletes have to retire by age thirty-five?

What's the definition of minor surgery?
An operation performed on somebody else.

When Jackie went to the dentist for the first time in years, she was prepared for bad news. Nevertheless, she was a little put out when, after some time, the dentist gasped, "Jesus, what happened to your teeth? They're all gone, and your gums are in terrible shape!"
"If it's such a big problem," Jackie retorted, "then get your face out of my lap."

You have a cough? Go home, eat a whole box of ex-lax, and tomorrow you'll be *afraid* to cough.

—PEARL WILLIAMS

A man with a frog perched on top of his head goes to see a doctor.

"What seems to be the problem?" the physician asks.

"My ass," the frog responds, to the amazement of the doctor.

"And . . . uh . . . what's wrong with your ass?" the doctor inquires further, somewhat perplexed.

"Would you believe," complains the frog, "this started as a wart?"

I used up all my sick days, so I'm calling in dead.

What's the good part about Alzheimer's disease?
You keep meeting new friends.

"Tell me the truth, Doctor Hill," said the emaciated fellow. "How much longer am I going to live?"

"It's always hard to predict," she replied brightly, "but let's just say that if I were you, I wouldn't start watching any miniseries on TV."

Apparently, this woman's miniature schnauzer had an infection in its ear. The vet told her that it was due to an ingrown hair and that the best treatment would be to remove the hair with a depilatory cream.

The women went to a drugstore and asked the pharmacist for assistance in selecting the appropriate product.

He went on about how some depilatory creams were better for use on the legs and how some were gentler and better for removing facial hair. Then he said, "May I ask where you intend to use this?"

She replied "Well, it's for my schnauzer."

He said, "Okay, but you shouldn't ride a bike for two weeks."

Mrs. Johnson goes to a new gynecologist. He examines her and he says, "My goodness, Mrs. Johnson, that is the hugest vagina I have ever, ever seen."

When she gets home, she decides to have a look for herself. She takes a large mirror off the wall, puts it on the floor, takes off all her clothes, and stands on it. She's just about to look down when her husband comes home early from work.

He says, "What are you doing?"

She says, "Umm . . . I'm just exercising."

He says, "Well, be careful not to fall in the hole."

What's the best thing about having Alzheimer's disease?
You never have to watch reruns on television.

Holidays

Santa Claus? You have to look very carefully at a man like this. He comes but once a year? Down the chimney? And in *my* sock?

—PROFESSOR IRWIN COREY

Thanksgiving is an emotional time. People travel thousands of miles to be with people they see only once a year. And then discover once a year is way too often.

—JOHNNY CARSON

I never believed in Santa Claus because I knew no white man would be coming into my neighborhood after dark.

—DICK GREGORY

I must say, when the doorman where I live puts up the Christmas tree in the lobby, he has the same friendly smile for those who have remembered him at Christmas and for those who have not. Except that when he trims the tree, if you have not, there you are on the tree, hanging in effigy.

—SELMA DIAMOND

The Supreme Court ruled against having a Nativity scene in Washington, D.C. This wasn't for religious reasons. They couldn't find three wise men and a virgin.

—Jay Leno

I wanted our street to have the prettiest Christmas decorations in the neighborhood, so I strung colored balls from house to house, all the way down the block. And I did all the electrical wiring myself. If you'd like further information, just drive down Moorpark Street in North Hollywood. We're the third pile of ashes from the corner.

—Bob Hope

The main reason Santa is so jolly is because he knows where all the bad girls live.

—George Carlin

"Have you been a good boy all year?" Damn him! Damn Santa Claus—has anybody ever been a good boy all year? . . . "He's making a list, checking it twice. He's gonna find out who's naughty or nice." Who the hell did he think he was, J. Edgar Hoover?

—Allan Sherman

I remember a Christmas years ago when my son was a kid. I bought him a tank. It was about a hundred dollars, a lot of money in those days. It was the kind of tank you could actually get inside and ride.

Instead, he played in the box it came in.

It taught me a valuable lesson. Next year he got a box, and I got a hundred dollars' worth of scotch.

I had a big New Year's Eve—they tell me. But New Year's Eve is a lot of fun. We had a big party. We didn't like our furniture anyway. It was eighteenth-century Provincial. Now it's twentieth-century splinters. I invited Les Brown and the band over. We didn't like our neighbors either. I invited the brass section, too. We don't even like ourselves.

—Bob Hope

It sure would be nice if we got a day off for the president's birthday, like they do for the queen. Of course, then we would have a lot of people voting for a candidate born on July third or December twenty-sixth, just for the long weekends.

Home

My bathroom has a digital sink. Every time I want the water to stop running, I put my finger in the faucet.

—Ron Smith

I'm moving out, but first I'm getting a thousand roaches. 'Cause it said in the rent book, "Leave the place the way you found it."

—Dolly Allen

We are in the process of buying a home. When you buy a home, you deal with Realtors. Realtors are people who did not make it as used-car salesmen.

—Bob Newhart

The homeowner got into his grubbiest clothes one Saturday morning and set about all the chores he'd been putting off for weeks. He'd cleaned out the garage, pruned the hedge, and was halfway through mowing the lawn when a woman pulled up in the driveway and yelled out her window, "Say, what do you get for yard work?"

The fellow thought for a minute, then answered, "The lady who lives here lets me sleep with her."

We have one of those floor lamps with three degrees of brightness: dim, flicker, and out.

This morning there was ice on the pipes in my apartment, but the landlord fixed it. He put antifreeze in the radiator.

—HERB SHRINER

I can't believe I actually own my own house. I'm looking at a house and it's two hundred grand. The Realtor says, "It's got a great view." For two hundred grand I better open up the curtains and see breasts against the window.

—GARRY SHANDLING

I'm living on a one-way, dead-end street. I don't know how I got there.

—STEVEN WRIGHT

Homosexuality

Did you hear about the gay pickpocket? After he takes your wallet, he kisses your ass.

—RED BUTTONS

My doctor said, "I have some bad news and some good news."
   I said, "Okay, give me the bad news."
   He said, "Well it's all how you regard something like this, but you show very definite signs of homosexuality."
   I said, "Oh, come on. What in the world is the good news?"
   He said, "The good news is I think you're cute."

—FOSTER BROOKS

What's the definition of a lesbian?
   Just another damn woman trying to do a man's job.

Philip and Michael were live-in lovers. One day Philip called in sick, and Michael called home in the middle of the morning to see how he was feeling. "Oh, by the way," he asked, "did the paper boy come yet?"

"No," answered Michael, "but he's got that glassy look in his eye. . . ."

A gay church is like any other church, except that every other person is kneeling.

—Norm Crosby

"My dildo can do anything a man can do," boasted a lesbian in a bar one night.

"Oh yeah?" replied a nearby drunk. "Let's see your dildo get up and order a round of drinks."

"Mommy, one of the kids at school called me a sissy."
"So what did you do, Benny?"
"I hit him with my purse."

Some men think that they can convert gay women, make them straight. I couldn't do that. I could make a straight woman gay, though.

—Jeff Stilson

I am the biggest fag hag. I love my gay male friends so much. But when I was a little girl, I always wished I would be constantly surrounded by gorgeous guys. And I am, but I should have been more specific.

—Margaret Cho

Heard about the new gay sitcom?
It's called, "Leave It, It's Beaver."

Three rednecks were having a few in a bar and bragging about how big their dicks were. Finally the boasting grew so extravagant that there was only one way to resolve the dispute: Each man unzipped his fly and laid it out on the bar.

At this very moment a homosexual happened into the bar. "What'll you have?" asked the bartender.

"Gee," said the gay man, "I was gonna have a Bloody Mary . . . but I think I'll take the buffet."

Zabiski saved up his money for an excursion to Reno, where he soon found himself at the bar next to a very attractive brunette. "Say, could I buy you a drink?" he asked boldly.

"Forget it, buddy," she replied, not unkindly. "I'm gay."

Zabiski looked blank.

"I'm a lesbian," she elaborated.

Zabiski shook his head. "What's a lesbian?"

"See that woman over there?" She pointed at a lovely blond waitress serving drinks on the far side of the room.

Zabiski nodded, perking up.

"Well, I'd like to take her up to my room," the brunette elaborated, "take all her clothes off, and nibble her tits and lick every curve and suck every inch of that sweet young thing, all night long."

At this, Zabiski burst into tears and buried his head in his arms.

"Why the hell're you crying?" asked his companion gruffly.

"I think I'm a lesbian, too," he sobbed.

My brother is gay and my parents don't care—as long as he marries a doctor.

—ELAYNE BOOSLER

Gay people invented sports. Think about it. Boxing. Two topless men . . . in silk shorts . . . fighting over a belt and a purse.

—ANT

231

The law against sodomy is to stop homosexual men from enjoying themselves. That's what the law is all about. But this is stupid. What do you do according to the law? You find two men enjoying themselves sexually. You arrest them and throw them in . . . prison? That oughta do it.

—KEVIN POLLAK

What's the army afraid is going to happen if gay people are in it? "Private, shoot that man!"
"I can't, he's adorable."

—JON STEWART

I got even with my parents by telling them I'm gay. You see, because I'm going out with this guy I know they would otherwise hate, now I know that when they meet him, they'll love him.

—MARGARET SMITH

Two gay guys are in an elevator.
The elevator operator says, "You going down?"
The first guy says, "Heaven's no. We're just conversing."

What's another term for lesbian?
Vagitarian.

Did you hear about the gay Indian?
He was a brave sucker.

Two gay guys live together.
The first guy says, "Let's play hide-and-seek. I'll hide, and if you find me, I'll blow you."
The second guy says, "What if I can't find you?"
He says, "I'll be behind the piano."

What's the lesbian motto?
"No penis between us."

One lesbian frog says to the other, "You know, we really do taste like chicken."

—BRUCE KIRBY

One gay guy says to another, "Your chest is so hairy. . . ."

The second one says, "Well, I put Vaseline on it every night."

The first one says, "That can't be the reason. . . . If it was, I'd have a ponytail growing out of my ass."

Honesty

At long last the good-humored boss felt compelled to call Fitch into his office. "It has not escaped my attention," he pointed out gently, "that every time there's a big home game, you have to take your aunt to the doctor."

"You know, you're right, sir," exclaimed Fitch. "I hadn't realized. You don't suppose she's faking it now, do you?"

It's said that Abraham Lincoln once sized up the case of a prospective client as follows: "You have a pretty good case, technically, but in terms of justice and equity, it's got problems. So you'll have to look for another lawyer to handle the case, because the whole time I was up there talking to the jury, I'd be thinking, 'Lincoln, you're a liar!' and I just might forget myself and say it out loud."

King Arthur was preparing to go out on an expedition and would be away from Camelot for an indefinite period of time. But he was worried about leaving Queen Guinevere alone with all those horny Knights of the Round Table. So he went to Merlin for some advice. After he explained his predicament to Merlin, the wizard looked thoughtful and asked the king to come back in a week.

A week later King Arthur was back in Merlin's laboratory, where the good wizard showed him his latest invention. It was a chastity belt . . . except that it had a rather large hole in the most obvious place.

"This is no good, Merlin!" the king exclaimed. "Look at this opening. How is this supposed to protect m'lady, the queen?"

"Ah, sire, just observe," said Merlin as he searched his cluttered workbench until he found what he was looking for. He then selected his most worn-out wand, one that he was going to discard anyway. He inserted it into the gaping aperture of the chastity belt, whereupon a small guillotine blade came down and cut it neatly in two.

"Merlin, you are a genius!" said the grateful monarch. "Now I can leave, knowing that my queen is fully protected."

After putting Guinevere in the device, King Arthur set out upon his quest. Several years passed before he returned to Camelot.

Immediately, he assembled all his knights in the courtyard and had them drop their trousers for an informal "short arm" inspection. Sure enough! Each and every one of them was either amputated or damaged in some way. All of them except Sir Galahad.

"Sir Galahad," exclaimed King Arthur. "The one and only true knight! Only you among all the nobles have been true to me. What is it in my power to grant you? Name it and it is yours!"

But Sir Galahad was speechless.

A woman walks into a butcher shop and asks the butcher how much a pound of tenderloin is.

"Twelve dollars per pound," replied the butcher.

"Are you sure? That can't be," said the lady.

"Look, ma'am, it says right here on the card, 'twelve dollars per pound.'"

"But that seems so high compared to other butchers in the area," she said.

"Lady, maybe they gave you the price for a poorer cut of beef," said the butcher.

"No, the butcher across the street said it was nine dollars per pound."

"Well, then why don't you go buy it there?" asked the butcher.

"Because they are all out."

"When I'm all out, I sell it for eight dollars per pound," retorted the butcher.

Hospitals

A hospital bed is a parked taxi with the meter running.

—Groucho Marx

Did your wife recover from her operation?

Not yet, she's still talking about it.

Today's hospitals don't kid around. I won't say what happens if you don't pay a bill, but did you ever have tonsils put back in?

—Joey Adams

I said, "Officer, I'm speeding because I'm taking my mom to the hospital. She OD'd on reducing pills."

He said, "I don't see any woman in the car with you."

I said, "I'm too late."

—Emo Philips

Nate was in a nasty accident, and broke so many bones that it was necessary for him to be placed in a body cast, with all four limbs in traction and his neck immobilized. And during his lengthy hospitalization, he had to be fed rectally.

The attending nurse felt especially sorry for him when his birthday came around, so she decided to give him a special treat: some ice cream through the food tube. But she'd barely left the room before Nate's screams of, "Nurse! Nurse!" echoed down the corridor.

Rushing back in, she cried, "What's the matter? Is it too cold? I'm so sorry—"

"No, no, no," Nate howled back. "I hate rum raisin!"

They try to humiliate you in the hospital. They make you pee in a bottle. I hate that. I was in the hospital. The nurse said, "You have to pee in this bottle." She left and I filled it with Mountain Dew. She came back and I chugged it. She was puking for days. It's a sick world and I'm a happy guy!

—LARRY REEB

I had general anesthesia. That's so weird. You go to sleep in one room and then you wake up four hours later in a totally different room. Just like college.

—ROSS SHAFER

If I'm ever stuck on a respirator or a life support system, I definitely want to be unplugged—but not until I'm down to a size eight.

—HENRIETTE MANTEL

It's a good thing I'm covered by Red, White, and Blue Cross. I was operated on at a great hospital—Our Lady of Malpractice! Five years ago they spent three million dollars on a recovery room. It hasn't been used yet. After the operation, the doctor told me, "Soon, your sex life's gonna be terrific—especially the one in the winter."

—MILTON BERLE

I don't blame hospitals for trying to keep costs down, but I really think a coin-operated bedpan is going a little too far.

—JOEY ADAMS

Hotels

My hotel room is so small that when I die, they won't have to put me in a casket. They'll just put handles on the room.

—HERB SHRINER

My friend and his wife stayed in a hotel and got a bill for ninety bucks. He screamed, "For what, ninety dollars?"

The desk clerk said, "For room and board, sir."

My friend said, "Room and board? We didn't eat here."

The clerk said, "It was here for you. If you didn't get it, it's your fault."

My friend said, "You take forty dollars. I'm charging you fifty dollars for fooling around with my wife."

The clerk said, "I never touched your wife!"

My friend said, "It was there for you."

—NORM CROSBY

Why is it they have Bibles in every motel room? Why should a man want to read the Bible when he's alone with a woman in a hotel room? Why would he be interested? Whatever he's praying for, he's already got!

—MILTON BERLE

Housework

Oh, give me a home where the buffalo roam—and I'll show you a houseful of dirt.

——MARTY ALLEN

I haven't cleaned up in a while. I've got a messy house—a milk carton with a picture of the Lindbergh baby on it.

—GREG RAY

Who invented the brush they put next to the toilet? That thing hurts!

—ANDY ANDREWS

If you want to get rid of stinking odors in the kitchen, stop cooking.

—ERMA BOMBECK

The efficiency expert concluded his lecture with a note of caution. "You don't want to try these techniques at home."

"Why not?" asked someone from the back of the audience.

"I watched my wife's routine at breakfast for years," the expert explained. "She made lots of trips to the refrigerator, stove, table, and cabinets, often carrying just a single item at a time. 'Hon,' I suggested, 'Why don't you try carrying several things at once?'"

The voice from the back asked, "Did it save time?"

The expert replied, "Actually, yes. It used to take her twenty minutes to get breakfast ready. Now I do it in seven."

Humility

Observing a light across the water, the captain had his signalman instruct the other vessel to change her course ten degrees south.

The response was prompt: "Change your course ten degrees north."

"I am a captain," he responded testily. "Change your course ten degrees south."

The reply: "I'm a seaman first class—change your course north."

The captain was furious. "Change your course now. I'm on a battleship."

"Change your course ten degrees north, sir—I'm in a lighthouse."

It's going to be fun to watch and see how long the meek can keep the earth after they inherit it.

—Kin Hubbard

It's like what the beaver said to the rabbit as they stared up at the immense bulk of Hoover Dam: "No, I didn't actually build it—but it's based on an idea of mine."

A man walks along a lonely beach. Suddenly he hears a deep voice: "dig!"

He looks around; nobody's there. I am having hallucinations, he thinks. Then he hears the voice again: "I said, dig!"

So he starts to dig in the sand with his bare hands, and after digging for some time, he finds a small chest with a rusty lock.

The deep voice says, "Open!"

Okay, the man thinks, let's open the thing. He finds a rock with which to break the lock, and when the chest is finally open, he sees a lot of gold coins.

The deep voice says, "To the casino!"

Well, the casino is only a few miles away, so the man takes the chest and walks to the casino.

The deep voice says, "Roulette!"

So he changes all the gold into a huge pile of roulette tokens and goes to one of the tables, where the players gaze at him in disbelief.

The deep voice says, "Twenty-seven!"

He takes the whole pile and drops it at the twenty-seven. Everybody is quiet when the croupier throws the ball.

The ball stays at the twenty-six.

The deep voice says, "Shit!"

When you're as great as I am, it's hard to be humble.

—Muhammed Ali (attributed)

You probably wouldn't worry about what people think of you if you knew how seldom they do.

—OLIN MILLER

If there is such a thing as genius, which is just what?—what the fuck is it?—I am one, you know. And if there isn't, I don't care.

—JOHN LENNON

I don't deserve any credit for turning the other cheek, as my tongue is always in it.

——FLANNERY O'CONNOR

The city slicker was fishing with a fancy new rod and all the latest lures, but he hadn't had a nibble by lunchtime. Adding to his irritation was the fact that a farm boy in a rowboat not far away had pulled in a number of good-sized bass. They quit about the same time, and the man couldn't help going over to him. "You caught all those fish with that old stick—and a bent pin for a hook?" he croaked disbelievingly. "What's your secret?"

The boy shrugged and hitched up his overalls. "I guess I just keep myself out of sight."

Humor

I don't make jokes; I just watch the government and report the facts.

—WILL ROGERS

The man who laughs has not yet heard the news.

—BERTOLT BRECHT

Repartee is something we think of twenty-four hours too late.

—MARK TWAIN

"Laughter is God's gift to mankind," proclaimed the preacher ponderously.

"And mankind," responded the cynic, "is the proof that God has a sense of humor."

Gracie: What's the difference between an umbrella and a pickle?

George: You're making this up?

Gracie: Yes.

George: What's the difference between an umbrella and a pickle? (Thinks for a moment.) I give up.

Gracie: Oh? I give up, too.

George: I thought you said you made up riddles.

Gracie: I do. I make up riddles. I don't make up answers.

—GEORGE BURNS AND GRACIE ALLEN

Whatever you have read I have said is almost certainly untrue, except if it is funny, in which case I definitely said it.

——TALLULAH BANKHEAD

Everything is funny as long as it is happening to somebody else.

—WILL ROGERS

Husbands

A husband is what's left of a man after the nerve has been extracted.

—HELEN ROWLAND

My wife thinks that I'm too nosy. At least that's what she keeps scribbling in her diary.

—DRAKE SATHER

I've been asked to say a couple of words about my husband, Fang. How about "short" and "cheap"?

—PHYLLIS DILLER

The new bride gushed to her mother, "My husband is very good to me. He gives me everything I ask for."

Her mother said, "That only shows you're not asking for enough."

—JOEY ADAMS

The wedding night found Dan and Lorraine in a posh suite at the Hyatt, a bottle of champagne by the bed. Pulling a sexy negligee out of her suitcase, Lorraine was startled when Dan tossed her a pair of his pants and told her to put them on.

They fell down in a pool around her ankles. "Honey, I can't wear your pants," she protested, coming around the bed to hand them back to him.

"Damn straight, and don't you forget it," ordered the new husband. "I'm the man and I wear the pants in this family."

Lorraine slipped out of her panties and tossed them to Dan. "Put these on, darling," she asked sweetly.

Of course Dan couldn't pull the little scrap of lace past his knees. "I can't get into your pants, Lorraine," he complained.

"That's right," she snapped. "And it's going to stay that way until you change your damn attitude!"

I look at husbands the same way I look at tattoos. I want one but I can't decide what I want and I don't want to be stuck with one I'm just going to grow to hate and have to have surgically removed later.

—MARGARET CHO

Noting that she and her husband made love more and more in-frequently, Sandy tried everything she could think of: romantic dinners and cruises, greeting him at the door in sexy lingerie, trying out exotic paraphernalia from a sex boutique. But nothing seemed to work, and finally he yielded to her urgings that he consult a sex therapist.

To her amazement, a single visit restored her husband's ardor to honeymoon dimensions. The only quirk was that every so often during lovemaking, her husband would dash into the bathroom for a minute or two. Finally her curiosity overcame her better judgment, and she followed him to the bathroom door. Looking in, she saw him peering intently into the mirror and repeating, "She's not my wife . . . she's not my wife. . . ."

A woman went into the neighborhood grocery store and asked the grocer for a can of cat food. Knowing that she didn't have a cat, the grocer asked why she was buying the stuff. "It's for my husband's lunch," was the answer.

Shocked, the grocer said, "You can't feed cat food to your husband. It'll kill him!"

"I've been giving it to him for a week now and he likes it fine," was her answer, and each day the woman continued to come in and purchase a can of cat food for her husband's lunch.

It wasn't too much later that the grocer happened to be scanning the obituary column in the local paper and noticed that the woman's husband had passed away. When the woman came into the store, he couldn't resist saying, "I'm sorry to hear about your husband, but I warned you that he'd die if you kept feeding him cat food."

"It wasn't the cat food that killed him," she retorted. "He broke his neck trying to lick his ass!"

I feel like Liz Taylor's fourth husband: I know what I am supposed to do, but I am at a loss as to how to make it different.

As soon as they had finished making love, Susie jumped up from the bed and started packing her suitcase.

"What on earth are you doing?" asked her puzzled husband.

"In Las Vegas I could get two hundred dollars for what I just gave you for free," she pointed out, "so I'm moving to Las Vegas."

This was enough to provoke her husband to jump up and began packing *his* bags.

"What're you up to?" asked Susie in surprise.

"I'm following you to Las Vegas," he replied. "I've *got* to see you live off six hundred dollars a year."

I

Imagination

It was an elegant dinner party and the hostess had left nothing to chance—except that a little water had splashed on the marble floor. And when the waiter came into the dining room carrying the beautiful roast suckling pig, he slipped and fell flat, sending the roast flying.

"Don't worry, Charles," said the hostess calmly. "Just take the roast back to the kitchen and bring out the other one."

Requesting an interview with a loan officer, an inventor explained that he was working on a substance which, applied locally, would make a woman's pussy smell like an orange. The skeptical banker refused the loan.

A year or so later, the banker noticed that the man now had an enormous account. Inviting him in, the banker graciously apologized. "I do hope you don't bear us any hard feelings for turning down your loan request."

"Far from it," replied the inventor cheerfully. "It got me thinking. Instead, I developed a way to make an orange smell like pussy, and it's been very successful."

Phyllis came into the office all aflutter about her husband. "You won't believe this, Susie, but Rick takes a fishing pole into the bathroom and tosses the hook into the tub."

"You've got to be kidding," gasped her friend. "Don't you think you should take him to a psychiatrist?"

"No time," replied Phyllis with a shrug. "I'm too busy cleaning fish."

A man goes to the U.S. Patent Office and asks to patent the apple he's carrying. "You can't do that," says the Patent Office official. "Mother Nature invented the apple."

"Not this apple. It's special," says the man. "Take a bite,"

The officer takes a bite and says, "So? It tastes like any old apple."

"Turn it around, turn it around."

"Wow—it tastes like a pear!"

"Turn it again."

"This is incredible," says the official, "it tastes like a peach." And he gives the guy a patent on his three-flavored apple.

As the man's walking through the lobby on his way out he sees a man with a bagful of cookies. "What've you got there?" he asks cheerfully.

"Special cookies," explains the second guy. "Take a bite and it tastes like pussy."

"I don't believe it—let me try one." He takes a big bite, only to make a face and sputter, "Goddamn, this tastes like shit."

"Turn it around, turn it around!"

Work is a fine thing if it doesn't take up too much of your free time.

This guy was down on his luck. He lost his job and was really in debt, so he decided to end it all. He went to a bridge outside town and was ready to jump, when out of the gathering fog he saw a figure coming slowly toward him. It was the ugliest woman he'd ever seen and she was wearing a conical hat. "Who the hell are you?" he asked.

"I'm a witch," she said. "And I have magic powers. I'll make you a deal. If you make love to me for twenty-four hours, I'll cast a spell on every one you owe money to. I'll cast a spell on your boss. I'll make your life good again with my powers."

He looked at her again. She was really ugly and he didn't want to cheat on his wife, but he figured he had nothing to lose since he was going to kill himself. So they went to a local motel and, ugly as she was, they made love all day and all night.

The next morning when he got up, he looked over at her. She was still ugly. She looked at him and asked, "How old are you?"

"I'm forty-five," he answered.

She looked at him and said, "Aren't you a little old to believe in witches?"

—DAN AYKROYD

You can do anything with a bayonet except sit on it.

—NAPOLEON BONAPARTE

Infidelity

My wife likes to talk to me during sex. In fact, the other day she called me from a motel.

—SCOTT RECORD

A young couple hadn't been married for long when, one morning, the man came up behind his wife as she got out of the shower and grabbed her by the buttocks. "Y'know, honey," he said smugly, "if you firmed these up a little bit, you wouldn't have to keep wearing a girdle."

Her feelings were so hurt that she refused to speak to him for the rest of the day.

Only a week later he again stepped into the bathroom just as she was drying off from her shower. Grabbing both breasts, he said, "Y'know, honey, if you firmed these up a bit, you wouldn't have to keep wearing a bra."

The young wife was infuriated, but she had to wait until the next morning to exact her revenge. Waiting until her husband stepped out of the shower, she grabbed him by the penis and hissed, "Y'know, honey, if you firmed this up a little bit, I wouldn't have to keep using your brother."

Tim and Elaine decided to tie the knot and went to the doctor for physical exams. Afterward the doctor called Tim into his office and told him he had some good news and some bad news. "The good news," he explained, "is that your fiancée has gonorrhea."

Tim paled. "If that's the *good* news, Doctor, then what the hell's next?"

The doctor elaborated. "Tim, the bad news is that she didn't get it from you."

When a man steals your wife, there is no better revenge than to let him keep her.

—SACHA GUITRY

Houndslow had handled all of Harrington's legal affairs for years, and one day he had to make a difficult telephone call to his old acquaintance. Being a forthright type, he got right to the point. "Harrington, I have some terrible news and some really awful news."

The businessman sat down and disconnected the speaker-phone. "Shoot, Houndslow."

"The terrible news is that your wife found a picture that's going to be worth several hundred thousand dollars," the lawyer informed him.

"That's the terrible news?" Harrington was intrigued. "I can hardly wait to hear the really awful news."

"It's a picture of you and your receptionist."

It's after dinner when this guy realizes he's out of cigarettes. He decides to pop down to the corner bar for a pack, telling his wife he'll be right back. The bartender offers him a draft on the house and he decides he has time for just one. He's nursing it along when a gorgeous blond comes in the door, but he looks the other way because he knows he has no time to fool around. So can he help it if she comes and sits right next to him and says how thirsty she is?

One thing leads to another and eventually the girl says how much she likes him and invites him back to her apartment to get better acquainted. How can he refuse? They go back to her place and go at it like crazy, and the next thing he knows, it's four o'clock in the morning. Jumping out of bed, the guy shakes the girl awake and asks if she has any baby powder.

"Yeah, in the bathroom cabinet," she says groggily.

He dusts his hands liberally with the powder, drives home at ninety miles an hour, and pulls into the driveway to find his wife waiting up for him with a rolling pin in her hand. "So where've you been?" she screeches.

"Well, you see, honey," he stammers, "I only went out for cigarettes, but Jake offered me a beer and then this beautiful bombshell walked in and we got to talking and drinking and we've been back at her apartment fucking like bunnies. . . ."

"Wait a minute," snaps his wife. "Let me see your hands." Turning on him furiously, she says, "Don't you ever try lying to me again, you rotten little skunk—you've been bowling again!"

I will not cheat on my wife. Because I love my house.

—CHAS ELSTNER

A man from the city decided to buy himself a pig, so he took a drive in the country until he saw a sign reading, "Pigs for Sale." Turning into the drive, he parked next to an old farmer standing next to a pen full of pigs, and explained his mission. Agreeing to a price of a dollar a pound, he picked out his pig, whereupon the old man picked up the pig by the tail with his teeth. "Ayuh," he pronounced, setting the squealing animal down, "that there pig weighs sixty-nine pounds."

Noting his customer's astonishment, the farmer explained that the ability to weigh pigs in this manner was a family trait passed down through the generations. Skeptical, and not wanting to be taken for a city slicker, the man insisted on a second opinion. So the old farmer called his son over from the barn, and the boy, after weighing the pig in the same fashion, pronounced its weight to be sixty-nine pounds.

Convinced, the man pulled out his wallet, but the farmer asked him to go up to the farmhouse and pay his wife, who would give him a receipt. The man was gone for a long time, and when he finally returned to the pigpen, it was without a receipt.

"What's the problem, son?" asked the old man.

"I went up there just like you said," recounted the man from the city, "but your wife was too busy to give me a receipt."

"Too busy doing what?" wondered the farmer.

"Well, sir, I'm not exactly sure," stammered the man, "but I think she's weighing the milkman."

What are three words you never want to hear when you're making love?

"Honey, I'm home!"

One night little Johnny walked in on his parents while they were screwing. "Daddy," he cried, "what are you and Mommy doing?"

"Uh . . . we're making a little sister for you to play with," stammered his father.

"Oh, neat," said Johnny, and went back to bed.

The next day his dad came home to find the little boy sobbing his eyes out on the front porch.

"What's wrong, Johnny?" he asked, picking him up.

"You know the little sister you and Mommy made me?"

"Yes," said his father, blushing.

The little boy wailed, "Today the milkman ate her."

A guy goes home and finds his best friend in bed with his wife. He says, "Sam, I have to, but you?"

—GENE BAYLOS

Jake and Jim were about to head out for another long winter trapping in the northernmost wilds of Saskatchewan. When they stopped for provisions at the last tiny town, the proprietor of the general store, knowing it was going to be a good many months without female companionship, offered them two boards each featuring a fur-lined hole.

"We won't be needing anything like that," Jake protested, and Jim shook his head righteously. But the storekeeper pressed the boards on them, pointing out that they could always be burned as firewood.

Seven months later, bearded and gaunt, Jake walked into the general store. After a little chitchat about the weather and the trapping, the storekeeper asked where his partner was. "I shot the son of a bitch," snarled Jake. "Caught him dating my board."

Laurie fell for her handsome new dentist like a ton of bricks, and pretty soon had lured him into a series of passionate encounters in the dental clinic after hours. But one day he said sadly, "Laurie, honey, we've got to stop seeing each other. Your husband's bound to get suspicious."

"No way, sweetheart, he's dumb as a post," she assured him. "Besides, we've been screwing for six months now and he doesn't suspect a thing."

"True," agreed the dentist, "but you're down to one tooth."

"Sheila," asked Lucy thoughtfully one day, "what would you do if you caught another woman in bed with your husband?"

"With Ralph?" Sheila thought it over. "Let's see: I'd break her cane, shoot her Seeing Eye dog, and call a cab to take her back to the institution she escaped from."

Two fellows were sitting in a coffee shop, when suddenly the town's fire alarm went off. One jumped up and headed for the door.

His friend shouted, "Hey, Tom, I didn't know you were a fireman!"

Tom replied, "I'm not, but my girlfriend's husband is. . . ."

A woman went to a psychiatrist because she was having serious problems with her sex life. The psychiatrist asked her many questions, but he did not seem to be getting a clear picture of her problems. Finally he asked, "Do you ever watch your husband's face while you are having sex?"

"Well, yes, I did once."

"Well, how did he look?"

"Very angry."

At this point the psychiatrist felt that he was really getting somewhere and he said, "Well that's very interesting, we must look into this further. Now tell me, you say that you have only seen your husband's face once during sex. That seems somewhat unusual. How did it occur that you saw his face that time?"

"He was looking through the window."

One day, Bobby Shapiro goes to the local brothel and, to his astonishment, meets his father there.

"Papa," he says, "what are you doing here?"

"Son," the father replies, "for fifty bucks, why should I bother your mother?"

A married woman is having an affair. Whenever her lover comes over, she puts her nine-year-old son in the closet. One day the woman hears a car in the driveway and puts her lover in the closet, too.

Inside the closet, the little boy says, "It's dark in here, isn't it?"

"Yes, it is," the man replies.

"You wanna buy a baseball?" the little boy asks.

"No, thanks," the man replies.

"I think you do want to buy a baseball," the little extortionist continues.

"Okay. How much?" the man replies after considering the position he is in.

"Twenty-five dollars," the little boy replies.

"Twenty-five dollars!" the man repeats incredulously, but complies to protect his hidden position.

The following week, the lover is visiting the woman again, when she hears a car in the driveway and, again, she puts her lover in the closet with her little boy.

"It's dark in here, isn't it?" the boy starts off.

"Yes, it is," replies the man.

"Wanna buy a baseball glove?" the little boy asks.

"Okay. How much?" the hiding lover responds, acknowledging his disadvantage.

"Fifty dollars," the boy replies and the transaction is completed.

The next weekend, the little boy's father says, "Hey, son. Go get your ball and glove and we'll play some catch."

"I can't. I sold them," replies the little boy.

"How much did you get for them?" asks the father, expecting to hear the profit in terms of lizards and candy.

"Seventy-five dollars," the little boy says.

"*Seventy-five dollars!* That's thievery! I'm taking you to the church right now. You must confess your sin and ask for forgiveness," the father says as he hauls the child away.

At the church, the little boy goes into the confessional, draws the curtain, sits down, and says, "It's dark in here, isn't it?"

"Don't you start that shit in here now," the priest says.

Jake was on his deathbed, with his wife, Becky, at his side. With tears streaming down his face, he said, "Becky, I must confess. . . ."

Becky interrupted, "Hush. Don't try to talk."

But Jake insisted, "No, I want to die with a clean conscience. I must confess. I've been unfaithful to you."

Becky replied, "Yes, I know. Why else would I have poisoned you?"

Gary matched Dan drink for drink, trying to get him to talk about what was troubling him. Gentle prodding was ignored until finally, after downing the sixth, when Dan blurted out, "Okay, it's your wife."

"My wife?" his friend demanded. "What about my wife?"

Dan replied, "I think she's cheating on us."

Don't keep him in the doghouse too often or he might give his bone to the woman next door

A man needs a mistress, just to break the monogamy.

Take an interest in your husband's activities: hire a detective.

A man and his wife were at a party. When a young woman walked in, the man said to his wife very matter-of-factly: "Look, that's our neighbor's mistress." His wife was rather shocked, but said nothing. Then, when a few minutes later another young woman walked in, he added, "And that's mine." His wife was silent for a few moments. Then she said, "Ours is prettier."

A doctor and his wife were having a big argument at breakfast.
"You aren't so good in bed either!" he shouted and stormed off to work But by midmorning he decided that he would try to make amends and he phoned home.
After many rings, the wife finally picked up the phone.
"What took you so long to answer?" he asked.
"I was in bed."
"What were you doing in bed this late?"
"Getting a second opinion!"

A man was complaining to his friend: "I had it all . . . money, a beautiful house, a nice car, the love of a beautiful woman . . . then poof! It was all gone."
"What happened?" asked the friend.
The first man replied, "My wife found out."

A little boy walks in on his mother and father when they're having sex. His mother is on top of his father and she's bobbing up and down.
The little boy asks, "What are you doing, Mommy?"

She replies, "Well, Daddy is getting fat, so I thought I would try to flatten his tummy."

The little boy says," I don't know why you bother, the minute you leave for work the maid comes in and blows it right back up again."

A wife and her husband were having a dinner party for all the high-society people in town. To show how classy they were, she decided at the very last minute that snails should be served, but all the stores were closed. So, she asked her husband to run down to the beach with the bucket she was handing him to gather some snails. Very grudgingly he agreed. He took the bucket and walked out the door, down the steps, and out to the beach. As he was collecting the snails, he noticed a beautiful woman strolling alongside the water just a little farther down the beach. He kept thinking to himself, "Wouldn't it be great if she would even just come down and talk to me?" He went back to gathering the snails. All of a sudden he looked up, and the beautiful woman was standing right over him. They got to talking, and she invited him back to her apartment a little ways down the beach. When they got there, they started fooling around. It got so hot and heavy that he was exhausted afterwards and passed out. At six thirty the next morning, he woke up and yelled, "Oh my gosh! My wife's dinner party! She'll kill me!!" He gathered all his clothes, put them on real fast, grabbed his bucket of snails, and ran out the door.

He ran down the beach all the way to his apartment. As he started running up the stairs, he dropped the bucket of snails. Snails went flying and were all over the stairs. Just then the door opened, and his angry wife was standing there, wondering where he'd been all this time.

He looked at the snails scattered on the steps, then he looked at her, then back at the snails and said: "Come on, little guys, we're almost there!"

Three men died and went to heaven. Upon their arrival, St. Peter asked the first man if he had been faithful to his wife. The man

admitted to two affairs during his marriage. St. Peter told him that he could receive only a compact car to drive in heaven.

Then St. Peter asked the second man if he had been faithful to his wife and the man admitted to one affair. St. Peter told him he would be given a midsize car to drive.

The third man was asked about his faithfulness, and he told St. Peter he had been true to his wife until the day he died. St. Peter praised him and gave him a luxury car.

A week later, the three men were driving around, and they all stopped at a red light. The men in the compact and midsize cars turned to see the man in the luxury car crying. They asked him what could possibly be the matter—after all, he was driving a luxury car.

"I just passed my wife," he told them, "and she was on a skateboard."

Two friends are having a drink at a bar. One says to the other, "You know, I ran into George on the street yesterday. He looked terrible, all beat up."

"Really?" the friend said. "What happened to him?"

"That's what I said. I said, 'George, What happened to you? I thought you were living the life of Riley.' And then George says to me, 'I was, but he came home unexpectedly.'"

Ever since they got married, Jan had a padlocked chest by the foot of their bed. Despite his pleading from time to time, she never revealed the contents to her husband, Bill. Finally, on their silver anniversary, she agreed to let him see the contents. He watched anxiously as she unlocked the chest and opened the lid. Inside were two ears of corn and fifteen thousand dollars. He looked at the chest and looked at his wife. Jan said, "It is like this: Every time I cheated on you, I put in an ear of corn." He was surprised to learn she has been unfaithful. But twice in twenty-five years wasn't that bad, so he smiled and asked, "What about the money?"

"Well, every time I reached a bushel, I sold it."

Initiative and Incentive

When the aged president of the company was out of town, half a dozen of his senior executives got together to plan some way to ease the old coot out of the driver's seat. To their horror, the executive VP's secretary buzzed him halfway through the meeting and informed him that the president had come back early and was on his way to see him.

"If he catches us all here, he'll know exactly what we're up to," cried the VP. "Quick—you five, jump out the window!"

"But we're on the thirteenth floor," protested the company treasurer. "Jump!" yelled the VP. "This is no time for superstition."

At the conclusion of his lecture to a group of young recruits, the legendary paratrooper asked for questions. A hand shot up. "What made you decide to make that first jump, sir?"

Without hesitating, the paratrooper replied, "An airplane at eighteen thousand feet with three dead engines."

Two guys are being chased by a bear, when one stops to put on his sneakers.

The other guy yells, "You idiot, you can't outrun a bear."

The first guy gasps, "I don't have to outrun a bear—I just have to outrun you."

Never put off until tomorrow what you can forget about entirely.

Adultery is the application of democracy to love.

—H. L. MENCKEN

I'd kill for a Nobel Peace Prize.

—STEVEN WRIGHT

Two skeletons used by the professor of anatomy found themselves stowed away in a dusty closet, and after several weeks of boredom, one turned to the other and asked, "What are we doing shut up in here anyway?"

"Got me," admitted his companion. "But if we had any guts, we'd get out of here."

There are three ways to get something done: do it yourself, hire someone, or forbid your kids to do it.

Insurance

Customer: I'd like to insure my house. Can I do it over the phone?

Insurance agent: No, I'm afraid a personal inspection is necessary.

Customer: Okay, but you better get over here quick—it's on fire.

"Don't let me pressure you, Mrs. Schmidt," said the aggressive life insurance salesman. "Why don't you sleep on my offer and call me in the morning. If you wake up."

What's the best thing about turning sixty-five?

No more calls from insurance salesmen.

I used to sell life insurance. But life insurance is really a weird concept. You really don't get anything for it. It works like this: You pay *me* money. And when you die, I'll pay *you* money.

—BILL KIRCHENBAUER

The investigation into the fire that had destroyed Biaggi's warehouse took almost a year. So when he received word that the case had finally been settled, Biaggi headed right over to his lawyer's office to collect the insurance money. Once there, he was stunned by just how large a percentage the lawyer was retaining to cover his services.

"Face it, Mr. Biaggi," said the lawyer smoothly, "I've earned it, now, haven't I?"

"Jesus," muttered the businessman under his breath, "you'd think *you* started the fire."

When Dan's house burned down, his first phone call was to the guy who'd sold him his homeowner's policy. "I need a check for the cash value of my house, and I need it as soon as possible," he said firmly.

"I'm afraid it doesn't work that way," explained the insurance agent politely. "See, yours was a replacement policy, which means that we'll be rebuilding the house exactly as it was before."

"I see," said Dan, after a long pause. "In that case, I want to cancel the policy on my wife."

Why is sex like insurance?

The older you get, the more it costs.

"Mommy, can I swim out to where the waves are breaking?" asked the little girl. The mother shook her head firmly.

"Pleeeease?" she begged. "Daddy's swimming out there."

"I know, darling, but he's insured."

How many doctors does it take to change a lightbulb?

It depends on what kind of insurance the bulb has.

J

Jewish American Princesses

How about the new disease affecting Jewish women?
    It's called MAIDS—if they don't get one, they die.

What's the hardest thing for a JAP about having a colostomy?
    Trying to find shoes to match the bag.

What's a JAP's idea of natural childbirth?
    Absolutely no makeup.

What does a JAP say when she's having sex?
    "Mom, I've got to hang up now. . . ."

How do you give a JAP an orgasm?
    Scream, "Charge it to Daddy!"

How many Jewish girls does it take to change a lightbulb?
    **Two. One to hold the Diet Pepsi and the cigarette and one to
call her father.**

Did you hear about the new Jewish army doll for girls?
    It's called G.I. JAP.

**Why did the Jewish mother have herself entombed at
Bloomingdales?**
    So she could see her daughter at least twice a week.

A Jewish princess is a girl who makes love with her eyes closed—because she can't bear to see another person's pleasure.

—CHARLES SIMMONS

What do you call a Japanese JAP?
    An Orienta.

Why don't JAPs like blow jobs?
    JAPs don't like any kind of job.

A Jewish girl pulls into a gas station.
    She says, "Do you charge batteries?"
    The kid says, "Yeah."
    She says, "Well then, put in a battery and charge it to my father."

Did you hear about the JAP who asked her father for fifty dollars to go shopping?
    "Forty dollars," he screamed, "what're you gonna buy with thirty dollars?"

What's the difference between Jewish women and Catholic women?
    Catholic women have fake jewelry and real orgasms.

Jewish Mothers

There are only two things a Jewish mother needs to know about sex and marriage: 1. Who is having sex? 2. Why aren't they married?

—DAN GREENBURG

How ambitious was the Jewish mother when it came to her offspring?
    Well, when a stranger inquired as to their ages, she replied,

"The doctor's in third grade and the lawyer will be starting kindergarten in the fall."

What's a Jewish mother's dilemma?
Having a gay son who's dating a doctor.

Three Jewish mothers were sitting around comparing notes on their exemplary offspring. "There never was a daughter more devoted than my Judy," said Mrs. Levine with a sniff. "Every summer she takes me to the Catskills for a week, and every winter we spend a week at Delray Beach."

"That's nothing compared to what my Lois does for me," declared Mrs. Stein proudly. "Every winter she treats me to two weeks in Miami, and in the summer, two weeks in the Hamptons, in my own private guest house."

Mrs. Lipkin sat back with a proud smile. "Nobody loves her mother like my Patty does, nobody."

"So what does she do?" asked the two women, turning to her.

"Three times a week she gets into a cab, goes to the best psychiatrist in the city, and pays him a hundred and fifty dollars an hour—*just to talk about me!*"

I'm Jewish, but we're not religious. My mother had a menorah on a dimmer.

—Richard Lewis

My mother's a typical Jewish mother. Once she was on jury duty. . . . They sent her home. She insisted *she* was guilty.

—Cathy Ladman

A young Jewish man takes his mother to a movie about life in ancient Rome. She has a little difficulty following the storyline, so at one point she asks her son to explain a scene in progress. "This particular scene," he whispers, "shows how in those days the Romans often persecuted the Christians by throwing them into the arena to be devoured by lions."

Studying the gory image for a few moments, she points her finger at a lion in the far corner and shouts, "And dat vun—vy isn't he eating?"

How many Jewish mothers does it take to change a lightbulb?
None—"I'll just sit in the dark."

All Jewish mothers carry a card in their wallets. What does it say?
"In case of an accident, I'm not surprised."

This isn't about my mother, it's about Jackie Clark's mother. He got a job in a nightclub and he came home with a Kodachrome transparency of a beautiful girl. She was wearing dark-blue leotards. From the waist up, nothing. He said, "Ma, when I work in nightclubs, that's the kind of girl I work with."

She looked at the picture and said, "That's the color I want the drapes."

—BILL DANA

What's the difference between a Jewish mother and an elephant?
Elephants eventually forget.

Why aren't Jewish mothers attacked by sharks?
Professional courtesy.

How can you tell the mother-in-law at a Jewish wedding?
She's the one on her hands and knees picking up the rice.

How can you tell it's a Jewish mother's home?
There's a safety mat in the bird bath.

Her anthropologist daughter has been off in the darkest jungle for fourteen months and has just announced her engagement to the man of her dreams. So the Jewish mother is almost beside herself with excitement that they are arriving home in time for the holidays. But at the airport, she is struck speechless when she sees her daughter come through the gate accompanied by a tall man with a bone through his nose, clad only in a grass skirt and bead necklace. Then she sobs, "Oh, Rachel, I wanted for you a rich doctor, not a witch doctor!"

The first Jewish woman is elected president. She calls her mother:
"Mama, I've won the election, you've got to come to the swearing-in ceremony."

"I don't know, what would I wear?"

"Don't worry, I'll send you a wonderful dressmaker."

"But how will I get there?"

"I'll send an airplane just for you."

"But it's such a schlep to the airport."

"Mama, I'll send a limousine to take you to the airport."

"And what will I do when I get to Washington?"

"There'll be a helicopter waiting. And after the ceremony, you'll come with me to a lovely dinner party."

"But you know I only eat kosher."

"I'll be sure the food for you is kosher. Just come, Mama."

"Okay, okay, if it makes you happy."

The great day comes and Mama, beautifully dressed, is seated between two Supreme Court Justices. She nudges the gentleman on her right and says, "You see that girl, the one with her hand on the Bible . . . her brother's a doctor!"

Jews and Judaism

Montgomery Epstein was taking an oral examination. He was asked to spell "cultivate," and he did so correctly. "But do you know what the word means?" asked the teacher. "Can you use it in a sentence?"

For a moment Montgomery looked puzzled. Then he bright-
ened up and said, "Last vinter on a very cold day, I vas vaiting for
a streetcar. But it vas too cultivate, so I took the subvay."

Jews don't mind drinking as long as it doesn't interfere with their
suffering.

—Milton Berle

Did you hear about the Jewish porn movie?
It's called *Debbie Does Bubkis.*

—Milton Berle

How can you spot a disadvantaged Jewish teenager?
He's driving a domestic car.

The two old ladies were enjoying their after-dinner coffee at the
Catskills resort when a flasher darted over to their table and
opened his coat.
"Hmmphhh," snorted Sadie without blinking an eye. "You
call *that* a lining?"

An old Jewish man is talking long-distance to California when all of a
sudden he gets cut off. He hollers, "Operator, giff me beck the
party!"
She says, "I'm sorry, sir, you'll have to make the call all over
again."
He says, "What do you want from my life? Giff me beck de party."
She says, "I'm sorry, sir, you'll have to place the call again."
He says, "Operator, ya know vat? Take da telephone and shove it
in you know vere!" And he hangs up.
Two days later he opens the door and there are two big, strapping
guys standing there who say, "We came to take your telephone out."
He says, "Vy?"
They say, "Because you insulted Operator Twenty-eight two days

ago. But if you'd like to call up and apologize, we'll leave the telephone here."

He says, "Vait a minute, vat's da rush, vat's da hurry?" He goes to the telephone and dials. "Hello? Get me Operator Twenty-eight. Hello, Operator Twenty-eight? Remember me? Two days ago I insulted you? I told you to take da telephone and shove it in you know vere?"

She says, "Yes?"

He says, "Veil, get ready—dey're bringin' it to ya!"

I knew a fellow named Otto Kahn. He was a very rich man, and his close friend was Marshall P. Wilder, who was a hunchback. They were walking down Fifth Avenue and they passed a synagogue. Kahn stopped for a moment and said, "You know, I used to be Jewish."

Wilder said, "Really? I used to be a hunchback."

—GROUCHO MARX

Reuben and Meyer were both gin rummy addicts. One day they met in the card room at the country club, and it just happened to be the day after Reuben's wife had been discovered in bed with Meyer.

"Look," said Reuben, "I know you've been screwing my wife, but I still love her, so let's settle this in a civilized way. We'll play a game of gin and the winner gets to keep her."

"Okay," agreed Meyer, "but just to make it interesting, let's play for a penny a point."

A devout Jew, Mrs. Feinstein offered up her prayers each week in temple. One week she prayed especially fervently. "Lord, I have always been a good Jew, and I've had a good life. I only have one complaint: I'm poor. Please, Lord, let me win the lottery."

The next week, Mrs. Feinstein was a little more strident. "Lord," she prayed, "have I ever missed a High Holy Day? Have I not fasted every Yom Kippur? Why must I go to my grave a pauper? One lottery win is all I'm asking You for."

The third week, Mrs. Feinstein made no bones about her displeasure. "A faithful Jew such as myself, Lord, always observant, always dutiful, asks for one little favor, and what do I get?"

A glowing, white-bearded figure stepped down from the heavens into the temple. "Now, Mrs. Feinstein," boomed God, "don't you think you could at least meet me halfway, and buy a ticket?"

A Jewish guy's idea of oral sex is talking about himself.

—Abby Stein

How many Jewish women does it take to screw in a lightbulb?

Three. One to call the cleaning lady, and the other two to feel guilty about having to call the cleaning lady.

What did the dyslexic rabbi say after a particularly rough day?

"Yo!"

A man struck up a conversation with an attractive woman at the bar, and when she went to the ladies room, he beckoned the bartender to come over. "Listen, I'd really like to get lucky with this girl," he explained, "but I think I'm going to need a little help. Got any Spanish Fly to put in her drink?"

"We're out of Spanish Fly, but I can let you have some Jewish Fly for half the price," said the bartender.

"Jewish Fly? Never heard of it," admitted the horny guy. "But I'll give it a shot if you recommend it." So he paid for the little packet and poured the contents into her cocktail.

Sure enough, the women grew friendlier by the sip. Halfway through the drink, she began holding his hand, and by the time the glass was empty, she was stroking his thigh. "What say we get out of this joint?" she whispered in his ear.

"Great!" he replied with a gulp. "Where to?"

"We'll pick up my mother, go shopping, and talk about medical school."

One Sunday, an old Jewish man walks into a Catholic Church and sits down in a confessional.

"Forgive me, Father, for I have sinned," he says humbly. "Yesterday afternoon a beautiful girl with gigantic breasts and a cute little tush valked into my delicatessen and started making nice to me. Veil, what can I tell you, I closed the store and for the next six hours I fucked her. I vas like a crazy man or something."

"Excuse me, Mr. Epstein," interrupts the perplexed priest. "But you're Jewish. Why are you telling me?"

"Telling *you*?" yelled old Epstein. "I'm telling everyone!"

I know a guy who wanted to get in the temple on Yom Kippur, but without a ticket, they don't let you in. He said, "Look, I just want to say something to someone."

The guy at the door says, "You gotta have a ticket."

He says, "Let me in for one second, I just have to say something to somebody."

The guys says, "Okay, I'll let you in. But if I catch you praying. . . ."

—Pearl Williams

I'm from a very liberal Jewish family. My parents believe in the Ten Commandments, but they believe you can pick five.

—Bill Scheft

This Hasidic Jew from New York decides to go to Birmingham, Alabama, to see what it's like there. When he gets off the bus in Birmingham, he notices that all the kids are staring at him. Not being accustomed to being stared at, he find, this a bit unnerving, so he turns to the kids and says, "Watsa mattah? You nevah saw a Yhankee before?"

It's the yearly party at the temple and they're having the drawing for the door prizes. Goldstein wins third prize and gets a color television set. Rosenberg wins second prize, goes up to collect, and is presented

with a plate of cookies. He comes back to the table and says,
"Goldstein, I don't understand it. You won third prize, you got a color
TV. I won second prize, I got a goddamned plate of cookies." Goldstein
says, "Rosenberg, you don't understand. The cookies were baked by
the rabbi's wife."

Rosenberg says, "Fuck the rabbi's wife."

Goldstein says, "Shh . . . that's first prize."

A blind guy goes to a Passover seder.
The hostess hands him a piece of matzah.
He says, "Who wrote this shit?"

A Jewish couple have a son who is very bright but a bit troublesome.
At the age of five they send him to a yeshiva and within a week they
hear that things aren't going well. After a couple of months they are
asked to take him out of school, since he is not setting a good example for the other children.

Things go from bad to worse. They send him to the local public
school and by the end of the first term they are asked to remove him
because he's a serious behavior problem. Then they send him away
to military school and, to their dismay, there, too, he's considered
incorrigible.

Finally, in desperation, the parents take him to the only place
left—the local parochial school. A week passes, and then another, and
a month goes by and they don't hear anything from the school. There
are no compaints about his performance, no reports of trouble. Their
curiosity is really aroused when he comes home at the end of the
term with a report card showing three Bs and the rest As. And at the
end of the second term he has straight As on his report card, and his
performance has been so good that he is the top student in his class.

Finally, his mother can contain herself no longer and she says to
him, "What's going on? We send you to the yeshiva and they throw
you out. The public school can't deal with you, and even at military
school you were considered incorrigible. But now, with these

Catholics, you're not only behaving yourself, you're getting wonderful grades."

"Well, Mama," says the boy, "I wasn't impressed by those other places, but the first thing I see when I go into this school is a Jewish guy nailed to a cross and I know it's time to get my act together."

I belong to a reform congregation. We're called Jews R Us.

—Dennis Wolfberg

A Jewish man is on his deathbed, and very feebly, his eyes closed, he asks, "Are you there, dear wife?"

She answers, "Of course, my love."

Then he asks, "Are you there, beloved son?"

"Yes, of course I'm here, Father," the son replies.

The man opens his eyes, gathers all his strength, and says, "Then who the fuck is minding the store?"

What does the Jewish Superman say?
"Up, up, and oy vey!"

God offered his tablet of commandments to the world. He first approached the Italians. "What commandments do you offer?" they asked.

"Thou shalt not murder," God replied.

"Sorry, we are not interested," said the Italians.

Next God offered the tablet to the Rumanians.

"What commandments do you offer?" they asked.

"Thou shalt not steal," God replied.

They answered, "Sorry, we are not interested."

Next God offered them to the French.

"What commandments do you offer?" they asked.

"Thou shalt not covet thy neighbor's wife," God replied.

"Sorry, we are not interested," they answered.

Finally God approached the Jews. "How much?" they asked.

"They are free," God replied.

"We'll take all ten of them!"

Did you hear about the Jewish guy at the nudist colony?
He got an erection, walked into a wall, and broke his nose.

What's the ultimate Jewish dilemma?
Pork on sale.

An old Jewish beggar was out on the street with his tin cup.
A man passed by and the beggar said, "Sir, could you spare
three cents for a cup of coffee?"
The man said, "Where do get coffee for three cents?"
And the beggar replied, "Who buys retail?"

A young Jewish boy starts attending a one-room school in a small
town. The teacher decides to use her position to try to influence the
new student. She asks the class, "Who was the greatest man that ever
lived?"

A girl raises her hand and says, "I think George Washington
was the greatest man that ever lived because he is the father of our
country."

The teacher replies, "Well . . . that's a good answer, but that's not
the answer I am looking for."

Another young student raises his hand and says, "I think
Abraham Lincoln was the greatest man that ever lived because he
freed the slaves and helped end the Civil War."

"Well, that's another good answer, but that is not the one I was
looking for," says the teacher.

Then the new Jewish boy raises his hand and says, "I think Jesus
Christ was the greatest man that ever lived."

The teacher's mouth drops open in astonishment. "Yes!" she
says. "That's the answer I was looking for." She then brings him up to
the front of the classroom and gives him a lollipop.

Later, during recess, another Jewish boy approaches him as he is
licking his lollipop. He says, "Why did you say, 'Jesus Christ'?"

The boy stops licking his lollipop and replies, "I know that the greatest man that ever lived was Moses, and *you* know it's Moses, but business is business."

I come from a very wealthy family. I was bar mitzvahed in the Vatican.

—LONDON LEE

Did you hear about the new brand of tires—Firestein?
    They not only stop on a dime, they pick it up.

A ship drops anchor off a small island that doesn't even seem to be on the charts, and the captain goes ashore to investigate. He walks inland a little way and is astonished to come upon a little town. There are houses and shops, flower gardens and vegetable gardens, even a fountain, but the place seems to be deserted. Then a short, bearded man walks out of one of the houses.
    "Who are you?" the captain asks. "How did you get here?"
    "My name is Irving Schwartz," replies the man. "I was ship-wrecked twenty, maybe twenty-five, years ago and I've lived here all this time."
    "And you built this town, all these buildings, by yourself?"
    "Sure. What else did I have to do?"
    "It's amazing," says the captain. "But Mr. Schwartz, I see that you've built two synagogues. Why is that?"
    "Every Jew," replies Mr. Schwartz, "has the right to have one synagogue he wouldn't set foot into."

—ARTHUR HALE

What is a Jewish pervert's favorite pick-up line?
    Hey, little girl, wanna buy a piece of candy?

Justice

Mrs. Swindon declined to serve on the jury because she was not a believer in capital punishment and didn't want her beliefs to get in the way of the trial.

"But, Madam," said the public defender, who had taken a liking to her kind face and calm demeanor, "this is not a murder trial. It is merely a civil lawsuit being brought by a wife against her husband. He gambled away the twelve thousand dollars he'd promised to spend on a sable coat for her birthday."

"Hmmm," mused Mrs. Swindon. "Okay, I'll serve. I could be wrong about capital punishment."

The three-time crook felt a wave of panic come over him as he surveyed the jury in the courthouse. Positive he'd never beat the murder rap, he managed to get hold of one of the kindlier-looking jurors, and bribe her with his life savings to go for a manslaughter verdict.

Sure enough, at the close of the trial, the jury declared him guilty of manslaughter. Tears of gratitude welling up in his eyes, the young man had a moment with the juror before being led off to prison. "Thank you, thank you—how'd you do it?"

"It wasn't easy," she admitted. "They all wanted to acquit you."

A judge was instructing the jury that a witness was not necessarily to be regarded as untruthful because he changed his statement from one which he had previously made to the police. "For example," he said, "when I entered my chambers today, I was sure I had my gold watch in my pocket. But then I remembered that I left it on my nightstand in my bedroom."

When the judge returned home, his wife asked him, "Why so much urgency for your watch? Isn't sending three men to get it a bit extreme?"

"What?" said the judge, "I didn't send anyone for my watch, let alone three people. What did you do?"

"I gave it to the first one," said the wife. "He knew exactly where it was."

Juries scare me. I don't want to put my fate in the hands of twelve people who weren't even smart enough to get out of jury duty.

—Monica Piper

Three sailors were stranded in a life raft with the captain after their ship had sunk in a typhoon. After going through the emergency rations, the captain gravely announced that there was only enough food for three people. "One of you will have to swim for it, I'm afraid," he said, averting his eyes from the sharks circling the raft, "but to make it fair and square, I'm going to ask each of you a question. If you answer correctly, you stay; if you blow it, out you go."

The three sailors nodded their agreement, and the captain turned to the first sailor. "What was the boat that was sunk by an iceberg?"

"The *Titanic*," answered the sailor with a sigh of relief.

"How many people were killed?"

"Three thousand, four hundred and seventy," blurted the second, mopping the nervous sweat off his brow."

"Correct," noted the captain, turning to the third sailor. "Name them."

Judge: The charge is the theft of sixteen radios. Are you the defendant?

Defendant: No, sir. I'm the guy that stole the radios.

Rubin and Katz, two judges, were each arrested on speeding charges. When they arrived in court on the appointed day, no one else was there, so instead of wasting time waiting around, they decided to try each other. Motioning Rubin to the stand, Katz asked, "How do you plead?"

"Guilty."

"That'll be fifty dollars and a warning from the court." Katz stepped down, and the two judges shook hands and changed places.

"How do you plead?" asked Rubin.

"Guilty."

Katz reflected for a moment or two. "These drunken driving incidents are becoming all too common of late," he pointed out sternly. "In fact, this is the second such case in the last quarter of an hour. That'll be one hundred dollars and thirty days in jail."

Judge Lipsky was presiding over a case of insurance fraud in which millions of dollars were at stake. It had taken almost a year for the case to come to trial, so she was especially eager that matters proceed without a hitch. She was, therefore, appalled when the court convened on the fourth day and the jury box held only eleven people. "And where is the twelfth member of the jury?" she inquired briskly of the foreman.

"Well, Your Honor, it's St. Patrick's Day, as you may know. The missing man is Brendan O'Rourke, and he'd never pass up marching in the parade. But don't worry—he left his verdict with me."

A little old man was escorted into the witness box. After being sworn in, the judge asked him to explain what happend. The man began to discuss his day work, and how things weren't going well, and how he was getting irritated by constant phone calls from his wife. As he rambled on, often incoherently, the entire courtroom seemed to be ready to nod off. Finally he ended by saying, "And then she hit me on my head with a maple leaf."

"Surely that couldn't have caused you any injury?" said the judge.

"Are you kidding?" exclaimed the old man. "It was the maple leaf from the center of our dining table, which seats ten!"

K

Kindness

A lonely stranger went into a deserted restaurant and ordered the breakfast special. When his order arrived, he looked up at the waitress and asked, "How about a kind word?"

She leaned over and whispered, "Don't eat the meat."

"Now, Bruno," said the teacher to the aggressive youngster, "what do you think your classmates would think of you if you were always kind and polite?"

"They'd think they could beat me up," responded the kid promptly.

A farmer in a beat-up old truck was driving to town when he spotted a hiker carrying a heavy backpack and a big suitcase. Being a caring man, the farmer pulled over and asked the young man if we wanted a ride. Even though the truck looked like it was about to fall apart, the young man put his suitcase in the cab and climbed aboard. But the farmer was confused when he noticed that the man was still wearing the backpack.

"Why don't you take a load off, sonny, and put that pack in the back with your suitcase?" asked the farmer.

The hiker responded, "That's very kind of you, sir, but I wasn't sure if the truck could carry the extra weight, so I thought I'd carry it myself."

L

Lawyers

What's the difference between a dead cat on the road and a dead lawyer on the road?

A dead cat has skid marks around it.

—Orson Bean

Know why laboratories have switched from rats to lawyers for their experiments?
1. There's no shortage of lawyers.
2. You don't get so attached to them.
3. After all, there are some things you can't get rats to do.

One day the gate between heaven and hell breaks down, so St. Peter arrives on the scene and calls out for the devil. The devil saunters over and says, "What do you want?"

St. Peter says, "Satan, it's your turn to fix it this time."

And the devil says, "I'm sorry, but my men are too busy to worry about fixing a mere gate."

St. Peter says, "Well then, I'll have to sue you for breaking our agreement."

And the devil says, "Oh yeah? Where are you going to get a lawyer?"

—Soupy Sales

If you can't find a lawyer who knows the law, find a lawyer who knows the judge.

A snake had the misfortune to be born blind, and although he managed to forage successfully, he was very lonely. So he was delighted to make the acquaintance of a little mole—which was very nearly blind, as such creatures are—who offered to be his friend.

They got together almost every day, and finally the snake mustered up his courage to ask the mole a question. "We have become dear friends, and yet I have no idea what you look like," he pointed out. "Would you mind if I coiled myself around you very gently so I could get an image of you?"

"Not at all," replied the mole graciously, and soon found himself in the center of a mountain of snake.

"Why, you are soft and furry, with a pointy little nose surrounded by bristly whiskers. Could it be that you are a mole?" hissed the snake.

"I am indeed," answered the mole. "And you—you are cold and slimy and are covered with scales and have no balls."

"Ssssshit," hissed the snake, "I must be a lawyer."

A doctor, a lawyer, and an architect were arguing about whose dog was the smartest, so they agreed to stage a contest. "Okay, Rover," said the architect, and Rover trotted over to a table and in five minutes had constructed a perfect scale model of Chartres Cathedral out of toothpicks. Pretty impressive, everyone agreed, and the architect gave Rover a cookie.

"Hit it, Spot," ordered the doctor, and Spot lost no time in performing an emergency Cesarean section on a cow, delivering healthy twin calves in less than three minutes. Not bad, the observers concurred, and Spot got a cookie from the doctor.

"Your turn, Fella," said the lawyer. So Fella trotted over, screwed the other two dogs, took their cookies, and went out to lunch.

A builder, an electrician, and a lawyer were arguing about which profession was the oldest.

The builder pointed out proudly that the first thing God had done was to build the earth.

"True," said the electrician, "but before that, He said, 'Let there be light.'"

"You're both right," said the lawyer agreeably, "but before the light, there was chaos—and who do you think created the chaos?"

Lawyers—they get together all day long and say to each other, "What can we postpone next?" The only thing they don't postpone, of course, is their bill, which arrives regularly. You've heard about the man who got the bill from his lawyer, which said, "For crossing the street to speak to you and discovering it was not you, twelve dollars."

—GEORGE S. KAUFMAN

It was one of the most gruesome cases ever to come before the court in the small town, and if found guilty, the defendant would spend the rest of his life behind bars. The case had not been proceeding well for the defense. Though there was no direct evidence, the circumstantial evidence was quite compelling. The only chance the lawyer had was to cast some doubt in the minds of the jurors. His only hope was to attack the testimony of the medical examiner.

Lawyer: "And prior to declaring the victim dead, did you check his pulse?"

Doctor: "No."

Lawyer: "Did you perform CPR?"

Doctor: "No."

Lawyer: "Did you do anything to determine if the victim was still alive prior to declaring him dead?"

Doctor: "No."

Lawyer: "Then, Doctor, isn't it possible that prior to your declaring the victim dead, he may in fact have been alive, and that it was your negligence that caused the death?"

Doctor: "Aside from the fact that his brain was in a jar, I suppose he could have been out practicing law."

Visiting New York City for a medical convention, a doctor from the University of Utah took the afternoon off to do some shopping. Wandering into a little antiques store, he came across a curious brass sculpture of a rat and inquired as to the price.

"I have to tell you the truth," said the proprietor. "I've sold that piece twice and it's been returned twice—so I'll let you have it for four hundred dollars. It's very old."

The doctor paid and headed out with his purchase in a bag under his arm. Not much later he noticed the shadowy forms of hundreds of live rats scuttling along in the gutters. A little while later the rats had swelled in number to several thousand, and it became evident they were following the doctor. His astonishment turned to disgust and alarm as the rat pack grew to fill up the whole street, so he picked up speed and headed east. When he reached the river, he chucked the brass rat right in, and to his considerable relief, the horde of rats followed it to a watery death.

The next morning the doctor was the very first customer in the antiques store.

"No way, buddy, I'm not taking it back a third time," protested the owner.

"Relax, I'm not bringing the rat back," soothed the doctor. "I just wanted to know . . . do you have a brass lawyer?"

A lawyer shows up at the pearly gates and St. Peter says, "Normally, we don't let you people in here, but you're in luck. We have a special this week. You go to hell for the length of time you were alive, then you get to come back to heaven for eternity.

The lawyer says, "I'll take the deal."

St. Peter says, "Good, I'll put you down for two hundred and twelve years in hell. . . ."

The lawyer says, "What are you talking about? I'm sixty-five years old!"

St. Peter says, "Up here we go by billing hours."

—Orson Bean

The comely redhead was thrilled to have obtained a divorce and was dazzled by the skill and virtuosity of her lawyer, not to mention his healthy income and good looks. In fact, she realized, she had fallen head over heals in love with him, even though he was a married man.

"Oh, Sam," she sobbed at the conclusion of the trial, "isn't there some way we can be together, the way we were meant to be?"

Shaking her by the shoulders, Sam proceeded to scold her roundly for her lack of discretion and good judgment. "Snatched drinks in grimy bars on the edge of town, lying on the phone, hurried meetings in sordid motel rooms—is that really what you want for us?"

"No . . . no . . ." she sobbed, heartsick.

"Oh," said the lawyer. "Well, it was just a suggestion."

A lawyer and an engineer were fishing in the Caribbean. The lawyer said, "I am here because my house burned down and everything I owned was destroyed. The insurance company paid for everything."

"That is quite a coincidence," said the engineer, "I'm here because my house and all my belongings were destroyed by a flood, and my insurance company also paid for everything."

The lawyer looked somewhat confused and asked, "How do you start a flood?"

Two men meet on the street.

"It was very cold this morning."

"How cold was it?"

"I don't know exactly what the temperature was, but I saw a lawyer with his hands in his own pockets."

The receptionist at a law firm answered the telephone the morning after the firm's senior partner had died unexpectedly.

"Is Mr. Smith there?" asked the client on the phone.

"I am very sorry, but Mr. Smith passed away last night," the receptionist answered.

"Is Mr. Smith there?" repeated the client.

The receptionist was perplexed. "Perhaps you did not understand me. I am afraid Mr. Smith passed away last night."

"Is Mr. Smith there?" asked the client again.

"Madam, do you understand what I am saying?" asked the exasperated receptionist. "Mr. Smith is dead."

"I understand you perfectly," the client sighed. "I just cannot hear it often enough."

A lawyer is standing at the gate to heaven, and St. Peter is listing his sins:

1. Defending a large corporation in a pollution suit when he knew they were guilty.

2. Defending an obviously guilty murderer because the fee was high.

3. Overcharging many clients.

4. Prosecuting an innocent woman because a scapegoat was needed in a controversial case.

And so the list continued.

The lawyer objects and begins to argue his case. He admits all these things, but argues, "Wait, I've done some charity in my life, too."

St. Peter looks in his book and says, "Yes, I see. Once you gave a dime to a panhandler and once you gave an extra nickel to the shoeshine boy, correct?"

The lawyer gets a smug look on his face and replies, "Yes."

St. Peter turns to the angel next to him and says, "Give this guy fifteen cents and tell him to go to hell."

Four surgeons were taking a coffee break and were discussing their work.

The first one said, "I think accountants are the easiest to operate on. Everything inside is numbered."

"I think librarians are the easiest" said the second surgeon. "When you open them up, all their organs are alphabetically ordered."

The third surgeon said, "I prefer to operate on electricians. All their organs are color coded."

The fourth one said, "I like to operate on lawyers. They're heartless, spineless, gutless, and their heads and their behinds are interchangeable."

"You seem to have more than the average share of intelligence for a man of your background," sneered the lawyer at a witness on the stand.

"If I wasn't under oath, I'd return the compliment," replied the witness.

Santa Claus, the tooth fairy, an honest lawyer, and an old drunk are walking down the street together when they simultaneously spot a hundred-dollar bill. Who gets it?

The old drunk, of course, the other three are mythological creatures.

A rabbi, a Hindu, and a lawyer were driving late at night in the country when their car expired. They set out to find help, and came to a farmhouse. When they knocked at the door, the farmer explained that he had only two beds, and one of the three men would have to sleep in the barn with the animals.

The rabbi said he would sleep in the barn and let the other two have the beds. Ten minutes after the rabbi left, there was a knock on the bedroom door. The rabbi entered exclaiming, "I can't sleep in the barn; there is a pig in there. It's against my religion to sleep with a pig!"

The Hindu said he would sleep in the barn, since he had no religious problem with pigs. However, about five minutes later, the Hindu burst through the bedroom door, saying "There's a cow in the barn! I can't sleep in the same room as a cow! It's against my religion!"

The lawyer, anxious to get to sleep, said he would go to the barn, since he had no problem sleeping with animals.

In two minutes, the bedroom door burst open and the pig and the cow entered. . . .

There was a terrible accident at the building site, and the construction worker rushed over to where a well-dressed woman was pinned beneath an iron girder.

"Hang in there, lady," he said helplessly, "the ambulance will be here soon. Are you badly hurt?"

"How should I know?" she snapped. "I'm a doctor, not a lawyer."

WARNING: **Prosecuters Will Be Violated.**

A man calls his lawyer and asks: How much would you charge me to answer three questions?

Lawyer: Four hundred dollars.

Man: That's a lot of money isn't it?

Lawyer: I guess so. What's your third question?

Two lawyers are walking down the street and they see a beautiful woman walking toward them.

The first lawyer says, "See that woman? Boy, would I love to screw her."

The second lawyer says, "Out of what?"

Two lawyers are in a bank when, suddenly, armed robbers burst in. While several of the thieves take the money from the tellers, others line the customers, including the lawyers, up against a wall, and proceed to take their wallets, watches, and other jewelry.

While this is going on, one lawyer jams something into the other lawyer's hand.

Without looking down, the second lawyer whispers, "What is this?" to which the first lawyer replies, "It's that fifty dollars I owe you."

We have 35 million laws to enforce the ten commandments.

What is the difference between a lawyer and a rooster?

When a rooster wakes up in the morning, its primal urge is to cluck defiance.

Running into the local attorney on a street corner, the man asked her a business question. He was startled when a bill for her services arrived a few days later, to the tune of seventy-five dollars.

Not long afterward they ran into each other on the street again, and the lawyer greeted him cheerfully.

"Good morning," he responded, "but I'm telling you, not asking you."

Discovering a leak in the bathroom, the lawyer's secretary called the plumber, who fixed it in a matter of minutes. The bill, however, was substantial, so substantial that the lawyer called to complain. "You weren't here for more than ten minutes," he said, "and I don't charge that much for an hour."

"I know," responded the plumber sympathetically. "I didn't either, when I was a lawyer."

An engineer, a physicist, and a lawyer were being interviewed for a position as chief executive officer of a large corporation. The engineer was interviewed first, and was asked a long list of questions, ending with "How much is two plus two?" The engineer excused himself and made a series of measurements and calculations before returning to the boardroom and announcing, "Four."

The physicist was next interviewed, and was asked the same questions. Again, the last question was, "How much is two plus two?" Before answering the last question, he excused himself, made for the library, and did a great deal of research. After a consultation with the United States Bureau of Standards and many calculations, he also announced, "Four."

The lawyer was interviewed last, and again the final question was, "How much is two plus two?" The lawyer drew all the shades in the room, looked outside to see if anyone was there, checked the telephone for listening devices, and finally whispered, "How much do you want it to be?"

After successfully passing the bar exam, a young man opened his own law office. One day he was sitting idle at his desk when his secretary announced that a Mr. Jones had arrived to see him.

"Show him right in!" the lawyer replied. As Mr. Jones was being ushered in, the lawyer had an idea. He quickly picked up the phone and shouted into it ". . . and you tell them that we won't accept less than fifty thousand dollars, and don't even call me until you agree to that amount!"

Slamming the phone down, he stood up and greeted Mr. Jones. "Good morning, Mr. Jones, what can I do for you?"

"I'm from the telephone company," Mr. Jones replied. "I'm here to connect your phone."

Life

Life is a sexually transmitted disease.

—Guy Bellamy

"Daddy, what are those dogs doing?" asked little Tiffany, catching sight of two dogs across the street stuck together in the act of intercourse.

"Uh . . . one dog's hurt and the other one's helping him out, honey," explained her red-faced father hastily.

"What a fuckin' world, huh, Dad?" remarked Tiffany, looking up at him sweetly. "Just when you're down and out, somebody gives it to you up the ass."

Life was a lot simpler when what we honored was father and mother rather than all the major credit cards.

—Robert Orben

Life is not for everyone.

—Michael O'Donoghue

Milton came into his wife's room one day. "If I were, say, disfigured, would you still love me?" he asked her.

"Darling, I'll always love you," she said calmly, filing her nails.

"How about if I became impotent, couldn't make love to you anymore?" he asked anxiously.

"Don't worry, darling, I'll always love you," she told him, buffing her nails.

"Well, how about if I lost my job as vice president?" Milton went on, "if I weren't pulling in six figures anymore. Would you still love me then?"

The woman looked over at her husband's worried face. "Milton, I'll always love you," she reassured him, "but most of all, I'll really miss you."

If you want my final opinion on the mystery of life and all that, I can give it to you in a nutshell. The universe is like a safe to which there is a combination. But the combination is locked up in the safe.

—Peter De Vries

The theology student decided his academic pursuits were a travesty and that he should go forth and seek the meaning of life for himself. In the course of his travels, he was directed to a distant peak in the Himalayas where a great sage resided. Arriving at the sage's austere cave after a trek of many days, the student prostrated himself and asked humbly, "Oh, revered Master, what is life?"

"Life," pronounced the wizened old man gravely, "is the scent of jasmine after a spring rain."

The student frowned. "But, Master," he objected gently, "an Incan wise man I encountered on the steps of Machu Picchu told me life was a thorn like a needle of tempered steel."

The sage nodded calmly and said, "That's *his* life."

I believe you should live each day as if it is your last, which is why I don't have any clean laundry because, come on, who wants to wash clothes on the last day of her life?

Losers

My friend hit it big in Las Vegas. He drove there in an $8,000 car, and returned home in a $20,000 bus.

How can you tell when a guy's a loser?

When he's making love, he fantasizes he's someone else.

Dial-a-Prayer hung up on me.

—JACKIE VERNON

How can you tell a guy really doesn't have much to offer?

His bride shows up at the wedding with a date.

Three high-school pals were walking on the boardwalk when they saw the most gorgeous girl in a string bikini. Two of the guys let out wolf whistles and stared their eyes out, but Norman, the third guy, took to his heels in the opposite direction.

A few days later, all three were walking on the boardwalk again and saw the same girl, this time wearing nothing but the bikini bottom. And again, two of the guys went ape while Norman ran for his life.

So when the guys saw the girl a third time—this time she's stark naked—the other two grabbed Norman before he could get away. Shaking him by the shoulders, they shouted, "Why're you running away from a gorgeous sight like that, you jerk?"

Trembling, Norman blurted, "See, it's like this: my mother told me if I ever looked at a naked woman, I'd turn into stone . . . and I felt something getting hard."

How can you tell if a guy is a loser?

When he calls a porn service and the girl says, "Not tonight, I've got an earache."

He was so lonely, he couldn't eat Jell-O without fondling it first.

How can you tell if a guy is a loser?

His therapist sends him hate mail.

—Bob Hope

I know a guy who's so square that he went to an orgy and all he did was steal the grapes.

—Red Buttons

How do you know if a guy's a loser?

If the only way he gets to see a woman naked is by buying the clothes off a store mannequin.

He can remember the night he lost his innocence in the backseat of the family car. It would have been even more memorable if he hadn't been alone.

—Red Buttons

Love

If love is the answer, could you rephrase the question?

—Lily Tomlin

Love is like an hourglass, with the heart filling up as the brain empties.

—Jules Renard

Love is an ocean of emotions, entirely surrounded by expenses.

—James Dewar

If it is your time, love will track you down like a cruise missile. If you say, "No, I don't want it right now," that's when you'll get it for sure. Love will make a way out of no way. Love is an exploding cigar that we willingly smoke.

—Lynda Barry

A lot of people wonder how you know if you're really in love. Just ask yourself this one question: "Would I mind being financially destroyed by this person?"

—Ronnie Shakes

Love is what happens to a man and woman who don't know each other.

—W. Somerset Maugham

Love is like the measles—all the worse when it comes late in life.

—Douglas Jerrold

Love is staying awake all night with a sick child. Or a very healthy adult.

—David Frost

A Love Poem: "Hey, Wait a Minute"
> Her long tan legs
> Those dark bedroom eyes
> Her deep, sexy voice
> Her huge protruding Adam's apple . . . hey, wait a minute?

—JEFFREY ROSS

Make love, not war, or do both—get married.

Luck

Some of you at the Friars may remember a guy named Charlie Schlossel, a very successful manufacturer who seemed to disappear from our midst. Last night I was about to enter my limousine when I saw this homeless person going through a garbage can and I realized it was Charlie Schlossel. It was a sobering moment. I said, "Charlie, what happened?"

"Well, I went through fifteen million like this," he said, snapping his fingers. "You know, after I sold my business, I always wanted a jet airplane, so I bought one. I'm coming out of Manila Airport, we had to abort the takeoff, the wing hits the tarmac, bursts into flame, thank God we were all safe. Five million dollars, no insurance, out the window."

He said, "I was sitting in the south of France, I saw this yacht and I hear somebody's saying that the guy's going belly up. I give him five million for the yacht. We're coming out of the fjords in Norway, hit an iceberg, sunk, thank God we got out."

He said, "I saw this little girl in the Greek Islands . . . breasts, ass firm, tight, maybe twenty, twenty-three years old. I married her. Two years later she took me for five million in the settlement."

The lesson, I guess, that we can all learn is that if it flies, floats, or fucks—rent it.

—ALAN KING

Don't believe in superstition—it brings bad luck.

When Doug came in for the results of his routine physical, the doctor said gently, "Doug, you'd better sit down. I've got some good news and some bad news."

"Okay," said Doug, taking a seat, "give me the bad news first."

"Well," said the doctor, "you've only got three weeks to live."

"Jesus!" gasped Doug, wiping the sweat off his brow. "What the hell's the good news?"

"You know that really gorgeous receptionist out in the front office?"

"You bet!" answered Doug.

"The one with the body that won't quit?"

"Right."

"And the blond hair and big baby blues—"

"Yeah, yeah," interrupted Doug. "Where's the good news?"

Leaning forward, the doctor announced with a grin, "I'm sleeping with her!"

Ever notice how the person who remarks, "Well, that's the way the ball bounces," is usually the one who dropped the ball?

For every set of horseshoes human beings use for luck, somewhere in this world there's a barefoot horse.

—ALLAN SHERMAN

Michael was never considered the brightest man in town. And one day, when he was seen driving around in a new sports car, everyone asked him what happend. "I won the lottery," he answered.

"How did you guess the number?" a person asked.

"Well, for three consecutive nights, I dreamed of the number eight. Then I realized that three times eight is thirty-two, so I picked number thirty-two. Sure enough, number thirty-two came up, and now I'm a rich man."

"You numbskull," said the person, "three times eight is twenty-four!"

"Really?" said Michael. "Well, thirty-two won anyway."

Two clerics get into a car accident and it's a bad one. Both cars are totally demolished, but, amazingly, neither of the men are hurt. After they crawl out of their cars, one says to the other, "There's nothing left, but we are unhurt. This must be a sign from God. God must have meant that we should meet and be friends and live together in peace the rest of our days."

The other replies, "I agree with you completely. This must be a sign from God."

"And look at this," says the other. "Here's another miracle. My car is completely demolished but this bottle of wine didn't break. Surely God wants us to drink this wine and celebrate our good fortune."

He then hands the bottle to the other man, who takes a few big swigs and hands the bottle back. The man takes back the bottle and immediately puts the cap on. The other man asks, "Aren't you going to take a drink?"

"No, I think I'll wait for the police to join us," the man said.

A man rushes into his house and yells to his wife, "Martha, pack up your things. I just won the California lottery!"

Martha replies, "Shall I pack for warm weather or cold?"

The man responds, "I don't care. Just so long as you're out of the house by noon!"

Why are builders afraid to have a thirteenth floor, but book publishers aren't afraid to have a Chapter Eleven?

A guy on his deathbed looks at his wife and says, "You know, honey, when we left Russia, you left with me, you stuck with me. When we moved to Cleveland, we had a little store, they burned us out, you stuck with me. We went to Watts, we tried to help the black people, they burned us out, you stuck with me."

She said, "You know, you're a jinx."

—HENNY YOUNGMAN

Lust

If her lips are on fire and she trembles in your arms, forget her.
She's got malaria.

—JACKIE KANNON

The biggest myth, as measured by square footage, is that as you
grow older, you gradually lose your interest in sex. This myth
probably got started because younger people seem to want to have
sex with each other at every available opportunity, including
traffic lights, whereas older people are more likely to reserve
their sexual activities for special occasions, such as the installa-
tion of a new pope.

But does this mean that, as an aging person, you're no longer
capable of feeling the lust that you felt as an eighteen-year-old?
Not at all! You're attracted just as strongly as you ever were
toward eighteen-year-olds! The problem is that everybody your
own age seems repulsive.

—DAVE BARRY

The fraternity boy went into the pharmacy and asked for the most reli-
able aphrodisiac available. "I got a couple of coeds coming over this
weekend and they're gonna be horny as hell," he whispered confiden-
tially. "I wanna be able to handle them all myself, know what I mean?"

The pharmacist handed him a little jar with a conspiratorial wink,
and wished him a happy weekend.

Monday morning the young man crawled into the pharmacy and
croaked, "Bengay . . . I need some Bengay."

"For your pecker?" asked the incredulous pharmacist. "It'll sting
like hell."

"No, for my elbow. The women didn't show."

Especially horny one night, Sam rolled over and nuzzled his wife. "How about it, honey?" he asked tenderly.

"Oh, Sam, I've got an appointment with the gynecologist tomorrow," said his wife, going on to explain that the doctor had requested that she abstain from intercourse for twenty-four hours before an appointment.

Sam sighed deeply and turned over to his side of the bed. A few minutes later he rolled back and asked hopefully, "You don't have a dentist appointment, do you?"

The difference between love and lust is that lust never costs more than two hundred dollars.

M

Male Anatomy

When Mike came into the office for the results of some medical tests, the doctor told him he had some good news and some bad news. Mike asked for the good news first.

"Your penis is going to grow two inches in length and an inch in circumference."

"That's terrific," Mike exclaimed, breaking into a big smile. "So what could be bad?"

The doctor answered, "Malignant."

Three couples traveling from out of town to a convention had to share two rooms at the overbooked hotel. They decided that the three husbands would sleep in one room, and the three wives would sleep in the other room. In the middle of the night, the guy in the middle woke up and started to climb over the fellow on the end, who woke up, and said, "What are you doing?"

"I'm going to go find my wife," he said. "I just woke up with the biggest erection that I have had in years."

And the fellow underneath said, "Do you want me to go with you?"

And the guy on top said, "Why should I want you to go with me?"

He said, "Because that's my cock you're holding."

—Norm Crosby

Why do men have more brains than dogs do?

So they won't hump women's legs at cocktail parties.

Who's the most popular guy at the nudist camp?

The one who can carry two cups of coffee and a dozen doughnuts at the same time.

I went to my doctor and told him, "My penis is burning." He said, "That means somebody is talking about it."

—Garry Shandling

Who wants to blow their husband? You want to blow a guy that you've been dating and he's mysterious and you suck his cock and go home. Who wants to blow a guy and then go to IKEA with him all day?

—Louis C.K.

When I was in college I had this hippie girlfriend and she said, "Well, it's like, when we make love, there's no me and no you. Our bodies are like one continuous being." I said, "Okay, but how about paying some attention to our dick?"

—Bill Maher

Every time a woman leaves something off, she looks better, and every time a man leaves off something, he looks worse.

—Will Rogers

Two very nervous young men got to talking in the doctor's waiting room and discovered they had similar symptoms: one had a red ring around the base of his penis and the other one had a green ring. The fellow with the red ring was examined first. In a few minutes he came out, all smiles, and said, "Don't worry, man, it's nothing!"

Vastly relieved, the second patient went into the examining room, only to be told a few minutes later by the doctor, "I'm very sorry, but you have an advanced case of VD and your penis will have to be amputated."

Turning white as a sheet, the young man gasped, "But the first guy . . . he said it was no big deal!"

"Well, you know," said the doctor, "there's a big difference between gangrene and lipstick."

One day Gary went into the local tattoo parlor with a somewhat odd request. He had this great new girlfriend named Wendy, he explained, and while their sex life was dynamite, he was sure it would be even better if he had her name tattooed on his prick.

The tattoo artist did her best to dissuade him, pointing out that it would be very painful, and that most of the time the tattoo would just read "Wy" anyway. But Gary was undeterred, and went ahead with the tattoo. Sure enough, Wendy was crazy about the tattoo, and their sex grew even wilder and more frequent. Gary was a happy man.

One day he was downtown and had to take a leak in a public men's room. At the next urinal was a big, tall guy, and when Gary looked over he was surprised to see "Wy" on this guy's penis as well. "How about that!" he exclaimed. "Say, is your girlfriend's name Wendy, too?"

"Dream on," answered the guy. "Mine says, 'Welcome to my place and Have a Nice Day.' "

What does a dumb bridegroom say on his wedding night?

"Where's the reset button?"

Joe and Moe went outside to take a leak and Joe confessed, "I wish I had one like my cousin Junior. He needs four fingers to hold his."

Moe looked over and pointed out, "But you're holding *yours* with four fingers."

"I know," said Joe with a sigh, "but I'm peeing on three of them."

Harry stopped by the funeral parlor to see his friend Joe, who was an embalmer, and found him at work on a corpse with a gigantic penis. The man's apparatus was so spectacular that Harry blurted out, "Wouldn't I love to have that cock!"

"You might as well—this guy doesn't need it anymore," said Joe, and he proceeded to cut off the organ and hand it to Harry. Harry wrapped it up carefully and took it home, where he found his wife in the kitchen making dinner. Deciding to have a little fun, Harry unwrapped the package, stuck it between his legs, and rushed into the kitchen, shouting, "Look, honey, look!"

His wife took one look and asked, "What happened to Sidney?"

What were the first words Adam said to Eve?
"Stand back—I don't know how big this thing's going to get!"

What goes "Ha! Ha! Thump! Thump!"?
A man laughing his balls off.

"Why do you iron your bra when you have nothing to put into it?"
asked the husband snidely.
"I iron your shorts, don't I?" retorted the wife.

What did the elephant say to the naked man?
"How do you breathe through that thing?"

Male dentists are the only men in our society who can routinely tell women to shut their mouths and not be slapped for telling them.

What did the patient tell the plastic surgeon when he helped her out of the examining chair?
Thanks for the lift.

The doctor was examining a young model who was having tremendous pain in her side.

"My dear, you have acute appendicitis," the doctor said.

The woman became quite angry and said, "Don't try hitting on me doctor, I just want to be examined, not complimented."

What's six inches long that women love?

Folding money.

Jack was delighted by the opportunity to use the golf course at the swank country club, and even more so when he hit a hole-in-one on the eighth hole. As he bent over to take his ball out of the cup, a genie popped out.

"This club is so exclusive that my magical services are available to anyone who hits a hole-in-one on this hole," the genie explained. "Any wish you desire shall be granted."

"How about that!" Jack was thrilled, and immediately requested a longer penis.

"Your wish is granted," intoned the genie solemnly, and disappeared down the hole in a puff of incense.

The golfer went on down the green, and as he walked, he could feel his dick slowly lengthening. As the game progressed, Jack could feel it growing and growing, down his thigh, out from his shorts, down past his knee.

"Maybe this wasn't such a great plan after all," muttered Jack to himself, and headed back to the eighth hole with a bucket of balls. Finally he managed a hole-in-one, and when he went to collect the ball, he had to hold up the head of his penis to keep it from dragging on the ground.

Out popped the genie. "This club is so exclusive that my magical services are available to anyone who hits a hole-in-one on this hole. Any wish you—"

"Yeah, yeah, yeah," interrupted Jack. "Could you make my legs longer?"

The voluptuous blond was enjoying a stroll around Plato's Retreat, arrogantly examining everyone's equipment before making her choice. In one room she happened against a scrawny, bald fellow with thick glasses, and to complete the picture, his penis was a puny four inches long.

Checking it out with a sneer, the blond snickered, "Just who do you think you're going to please with *that*?"

"Me," he answered, looking up with a grin.

A certain couple loved to compete with each other, comparing their achievements in every aspect of their lives: salaries, athletic abilities, social accomplishments, and so on. Everything was a contest, and the husband sank into a deep depression because he had yet to win a single one. Finally, he sought professional counsel, explaining to the shrink that while he wouldn't mind losing once in a while, his unbroken string of defeats had him pretty down.

"Simple enough. All we have to do is devise a game that you can't possibly lose." The shrink thought for a moment, then proposed a pissing contest. "Whoever can pee higher on the wall wins—and how could any woman win?"

Running home, the husband called up, "Darling, I've got a new game!"

"Oooh, I love games," she squealed, running down the stairs. "What is it?"

"C'mon out here," he instructed, pulling her around to the patio. "We're going to stand here, piss on this wall, and whoever makes the highest mark wins."

"What fun! I'll go first." The woman proceeded to lift her dress, then her leg, and pee on the wall about six inches up from the ground. She turned to him expectantly.

"Okay, now it's my turn," said the beleaguered husband eagerly. He unzipped his fly, pulled out his penis, and was just about to pee when his wife interrupted.

"Hang on a sec," she called out. "No hands allowed!"

Male Performance

Joe was in the corner bar having a few when his friend Phil dropped in and joined him. It didn't take long for Phil to notice a string hanging out of the back of Joe's shirt collar, which his friend kept tugging on.

Finally, Phil couldn't contain his curiosity and asked, "What the hell's that string for?"

"Two weeks ago I had a date with that dish Linda," Joe explained, "and when I got her into the sack, would you believe I couldn't perform? Made me so mad that I tied this string on it, and every time I think of how it let me down, I pull the string and make it kiss my ass."

I went to a meeting for premature ejaculators. I left early.

—RED BUTTONS

For Christmas, Freddy got the chemistry set he'd been begging for, and he promptly disappeared with it into the basement. Eventually his father went down to see how he was doing and found Freddy surrounded by test tubes, pounding away at the wall.

"Son, why're you hammering a nail into the wall?" he asked.

"That's no nail, that's a worm," explained Freddy, and showed his dad the mixture in which he'd soaked the worm.

"Tell you what, pal," suggested Freddy's father, his eyes lighting up. "Lend me that test tube and I'll buy you a Toyota."

Needless to say, Freddy handed it over, and the next day when he got home from school, he spotted a brand new Mercedes-Benz in the driveway. "Hey, Dad, what's up?" he called, running into the house.

"The Toyota's in the garage," explained his father, "and the Mercedes is from your Mom."

To be honest with you, I adore Viagra. I take one every night. It keeps me from rolling out of bed at night.

—FREDDIE ROMAN

Here's to the guy who loves me terribly. May he soon improve.

I love her for what she is.
Wealthy.

Hungry for company, the young couple is delighted when a spaceship lands in a field on their very isolated farm and out steps a young, very humanoid Martian couple. They get to talking and soon the wife invites the Martians to dinner. During dinner the conversation is so stimulating and all four get along so well that they decide to swap partners for the night.

The farmer's wife and the male Martian get the master bedroom, and when he undresses, she sees that his phallus is very small indeed. "What are you going to do with that?" she can't resist asking.

"Watch," he says smartly. He twists his right ear and his penis suddenly grows to eight inches in length—but it's still as skinny as a pencil. And again the farmer's wife can't suppress a disparaging comment.

So the Martian twists his left ear, at which his prick grows as thick as a sausage. And he and the woman proceed to screw like crazy all night long.

The next morning the Martian couple take off after cordial farewells, and the farmer turns to his wife. "So how was it?" he asks curiously.

"It was fabulous, really out of this world," reports the wife with a big smile. "How about you?"

"Nothing special," admits the farmer. "Kinda weird in fact. All night long she kept playing with my ears."

Why don't women blink during foreplay?
They don't have enough time.

One day God came to Adam to pass on some news. "I've got some good news and some bad news," God said.

Adam looked at God and said, "Well, give me the good news first."

Smiling, God explained, "I've got two new organs for you. One is called a brain. It will allow you to be very intelligent, create new things, and have intelligent conversations with Eve. The other organ I have for you is called a penis. It will allow you to reproduce your now intelligent life form and populate this planet. Eve will be very happy that you now have this organ and can give her children."

Adam, very excited, exclaimed, "These are great gifts you have given to me. What could possibly be bad news after such great tidings?"

God looked upon Adam and said with great sorrow, "The bad news is that when I created you, I only gave you enough blood to operate one of these organs at a time."

There are these two friends, a Latin man and an American man. One evening, they're in a bar arguing over which of them can have sex the most times in one night. They decide to settle the issue by going to the local brothel and gathering experimental evidence.

So they get to the brothel, pair off with a couple of the ladies, and go to their respective rooms. The American guy energetically balls his woman and, reaching up with a pencil, makes a "1" mark on the wall. Then he falls asleep. He wakes up in a couple of hours and screws her again, albeit a little less enthusiastically this time. Again, he reaches back and marks a "1" on the wall. Again, he falls asleep. He wakes up again in a couple of hours and lethargically humps the hooker again. He drowsily marks another "1" on the wall. Then he falls asleep for the rest of the night.

The next morning, the Latin guy barges into the other guy's room to see how he did. He takes one look at the wall and exclaims, "A hundred and eleven? You beat me by three!"

Manners

A car is useless in New York; essential everywhere else. The same with good manners.

—Mignon McLaughlin

Never drink from your finger bowl—it contains only water.

—Addison Mizner

I dreamed that God sneezed, and I didn't know what to say to him.

—Henny Youngman

The woman was more than a little upset when her car stalled in the middle of the main street, and even more so when no amount of cajoling could get it started again. As the light turned from red to green a third time and the car still failed to respond, the honking of the fellow in the car behind her grew even more insistent. Finally the woman got out and walked over to his door. "Excuse me, sir," she said politely, "if you'd like to help out by trying to get my car started yourself, I'll be glad to sit here and honk your horn for you."

What do you get when you cross a great painter with a really rude person?

Vincent Van Go Fuck Yourself.

A good listener is generally thinking about something else.

—Kin Hubbard

Monroe's mother couldn't wait for her first visit to the Air Force base in Nevada where he was stationed. Dutifully he showed her around and answered her many questions—except one about where the road behind the mess hall led. He ignored the question a second time, which was enough for his mother to launch into a lecture about good manners, respecting one's elders—

"Mom," Monroe interrupted, "lay off, will you? If I tell you, I'll have to shoot you."

The very well-dressed man was approached by a shabby, unkempt fellow. "Could you spare a dollar for a cup of coffee?" asked the bum.

"A cup of coffee is only fifty cents," he responded icily.

"Oh, I know," replied the bum breezily. "I was hoping you'd join me."

The trouble with being punctual is that there's nobody there to appreciate it.

—HAROLD ROME

Marriage

Bigamy is having one wife too many. Monogamy is the same thing.

When a man brings his wife flowers for no reason, there's a reason.

—MOLLY McGEE

Ohrenstein was less than pleased with the doctor's remedy for the constant fatigue that was plaguing him. "Give up sex completely, Doctor?" he screamed. "I'm a young guy. How can you expect me to just go cold turkey?"

"So get married and taper off gradually," advised the physician.

I told my wife that black underwear turns me on, so she didn't wash my shorts for a month.

—MILTON BERLE

Many poor husbands were once rich bachelors.

We're happily married. We wake up in the middle of the night and laugh at each other.

—Bob Hope

Marriage is a wonderful institution, but who wants to live in an institution?

—Groucho Marx

My parents have been married for fifty years. I asked my mother how they did it. She said, "You just close your eyes and pretend it's not happening."

—Rita Rudner

When the traveling salesman got the message at the hotel desk that his wife had given birth, he rushed to the phone. "Hi, honey," he cried happily. "Is it a boy or a girl?"

"Irving, Irving," sighed his wife wearily, "is that all you can think about? Sex, sex, sex?"

Sex when you're married is like going to a 7-Eleven. There's not as much variety, but at three in the morning, it's always there.

—Carol Leifer

Did you know that once you get married, you can look forward to three different kinds of sex?

First there's house sex, when you make love all over the house; on the floor, on the kitchen table, in the garage, any-where, any time.

Then comes bedroom sex; after the kids are bathed and fed and asleep, the shades are pulled down and the door locked, you make love in the bedroom.

Last comes hall sex. That's when you pass each other in the hall and snarl, "Fuck you."

My wife and I were happy for twenty years. Then we met.

—HENNY YOUNGMAN

Do you know what it means to come home at night to a woman who'll give you a little love, a little affection, a little tenderness? It means you're in the wrong house, that's what it means.

—HENNY YOUNGMAN

There is something magical about the fact that success almost always comes faster to the guy your wife almost married.

An extravagance is anything you buy that is of no use to your spouse.

As he got into bed, the husband was very much in the mood, but was hardly surprised when his wife pushed his hand off her breast. "Lay off, honey. I have a headache."

"Perfect," he responded, without missing a beat. "I was just in the bathroom powdering my dick with aspirin."

We would have broken up except for the children. Who were the children? Well, she and I were.

—MORT SAHL

George Bush says that gay people getting married would violate the sanctity of marriage. Is anybody here married? Does it feel like a gift from God to you?

—GREG GIRALDO

A girl is getting married and she asks the priest what she should wear. The priest says, "If it's your first marriage, to signify pu-

rity, you wear white. If you've been married before, you wear lavender." So he asks what she's going to wear and she says, "A white dress with a little bit of lavender."

—Stewie Stone

A middle-aged man confided to his doctor that he was tired of his wife and wished there were some way of doing her in so that he could have some good years left to himself. "Screw her every day for a year," counseled the doctor. "She'll never make it."

As chance would have it, it was about a year later when the doctor happened to drop by his patient's house. On the porch sat the husband looking frail and thin; his wife, tan and robust, could be seen out back splitting wood.

"Say, Sam, you're looking good," said the doctor uneasily, "and Laura certainly is the picture of health."

"Little does she know," hissed Sam with a wicked little smile, "she dies tomorrow."

One day the Israeli soldier at the checkpoint on the military highway addressed the Arab riding along on his donkey, his aged wife trudging before him. "I've been watching you go by every morning for months," the guard commented, "and you always ride and your wife is always on foot. Why?"

"Wife no have donkey," replied the Arab with a shrug.

"I see. But why does she walk in front of you? Is that the custom of your people?"

The Arab shook his head. "Land mines," he explained.

My wife's an earth sign. I'm a water sign. Together we make mud.

—Henny Youngman

The aged farmer and his wife were leaning against the edge of the pigpen when the old woman wistfully recalled that the next week would mark their golden wedding anniversary. "Let's have a party, Homer," she suggested. "Let's kill the pig."

The farmer scratched his grizzled head. "Gee, Elmira," he finally answered, "I don't see why the pig should take the blame for something that happened fifty years ago."

Sex in marriage is like medicine. Three times a day for the first week. Then once a day for another week. Then once every three or four days until the condition clears up.

—PETER DE VRIES

An aspiring actor called home to announce with great pride that he'd been cast in an off-Broadway play. "It's a real opportunity, Dad," he said. "I play this guy who's been married for twenty-five years."

"That's great, son," enthused his father. "And one of these days you'll work up to a speaking part."

[He] has decided to take himself a wife, but he hasn't decided yet whose. . . .

—PETER DE VRIES

Having been invited to his friend's wedding anniversary party, the man asked which apartment he should go to.

"Go to the eleventh floor," the friend instructed. "Find apartment G, push the buzzer with your elbow, and when the door opens, quickly put your foot against it."

"Why such an elaborate plan?" asked the perplexed guest.

"Well," cried the host, "you're not planning on coming empty-handed are you?"

The only thing that holds a marriage together is the husband bein' big enough to step back and see where his wife is wrong.

—ARCHIE BUNKER

Woman to marriage counselor: "The only thing my husband and I have in common is that we were married on the same day."

Marrying a man is like buying something you've been admiring for a long time in a shop window. You may love it when you get it home, but it doesn't always go with everything else in the house.

—JEAN KERR

Wife: Honey, what is the meaning of this vase of flowers on the breakfast table?

Husband: Today's your wedding anniversary.

Wife: Really! Well, do let me know when yours is so I can reciprocate.

I belong to Bridegrooms Anonymous. Whenever I feel like getting married, they send over a lady in a housecoat and hair curlers to burn my toast for me.

—DICK MARTIN

In Hollywood all marriages are happy. It's trying to live together afterward that causes all the problems.

—SHELLEY WINTERS (ATTRIBUTED)

The dread of loneliness is greater than the fear of bondage, so we get married.

—CYRIL CONNOLLY

One day during his lunch hour, a careworn man went to consult a fortuneteller.

She gathered her shawl around her, gazed deeply into her crystal ball, and solemnly intoned, "I see . . . I see a buried treasure. . . ."

"I know, I know," her customer interrupted wearily, "my wife's first husband."

A man in love is incomplete until he has married. Then he's finished.

—ZSA ZSA GABOR

Before marriage, a man will lie awake all night thinking about something you said; after marriage, he'll fall asleep before you finish saying it.

—HELEN ROWLAND

Easy-crying widows take new husbands soonest; there's nothing like wet weather for transplanting.

—OLIVER WENDELL HOLMES, SR.

Whoever perpetrated the mathematical inaccuracy, "Two can live as cheaply as one," has a lot to answer for.

—CAREN MEYER

The trouble with marrying your mistress is that you create a job vacancy.

—SIR JAMES GOLDSMITH

First guy: I've got a big problem. I'm married to a wonderful cook, a marvelous lover, and the best-looking woman in town.
Second guy: So what's the problem?
First guy: Having more than one wife is illegal.

Are you living a life of quiet desperation, or are you married?

One time, Billy was in Chicago to speak, and there was a problem with the hotels because there was a big convention in town. And he was with his assistant, Lacy. All the rooms were booked and there was only one room left, but it had two beds in it and they decided to share the room.
Lacy said, "You know, Billy, I'm cold."
And Billy said, "Well, Lacy, how'd you like to be Mrs. Crystal for the night?"
She said, "I'd love to be Mrs. Crystal for the night."
And Billy said, "Then get up and shut the fuckin' window."

—JIM BELUSHI, ABOUT BILLY CRYSTAL

My parents want me to get married. They don't care who anymore, as long as he doesn't have a pierced ear, that's all they think about. I think men who have pierced ears are better prepared for marriage. They've experienced pain and bought jewelry.

—RITA RUDNER

I've been in love with the same woman for forty-one years. If my wife finds out, she'll kill me.

—HENNY YOUNGMAN

Marriage is not a man's idea. A woman must have thought of it. Years ago some guy said, "Let me get this straight, honey. I can't sleep with anyone else for the rest of my life, and if things don't work, you get to keep half my stuff? What a great idea."

—BOBBY SLAYTON

Extramarital sex is as overrated as premarital sex. And marital sex, come to think of it.

—SIMON GRAY

Harry was stunned to come home from work one evening and find his wife stuffing all her belongings into a suitcase. "What on earth are you doing?" he cried.

"I can't stand it anymore!" she shrieked. "Thirty-two years we've been married, and all we do is bicker and quarrel and ignore each other. I'm leaving!"

Stunned, Harry watched his wife close the suitcase, lug it down the stairs, and proceed to walk out of the house . . . out of his life.

Suddenly, he was galvanized into action. Running into the bedroom and grabbing a second suitcase, he yelled back at his wife, "Sylvia, you're right, you're absolutely right—and I can't bear it either. Wait a minute, and I'll go with you."

It is difficult to tell who gives some couples the most happiness, the minister who marries them or the judge who divorces them.

—MARY WILSON LITTLE

The other night I said to my wife, "Do you feel that the sex and excitement have gone out of our marriage?"

She said, "I'll discuss it with you during the next commercial."

—MILTON BERLE

The newlyweds were married for five days. He turns to her and says, "Honey, we're gonna make love a new way tonight. We're gonna lie back to back."

She says, "How can that be any fun?"

He says, "I've invited another couple."

—WOODY WOODBURY

I hate singles bars. Guys come up to me and say, "Hey, cupcake, can I buy you a drink?"

I say, "No, but I'll take the three bucks."

—MARGARET SMITH

The wise old man pointed out that it was impossible to judge the happiness of a married couple from observation alone. "Some couples hold hands because, if they let go, they're afraid they'd kill each other."

One day a farmer went out to the barn to feed his cow. As he was pouring the food into the cow's trough, the cow kicked it over, spilling feed everywhere.

"That's one," said the farmer.

The next day, the cow knocked down a fence the farmer had spent two weeks repairing.

"That's two," warned the farmer.

The following morning, while the farmer was milking the cow, it knocked the bucket over, spilling milk all over the ground.

"That's three," said the farmer, and he got his shotgun and shot the cow through the head.

His wife heard the gun blast and ran out to the barn. "Why the hell did you kill the cow?" she yelled when she saw the dead cow and her husband with a smoking shotgun in his hands.

"That's one," he said.

President and Mrs. Coolidge once visited a state fair, where the prize rooster was brought to Mrs. Coolidge's attention. "This here rooster does his duty up to eight times a day, ma'am," the proud owner informed her.

The first lady's eyes opened wide. "Please see to it that that piece of information reaches the president," she instructed crisply.

Not long after, the president's party passed through the poultry barn, and the rooster's owner dutifully informed Coolidge of the bird's prowess.

"Eight times a day, eh?" the president marveled. "With the same hen?"

"No sir—with a different hen each time."

"Pass that on to Mrs. Coolidge!"

Marriage, as far as I'm concerned, is one of the most wonderful, heartwarming, satisfying experiences a human being can have. I've only been married seventeen years, so I haven't seen that side of it yet.

—George Gobel

How does a WASP propose marriage?
He asks, "How would you like to be buried with my people?"

Married men live longer than single men. But married men are a lot more willing to die.

Don't marry for money; you can borrow it cheaper.

—SCOTTISH PROVERB

Thoroughly fed up with his wife's incessant pissing and moaning, Joe finally agreed to accompany her to a meeting with her therapist. Once there, he made his reluctance quite clear, along with the fact that he had no idea how she found so much to complain about all the time.

"Well, Mr. Johnson," the therapist pointed out gently, "it is customary for married people to have sexual intercourse regularly, even frequently. Mrs. Johnson tells me that even on the nights when you don't fall asleep in front of the TV, you never respond in any way to her sexual advances."

"Yeah, well, so?" Joe scratched his head. "So whaddaya recommend?"

"Well, a reasonable minimum might be sexual intercourse at least twice a week," suggested the counselor.

"Twice a week, huh?" grunted Joe, thinking it over. "Okay, I could drop her off on Mondays—but on Fridays she's gotta take the bus."

Listening to Winston Churchill expound at length on his political opinions, Lady Astor grew more and more furious. Finally, unable to contain herself, she snapped, "If you were my husband, I'd put poison in your coffee."

"And if I were your husband," returned Churchill, "I'd drink it."

A marriage license costs ten dollars down, and your income for life.

Jimmy and Kathy are newlyweds in the honeymoon suite on their wedding night, and Kathy's in the bathroom. As Jimmy's getting undressed, he says to himself, "How am I going to tell her? How am I going to tell my new wife that I have the world's smelliest feet?" Then he throws his socks under the bed.

Kathy walks out of the bathroom, and, too chicken to face her, Jimmy runs past her and goes into the bathroom.

Kathy sits on the edge of the bed and says to herself, "How am I going to tell him? How am I going to tell my new husband that I have the world's worst breath? I've got to tell him." Just then Jimmy walks out of the bathroom. Kathy runs up to him, gives him a huge wet kiss, pulls back and says, "Honey, I've got to tell you something."

Jimmy says, "Yeah, I know. You just ate my socks."

A girl brings her boyfriend over to her house so that he can meet her parents. They're sitting on the couch when her parents walk in. He's got a surprise question to ask them, which even surprises her. He wants to marry her. He is nervous, and says to her father, "Sir, may I have your daughter's hole in handy matrimony?"

A lady says to her husband, "Arnie, I want breast implants."

He says, "We can't afford it. Go grab a wad of toilet paper and rub it up and down between your tits."

She says, "Will it make them bigger?"

He says, "It worked on your ass."

Besides "I love you," what three words does a wife want to hear most?
"I'll fix it."

What's the best way to have your husband remember your anniversary?
Get married on his birthday.

A couple are celebrating their twentieth anniversary in the same hotel where they spent their honeymoon. They're even in the same room, on the same bed.

She says, "Harry . . . what were you thinking twenty years ago on this night?"

He says, "I was thinking I'd like to fuck your brains out."

She says, "What are you thinking now?"

He says, "I think I did it."

An older man was married to a younger woman. After several years of a very happy marriage, he had a heart attack. The doctor advised him that to prolong his life, he should cut out sex.

He and his wife discussed the matter and decided that he should sleep in the family room downstairs to save them both from temptation.

One night, after several weeks, he decided that life without sex wasn't worth living, so he headed upstairs. He met his wife on the staircase and said, "I was coming up to die."

She laughed and replied, "I was coming down to kill you!"

A miserably married guy decides he needs some companionship, so he goes to a pet store.

The salesman says, "I have a great pet for you. A toothless hamster."

The guy says, "Nah."

The salesman says, "But it gives great head."

The guy takes it home.

His wife screams, "What the hell is that thing?"

He says, "Never mind what it is. Teach it to cook and then get the fuck out."

Marriage means commitment. Of course, so does insanity.

Marriage is a ceremony that turns your dreamboat into a barge.

Marriage is bliss. Ignorance is bliss. Ergo. . . .

A guy goes to buy a train ticket and the girl selling tickets has an incredible set of jugs. He says, "Give me two pickets to Titsburgh . . . umm . . . I mean, two tickets to Pittsburgh." He's really embarrassed.

The guy in line behind him says, "Relax, pal. We all make Freudian slips like that. Just the other day at the breakfast table I meant to say to my wife, 'Please pass the sugar,' but I accidentally said, 'You fucking bitch, you wrecked my life.'"

Marriage is like a hot bath. Once you get used to it, it's not so hot.

Marriage is the high sea for which no compass has yet been invented.

Marriage is the only sport that requires the trapped animal to buy the license.

Marriage is the triumph of imagination over intelligence. Second marriage is the triumph of hope over experience.

A honeymoon should be like a table . . . four bare legs and no drawers.

A wedding is a funeral where a man smells his own flowers.

A smart husband buys his wife fine china so she won't trust him to wash it.

Anybody who claims that marriage is a fifty-fifty proposition doesn't know the first thing about women or fractions.

Getting married is like buying a dishwasher: You'll never need to do it by hand again.

A best man's speech should be like a miniskirt; short enough to be interesting, but long enough to cover the bare essentials.

I married Miss Right. I just didn't know her first name was Always.

If love is blind, then marriage is a real eye-opener!

In marriage, the bride gets a shower; but for the groom, it's curtains!

I had some words with my wife, and she had some paragraphs with me.

I want a husband who is decent, God-fearing, well-educated, smart, sincere, respectful, treats me as an equal, has a great body, and has the same interests in life as me. Now, I don't think that's too much to ask of a billionaire, do you?

I was engaged myself once. To a contortionist. But she broke it off.

Losing a wife can be hard. In my case, it was almost impossible.

May the bluebird of happiness crap all over your wedding cake.

My wife has a split personality, and I hate both of them.

My wife ran off with my best friend last week. Gawd, I miss him!

My wife submits and I obey.
  She always lets me have her way.

She offered her honor, he honored her offer, and all night he was on her and off her.

Sorry I cannot be at the wedding . . . please send me a photo of the bride and groom mounted.

The gods gave man fire and he invented fire engines. They gave him love and he invented marriage.

The three stages of sex in marriage: tri-weekly; try-weekly; try-weakly.

Their marriage is a wonderful partnership. He's the silent one.

The trouble with being the best man at a wedding is that you never get to prove it.

She's a lovely person. She deserves a good husband. Marry her before she finds one.

—Oscar Levant to Harpo Marx upon meeting Harpo's fiancée

Marriage is a three-ring circus: engagement ring, wedding ring, and suffering.

Before marriage, a man yearns for the woman he loves. After marriage, the Y becomes silent.

One of the reasons ballet is so popular today is that married men are able to watch a number of ladies who for more than two hours never say a word!

I wouldn't say that my wife is cold, but every time she opens her mouth, a little light comes on inside.

At the cocktail party, one woman said to another, "Aren't you wearing your wedding ring on the wrong finger?" The other woman responded, "Yes, I am. I married the wrong man."

Married life is very frustrating. In the first year of marriage, the man speaks and the woman listens. In the second year, the woman speaks and the man listens. In the third year, they both speak and the neighbors listen.

Marriage is grand, divorce is about ten grand.

As was common, the baseball player and his wife got into a nasty quarrel at breakfast. "You're not good in bed either," yelled the husband.

"Oh, like you're Don Juan," his wife replied sarcastically.

"You keep up that language and you're asking for trouble," shouted the husband.

"What are you going to do, try to hit me?"

"If that's what it takes," said the baseball player.

"Listen, superstar, you couldn't hit water if you fell out of a boat!"

Before we got married, I caught her in my arms. Now I catch her in my pockets.

After a quarrel, a wife said to her husband, "You know, I was a fool when I married you." And the husband replied, "Yes, dear, but I was in love and didn't notice it."

When a man opens the door of his car for his wife, you can be sure of one thing: either the car is new or the wife is.

There are two lines for men waiting to enter the pearly gates of heaven. One line is marked for men who have been dominated by their wives. The line is huge and extends for miles and miles. The second line is marked for men who have dominated their wives. In that line is standing one meek-looking man. St. Peter walks up to the man and says, "Excuse me, are you supposed to be in this line?" And the little old man responded, "I think so. My wife told me to stand here."

After paying for a wedding, all a father has left to give away is the bride.

Man: Rules the roost. Woman: Rules the rooster.

Masturbation

A recent poll disclosed the fact that 90 percent of all men masturbate in the shower. The other 10 percent sing. Do you know what they sing?

You say you don't know? I didn't think so. . . .

Do you hear about the young boy whose mother caught him jerking off in the bathroom?

She told him to stop because he'd go blind . . . and he asked if he could keep going just until he needed glasses.

What do video games and *Playboy* have in common?

They both improve eye-hand coordination.

What did the seven dwarfs say when the prince awoke Snow White?

"Guess it's back to jerking off."

A Wyoming cowhand went to Denver for a little rest and relaxation, but he didn't succeed in coping well with the complexities of city life. In fact, midnight found him alone in his hotel room, jerking off.

Suddenly the door was opened by a bellhop carrying a drink intended for the room next door. "Pardon me, sir," said the flustered bellhop, "but where would you like me to set down your drink?"

"I didn't order a drink, " retorted the cowhand, thinking fast. "Can't you see I'm already so drunk that I'm taking advantage of me?"

A man said to his son, "Son, if you masturbate, you'll go blind."

The son replied, "I'm over here, Dad."

—DICK CAPRI

If sex is so personal, why are we expected to share it with somebody else?

—Lily Tomlin

Don't knock masturbation. It's sex with someone I love.

—Woody Allen

Early one morning, while his son was getting ready for his first day of school, his father took him aside and proceeded to instruct him on the appropriate way to urinate: "Okay, son: one, unzip your pants. Two, take out your penis. Three, pull back the foreskin. Four, pee into the urinal. Five, shake your penis off. Six, push back your foreskin. And, finally, replace your penis and zip your fly back up."

Later that day the father received a call from his son's teacher. "What seems to be the problem?" he asked.

"Well," the teacher said somewhat perplexed, "it appears that your son doesn't want to leave the bathroom."

"Oh, really? What's he doing in there?"

"We're not sure. He just keeps repeating, 'Three-six, Three-six.'"

One day little Herbie heard a noise from his parents' room and opened the door to see them screwing. "What're you doing, Dad?" he asked.

"Just playing gin rummy with your mother," was the answer.

On the way back downstairs, little Herbie heard a noise coming from his grandparents' room, opened the door, and asked what was going on. His granddad explained he was just playing gin rummy with his grandmother.

Not too much later, dinner was served and everyone came to the table except little Herbie. Looking in his room, Herbie's father found him lying on his bed, the sheets flapping up and down. "I'm just playing gin rummy," explained the boy.

"But you've got no one to play with," said his dad sternly.

"That's okay, Dad, with a hand like this, you don't need a partner."

The reason I feel guilty is that I'm so bad at it.

—David Steinberg

Schmendrick was having problems with premature ejaculation and his doctor recommended a topical cream guaranteed to prolong erection. When asked later whether it worked, Schmendrick replied, "I came rubbing the stuff on."

Memory

I have a memory like an elephant. In fact, elephants often consult me.

—Noel Coward (attributed)

When Robinson stretched out on the psychiatrist's couch, he was clearly in a bad state. "Doctor," he pleaded, voice quavering and hands twitching, "you've got to help me. I really think I'm losing my mind. I have no memory of what happened to me a year ago, nor even of a few weeks back. I can't even recall yesterday with any clarity. I can't cope with daily life—in fact, I think I'm going insane."

"Keep calm, Mr. Robinson," soothed the shrink. "I'm sure I'll be able to help you. Now tell me, how long have you had this problem?"

Robinson looked up blankly. "What problem?"

Nobody ever forgets where he buried the hatchet.

—Kin Hubbard

Mort's short-term memory was getting worse. So one afternoon he resorted to the time-honored remedy of tying a string around his finger to remind himself that there was something he wanted to do when he got home that day. He forgot all about it until after dinner, when the string caught his attention—but he had no idea why it was there. Frustrated, Mort decided that if he sat up long enough, the reason would come to him. And sure enough, at one in the morning it did: he wanted to go to bed early that night.

Harold saved for years and years for a his dream vacation— a weekend in Nevada, where prostitution was legal. However, since Harold worked for barely the minimum wage, the years stretched into decades, and he was ninety-one when he got off the bus in Reno in front of a glitzy bordello.

Harold tottered up to the front desk. "Isn't this Adelaide's famous Pleasure Palace?" he asked.

"Why, yes," replied the incredulous receptionist. "How can I help you?"

"Don't you have the most beautiful gals in town lined up and waiting?" Harold quavered. The receptionist nodded. "Well, I'm here to get laid," Harold said.

"How old are you, Pops?" she asked bluntly.

"I'm ninety-one."

"Ninety-one! Pops, you've *had* it."

"Oh, really?" A disconcerted look passed over the old man's face as his trembling fingers reached for his wallet. "What do I owe you?"

What did you dream last night?

I don't remember, I slept through most of it.

My grandfather's a little forgetful, and he likes to give me advice. One day he took me aside and left me there.

—RON RICHARDS

A young woman was walking toward the bus stop when she saw a little old man sitting on the curb, sobbing his heart out. Moved by his grief, the woman bent over and asked him what was so terribly wrong.

"Well, you see," choked the old man, "I used to be married to this awful bitch. She was fat and ugly, never put out, the house was a pigsty, and she spent my money like water. She wasn't even a decent cook. My life was hell."

His listener clucked sympathetically.

"Then she died," sobbed the old man, "and I met this beautiful woman. Twenty-eight years old, a body like Sophia Loren and a face like an angel, a fabulous cook and housekeeper, the hottest thing in bed you could possibly imagine, and—can you believe it?—crazy about me! She couldn't wait to marry me, and treats me like a prince in my own home."

"This doesn't sound so bad," said the young woman.

"I tell you, I'm the luckiest man in the world." The old coot bent over in a racking spasm, convulsed with sorrow.

"Well, then," said the woman tentatively, "what's to be so un-happy about? Why are you sobbing on the street corner?"

"Because," he sobbed, "I can't remember where I live!"

"I just hope it's not Alzheimer's," confessed Lundquist. "Maybe there's some kind of memory medicine you can give me. See, I'm getting terribly forgetful; I lose track of where I'm going or what I'm supposed to do when I get there. What should I do?" he asked glumly.

"Pay me in advance," the doctor promptly suggested.

"My teeth may be gone, my digestion a mess," remarked the old codger as he rocked back and forth on the porch, "but thank heavens I still have my memory, knock wood [he knocks on the arm of his chair]. . . . Who's there?"

The retired couple was sitting at the table after their Sunday lunch when the wife looked over and said, "Know what I feel like? An ice cream. Will you go get me one?"

"Okay, honey," said the long-suffering husband, getting up.

"But not just any ice cream," she interrupted. "A sundae."

"Okay, dear, a sundae it is."

"But not just any sundae, a banana split. Should I write it down and put the note in your coat pocket?"

"No, dear," said the husband, pulling on his coat. "You want a special sundae, a banana split."

"Right, but not just any banana split. I want a scoop of chocolate on one side and a scoop of vanilla on the other. Sure you don't want me to write it down?"

"I got it, I got it," said the beleaguered husband, heading for the door.

"But that's not all," she shouted after him. "I want it to be special. I want whipped cream and a cherry on top. Let me write it down for you."

"No, no, no," protested her husband. "You want a special ice cream sundae: a banana split with a scoop of vanilla here, a scoop of chocolate there, some whipped cream, and a cherry on top."

"And don't forget the chopped nuts."

"Chopped nuts," repeated the husband as the door closed after him.

Two hours later the husband returned and put a greasy paper bag on the kitchen table. The wife walked over, looked inside, and saw four bagels. Looking up at him in intense irritation, she snapped, "I knew it—you forgot the cream cheese."

Men

Is there a way to accept the concept of the female orgasm and still command the respect of your foreign-auto mechanic?

—Bruce Feirstein

Guys will actually judge women based on the way they're built. . . . A lot of guys think the larger a woman's breasts are, the less intelligent she is. I don't think it works like that. I think it's the opposite. I think the larger a woman's breasts, the less intelligent the men become.

—ANITA WISE

I was talking to a businessman and I said, "Don't you think most men are little boys? And he said, "I'm no little boy! I make seventy-five thousand dollars a year."

And I said, "Well, the way I look at it, you just have bigger toys."

—JONATHAN WINTERS

No nice men are good at getting taxis.

—KATHERINE WHITEHORN

I hate when women compare men to dogs. Men are not dogs. Dogs are loyal. I've never found any strange panties in my dog's house.

—WANDA SYKES

Giving a man space is like giving a dog a computer. The chances are he will not use it wisely.

—BETTE-JANE RAPHAEL

The male is a domestic animal, which, if treated with firmness and kindness, can be trained to do most things.

—JILLY COOPER

I require only three things of a man. He must be handsome, ruthless, and stupid.

—DOROTHY PARKER

A smart husband is one who thinks twice before saying nothing.

How can a real man tell when his girlfriend's having an orgasm?
Real men don't care.

I like two kinds of men: domestic and foreign.

—MAE WEST

Why did God create men?
Because a vibrator can't mow the lawn.

Why are men like paper cups?
They're dispensable.

How is a man like the weather?
Nothing can be done to change either one of them.

Where do you have to go to find a man who is truly into commitment?
A mental hospital.

How can you tell if a man's playing around?
He sends you love notes that are photocopied and begin with the line, "To whom it may concern . . ."

What is the difference between men and pigs?
Pigs don't turn into men when they drink.

How many men does it take to wallpaper a feminist's house?
Only four if you slice them thin enough.

How does a man show he is planning for the future?
He buys two cases of beer instead of one.

Middle Age

Middle age occurs when you are too young to take up golf and too old to rush the net.

—FRANKLIN P. ADAMS

I may be forty, but every morning when I get up, I feel like a twenty-year-old. Unfortunately, there's never one around.

He must have had a magnificent build before his stomach went in for a career of its own.

—Margaret Halsey

When you are about thirty-five years old, something terrible always happens to music.

—Steve Race

I don't think it's fair to call people middle-aged just because they're not so young anymore.

—Syd Hoff

An enthusiastic tennis player, Supreme Court Justice Hugo Black was advised by his doctor that the sport was inadvisable for someone in his forties.

"In that case," rejoined the judge, "I can't wait to turn fifty so I can play again."

Miscellaneous

Sister Christen's first post as a missionary was in a remote tribal area in East Africa. She realized that the first step in converting the heathen would be to teach them her language. She began with the tribal chieftain. Leading him into the countryside, she pointed out a banyan tree and said, "Tree."

"Tree," the chief repeated obligingly.

Next they came across a herd of monkeys. "Ba-boons," explained Sister Christen.

"Ba-boons," he repeated.

"Very good." The nun beamed.

At the riverbank they encountered a herd of hippopotami.

"Hip-po-pot-a-mus," repeated the tribesman dutifully. And then, what should they encounter in the rushes at the water's edge but a couple making love. Blushing scarlet, the nun blurted, "Man on bicycle."

Paying no attention, the chief thrust his spear into the man's back.

"Chief, why did you kill him?" screamed the horrified nun.

"Him on my bicycle," he explained with a shrug.

Ever since Eve gave Adam the apple, there has been a misunderstanding between the sexes about gifts.

—Nan Robertson

Why does the crack in your ass go up and down instead of across? So that when you're sliding downhill, you don't mumble.

A nymphomaniac goes to the supermarket and gets all hot and bothered eyeing the carrots and cucumbers. By the time she gets to the checkout line, she can't hold out much longer, so she asks one of the supermarket baggers to carry her groceries out to the car for her. They're halfway across the lot when she slips her hand down his pants and whispers, "You know, I've got an itchy pussy."

"Sorry, lady," says the bagger, "but I can't tell one of those Japanese cars from another."

Three traveling salesmen ran out of gas not far from a hospitable farmer's house. He and his eighteen beautiful daughters invited them in out of the rain and said they could spend the night, although the farmer apologized because there was only one spare bedroom and two salesmen would have to sleep in the barn. The three salesmen gratefully accepted his offer, for there were no towing services available at that time of night.

The next morning the salesmen went on their way and in the car they began to compare notes about the evening's experience.

"All I dreamed about was straw," said the first guy, "because I had to sleep with the horses."

"You think that's bad," piped up the second guy. "All I dreamed about was mud, because I was down there with the pigs. How 'bout you, Phil?"

"I'll tell ya," said Phil blearily, "all I could think about was golf."

"Why golf?" asked the driver.

"Hey, if you shot eighteen holes in one night, that's all you'd be able to think about either."

It was a little town—when I was a kid we used to play Monopoly on it.

—DONNA JEAN YOUNG

How can you tell when a town's really small?
The local hooker stands under a flashlight.

It was a really formal event. There were so many limousines it looked like a Mafia Tupperware party.

—BOB HOPE

Andy wants a job as a signalman on the railways and he is told to meet the inspector at the signal box.

The inspector puts this question to him: "What would you do if you realized that two trains were heading for each other on the same track?"

Andy says, "I would switch the points for one of the trains."

"What if the lever broke?" asked the inspector.

"Then I'd dash down out of the signal box," said Andy, "and I'd use the manual lever over there."

"What if that had been struck by lightning?"

"Then," Andy continued, "I'd run back into the signal box and phone the next signal box."

"What if the phone was busy?"

"Well, in that case," persevered Andy, "I'd rush down and use the public emergency phone along the track."

"What if that was vandalized?"

"Oh, well, then I'd run into the village and get my uncle Silas." This puzzled the inspector, so he asked, "Why would you do that?"

"Because he's never seen a train crash."

Why don't lobsters share?
    They're shellfish.

What's white and crawls up your leg?
    Uncle Ben's Perverted Rice.

I have a friend who's so cold he once sent artificial flowers to an artificial heart recipient.

—Red Buttons

When Selma answered her telephone, it happened to be an obscene phone call. The man on the other end began describing in detail all the kinky, perverted sexual acts he wanted to engage in with her.

"Now hang on, wait just a minute," Selma interrupted. "All this you know from me just by saying hello?"

A talking horse, Plug, had problems getting out of the starting gate. He would hesitate whenever there was the announcement over the loudspeaker, *"They're off!"*

The jockey complained to Plug's owner, and suggested that, perhaps, since Plug was a stallion, his hormones were interfering with his attention to the rider. So the owner had Plug gelded.

After a period of soreness and healing, Plug was once again in the starting gate. But when the race started, he sat down on his haunches.

"What the hell are you doing?" angrily shouted the jockey.

"Well," said the horse, "I was really going to win this race, and I was thinking about how being a gelding would be helpful, but when the gate opened, and there was the announcement over the loudspeaker, *'They're off!'* I just sat down and cried."

The newly rich real estate developer splurged on a Rolls-Royce Silver Shadow and couldn't wait to show it off. So after a meeting with the manager of his bank, he offered him a ride home.

"Whaddaya think?" he couldn't resist asking his passenger after a mile or two. "Pretty snappy, eh? I bet you've never ridden in one of these before."

"Actually I have," replied the banker graciously, "but this is my first time in the front seat."

Once there was a beautiful woman who loved to work in her vegetable garden, but no matter what she did, she couldn't get her tomatoes to ripen. Admiring her neighbor's garden, and his beautiful bright red tomatoes, she went over one day and asked him to tell her his secret.

"It's really quite simple," the old man explained. "Twice each day, in the morning and in the evening, I expose myself in front of the tomatoes and they turn red with embarrassment."

Desperate for the perfect garden, she decided to try the same thing and proceeded to expose herself to her plants twice daily.

Two weeks passed and her neighbor stopped by to check her progress.

"So," he asked, "any luck with your tomatoes?"

"No," she replied excitedly, "but you should see the size of my cucumbers!"

If an athlete gets athlete's foot what does an astronaut get?
Mistle toe.

A guy works in the circus, following the elephants with a pail and shovel. One day, his brother comes to see him. He says, "Sam, I've got great news. I've got you a job in my office. You'll wear a suit and tie, work regular hours, and start at a nice salary. How about it?"

Sam says, "What? And give up show business?"

Burford gets his jaw badly broken in a barroom brawl and goes to the hospital. The doctors have to wire his jaw shut, so he's forced to eat through his rear end.

One day, he mumbles to his wife, "Honey, I gotta have a cup of coffee."

His wife starts feeding him a cup of coffee through the tube that goes into his ass, and Burford starts kicking and jumping around.

She says, "Is it too hot?"

Burford grunts, "No, it's too sweet."

The freeloading son of a wealthy businessman said to his father one morning, "Have a great day, Dad!"

"Thank you, son. But why did you say that?"

"Because if you have a great day, I'll have a great day."

I saw a bumper sticker the other day that said, "Jesus is my best friend." Boy, his dog must be pissed.

Furniture is the other thing my wife likes to push around.

Three students at the CIA Academy were about to graduate. The instructor called them into a room and said to the first one, "Take this gun and go into the next room. I want you to assassinate whomever you find there. If you don't do this, you don't graduate."

The man took the gun and went into the next room, where he found his wife.

Taking one look at her, he returned to the instructor, threw down his gun and quit, saying, "I can't do this."

The next man went into the room and saw his own wife. He hesitated a moment, then he, too, resigned.

The third man took the gun and went into the room. The instructor heard six rapid shots, followed by screams, thuds, crashes, then silence. Then the door opened and out came the third agent all bloody, and his shirt in shreds. He said to the instructor, "You idiot, you gave me blanks! I had to strangle her!"

Why do Japanese Sumo wrestlers shave their legs?
So you can tell them apart from feminists.

Why are elephants wrinkled?
Have you ever tried to iron one?

If a pickpocket would go through my pockets now, all he'd get is exercise.

After about his seventh or eighth drink, the bum looks up from his glass on the bar and sees a horse standing next to him. This would have struck him as odd, except that he was too drunk to notice anything out of the ordinary.

"Hey," he said to the bartender, "there's a horse standing next to me."

"I know," replied the bartender, wiping a glass. "That horse comes in here all the time—and you know, once, just once, I'd like to see him show some kind of expression. He must be part Vulcan or something."

The bum looked at the horse's face. A better poker player could not exist on this earth. "Uh-huh."

"Tell ya what," the bartender suggested, "I'll give you a free round of drinks if you can make him laugh."

The bum thought for a second or two, then said, "Sure." He took the horse by the reins and led him into the men's bathroom. A moment later, he and the horse came out again, and the horse was laughing uproariously.

Stunned, the bartender poured the bum's free round of drinks without taking his eyes off the animal.

"That was *amazing!*" he told the bum as he finished off his last drink. "I'll give you another free round of drinks if you can make him cry!"

Smiling, the bum said, "All right," and once again led the horse into the men's room. When they came out a minute later, the horse was wallowing in tears. Shaking his head and rubbing his disbelieving eyes, the bartender poured the bum his second round of drinks.

"You've gotta tell me," he said as the bum finished his drink, "*how* on *earth* did you get that horse to laugh and cry?"

"Well," said the bum, clearing his throat with pride, "First I told him that my dick was longer than his, and then I proved it."

Fighting for peace is like fucking for virginity.

There are these two nude statues, one of a man and the other of a woman, standing across from each other in a secluded park. A few hundred years after they've been put in place, an angel flutters down to them. A wave of his hand, and suddenly the statues come to life and the man and the woman step down from their pedestals.

The angel says, "I have been sent to grant the mutual request you both have made after hundreds of years of standing across from each other, unable to move. But be quick—you only have fifteen minutes until you must become statues again."

The man looks at the woman. They both flush and giggle, and then run off into some underbrush. The sound of great rustling comes from the bushes, and seven minutes later, they come back to the angel, obviously satisfied.

The angel smiles at the couple. "That was only seven minutes—why not go back and do it again?"

The former statues look at each other for a minute, and then the woman says, "Why not? But let's reverse it this time—you hold down the pigeon, and I'll shit on it."

A yuppie opened the door of his BMW, when suddenly a car came along and hit the door, ripping it off completely. When the police arrived at the scene, the yuppie was complaining bitterly about the damage to his precious BMW.

"Officer, look what they've done to my Beeeeemer!" he whined.

"You yuppies are so materialistic, you make me sick!" retorted the officer. "You're so worried about your stupid BMW, that you didn't even notice that your left arm was ripped off!"

"Oh my gaaawd," replied the yuppie, finally noticing the bloody left shoulder where his arm once was. "Where's my Rolex?"

How many mice does it take to screw in a lightbulb?
Only two, but the hard part is getting them into the lightbulb.

A man was found murdered in his home. Detectives at the scene found the man facedown in the bathtub. The tub had been filled with milk, and the deceased had a banana protruding from his buttocks.

The police suspect a cereal killer.

Did you hear that one of Santa's elves tried to commit suicide?
It seems he had very low elf-esteem.

Why isn't there mouse-flavored cat food?

Did you here about the psychic amnesiac?
He knew in advance what he was going to forget.

What is the definition of a WASP?
Someone who gets out of the shower to take a leak.

Mistakes

I don't want to make the wrong mistake.

—Yogi Berra

To err is human, but to really screw up requires a computer.

As long as the world is turning and spinning, we're gonna be dizzy and we're gonna make mistakes.

—MEL BROOKS

The only thing I regret about my life is the length of it. If I had to live my life again, I'd make all the same mistakes—only sooner.

—TALLULAH BANKHEAD

A company we know is encountering so many errors, it's thinking of buying a computer to blame them on.

Money

A study of economics usually reveals that the best time to buy anything is last year.

—MARTY ALLEN

Inflation is when you pay cash for something and they ask to see your driver's license.

Among the things money can't buy is what it used to.

—MAX KAUFFMANN

Bills travel through the mail at twice the speed of checks.

—STEVEN WRIGHT

There's a phrase we live by in America: "In God We Trust." It's right there where Jesus would want it: on our money.

—STEPHEN COLBERT

The seventy-seven-year-old tycoon and his twenty-six-year-old bride were on their way from the wedding reception to the honeymoon suite at the Plaza when he had a tremendous heart attack. Paramedics labored furiously over his frail body as the ambulance rushed across town.

The millionaire's pulse remained feeble and erratic, however, and one of the medics turned to the young bride. "How about giving your husband a few words of encouragement, Mrs. Dillon? I think he could use them," he suggested.

"Okay," she agreed with a shrug, leaning toward the stretcher. "Bill, honey, I hope you perk up real fast. I'm so horny I'm ready to hop on one of these cute guys in white."

The best things in life are free. And the cheesiest things in life are free with a paid subscription to *Sports Illustrated*.

One dark night outside a small town, a fire started inside the local chemical plant. Before long it exploded into flames and an alarm went out to fire departments from miles around. After fighting the fire for over an hour, the chemical company president approached the fire chief and said, "All of our secret formulas are in the vault in the center of the plant. They must be saved! I will give fifty thousand dollars to the engine company that brings them out safely!"

As soon as the chief heard this, he ordered the firemen to strengthen their attack on the blaze. After two more hours of attacking the fire, the president of the company offered $100,000 to the engine company that could bring out the company's secret files. In the distance, a long siren was heard and another fire truck came into sight. It was a local volunteer fire company composed entirely of men over sixty-five. To everyone's amazement, the little fire engine raced through the chemical plant gates and drove straight into the middle of the inferno. In the distance the other firemen watched as the old-timers hopped off their rig and began to fight the fire with an effort that they had never seen before.

After an hour of intense fighting, the volunteer company had extinguished the fire and saved the secret formulas. Joyous, the chemical company president announced that he would double the reward to $200,000 and walked over to personally thank each of the volunteers. After thanking each of the old men individually, the president asked the group what they intended to do with the reward money. The fire truck driver looked him right in the eye and said, "The first thing we're going to do is fix the damn brakes on that truck!"

I've been rich and I've been poor; rich is better.

—SOPHIE TUCKER

Beverly Hills is so exclusive—it's the only town in America where Taco Bell has an unlisted number. And so rich—it's the only place I've seen a Salvation Army Band with a string section.

People who say money can't buy happiness just don't know where to shop.

—TOM SHIVERS

My father got my mother a telephone in the limousine. Big deal, every time it rings he has to run down to the garage and answer it.

—LONDON LEE

Money is better than poverty, if only for financial reasons.

—WOODY ALLEN

Money really isn't everything. If it was, what would we buy with it?

—TOM WILSON

The kid had swallowed a coin and it got stuck in his throat, and so his mother ran out in the street yelling for help. A man passing by took the boy by his shoulders and hit him with a few strong strokes on the back, and he coughed the coin out.

"I don't know how to thank you, Doc . . ." his mother began.

"I'm not a doctor," the man replied. "I'm from the IRS."

When a fellow says, "It ain't the money but the principle of the thing," it's the money.

—ELBERT HUBBARD

Mothers and Motherhood

My friend Myron tells me, "Last year on Mother's Day the whole family got together for a big dinner, and afterward, when Mom started to clean up, I said to her, 'Don't bother with those dishes, Mom. Today is Mother's Day. You can always do them tomorrow.' "

—JOEY ADAMS

There's not a lot of warmth between me and my mother. I asked her about it. I said, "Mrs. Stoller. . . ."

—FRED STOLLER

If it's five o'clock and the children are still alive, I've done my job.

—ROSEANNE

I think I'd be a good mother. Maybe a little overprotective. Like I would never let the kid out—of my body.

—WENDY LIEBMAN

An angry mother took her son to the doctor and asked, "Is a nine-year-old boy able to perform an appendectomy?"

"Of course not," the doctor said impatiently.

The mother turned to her son and said, "What did I tell you? Now put it back."

The child had his mother's eyes, his mother's nose, and his mother's mouth. Which leaves his mother with a pretty blank expression.

—ROBERT BENCHLEY

A woman came to ask the doctor if a woman should have children after thirty-five. The doctor said, "Thirty-five children is enough for any woman!"

—Gracie Allen

When my mom got really mad, she would say, "Your butt is my meat." Not a particularly attractive phrase. And I always wondered, Now, what wine goes with that?

—Paula Poundstone

My mom was a little weird. When I was little she would make chocolate frosting. And she'd let me lick the beaters. And then she'd turn them off.

—Marty Cohen

The boy's mother had bought him two new ties. He hurried into his bedroom, immediately put on one of them, and hurried back.

"Look, Mama! Isn't it gorgeous?"

His mother said, "What's the matter? You don't like the other one?"

Mothers-in-Law

I haven't spoken to my mother-in-law for eighteen months—I don't like to interrupt her.

—Ken Dodd

Behind every successful man stands a proud wife and a surprised mother-in-law.

—Brooks Hays

First guy: I got this bottle of brandy for my mother-in-law.

Second guy: What a great trade!

Over a beer one evening, Fred was going on and on about his mother-in-law—how cheap she was, how meddlesome, how petty, how overbearing, how boring. But then he leaned over and confessed that he had to give the old bird credit for one thing. There was one moment when he'd have cut his throat if it weren't for her.

"Huh?" His buddy was startled.

"She was using my razor."

For Mothers-in-Law Day do something nice for the lady: take her out to dinner, send her flowers, divorce her daughter.

—JOEY ADAMS

What do you call a blond mother-in-law?

An air bag.

The Movies

If my fanny squirms, it's bad. If my fanny doesn't squirm, it's good. It's as simple as that.

—HARRY COHN

The big guns in the movie business are usually those who have never been fired.

You're never disappointed in an X-rated movie. You never say, "Gee, I never thought it would end *that* way."

—RICHARD JENI

Did you hear about the new nature movie?

It's the epic story of a dysfunctional salmon who only wanted to float downstream.

After Groucho Marx introduced Sam Goldwyn [at a Friars roast], Goldwyn made a less than thrilling speech about the glories of being an independent producer. When he sat down, Groucho slunk to the microphone, flicked the ashes from his cigar, glared at Goldwyn, and sneered, "Do you suppose I could buy back that introduction?"

Then he turned to the audience and growled, "I saw Mr. Goldwyn's last picture, and what he's got to be independent about, I'll never know."

— Groucho Marx, according to Joey Adams

An adult Western is where the hero still kisses his horse at the end, only now he worries about it.

— Milton Berle

Music

At a party to celebrate the success of the musical *Showboat,* Mrs. Kern, the wife of the composer, was approached by a gushing fan. "And to think your husband wrote that fabulous song 'Old Man River'! It's absolutely my favorite—"

"No, you've got it wrong," interrupted Mrs. Hammerstein. "My husband wrote 'Old Man River.' Her husband wrote, 'Dum dum dum-dum, da dum dum dum-dum.'"

Opera in English is, in the main, just about as sensible as baseball in Italian.

— H. L. Mencken

Opera is when a guy gets stabbed in the back, and instead of bleeding, he sings.

— Ed Gardner

What's Beethoven doing now?
Decomposing!

When the orchestra began playing Tchaikovsky's *Romeo and Juliet* overture, a woman noticed tears beginning to run down the cheeks of the elderly man she was seated next to. Before long he was sobbing outright, so she turned to him and said gently, "You must be an incurable romantic."

"Not at all," he gulped. "I'm a musician."

The trouble with jazz is that there is not enough of it; some of it we have to listen to twice.

—Don Herold

Did you know Mozart had no arms and no legs? I've seen statues of him on people's pianos.

—Victor Borge

You know you're going out with someone too young for you when they say, "Did you know Paul McCartney was in a band before Wings?"

Why can't you go to the bathroom at a Beatles reunion concert?
    There's no John.

Either heaven or hell will have continuous background music. Which one you think it will be tells a lot about you.

—Bill Vaughan

What do you call a guy who hangs out with musicians?
    A drummer.

Q: What happens when you play country music backwards?
    A: Your dog comes back, you get your truck back, your momma gets out of jail. . . .

How many musicians does it take to change a lightbulb?
    One and ten on the guest list.

How do you know when there's a singer at the door?
    They can't find the key and they don't know when to come in.

What's the difference between a musician and a savings bond?
    A savings bond eventually matures and makes money

Why did the musician break open the drum?
    To look inside and see what makes all that noise.

What should you do when a musician comes to your door?
    Pay him and take your pizza.

N

Nature

I was walking along the ocean—that's generally where you'll find the beach—looking for ashtrays in their wild state.

—Ronny Graham

I have a large seashell collection. It's so large, I keep it on beaches all over the world.

—Steven Wright

Adam to Eve: Hey! I wear the plants in this family!

Negotiating

A girl walked into the corner hardware store, found the hinges she was looking for, and brought them up to the counter.

"Need a screw for those hinges?" asked the proprietor.

"No," she answered after reflecting for a bit, "but how about a blow job for the toaster in the back?"

A lady who took a cab from Beverly Hills to Malibu discovered that she had forgotten her purse. When she got out of the car, she said to the cab driver, "I'm sorry, I don't have any money with me." And she lifted her dress and she said, "Will this do?"

The cab driver turned around and sighed, "Gee, lady, don't you have anything smaller?"

—Norm Crosby

Levin was a notorious tightwad, and alleviated his few twinges of conscience by giving a quarter to the miserable-looking woman who sold bagels from a pushcart on the corner near his office. He never bought a bagel, having already breakfasted, but he always put a quarter into her grimy palm and felt himself a virtuous man.

This went on for months, until one day the bagel seller tugged at his immaculate cuff. "Mister, Mister, I gotta tell ya somethin'."

"Ah," acknowledged Levin with a gracious smile, "I suppose you wish to know why I give you a quarter every day but never take the bagel?"

"Nah, that's yer business," she snorted. "My business is tellin' ya the price's gone up to thirty-five cents."

I was selling tickets at the movie house when I got a phone call. This woman said, "How much is a ticket?"

I said, "Four dollars."

She said, "How much for children?"

I said, "Same price, four dollars."

She said, "The airlines charge half fare for children."

I said, "You come to the movie—put the kids on a plane."

—ALAN GALE

There was once a mobster who employed an accountant who was deaf and mute. He was satisfied with the guy's work until one year when he decided to double-check the books and found that he was short two million dollars. So he sent out a couple of goons to bring the guy in to his office. An hour or so later the cowering accountant arrived, accompanied by his brother, who could speak sign language. "You tell that son of a bitch I want to know where my two million bucks is at," boomed the mobster.

After a quick exchange with his brother, the translator reported that the accountant knew nothing about it.

The boss stood up, pulled out a gun, and came around the

desk to hold it against the accountant's neck. "You tell this son of a bitch that if he doesn't tell me where the dough is, I'm going to blow his brains out— after I have the boys work him over."

This was duly translated to the quaking accountant, who gestured frantically to his brother, explaining that the money was stashed in three shoe boxes in his closet. "So whaddid he say?" interrupted the gangster impatiently.

The translator turned and replied, "He says you haven't got the balls to blow his brains out."

The fellow was joined at the bar by a voluptuous woman who soon made her talents and charms abundantly clear. "I'll make your dreams come true," she whispered, "for a hundred and fifty dollars."

"That's a lot of money," the guy pointed out, admiring the cleavage set forth under his nose.

"I'm worth it," she assured him breathily. "For a hundred and fifty dollars, I'll act out your wildest, hottest fantasy. In fact, I can make any three words come true. Just dream them up, baby."

"Any three words? For a hundred and fifty dollars?" The man's voice grew husky as the woman's hand crept further and further up his inner thigh.

She nodded, reaching the other hand up to caress the back of his neck while he considered the offer. Finally he leaned back with a big smile and announced, "Okay, it's a deal!" He leaned over and whispered, "Paint my house."

One and one is two, and two and two are four, and five will get you ten if you know how to work it.

—Mae West

A verbal contract isn't worth the paper it's written on.

—Louis B. Mayer

A big-time negotiator was out fishing one day when he caught a strange-looking fish. He reeled the fish in, unhooked it, and threw it on the ground next to him. The fish started writhing in agony and, to the negotiator's surprise, said, "Please throw me back into the lake and I'll grant you three wishes."

"Any three wishes, huh?" the negotiator mused as visions of expensive fast cars and equally expensive and even faster women paraded through his head. "Fish," he finally exclaimed, "give me five wishes and I'll throw you back."

"Sorry," the fish answered while struggling for breath, "only three wishes."

The negotiator's pride was at stake and after giving the matter some thought he announced, "What do you take me for? A sucker? I'll settle for four wishes."

"Only three," the fish murmured weakly.

Fuming, the man debated the pros and cons of accepting the three wishes or continuing to bargain for that one extra wish. Finally, the negotiator decided it wasn't worth looking a gift fish in the mouth and said, "All right fish, you win, three wishes."

Unfortunately, the fish was dead.

New York

Crime in New York is getting worse. I was there the other week. The Statue of Liberty had both hands up.

—Jay Leno

Being a New Yorker is never having to say you're sorry.

—Lily Tomlin

If I had to live in New York City, I'm sure my life would be wider—but not so long.

—George M. Cohan

New York is a city where everyone mutinies but no one deserts.

—Harry Hershfield

Any time four New Yorkers get into a cab without arguing, a bank robbery has just taken place.

—JOHNNY CARSON

When you leave New York, you're camping out.

—JACKIE GLEASON

The National Council on Psychic Research has officially designated this to be true: The experience of changing planes in New York now officially counts as a near-death experience.

—DAVID LETTERMAN

Ask yourself why the New York subway system, alone of all the mass transit systems of the world, has maps inside rather than outside the trains. It's to force you to get on the wrong train in order to find out where you're going. . . . You decipher the map to discover that the first step in reaching your destination is to get off the wrong train at the next stop.

—CALVIN TRILLIN

How many New Yorkers does it take to screw in a lightbulb?
   None 'o yo' fuckin' business!

The two friends ran into each other on a street in New York's garment district.

   "I'm so sorry about the fire you had in your shop yesterday, is there anything I can do?"

   "For God's sake shut up. The fire isn't until tomorrow."

In yet another effort to clean up New York City, the mayor urged the City Council to pass legislation that would require alternate side of the street urination.

—DENNIS MILLER

353

How does a single woman in New York get rid of cockroaches?
She asks them for a commitment.

A woman from Texas and a woman from New York meet at a party.
The woman from Texas says to the woman from New York, "Hi!
Where y'all from?"

The woman from New York replies, "Where I come from we don't
end our sentences with prepositions. . . ."

So the woman from Texas says, "Fine! Where y'all from, bitch?"

I was sitting on the subway and a man came over, he said, "Are
you reading the paper?"

I said, "Yes," stood up, turned the page, and sat down again.

—David Brenner

O

Occupations

One of the sideshows at a circus featured a strong man who squeezed an orange until it appeared to be completely dry. When he finished, the strong man's manager challenged anybody in the audience to come forward and try to get one last drop out of the super-compressed piece of fruit. To make the offer a bit more enticing, the manager offered a thousand dollars to anyone who successfully eked out even one tiny drop of juice.

A weight lifter with bulging muscles bounced up onto the stage, grabbed the orange from the manager, and pressed it with all his might. Nothing came out. Next a big, burly construction worker sauntered up and took the orange from the exhausted weight lifter. After ten minutes of intense squeezing and a lot of grimacing, the construction worker finally admitted defeat.

"No other takers?" the manager asked with a satisfied sneer.

"May I try?" responded a short, skinny bespectacled man from the back row.

The manager couldn't keep a straight face as he and the rest of the crowd watched as the stranger made his way up to the front. Suddenly, the laughter stopped when, to everyone's amazement, the little guy picked up the orange and squeezed a puddle of juice onto the floor. Flabbergasted, the manager sputtered, "How the heck did you do that?"

"I'm an accountant."

A consultant is a man who knows 147 ways to make love, but doesn't know any women.

A stockbroker catches his wife in bed with another man.

He says to her, "What's going on?"

She says, "Believe it or not, John, I've gone public!"

—HENNY YOUNGMAN

Three college roommates got together regularly over the years, even though their professional lives differed widely. One had become an attorney, one a professor of Italian literature, and the third, a zoologist. When they next met, they were pretty gloomy, and it turned out that each had been told by his physician that he had only six weeks to live. Understandably, the conversation turned to the way in which each intended to live out his last days.

"I'm going to Tanzania," said the zoologist. "I've always wanted to see the rare mountain gorilla in its native habitat."

"Italy for me. I want to see where Dante was born, to be buried near the great man. And you?" asked the professor, turning to the third friend. "What would you like to see?"

"Another doctor," said the lawyer.

The company accountant had occasion to go on a business trip with one of the vice presidents. "Look," exclaimed his companion, gazing out the window of the train, "a flock of sheep—they've just been shorn."

Looking out to see for himself, the accountant noted, "On this side, at least."

I won't eat anything that has intelligence, but I would gladly eat a network executive or a politician.

—MARTY FELDMAN

What's the definition of an actuary?

Someone who wanted to be an accountant, but didn't have the personality.

The Fallons had a tomcat that insisted on going out every night to prowl around and chase after cats in heat. And week after week he'd return bloody and battered, ears torn, fur shredded. Finally, his owners had had enough, and took him to the vet to be neutered.

The cat lay low for a week or two, so the Fallons were delighted when one night the cat got dressed in black tie and tails, just as in the old days, and headed out the door. They were even more surprised when he was home by midnight without a spot or scratch on him. Crowding around and stroking him, they asked, "How'd you do it, old boy?"

"Easy," responded the cat, slicking back his whiskers. "Now I'm a consultant."

The high-school kid loved fast cars, and was thrilled to land a summer job with the local Alfa Romeo service center. "Gee, Mr. Vespucci," he gushed, grabbing a wrench, "I can't wait to learn all the ins and outs of fixing up these babies."

So he was startled when Mr. Vespucci told him to put down his tools and listen up. "The first thing you gotta learn how to do," he instructed the kid, "is to open the hood, stand back, and shake your head very, very sadly."

Anatoly was watching the May Day parade in Moscow with his friend Yevgeny. He beamed with patriotic fervor as a hundred ultra-modern tanks rumbled through Red Square, flushed with pride as crack battalions bristling with Kalashnikov rifles marched by in precise formation, then scratched his head in puzzlement: the next group to pass by consisted of ten men in rumpled gray business suits.

Finally he tugged on Yevgeny's arm. "I understand the tanks, the soldiers, the guns and missiles. But what's with those ten men?"

"Those, my friend, are economists," explained his friend. "Have you any idea how dangerous ten economists can be?"

I go to the world's wealthiest accountant. I'll tell you how rich he is: he takes his vacation in March.

Harry is at a banquet and keeps complaining that his false teeth are hurting him. The guy sitting to his left reaches into his pocket and pulls out a set of dentures. He hands them to Harry and says, "Try these."

Harry tries them, and says, "Thanks anyway, but they're too tight."

The guy pulls out another set and hands them to Harry. They fit perfectly, so Harry wears them for the entire night.

At the end of the banquet, Harry hands them back to the guy and says, "They fit me perfectly. Are you a dentist?"

The guy says, "No. An undertaker."

What does it mean when the flag at the Post Office is flying at half mast?

They're hiring.

Why can't Avon ladies walk fast?

Their lipstick.

How many mystery writers does it take to screw in a lightbulb?

Two, one to screw it almost all the way in and the other to give it a surprising twist at the end.

Old Age

Whitney woke up in the middle of the night and cried until his mother came in to see what was the matter. "I have to make pee pee," wailed the little boy.

"All right," said his mother, "I'll take you to the bathroom."

"No," insisted Whitney, "I want Grandma."

"Don't be silly, I can do the same thing as Grandma," said his mother firmly.

"Huh-uh. Her hands shake."

I'm now at the age where I've got to prove that I'm just as good as I never was.

—REX HARRISON (ATTRIBUTED)

Just as the elderly woman was turning her Mercedes into a parking space at the mall, she was edged out by a red Firebird. "You've got to be young and fast," jeered the teenaged driver as he jumped out from behind the wheel.

The woman reversed, revved her engine, and rammed the Firebird. As the Mercedes reversed and headed for his car again, the teenager turned and gaped, then ran over and banged on the woman's window. "What the hell do you think you're doing?" he screeched.

She smiled sweetly and explained, "You've got to be old and rich."

Sam wasn't happy about putting his dad in the state nursing home, but it was all he could afford—until a lucky investment paid off. The first thing he did with his newfound wealth was to move his father to the best nursing home available.

The old man was astounded by the luxury of his new surroundings. On the first day, as he was sitting in front of the television, he started to list to his right side. Instantly, a nurse ran over and tactfully straightened him out. Over lunch he started to lean a bit to the left, but within a few seconds a nurse gently pushed him upright again.

That night his son called. "How're you doing, Pop?" he asked eagerly.

"Oh, Sam, it's a wonderful place," said the father. "I've got my own color TV, the food is cooked by a French chef, the gardens look like Versailles, you wouldn't believe."

"Dad, it sounds perfect."

"There's one problem with the place, though, Sammy," the father whispered. "They won't let you fart."

The secret of staying young is to live honestly, eat slowly, and lie about your age.

—Lucille Ball

It's a good thing you didn't wait any longer to have this dinner. We're at a peculiar age. The other night Jack and I went to see a porno picture—and we fell asleep."

—George Burns, at seventy-six, about Jack Benny

Two old men meet while tottering around the park on their morning constitutional.

"Irving, how are you?" asks one, patting his friend on the arm.

"Terrible, terrible," mutters Irving. "Memory's going. For instance, I can't remember whether it was you or your brother who died."

I can tell I'm getting older. I'm starting to use "old people" clichés. The other day I actually told someone I slept like a baby. Like I woke up hungry every two hours with a mess in my pants.

—Jack Gallagher

An elderly man with a hearing problem suddenly lost his hearing completely. Concerned, he went to the doctor, who looked in his ear, picked up a pair of forceps, and extracted a suppository.

"Here's the trouble," the doctor announced, showing it to him.

The old man replied, "Now I know what I did with my hearing aid!"

Did you hear about the fifty-year-old hooker?

She sat down on a bar stool and fell all the way to the floor.

Grandpaw was sitting on the front porch talking to his grandson about growing old. "Why Teddy," he wheezed, "I remember goin' courting in the old buggy. On the way home I'd have to put my dong under a spoke in the buggy wheel to keep from peeing in my face, imagine that."

"Yeah, Grandpa? Go on," urged Teddy.

"Well, at seventy-five, things are a bit different. Now I have to rest it on one of the spokes to keep from peeing on my feet."

He's so old, his blood type was discontinued.

—BILL DANA

We're old enough to remember, George [Burns], Jack [Benny], and I, when hot pants was a condition. We recall that when there was no pill, the best method of birth control was a rusty zipper.

—ART LINKLETTER

Andrew was a dutiful son who accompanied his dad to his regular checkups with the urologist. "And how's your urine flow, Mr. Gunderson?" asked the doctor when they were seated in his office.

"Fine, just fine, Doctor, and God helps," quavered Gunderson cheerfully. "He turns the light on when I start, turns it off when I stop, and I don't have to do a thing."

"Oh, no," groaned the son as the puzzled urologist looked over at him. "Dad's peeing in the refrigerator again."

"Excuse me, Doctor," said the nurse, "but why is that old man sticking out his tongue and holding up his middle finger?"

"That's simple enough, nurse," answered the doctor, "I asked him to show me his sexual organs."

An eager-beaver young real-estate agent was doing his best to sell this old coot a condominium in Palm Beach. Having outlined its many attractions in detail, he confidently concluded his pitch: "And, Mr. Rosenblatt, this is an investment in the future."

"Sonny," croaked Mr. Rosenblatt, "at my age I don't even buy green bananas."

He's so old that when he orders a three-minute egg, they ask for the money up-front.

—MILTON BERLE

I'll never make the mistake of bein' seventy again!

—CASEY STENGEL

The girls in the brothel were frankly skeptical when a ninety-year-old man came in and put his money down on the front desk, but finally a good-hearted hooker took him up to her room. Imagine her surprised when he proceeded to make love to her with more energy and skill than any man she had ever known.

"I've never come so many times," she gasped. "How about once more, on the house?"

"All right," conceded the old geezer, "but I have to take a five-minute nap and you must keep your hands on my penis, just so, while I'm asleep." She agreed eagerly, and as soon as he woke up, he gave her an even better lesson in lovemaking.

"Oh God," gasped the hooker ecstatically, "I can't get enough of you. Please, just once more—I'll pay you."

The old man agreed, subject to the same conditions, and just before he nodded out, the hooker said, "Excuse me, but would you mind explaining about the nap and why I have to keep my hands on your privates?"

"I'm ninety years old," retorts the man, "so is it so surprising I need a little rest? As for the other, it's because the last time while I was napping they took my wallet."

Carla was well into her sixties when she went to her doctor complaining of nausea, exhaustion, and occasional cramps. After a thorough examination the doctor sent her to the hospital for a battery of tests, and finally confronted her with the results. "Mrs. Barber, medically impossible though it seems at your age, there's no doubt about it: you're pregnant."

"Impossible," she cried, and fainted dead away. When she came to, she staggered to the phone, dialed her seventy-eight-year-old husband, and screeched, "You've knocked me up, you randy old goat!"

There was a long pause at the other end of the line. Then a voice said, "And to whom am I speaking?"

I'm at that age now where just putting my cigar in its holder is a thrill.

—George Burns

There ain't nothin' an ol' man can do but bring me a message from a young one.

—Moms Mabley

The elderly man flattered himself that he was still a ladies' man, and decided to flirt with the comely waitress. "So tell me, sweetheart, where have you been all my life?" he crooned.

"Actually, sir," she pointed out sweetly, "for the first forty-five years of it, I wasn't even around."

A teenager was riding in an elevator with a very old woman when a horrible smell filled the car. Finally the kid said, "Excuse me for asking, lady, but did you fart?"

"Of course I did, sonny," she replied sharply. "Think I always smell like that?"

I am the oldest living white man, especially at seven in the morning.

—Robert Benchley

How do you know when you're really old?

You can remember championship fights between two white guys.

A man is as old as the woman he feels.

—GROUCHO MARX

Why are old people so wrinkled?
Ever try to iron one?

When an aged woman was asked if there were to be candles on her birthday cake, she responded curtly, "No, it's a birthday party, not a torchlight procession."

There's one advantage to being 102 years old. There's no peer pressure.

—DENNIS WOLFBERG

An old man concerned about his strength went to see his doctor. "Tell me what problem you are having," said the doctor.

"Well," said the old man, "at age twenty, I could bend back my erect penis about ten degrees. At age thirty, about twenty-five degrees. At age fifty, I could bend it back about forty degrees. At age sixty-five, I could bend it back about ninety degrees. Now at age seventy-eight, I can bend it back about a hundred and twenty degrees."

"And just what is it that concerns you?" asked the doctor again.

"Is it normal for my arm to keep getting stronger as I age?"

Herschel was astounded—and a little worried—when Reuben announced his upcoming marriage to a twenty-year-old girl. "At your advanced age," cautioned his friend, "couldn't that be fatal?"

Reuben shrugged philosophically. "If she dies, she dies."

Couples

My grandmother's ninety. She's dating. He's ninety-three. They're very happy. They never argue. They can't hear each other.

—CATHY LADMAN

A young woman was walking toward the bus stop when she came
across a little old man sitting on the curb, sobbing his heart out.
Moved by his grief, the woman bent over and asked him what was so
terribly wrong.

"I have sex with my wife almost every day of the week. Almost
Monday, almost Tuesday . . ."

—Milton Berle

**Senior citizens, good news! Of memory, hearing, all the faculties,
the last to leave us is sexual desire and the ability to make love.
That means that long after we're wearing bifocals and hearing
aids, we'll be making love. We just won't know with whom.**

—Jack Paar

The old couple sat through the porno movie twice, not getting up to
leave until the theater was closing for the night. "You folks must have
really enjoyed the show," commented the usher on the way out.

"It was revolting," retorted the old lady.

"Disgusting," added her husband.

"Then why did you sit through it twice?" asked the puzzled usher.

"We had to wait until you turned up the house lights," explained
the old woman. "We couldn't find my underpants, and his teeth were
in them."

My wife calls our waterbed the Dead Sea.

—Milton Berle

The newlyweds came back from their honeymoon at Niagara Falls
and moved into the apartment upstairs from the groom's parents,
Vito and Nina. That night Vito was awakened by a dig in the ribs from
his wife. "Vito, listen," she whispered. Sure enough, they could hear
the bedsprings in the room above them creaking rhythmically.
"Come on, Vito," she urged. So he rolled over on top of her and they
made love.

He had just fallen back asleep when the creaking of the bedsprings woke him again. "Vito, listen to them," said Nina in a stage whisper. "Come on." So he rolled over and made love to her again.

Vito was sound asleep when another dig in the ribs woke him to the sound of the bedsprings creaking away yet another time. "Vito, listen," began his wife, pulling off her nightgown.

At this the old man leaped to his feet, grabbed a broom, and started banging away on the ceiling like a maniac. "Cut it out, god-damnit!" he yelled. "You're killing your old man!"

"Doctor, I'm losing my sex urge," complained Ruth at her annual checkup.

"Mrs. Beeston, that's understandable at eighty-four," said the doctor, "but tell me, when did you first start noticing this?"

"Last night," she answered, "and then again this morning."

"Aha," said the doctor. "Your problem isn't a diminished sex drive, it's that you're not getting enough. You should be having sex at least fifteen times a month."

Thanking him and heading home, the old woman couldn't wait to report the doctor's prescription to her husband. "Guess what, Pop? He says I need it fifteen times a month!"

Pop put in his teeth and said, "That's just great, honey. Put me down for five."

When the elderly couple went in for their annual checkup, the wife stayed in the waiting room while her husband went in to be examined.

The doctor, kibitzing with him, said, "Sam, how's your sex life?"

"I'll tell you the truth," replied Sam. "The first time is great. But the second time, I start to sweat something terrible."

The doctor said, "Just a second. The second time? At your age? At eighty-five? That's remarkable." He excused himself and went out to the guy's wife in the waiting room and said, "Ma'am, I have to ask you this. I was asking your husband how his sex life is, and he said the first time was great, but the second time he starts to sweat something terrible."

"He wouldn't lie to you," responded the old woman. "In January, it's cold. In July, it's hot."

—Phil Stone

Two elderly men are sitting on a park bench, watching the young girls go by. One says to the other, "You know, I'm still sexually interested in women. In fact, I always get excited when I see the young girls walking by. The real problem is that at this age I don't see so good anymore."

This old man marries a girl barely out of her teens. Needless to say, she is asking for it, so when they get into bed on the wedding night, she asks him, "So are we going to have rampant sex tonight?"

The man responds by raising his hand and outstretching his fingers.

"What? Five times?" asks the eager girl.

"No," he replies. "Pick a finger."

There's a sweet old couple in Los Angeles. The wife went for a medical examination and when she came home she said to her husband, "The doctor said that I have the heart of a fifty-year-old person, I have the lungs from a forty-year-old person, and my blood pressure is like a person twenty-five years old."

"Oh really? And what did he say about your seventy-year-old ass?" asked her husband.

She said, "He never mentioned your name."

—Norm Crosby

The aged couple came into town for their annual physical. "You go in first, Paw," said the old woman, settling down to her knitting in the waiting room.

After a while, the old codger stuck his head out of the doctor's office. "Maw," he called out, scratching his head, "do we have intercourse?"

"If I've told you once, I've told you a dozen times, Paw," she scolded, "we have Blue Cross and Blue Shield."

An old couple are in bed one night and the woman wakes up and says, "Sam, get up and close the window. It's cold outside." The fellow keeps right on snoring.

A little while later she nudges him and says again, "Sam, get up and close the window! It's cold outside." He's about to go back to sleep, but she keeps shaking him, so finally he gets up and closes the window.

He gets back into bed and says, "So now it's warm outside?"

—Myron Cohen

An elderly man and his wife decided to separate. Before being allowed to do so legally, the family court insisted they undergo some marriage counseling to see if their union could be saved.

The therapist did her best, but to no avail. The old folks were absolutely determined to go through with separation leading to divorce.

Finally, in some desperation, the therapist said to the husband, "But you're ninety-five and your wife is ninety-three. You've been married for seventy-two years! Why do you want to separate now?"

To which the wife replied, "We haven't been able to stand each other for the last forty-six years. But we thought we should wait until all the children died before we split up."

Opinion

Desk sign: You may not think much of what I have to say, but remember, it's one six-billion-seven-hundred-millionth of the world's opinion.

In all matters of opinion, our adversaries are insane.

—Mark Twain

The degree of one's emotion varies inversely with one's knowledge of the facts—the less you know, the hotter you get.

—Bertrand Russell

Every man has a perfect right to his opinion, provided it agrees with ours.

—Josh Billings

Then there's the matter of half-truths. A certain sailor, celebrating a long-awaited ship's leave, got very inebriated. When he staggered back up the gangway, the captain sternly entered in the log: "Mate drunk tonight."

When he saw the entry, the mate objected violently. "Captain, the boat was moored—you know I've never been drunk on board before, never drunk on duty. If this stays on the record, I'll never get work on another ship."

Stone-hearted, the captain refused to modify his entry. "It is the truth, and it shall remain on the record."

A few days later the captain was checking over the log and came across an entry written by the mate: "Captain was sober today." The outraged captain summoned the mate and accused him of creating a false impression. "Anyone reading this will think my sobriety was unusual, that I'm usually drunk!" he bellowed.

"The statement is true," the mate calmly asserted, "and it will remain in the log."

I am free of all prejudice. I hate everyone equally.

—W. C. Fields

Optimism

What's the difference between an optimist and a pessimist?

An optimist created the airplane; a pessimist created the seat belts.

Hear about the easygoing guy who was given three weeks to live?

He took the last two weeks of July and the week between Christmas and New Years.

Confidence: what you start off with before you completely understand the situation.

Wife: You're always wishing for something you haven't got.

Husband: What else is there to wish for?

During his whistle-stop campaign for the presidency in 1948, Harry Truman is reputed to have asked a fellow in the crowd before him how he was intending to vote.

"Mr. Truman," came the reply, "I wouldn't vote for you if yours was the only name on the ballot."

Truman turned to an aide and instructed, "Put that man down as doubtful."

You know those seed catalogs? I think the pictures are posed by professional flowers getting fifty dollars an hour. I don't consider gardening so much growing flowers as burying seeds.

Things are bad. I saw two fellows downtown carrying those signs reading "The End Is Near"—and they were synchronizing their watches.

P

Paranoia

Friday afternoon I'm walking home from school and I'm watching some men build a new house. And the guy hammering on the roof calls me a paranoid little weirdo. In Morse code.

—Emo Phillips

I have an intense desire to return to the womb. Anybody's.

—Woody Allen

I've had a rough day. I put my shirt on and a button fell off. I picked up my briefcase and the handle fell off. I'm afraid to go to the bathroom.

—Scott Record, doing Rodney Dangerfield

I'm paranoid about everything. Even at home, on my stationary bike, I have an exercise mirror. . . . This is a rumor, but one of my uncles said that, apparently, at birth, I turned around and looked over my shoulder as I came out of the womb. I was paranoid. I thought maybe someone was following me.

—Richard Lewis

How many paranoid schizophrenics does it take to screw in a lightbulb?

Who wants to know?

It's hard to be nice to some paranoid schizophrenic *just because she lives in your body*!

—Judy Tenuta

I'm very insecure. I get depressed when I find out the people I hate don't like me. I'm kind of paranoid, too. I often think the car in front of me is following me the long way around.

—Dennis Miller

I wanted to go to the Paranoids Anonymous meeting, but they wouldn't tell me where it was.

Just because you're paranoid doesn't mean they're not out to get you.

Parenthood

My husband and I are either going to buy a dog or have a child. We can't decide whether to ruin our carpet or ruin our lives.

—Rita Rudner

Nowadays you can't even spank your kids. No, gotta give 'em a time-out. My dad would take time out of his busy day . . . to whip our ass.

—Jeff Foxworthy

Two law partners can't resist hiring a gorgeous young reception-ist, and despite promises to the contrary, neither can resist going to bed with her. And not too long afterward, their worst fears are realized. The blushing receptionist announces that she's preg-nant. No one even knows who the father is, and the partners are in a complete quandary. So toward the end of the pregnancy, they decide to chip in and send the girl off to Florida to have the baby.

Several months go by with no news. Finally, one of the part-ners feels so guilty that he hops on a flight to Miami to go check on the young mother. The next night the phone rings in their New York office.

"How is she?" asks his partner.

"Oh, she's fine," is the breezy answer, "but I've got some bad news and some good news."

"Oh yeah? What's the good news?"

"Well, like I said, Jeannette's fine. And she had twins."

"So what's the bad news?" asked the partner from New York.

"Mine died."

I will never understand children. I never pretended to. I meet mothers all the time who make resolutions to themselves. "I'm going to . . . go out of my way to show them I am interested in them and what they do. I am going to understand my children." These women end up making rag rugs, using blunt scissors.

—ERMA BOMBECK

One day Jason burst into the house and said, "Mom! Dad! I have great news: I'm getting married to the greatest girl in the world. Florence has agreed to marry me."

But that night Jason's dad took him aside for a little chat. "I have some bad news for you, son," he confessed. "See, I used to fool around a lot, and Florence is actually your half-sister. I'm afraid you can't marry her."

Jason was brokenhearted, and moped around for a good six months, but eventually he started dating again. And a year or so later he came home with happy tidings. "Vickie said yes! We're getting married in October, isn't that great?!"

Alas, Jason's father insisted on another private conversation and broke the bad news again. "Vickie's your half-sister, too, son. I'm awfully sorry."

This time Jason was beside himself with anger and grief, and he finally confessed to his mother. "At this rate I'm never going to get married," he moaned. "Every time I fall in love, Dad says the girl's my half-sister."

"Don't pay any attention to him, Jason," said his mother cheerfully. "See, I did some fooling around myself, and he's not your father."

When you're a parent, you're a prisoner of war. You can't go anywhere without paying someone to come and look after your kids. In the old days, babysitters were fifty cents an hour, they'd steam clean the carpet and detail your car. Now they've got their own union. I couldn't afford it, so I had my mother come over. The sitters called her a scab and beat her up on the front lawn.

—ROBERT G. LEE

You become about as exciting as your food blender. The kids come in, look you in the eye, and ask if anybody's home.

—ERMA BOMBECK

Mrs. Caesar to Caesar: No way we're naming this kid "Sid."

—RED BUTTONS

Politicians and Politics

The drinking age should be eighteen. When you're eighteen you're old enough to vote. You should be old enough to drink. Look who we have to vote for! You need a drink.

—MARC PRICE

Politics is the art of looking for trouble, finding it everywhere, diagnosing it incorrectly, and applying the wrong remedies.

—GROUCHO MARX

What's one advantage of electing a woman president of the United States?
   We wouldn't have to pay her as much.

Jack Benny told about the time Joe E. Lewis met Harry Truman at the White House. The president asked if there was anything he could do for him.

"Well," said Joe E., "I've had some bad horses lately, Mr. President. Can you get me an advance on my Social Security?"

If anybody comes up to you and says, "My kid is a conservative, why is that?" you say, "Remember in the sixties when we told you, if you kept using drugs, your kids would be mutants?"

—Mort Sahl

All the problems we face in the Unites States today can be traced to an unenlightened immigration policy on the part of the American Indian.

—Pat Paulsen

Voting in this election is like trying to decide which street mime to stop and watch.

—A. Whitney Brown

He who builds a better mousetrap will soon find the government spending eight hundred and fifty thousand dollars to build a better mouse.

There were four million people in the Colonies, and we had Jefferson and Paine and Franklin. Now we have two hundred and forty million and we have Bush and Quayle. What can you draw from this? Darwin was wrong.

—Mort Sahl

What's the difference between baseball and politics?
In baseball you're out if you're caught stealing.

It was a terrific election. Ninety-five million Americans took time off from work to vote, and sixty-eight million of them did.

The Homeland Security system. They had it color coded, like we're in fucking elementary school! Simplify it, there should be just three levels of security: Jesus Christ, Goddammit, FUCK ME!

—LEWIS BLACK

I went to the White House, met the president. We in trouble.

—RICHARD PRYOR

LBJ always told the truth, except when his lips moved.

—RED BUTTONS

About a month ago the president of the United States decided he had to get laid. Going to a high-class whorehouse, he found a blond, a redhead, and a brunette waiting in the downstairs lounge. "I'm the president of the United States," he said to the blond. "How much will it cost me to spend a little time with you?"

"Three hundred dollars," was her answer.

To the redhead he posed the same question.

She replied, "Five hundred dollars."

He made the same proposition to the brunette.

She replied, "Mr. President, if you can raise my skirt as high as my taxes, lower my panties as far as my wages, get your dick as hard as the times, keep it hard for as long as I have to wait in line at the store, keep me warmer than my apartment in the winter, and screw me like you do the public, believe me, Mr. President, it isn't going to cost you a dime."

A politician running for office was outraged at certain remarks that had been made about him in the local newspaper. Incensed, he barged into the editorial room of the paper and shouted, "You are printing lies about me, and you know it!"

"Relax," the editor said calmly, "What on God's green earth would you do if we told the truth about you?"

State legislators are merely politicians whose darkest secret prohibits them from running for higher office.

—Dennis Miller

Liberals think you can reform an ax murderer. They don't want to kill anything. They want to change the Listerine labels: "*Rehabilitate* the germs that can cause bad breath."

—Marc Price

The man with the best job in the country is the vice president. All he has to do is get up every morning and say, "How's the president?"

—Will Rogers

Folks, the President needs a break. He's like a Black & Decker vacuum. If you don't recharge his batteries, he can't suck.

—Stephen Colbert

Concluding a powerful and impassioned speech enumerating his many splendid qualities, the candidate finally asked if anyone had any questions.

"Yes, sir," called out a voice from the crowd. "Who else is running?"

Diplomacy is the art of saying, "Nice doggie," until you can find a rock.

—Will Rogers

If you've got 'em by the balls, their hearts and minds will follow.

—Sign in the White House office of Charles Colson

Ninety-eight percent of the adults in this country are decent, hardworking Americans. It's the other lousy two percent that get all the publicity. But then—we elected them.

—Lily Tomlin

How do you know when a liberal is really dead?
His heart stops bleeding.

I hear that the Democrats are considering changing their emblem from a donkey to a condom because a condom stands for inflation, halts production, discourages cooperation, protects a bunch of dicks, and gives one a sense of security while screwing others.

Democrats are better lovers than Republicans. You've never heard of a good piece of elephant, have you?

—MILTON BERLE

As far as the men who are running for president are concerned, they aren't even people I would date.

—NORA EPHRON

Political speeches are like a steer: A point here, a point there, and a lot of bull in between.

Being in politics is like being a football coach. You have to be smart enough to understand the game and dumb enough to think it's important.

What's a WASP's idea of affirmative action?
Hiring South American jockeys.

A farmer was out working in his field one day when a carload of politicians came flying by. They were going too fast for the curve and turned over in the ditch. Later the sheriff stopped by and asked the farmer if he has seen the car.
"Yep," replied the farmer.
"Where are they?" asked the sheriff.
"Over there," replied the farmer, pointing to the ditch filled with fresh dirt.

"You buried them?" asked the sheriff, "Were they still alive?"

Replied the farmer, "They said they were, but you know how those people lie."

How many presidents does it take to change a lightbulb?

None. They'll only promise change.

Reporter One: The cult members seem totally brainwashed, and still place their blind faith in a false savior offering hollow promises of salvation!

Reporter Two: And that concludes our report from the White House.

Poverty

I used to think I was poor. Then they told me I wasn't poor, I was needy. Then they told me it was self-defeating to think of myself as needy. I was deprived. Then they told me that underprivileged was overused. I was disadvantaged. I still don't have a dime. But I have a great vocabulary.

—Jules Feiffer

We were poor when I was young, but the difference then was the government didn't come around telling you you were poor.

—Ronald Reagan

The trouble with being poor is that it takes up all your time.

—Willem de Kooning

When Mike showed up for his appointment with the urologist, the doctor informed him a sperm sample was necessary and instructed him to go to Room Four. Dutifully going down the hall, Mike opened the door to Room Four and found two absolutely gorgeous women clad in scanty lingerie. They proceeded to arouse him beyond his wildest dreams, and Mike headed back down the hall with a dreamy smile and a terrific sperm sample.

Realizing he had to pee, Mike opened the door to the first bathroom he came across, only to interrupt a guy frantically beating off with a copy of *Hustler*. In the second bathroom a fellow was busy masturbating with the company of the *Penthouse* centerfold. Back in the doctor's office and curious as hell, Mike couldn't resist asking the doctor about the other two fellows.

"Oh, those guys?" replied the doctor dismissively. "Those're my Medicaid patients."

Thousands upon thousands are yearly brought into a state of real poverty by their great anxiety not to be thought poor.

—WILLIAM COBBETT

Problems

If at first you don't succeed, try, try again. Then quit. No use being a damn fool about it.

—W. C. FIELDS

No problem is too big to run away from.

—CHARLES M. SCHULZ

The shopkeeper was dismayed when a brand-new business much like his own opened up next door and erected a huge sign which read, "Best Deals." He was horrified when another competitor opened up on his right, and announced its arrival with an even larger sign, reading, "Lowest Prices." The shopkeeper was panicked, until he got an idea. He put the biggest sign of all over his own shop—it read, "Main Entrance."

Wendy found that her difficulty making even the simplest decisions was causing her problems on the job. Finally she decided to seek professional help.

"Tell me, Wendy," the psychiatrist began gently, "I understand you have trouble making decisions. Is that so?"

Wendy's brow furrowed. "Well," she finally answered, "yes . . . and no."

By trying, we can easily learn to endure adversity. Another man's, I mean.

—Mark Twain

Promiscuity

A man picks up a young woman in a bar and convinces her to come back to his hotel. When they are relaxing afterward, he asks, "Am I the first man you ever made love to?"

She looks at him thoughtfully for a second before replying. "You might be," she says. "Your face looks familiar."

What's the difference between Virginia and West Virginia?

In Virginia, moosehead is a beer. In West Virginia, it's a misdemeanor.

People in cars cause accidents. Accidents in cars cause people.

As the newlywed couple was checking into the hotel for their honeymoon, another couple at the desk offered to show them around the town that night. Thanking them for the kind offer, the bridegroom explained that it was their wedding night and that they'd prefer to take a rain check.

When the second couple came down to breakfast the next morning, they were astonished to catch sight of the groom in the hotel

bar apparently drowning his sorrows. "Why, you should be the happiest man in the world today," they said, coming over to him.

"Yesterday I was," said the man mournfully, "but this morning, without realizing it, I put three ten-dollar bills on the pillow and got up to get dressed."

"Hey, cheer up, she probably didn't even notice."

"That's the problem," the groom went on. "Without even thinking, she gave me five dollars change."

On their wedding night, a groom asks his new bride, "Honey, am I your first?"

She says, "Why does everyone ask me that?"

—GENE BAYLOS

"Doctor, I've got this problem," the man says. "My secretary, she loves to give blow jobs. Every morning when I get to work, I get a blow job. She gives me a quick one before I leave for lunch. And before I leave work at the end of the day, she really works me over."

"So what seems to be the problem?" the doctor asked.

"Well, you see, my wife is a nymphomaniac," the man continued. "I service her every morning when we get up. I go home for a quick half hour every day at lunchtime, and then we have a marathon session each night before we go to sleep."

"I still don't know what your problem is," said the doctor.

"You see, Doc, every time I masturbate, I get these dizzy spells."

A certain virginal and shy college freshman was lucky to have a roommate who was considerably more experienced. When the bashful boy broke down and explained his predicament, his roommate was quick to offer to set him up with the campus floozie. "Just take her out to dinner and a show and then let nature take its course," he explained reassuringly. "This girl knows what the score is."

The roommate arranged the date as promised, and the freshman took the coed out for a delightful evening of dining and dancing. On the way home, he parked his car in a dark lane, broke out in a cold sweat, and blurted out, "Gosh, I sure would love to have a little pussy."

"I would, too," she sighed. "Mine's the size of a milk pail."

An amateur golfer playing in his first tournament was delighted when a beautiful girl came up to him after the round and suggested he come over to her place for a while. The fellow was a bit embarrassed to explain that he really couldn't stay all night but that he'd be glad to come over for a while. Twenty minutes later they were in her bed making love. And when it was over, he got out of bed and started getting dressed.

"Hey," called the girl from beneath the covers, "where do you think you're going? Arnold Palmer wouldn't leave so early."

At that the golfer stripped off his clothes and jumped on top of her. After they'd made love a second time, he got out of bed and put his pants back on.

"What are you up to?" she called. "Jack Nicklaus wouldn't think of leaving now." So the golfer pulled off his pants and screwed her a third time, and afterward, he started getting dressed.

"C'mon, you can't leave yet," protested the girl. "Lee Trevino wouldn't call it a day."

"Lady, would you tell me one thing?" asked the golfer, looking at her very seriously. "What's par for this hole?"

What do you give the man who has everything?

Antibiotics.

The thing that takes up the least amount of time and causes the most trouble is sex.

—John Barrymore

A guy walks into a bar and says, "G-g-gimme a b-b-beer."

The bartender says, "Seems you've got a stuttering problem.

The guy says, "N-n-no sh-sh-shit."

The bartender says, "I used to stutter, but my wife cured me. One afternoon she sucked me off three times in a row, and I haven't stuttered since."

The guy says, "W-w-wow, th-th-that's great to kn-kn-know. . . ."

A week later, the same guy walks into the bar, and says, "G-g-gimme a b-b-beer."

The bartender says, "Why didn't you try what I told you?"

The guy says, "I d-d-did. It d-d-didn't w-w-work. B-b-but I m-m-must say, you have a r-r-really nice apartment."

A woman who had outlived no less than eight husbands finally passed away. Old friends and enemies alike gathered at the graveside and consoled or bitched with one another, as is so often the way.

"Oh, well, at least they'll be together again," sighed one of the departed's lady friends.

"Yes," replied a childhood friend with a sob, "but with which husband?"

"No, silly," said the first friend, "I meant her legs."

What do you call a New Zealander with four sheep?

A pimp.

What's the difference between kinky and perverted?

Kinky is when you use a feather. Perverted is when you use the whole chicken.

Prostitution

A guy walks up to a hooker and asks, "How much do you charge to rub the genitals?"

She says, "The same as the Jews."

—Norm Crosby

What chain of food stores do prostitutes patronize?
Stop 'n Blow.

A guy runs out of a burning hotel wearing only a hat and carrying his jacket and pants in his arms. He runs up to a fireman and asks, "Have you seen a redhead with big tits and a nice ass?"
The fireman says, "No."
The guy says, "Well if you see her, give her a fuck for me since I already paid for it."

—RED BUTTONS

A tired-looking old prostitute walked into a bar with a pigeon on her head and shouted, "Whoever can guess the weight of this bird can fuck me!"
Way in the back of the bar, a drunk yelled, "One thousand pounds!"
"Close enough," she answered cheerfully.

Did you hear about the prostitute who failed her driver's test three times?
She couldn't learn to sit up in a car.

The young Australian sailor couldn't wait for shore leave in the Big Apple. He lost no time picking up a hooker and bringing her back to his hotel room. Asking her to undress, he proceeded to lean the bed up against the wall and toss every other article of furniture out the window, down the air shaft.
"What on earth are you planning to do with me?" asked the hooker nervously.
"I'm not exactly sure, Ma'am," answered the Australian, "but if it's anything like it is with a kangaroo, we'll need all the room we can get."

Nussbaum the peddler was busted for selling woolen hats without a license, and he was hauled into court along with three prostitutes who had been arraigned on the same day.

"It's all a case of mistaken identity," protested the first street-walker to be summoned before the bench. "I'm mindin' my own business when this car pulls up—"

"Drop it," interrupted the judge. "I've seen you in this courthouse at least a dozen times before. That'll be a hundred and fifty dollars, and it'll be twice that if I set eyes on you again. Next!"

The second hooker whined, "I was just on my way to night school, Judge, to learn how to make an honest dollar, when—"

"Cut the crap," the magistrate broke in. "Two hundred and fifty bucks or ten days in jail—you choose. Next!"

The third woman came forward and declared, "Your Honor, I plead guilty: I'm a prostitute. It's not the living I'd choose, but it's the only way I can make enough to feed and clothe my family, so it's what I do."

The judge smiled. "Finally, someone who realizes a courtroom is a place to tell the truth. To reward your honesty, young woman, I'm dismissing your case. In fact, Mr. O'Brien"—he turned and summoned the bailiff— "make sure Miss Cardoza gets seventy-five dollars from the Policemen's Benevolent Fund. Next?"

Up stepped Nussbaum the peddler, who had been paying close attention. "Your Honor," he said frankly, "I'm not gonna lie to you either. I'm a prostitute."

What do you get when you cross an elephant and a prostitute?
A hooker who does it for peanuts and won't ever forget you.

Harry and his wife are having hard times, so they decide she'll become a hooker. She's not sure what to do, so Harry says, "Stand in front of that bar and pick up a guy. Tell him a hundred bucks. If you've got a question, I'll be parked around the corner."

She's not in front of the bar for five minutes when a guy pulls up in a car and says, "How much?"

She says, "A hundred dollars."

He says, "Shit. All I've got is thirty."

She says, "Hold on."

She runs back to Harry and says, "What can he get for thirty dollars?"

Harry says, "A hand job."

She runs back and tells the guy all he gets for thirty dollars is a hand job. He says okay, she gets in the car, he unzips his pants, and out pops a huge cock.

She stares at it for a minute, and then says, "I'll be right back."

She runs back around the corner and says, "Harry, can you loan this guy seventy bucks?"

A young hillbilly goes into a whorehouse and says, "I want a woman, but I've always been scared, because my momma told me a woman has teeth between her legs."

The whore says, "Don't be silly. I'll take care of you." She takes him up to a room, gets undressed, lies on the bed, and spreads her legs. "See," she says, "there's no teeth between my legs."

The kid says, "Of course you ain't got no teeth down there. Look at the shape your gums are in."

I broke into show business the hard way; I played piano in a whorehouse.

—RED BUTTONS

Psychiatrists and Psychiatry

A psychiatrist is a fellow who asks you a lot of expensive questions your wife asks you for nothing.

—JOEY ADAMS

The well-meaning social worker was seeing if Mrs. Englehardt qualified for admission to the local nursing home, and part of the stan-
dard procedure was a test for senility. "And what's this?" she asked
sweetly of the old German woman, who was sitting at the dinner
table.

"Dot? Dot's a spoon," answered Mrs. Englehardt.

"Very good," said the social worker. "And this?"

"Dot's a fork," answered the old woman.

"*Very* good. And this?" asked the social worker, holding up a
knife.

"Dot's a phallic symbol."

An assembly-line worker became increasingly obsessed with his
desire to stick his penis into the pickle slicer. Finally, worried
that he'd be unable to control the desire, he sought the advice of
a psychiatrist.

"You know, I had a case not unlike this one a few months ago,"
said Dr. Bernstein, thoughtfully rubbing his beard, "a man who
kept wanting to put his hand on a hot stove."

"So what happened?" asked the factory worker.

"He went ahead and did it," confessed the doctor, "and he
burned himself, but he never had the desire again. So my advice
is to go ahead and follow your impulse in order to free yourself."

"Okay, Doc." And the patient left.

At his next appointment, the doctor asked what had happened.

"I took your advice," said the man, "and stuck my penis into
the pickle slicer."

"So then what happened?" asked the psychiatrist, leaning
forward eagerly.

"We both got fired."

My superiority complex turned out to be an inferiority complex. I
said, "Great, that makes me the least of my problems."

—SARA B. SIRIUS

A man was attacked and left bleeding in a ditch. Two psychiatrists passed by and one said to the other, "We must find the man who did this—he needs help."

Why did the Siamese twins go to a shrink?
  They were co-dependent.

The man came into the psychiatrist's office, lay down on the couch, and told the doctor he needed help ridding his mind of an obsession. "All I can think of, day and night, is making love to a horse. It's driving me nuts."
  "I see," said the shrink, rubbing his goatee. "Now, would that be to a stallion or to a mare?"
  "A mare, of course," retorted the patient, pulling himself upright indignantly. "What do you think I am, a pervert or something?"

Nerve is going to a psychiatrist because of a split personality and asking for a group rate.

The seriously disturbed man slunk into the office of an eminent psychiatrist.
  "Doctor, you have to help me, it's gotten really bad," he pleaded. "I feel like nobody ever listens to me."
  The psychiatrist looked up and said, "Next!"

How many psychiatrists does it take to change a lightbulb?
  One. But the lightbulb has to really want to change.

I was in analysis. I was suicidal. As a matter of fact, I would have killed myself, but I was in analysis with a strict Freudian and if you kill yourself, they make you pay for the sessions you miss.

—WOODY ALLEN

Summoning the patient into his office, the psychiatrist shot her a radiant smile. "You know, Claudia, in this profession one rarely uses the word 'cure,' but after five years of therapy, it is my pleasure to pronounce you one hundred percent cured!" he announced proudly.

To his surprise, an unhappy look came over the woman's face. "What's wrong?" asked the doctor. "This is a success for me and a triumph for you—I thought you'd be thrilled."

"Oh, it's fine for you," she finally snapped, "but look at it from my point of view. Three years ago I was Joan of Arc. Now I'm nobody."

"I wouldn't worry about your son playing with dolls," the doctor told the middle-aged matron.

She said, "I'm not worried, but his wife is very upset."

—Joey Adams

I finally had an orgasm and my doctor told me it was the wrong kind.

—Woody Allen and Marshall Brickman

Aunt Jean was rattling along in her Oldsmobile when she got a flat tire. Being an independent sort, she jacked up the car and undid the nuts and bolts, but as she was pulling the tire off, she lost her balance and fell backward onto the hubcap holding the hardware. And it rolled right down into a storm sewer.

This entire incident occurred outside the state insane asylum and happened to be observed by an inmate watching carefully through an open but barred window.

"Listen, lady," he called out, "just use one bolt from each of the other three tires. They'll be plenty strong enough to get you to the gas station."

"Quick thinking," said Aunt Jean admiringly. "Now why on earth is a bright boy like you stuck in that place?"

"Lady, I may be crazy, but I'm not stupid."

You know how everyone wants a second opinion these days? Well, this lady had been going to a psychiatrist for years and finally she decided she'd had enough of it. "Doctor," she announced, walking into his office, "I've been seeing you every week for five years now. I don't feel any better, I don't feel any worse. What's the story? I want you to level with me. What's wrong with me?"

"All right," said the doctor, "I'll tell you. You're crazy."

"Now wait just a minute," she protested. "I think I'm entitled to a second opinion."

"Fine," he responded. "You're ugly, too."

—MEL CALMAN

I had to give up masochism—I was enjoying it too much.

Two women were comparing notes on their psychotherapists. "Frankly, mine drives me crazy," said Eileen. "Three years I've been going to her now and she never says a single word to me. Just sits there and nods."

"That's nothing," responded Ruthie. "After six years I finally get three words out of mine."

"Oh yeah? What'd he say?"

" '*No hablo ingles.*' "

I went to this conference for bulemics and anorexics. It was a nightmare. The bulemics ate the anorexics. It's okay—they were back again ten minutes later.

—MONICA PIPER

After the woman seated herself in the psychiatrist's office, the doctor asked, "What seems to be the problem?"

"Well, I, uh," she stammered. "I think I, uh, might be a nymphomaniac."

"I see," he said. "I can help you, but I must advise you that my fee is eighty dollars an hour."

"That's not bad," she replied. "How much for all night?"

A man goes to a psychiatrist and tells him, "Doc, I think I'm obsessed with sex."

"Well, let's do a few tests," the doctor says. He draws a square on a piece of paper and asks the man to identify it.

The man immediately says, "Sex."

Next the doctor draws a circle, which the man again identifies as sex.

Then the doctor draws a triangle, which, of course, the patient identifies as sex.

The doctor puts the drawings away and says to the patient, "Yes, I do believe you have an obsession with sex."

To which the man replies, "I'm not the one with the obsession! *You're* the one drawing all the dirty pictures!"

A writer from *Better Homes and Gardens* goes to an insane asylum to interview Horace Schmeeley, an inmate who is reported to be an amazing landscape gardener. As Horace shows the interviewer around the grounds, she is flabbergasted. Everything is immaculate. The flowers are beautiful, the grass is perfectly manicured, and the trees are expertly pruned. And his running commentary on each shrub and bush is equally impressive. She can't believe it. Here's this guy in an insane asylum, and he's probably the most talented gardener and landscape designer she's ever met, with an inexhaustable knowledge of every aspect of gardening.

At the end of the tour, she says to Horace, "I am enormously impressed with your work. Not only am I going to write a feature article about you and your work, but I'm going to petition my congressman to have you released from here, so you can get a good job on the outside. Your considerable talents shouldn't go to waste."

She turns and walks away. When she gets about twenty feet away from him, a huge brick flies into the back of her head and Horace yells, "You won't forget about me, will you?"

A man who had been in a mental institution for some years finally seemed to have improved to the point where it was thought he might be released. The psychiatrist who headed the institution, with commendable caution, decided, however, to interview him first.

"Tell me," said he, "if we release you, as we are considering doing, what do you intend to do with your life?"

The inmate said, "It would be wonderful to get back to real life and, if I do, I will certainly refrain from making my former mistake. I was a nuclear physicist, you know, and it was the stress of my work in weapons research that helped to put me here. If I am released, I shall confine myself to work in pure theory, where I trust the situation will be less difficult and stressful."

"Marvelous," said the psychiatrist.

"Or else," ruminated the inmate, "I might teach. There is something to be said for spending one's life in developing a new generation of scientists."

"Absolutely," said the psychiatrist.

"Then again, I might write. There is considerable need for books on science for the general public. Or I might even write a novel based on my experiences in this fine institution."

"An interesting possibility," said the psychiatrist.

"And finally, if none of these things appeals to me, I can always continue to be a teakettle."

How many psychoanalysts does it take to screw in a lightbulb?

How many do you think it takes?

Why is psychoanalysis a lot quicker for men than for women?

When it's time to go back to their childhood, men are already there.

R

Religion

Why is it when we talk to God, we're said to be praying, but when God talks to us, we're schizophrenic?

—LILY TOMLIN

If God's got anything better than sex to offer, he's certainly keeping it to himself.

—STING

A church is a place in which gentlemen who have never been to heaven brag about it to persons who will never get there.

—H. L. MENCKEN

And we are told in the Scriptures that at the beginning of time the Lord said, "Let there be light." But I've checked with a number of eminent Biblical scholars and they say the Lord's complete statement was as follows: "Let there be light. Well, maybe not all day."

—STEVE ALLEN

I'd like to come back as an oyster. Then I'd only have to be good from September until April.

—GRACIE ALLEN

When one of the angels asked God where he's going on holiday this year, God replied, "Certainly not to Earth again. I went there about two millennia ago, got a little Jewish girl pregnant—and they haven't stopped talking about it since!"

Hear about the New Age church in California?

It has three commandments and seven suggestions.

So . . . after Adam was created, there he was in the Garden of Eden. Of course, it wasn't good for him to be all by himself, so the Lord came down to visit.

"Adam," He said, "I have a plan to make you much, much happier. I'm going to give you a companion, a helpmate for you— someone who will fulfill your every need and desire. Someone who will be faithful, loving, and obedient. Someone who will make you feel wonderful every day of your life."

Adam was stunned. "That sounds incredible!"

"Well, it is," replied the Lord. "But it doesn't come for free. In fact, this is someone so special that it's going to cost you an arm and a leg."

"That's a pretty high price to pay," said Adam. "What can I get for a rib?"

Jesus was walking in the rain one day, and he passed the shop of Samson, who made clothes. Samson called out to Jesus and gave him a cloak he had just made. Jesus's cloak was admired by everyone. Everywhere he preached, people exclaimed about the workmanship of the cloak.

When Samson met Jesus six months from the day that he had given him the cloak, he said, "Jesus, we've got a great thing going here. Since people have seen you wearing your cloak, I have had so many orders for others like it. I think we should go into business together. The only problem I'm having is trying to decide what to call the business. Should it be called 'Samson and Jesus' or 'Jesus and Samson'?"

"How about Lord and Taylor?" Jesus responded.

If God dwells inside us like some people say, I sure hope He likes enchiladas, because that's what He's getting.

—JACK HANDEY

Going to war over religion is basically killing each other to see who's got the better imaginary friend.

—Richard Jeni

I was talking to Jesus, and I said, "Jesus, I feel like no one will ever accept me." And Jesus looked at me and said, "You know what my theory is? Accept me or go to hell."

—Gilbert Gottfried

Freaks everywhere. I went to a church in Chicago. Church had six commandments and four do-the-best-you-cans.

—George Wallace

Catholicism

A priest and a businessman were playing golf. After playing several holes, the businessman's game takes a turn for the worse.

"Damn! I missed!" he swears, as his ball lands in a sand bunker.

The priest is understandably shocked and admonishes the businessman, "Do not swear, my son. You will incur God's wrath."

The next time the businessman fails, however, he exclaims again, "Damn! I missed!"

The priest gets very angry and scolds him severely: "My son, you place yourself in great jeopardy by your words!"

But alas, as the businessman's ball again fails to roll where he wants it to, he yells loudly: "Damn, I missed!"

Suddenly a lightning bolt strikes from the clear sky and reduces the priest to a pile of smoldering ash, and a booming voice from heaven shouts: "Damn! I missed!"

"Someone stole my bike," complained a priest to his minister friend.

"Bring up the ten commandments in your sermon tomorrow and

as soon as you mention 'Thou shalt not steal,' the guilty party will come forward," the minister said confidently.

The next day, the priest visited the minister and happily reported he'd found his bike. "Yes," he went on, "when I came to 'Thou shalt not commit adultery,' I remembered where I'd left it."

A priest is sent to Alaska. After a few years the bishop goes to visit him. "How are you doing up here?" the bishop asks.

"It's really cold," the priest answers. "If it weren't for my Rosary and my two martinis every evening, I wouldn't make it. By the way, would you like a martini?"

"Sure," the bishop says.

The priest says, "Rosary, bring the bishop a martini."

—Henny Youngman

An ambitious new sales rep for Budweiser beer traveled all the way to Rome and managed to get an audience with the Pope himself. As soon as the two were alone together, he leaned over and whispered, "Your Holiness, I have an offer I think might interest you. I'm in a position to give you a million dollars if you'll change the wording in the Lord's Prayer to 'our daily beer.' Now whaddaya say?"

"Absolutely not," said the shocked pontiff.

"Hey, I understand; it's a big decision," sympathized the salesman. "How about five million dollars?"

"I couldn't think of it," sputtered the Pope.

"I know it's a tough one. Tell you what—I can go up to fifty million dollars," proposed the salesman.

Asking him to leave the room, the Pope called in the cardinal and whispered, "When does our contract with Pillsbury expire?"

I am one of those cliff-hanging Catholics. I don't believe in God, but I do believe that Mary was his mother.

—Martin Sheen

When the golfer went to retrieve his ball from deep in the woods, he was startled to come across a witch stirring a huge cauldron. Observing the steaming green brew with fascination, he finally asked, "What's in there?"

"A magic brew," hissed the witch. "One swig and you'll play better golf than anyone in the world. You'll be unbeatable."

"Fantastic!" exclaimed the golfer, his eyes lighting up. "Let me have some."

"Hold your horses," cackled the hag gleefully. "There's a catch. You'll pay for it with your sex life: it'll become the worst in the world."

The man stopped to think it over. "No sex . . . great golf . . ." he mused. "Give me a cup."

Finding his ball, the golfer headed out of the woods, finished his game in no time, and went on to whip the club champion that afternoon. Soon he became the best golfer in the country, constantly on tour, but a year later he found himself on the same course. Out of curiosity he went back into the woods, and sure enough the witch was still there, stirring her brew.

"You again," she wheezed, looking up blearily. "How's your golf game?"

He recited his latest triumphs on the circuit.

"And your sex life?" The witch tittered malevolently, but her expression changed to surprise when he answered, "Not bad."

"Not bad? How many times have you gotten laid this year?" The witch's curiosity had clearly gotten the best of her.

"Three, maybe four times," answered the golfer.

I'm a Catholic and I can't commit suicide, but I plan to drink myself to death.

—JACK KEROUAC

A nun was driving on the highway late on a chilly October afternoon and stopped to pick up a hitchhiker. He was a handsome fellow and the nun looked him over from head to toe, then blushed and quickly looked away. But soon enough her gaze wandered over to him again, and when it happened a third time, her passenger said bluntly, "Sister, I have to come right out and say I find you very attractive and I'd like to have sex with you right now."

Turning beet red, the nun began protesting that it would be absolutely impossible. Not only was she the bride of Christ, she had taken a vow of celibacy, and besides, it would be a sin.

"Good point," admitted the hitchhiker coolly, "but if you don't let me have sex with you, I'll kill myself—and that'll be a mortal sin for me. How could you have that on your conscience?"

The nun thought hard, then asked, "Are you Catholic?"

The hitchhiker assured her that he was.

"Are you married?"

"I'm as single as you are, Sister," he promised.

"All right," she said, "then I'll agree to having anal intercourse with you. That will only be a venial sin." She pulled over, they went off into the woods and had sex, and then got back in the car. A few miles down the road, the hitchhiker admitted he had a confession to make. "I really enjoyed that, Sister, but I lied to you: I'm Protestant."

The nun blanched.

"And that's not all," the hitchhiker went on unhappily. "I've got a wife and two kids."

The nun turned even paler, and her hands trembled on the steering wheel. But after a few minutes of silence, she said, "Well, there's something you should know about me, too. My name's Bob, and I'm on my way to a Halloween party."

Did you hear the one about the man who opened a dry-cleaning business next door to a convent? He knocked on the door and asked the Mother Superior if she had any dirty habits.

I like when people give up chocolate for Lent. Ooh, just like being nailed to a cross.

—GREG GIRALDO

Following the Vatican declaration that women cannot become priests because they do not resemble Christ, sources reported that Colonel Sanders declared that he would not employ anyone who didn't resemble a chicken.

—JANE CURTIN

The Pope and Jesse James die at the same time and meet on the way to their prospective destinations. After a brief discussion, they proceed on, but due to some unforeseen confusion, Jesse winds up in heaven and the Pope goes to hell!

After a few hours, the error is caught and they again meet on the way to their final resting places.

The Pope says, "Boy, I was worried for a while. I always wanted to meet the Virgin Mary."

Says Jesse, "I think you're too late."

Mother Superior: Sister Maria, if you were walking through town at night, and you were accosted by a man with bad intentions, what would you do?

Sister Maria: I would lift my habit, Mother Superior.

Mother Superior (shocked): And what would you do next?

Sister Maria: I would tell him to drop his pants.

Mother Superior: (even more shocked) And what then?

Sister Maria: I would run away. I can run much faster with my habit up than he can with his pants down.

Paddy O'Casey was on his deathbed when his wife, Colleen, tiptoed into the bedroom and asked if he had any last requests.

"Actually, my dear, there is one thing I really would like before I go off to that great shamrock patch in the sky," Paddy whispered. "A piece of that wonderful chocolate cake of yours."

"Oh, but you can't have that," his wife exclaimed. "I'm saving it for the wake."

A priest asks a nun if he can walk her back to the convent. She says, "Just this once." Upon arriving, he asks if he can kiss her.

She replies, "Well, all right, as long as you don't get into the habit."

A priest decides to pay a visit to a nearby convent. The convent is in a rundown neighborhood, and as the priest walks down the street, several prostitutes approach and proposition him, "Twenty bucks a trick!"

These solicitations embarrass the priest, who lowers his head and hurries on until he gets to the convent. Once inside, he displays his naiveté by asking the Mother Superior, "What is a trick?"

She answers, "Twenty bucks—just like on the outside!"

This guy went to confession. I went with him, we were kids. And he confessed that he had had sex with a girl in his parish. The priest asked, "Was it Mary Agnardi?" He said no.

"Was is Felice Endrini?" asked the priest. He said no.

"Was it Elise Guini?" He said no.

The priest said, "You're gonna do fifty Hail Marys and give me half your allowance on the plate for the next three weeks."

My friend came out of the confessional and I asked, "How'd you do?"

He said, "Not too bad, and I got three good leads!"

—BUDDY HACKETT

A nun goes to confession. "Oh, Father, I am ashamed. I was golfing with the other sisters, and I said the 'F' word."

"Oh, Sister, what made you say the 'F' word?"

"Well, I teed off the fifth hole, and sliced it into the woods."

"Sister, for that you said the 'F' word?"

"Oh no, I got out of that mess okay, only to land in a sand trap."

"Sister, for that you said the 'F' word?"

"Oh no! I got a good hit out of the trap, it bounced on the green, and rolled into the trap on the other side."

"Sister, for that you said the 'F' word?"

"Oh no, I hit it out of the trap, and came up six inches from the hole."

"Oh, Sister, for that you said the 'F' word?"

"Oh, heavens no, Father."

Then the priest interrupts and asks, "Sister, don't tell me you missed a fucking six-inch putt!"

Old Timothy O'Daly was clearly on his deathbed. So his son, Liam, was completely taken aback when the old man plucked at his sleeve, drew him close, and said, "My boy, it's time for you to go for the Protestant minister."

"But, Dad," gasped Liam, "what on earth would a good Catholic like yourself be wanting with a minister at a time like this—meaning no disrespect, of course."

"Get the minister," ordered O'Daly fiercely, and after a few more sputtering protests, his son hurried off to honor what might be his father's last request. He was back with the Reverend Wilson within forty-five minutes, and listened in dismay outside the door as the minister converted his father and administered the Protestant last rites.

His distress, however, paled beside that of Father McGuire, who hurried up the stairs past the departing Reverend Wilson. "Tim, Tim, why?" he cried, bursting into the old man's room. "We went to St. Joseph's together. We were altar boys at Our Lady of the Sacred Heart. I was there at your First Communion and you attended the first Mass I performed. How in the world could you do such a thing?"

"Paddy," said old O'Daly, leaning back against his pillows, "I figured if somebody had to go, better one of them than one of us."

Three nuns were walking along the street and one was describing with her hands the tremendous grapefruit she'd seen in Florida.

The second nun, also with her hands, described the huge banana she's seen in Jamaica.

The third nun, who was a little deaf, asked, "Father who?"

Old Andrzej was a priest in a small Polish town. He had always been a good man and lived by the Bible. One day, God decided to reward him with the answers to any three questions Andrzej would like to ask.

Old Andrzej did not need much time to consider, and his first question was: "Will there ever be married Catholic priests?"

God promptly replied, "Not in your lifetime."

Andrzej thought for a while, and then came up with the second question: "What about female priests then, will we have that one day?"

Again God had to disappoint old Andrzej: "Not in your lifetime, I'm afraid."

Andrzej was sorry to hear that, and he decided to drop the subject. Then, after thinking for a while, he asked the last question: "Will there ever be another Polish Pope?"

God answered quickly and in a firm voice: "Not in my lifetime."

Father Harris was motoring along a country lane in his parish on a spring afternoon when all of a sudden he got a flat tire. Exasperated, the priest stopped his car, got out, and assessed the damage. Luckily, a four-wheel-drive jeep rounded the bend and pulled to a stop behind the disabled vehicle. The door of the jeep opened and out stepped a powerful hulk of a man. "Good afternoon, Father," greeted the stranger. "Can I give you a hand?"

"Heaven be praised!" rejoiced the priest. "As you can see, my son, I have a flat tire, and I must admit, I've never changed one before."

"Don't worry about it, Father. I'll take care of it." And without skipping a beat, the bruiser picked up the front of the car with one hand and removed the lug nuts from the base of the flat tire with the other. "Why don't you get the spare from the trunk?" he asked.

"Why, ahh, yes, of course, my son," stuttered the amazed Father Harris. The priest rolled the spare around to the strong man, who casually lifted it up with his free hand, maneuvered it into place, and proceeded to tighten the lug nuts.

"Do you need the wrench?" the priest asked.

"That's okay," the fellow told him. "These nuts are as tight as the nuns I know."

"Hmmm," mused Father Harris. "I'd better get the wrench."

When the Mother Superior answered the knock at the convent door, she found two leprechauns shuffling their feet on the door sill. "Aye an' begorrah, Mother Superior," said the foremost one after an awkward pause, "would ye be havin' any leprechaun nuns in your convent?"

The nun shook her head solemnly.

The little man shuffled his feet a bit more, then piped up, "An' would there be any leprechaun nuns in the church?"

"No, my boys," said the Mother Superior gravely.

"Ye see, laddy," cried the first leprechaun, whirling around to his companion triumphantly. "I *told* you ye been fucking a penguin!"

Did you hear about the three nuns who were expelled from the nunnery?

They were caught doing pushups in the cucumber patch.

When the nuns were returning to their convent after their annual retreat in the mountains, the bus went over an embankment and four nuns were instantly killed. They materialized at the pearly gates, where St. Peter asked the first sister whether she had sinned during her time on earth. She blushed and confessed to having kissed a boy the day before taking her vows.

"Wash your lips in the holy water," ordered St. Peter, "and proceed into heaven. And you, Sister, have you sinned?"

The second nun blushed deeply and stammered, "St. Peter, I once touched a man's penis."

"Wash your hands in the holy water and you shall be cleansed and admitted into heaven." He turned expectantly to the remaining nuns, only to be startled by the sight of both of them fighting for position in front of the font of holy water. "Ladies, ladies," he remonstrated. "What in heaven's name is going on?"

"It's like this, St. Peter," replied one of the nuns. "I was last in line, but don't you think I should be allowed to gargle in the holy water before Bridget has to sit in it?"

The Pope calls a meeting of all the cardinals. After they have assembled in the meeting hall at the Vatican, the Pope says, "I have good news and bad news. The good news is that I just talked to Jesus. He has been resurrected, so our faith in his existence has been justified."

One of the cardinals stands up and says, "What's the bad news?"

The Pope replies, "He was calling from Salt Lake City."

When the Eisenbergs moved to Rome, little Jamie came home from school in tears. He explained to his mother that the nuns were always asking these Catholic questions and how was he, a nice Jewish boy, supposed to know the answers?

Mrs. Eisenberg's heart swelled with maternal sympathy and she determined to help her son out. "Jamie," she said, "I'm going to embroider the answers on the inside of your shirt and you just look down and read them the next time those nuns pick on you."

"Thanks, Mom," said Jamie, and he didn't bat an eye when Sister Michael asked him who the world's most famous virgin was. "Mary," he answered.

"Very good," said the nun. "And who was her husband?"

"Joseph," answered the boy.

"I see you've been studying. Now can you tell me the name of their son?

"Sure," said Jamie. "Calvin Klein."

A guy is walking into the doctor's office when a nun comes running out, screaming and crying.

The guy walks in and says, "Doc, what's with the nun?"

The doctor says, "Oh, I just told her she's pregnant."

The guy says, "The nun's pregnant?"

The doctor says, "No. But it certainly cured her hiccups."

During Bible study class, Freddie was much more interested in his new hot rod than in the lesson. His fidgeting didn't escape the nun's notice, so she decided to give him a spot quiz. "Who was God's son, Freddie?" she asked.

The girl behind Freddie poked him hard with her pencil and he cried out, "Jesus!"

"Very good," said the nun. "Now, who is the first member of the Holy Trinity?"

The girl poked Freddie even harder. "God Almighty!" he blurted.

"All right," said the Sister, deciding to throw him a trick question. "Now tell me what Eve said to Adam their first week together."

Once more the girl jabbed Freddie, and he screamed, "You prick me with that one more time and I'm going to shove it up your ass!"

When I was growing up, my mother wanted me to be a priest, but I think it's a tough occupation. Can you imagine giving up your sex life and then once a week people come in and tell you all the highlights of theirs?

—Tom Dreesen

"Father Reilly," the Mother Superior reported, "I just thought you should know that there's a case of syphilis in the convent."

"Oh, good," the priest replied. "I was really getting tired of the Chablis."

We were skeptical Catholics. We believed Jesus walked on water. We just figured it was probably winter.

—JOHN WING

Christianity

Born-again Christians . . . I'm a little indignant when they tell me I'm going to hell if I haven't been born again. Pardon me for getting it right the first time.

—DENNIS MILLER

Why don't Baptists make love standing up?

They're afraid it might lead to dancing.

Three fellows die and are transported to the pearly gates, where St. Peter explains that admission depends on a quick quiz, a mere formality. "I'm just going to ask each of you a single question," he explains, turning to the first guy. "What, please, is Easter?"

"That's easy. Easter is when you celebrate the Pilgrims' landing. You buy a turkey—"

"Sorry," interrupts St. Peter briskly, "you're out." And he asks the second man, "What can you tell me about Easter?"

"No problem," the fellow responded promptly. "That's when we commemorate Jesus's birth by going shopping, and decorating a tree—"

"No, no, no," St. Peter bursts out, and turns in exasperation to the last guy. "I don't suppose you know anything about Easter?"

"Certainly I do. See, Christ was crucified, and He died, and they took the body down from the cross and wrapped it in a shroud and put it in a cave and rolled this big stone across the entrance—"

"Hang on a sec," interrupts St. Peter excitedly, beckoning the other two over. "Listen. We've got someone here who actually knows his stuff."

"And after three days they roll the stone away," continues the third guy confidently, "and if He sees His shadow, there's going to be six more weeks of winter."

I was recently born again. I must admit, it's a glorious and wonderful experience.

I can't say my mother enjoyed it a whole lot.

—John Wing

When I was a kid my mother switched religions from Catholic to Episcopalian. Which is what, Catholic Lite? One-third less guilt than regular religion! You could eat meat on Friday, but not a really good cut.

—Rick Corso

How many Christian Scientists does it take to change a lightbulb?

One—to pray for the light to go back on by itself.

A man going into church was stopped cold by a huge sign the janitor had placed in front of the area of the floor that he just washed. It read: "Please Don't Walk on the Water."

Eastern Religions

My son has taken up meditation—at least it's better than sitting doing nothing.

—Max Kauffmann

What's the deal with incense? It smells like somebody set fire to a clothes hamper. Gym socks and jasmine. Do we need that smell? You know what incense smells like? If flowers could fart.

—WILLIAM CORONEL

There was a very strict order of monks who lived by a rule that permitted speaking only once on one day a year, one monk per year. When the day came around, the monk whose turn it was stood up and said, "I don't like the mashed potatoes here, they're too lumpy." And he sat down.

A year later, another monk stood up and said, "I rather like the mashed potatoes here, they're very tasty."

Another year went by and it was a third monk's turn. He stood up and said, "I'm leaving the monastery. I can't stand this constant bickering."

—HAL MCKAY

What did Buddha say to the hot dog vendor?
"Make me one with everything."

I believe in reincarnation. I've had other lives. I know, I have clues. First of all, I'm exhausted.

—CAROL SISKIND

How many Zen Buddhists does it take to screw in a lightbulb?
Two. One to screw it in and one to not screw it in.

Combination Acts

Probably the worst thing about being Jewish at Christmastime is shopping in stores, because the lines are so long. They should have a Jewish express line: "Look, I'm a Jew, it's not a gift. It's just paper towels!"

—SUE KOLINSKY

A priest, a minister, and a rabbi are all enjoying a beer together when a fly lands right in the priest's glass. Fishing it out, the priest shakes off the beer and throws it in the air, saying, "Be on your way, little creature."

Five minutes later the fly is back, this time making a nose dive for the minister's beer. Fishing it out and shaking it dry, the minister tosses it in the air, saying, "Be free, little bug."

But the fly is a slow learner and ends up five minutes later in the rabbi's glass. Picking it up and shaking it violently, the rabbi screams, "Spit it out, spit it out!"

When I was eight years old I sang in the Peewee Quartet and we worked at this Presbyterian church. And I got an Ingersoll watch. I went home and I said, "Ma, I've been a Jew for eight years and I never got anything. I was a Presbyterian for one day and I got a watch."

My mother said, "Help me hang the wash."

—GEORGE BURNS

Why didn't you tell me your mother was Jewish? With a Protestant father, you must have had the same kind of deal I had. I'm not upset that you're such a sly one, I'm upset over the missed opportunities. A million times I could have said, "Some of my best friend is Jewish."

Seated next to an aged rabbi on a transcontinental flight, the eager young priest couldn't resist the opportunity to proselytize. "You really should think about coming over to the Roman Catholic faith, being welcomed into the arms of the Holy Father," he enthused. "It is the only true faith, you know—only those who believe in the Sacraments shall be admitted to the Kingdom of Heaven when they die."

The rabbi nodded indulgently, but expressed no interest in the mechanics of conversion, and eventually the young priest fell silent, depressed by his failure. A little while later, the plane ran into a tremendous hurricane, lost power, and crashed into the Illinois countryside. Miraculously the priest was thrown, unhurt, from his seat. When he came to and looked back at the flaming wreckage, the first thing he saw was the rabbi, making the sign of the cross.

Crossing himself and whispering a brief prayer of gratitude, the priest ran over and took his arm. "Praise the Lord!" he babbled joyfully. "You *did* hear the Word after all, didn't you? And just in time for it to comfort you through mortal peril. And you do wish to be saved, to become one of us now. Alleluia!"

"Vat on earth are you talking about?" asked the elderly fellow, still rather dazed.

"Sir, I saw it with my own eyes. As you stepped out of the flames, you made the sign of the cross!"

"Cross? Vat cross?" asked the rabbi irritably. "I vas simply checking: spectacles, testicles, vallet, and vatch."

The priest became friends with the rabbi whose synagogue was across the street from his church. One day he couldn't help remarking that the church was in perfect repair, while the synagogue needed a new roof and was generally dilapidated.

"I don't seem to be able to get a penny out of my congregation," confessed the rabbi, "wealthy though they are. And while your parishioners are mostly blue-collar workers, you're obviously rolling in money."

"I'll show you how I do it," offered the priest generously, and beckoned for the rabbi to follow him into the confession booth.

Soon a penitent entered. "Father, I have sinned," she murmured. "I have committed adultery."

"Three Hail Marys and ten dollars in the collection box," ordered the priest. And so it went; for each of his sinning parishioners, the priest prescribed some Hail Marys and a donation. Eventually the priest turned to the rabbi and suggested that he handle the next one. "Professional courtesy," he said with a smile. "I'm sure you've gotten the point."

So the rabbi was behind the screen when the next person

came into the booth. "Father, I committed adultery three times last week," she confessed in a whisper.

"Thirty dollars and nine Hail Marys," ordered the rabbi.

"But, Father, I only have twenty-five dollars," she admitted in great distress.

"That's all right," the rabbi consoled her, not missing a beat. "Put the twenty-five in the collection box and go home and do it again. We've got a special this week—four for the price of two and a half."

A Christian, a Moslem, and a Jew, all very pious, met at an interfaith congress and got to talking about the experiences that had led to their religious devotion.

The Christian recounted being on a plane when it ran into a terrible storm over a remote wilderness area. "There was lightning and thunder all around us, and the pilot told us to brace for the crash. I dropped to my knees and prayed to God to save us—and then for a thousand feet all around us, the wind calmed and the rain stopped. We made it to the airport, and since then my faith has never wavered."

The Moslem then told of a terrifying incident on his pilgrimage to Mecca. "A tremendous sandstorm came up out of nowhere, and within minutes my camel and I were almost buried. Sure I was going to die, I prostrated myself toward Mecca and prayed to Allah to deliver me. And suddenly, for a thousand feet all around me, the swirling dust settled and I was able to make my way safely across the desert. Since then I have been the devoutest of believers."

Nodding respectfully, the Jew then told his tale. "One Sabbath I was walking back from the temple when I saw a huge sack of money just lying there at the edge of the road. It had clearly been abandoned, and I felt it was mine to take home, but obviously this would have been a violation of the Sabbath. So I dropped to my knees and prayed to Yahweh—and suddenly, for a thousand feet all around me, it was Tuesday."

A priest and a rabbi went to a prizefight at Madison Square Garden. One of the fighters crossed himself before the opening gong sounded. "What does that mean?" asked the rabbi.

"Not a damn thing if he can't fight," answered the priest.

—BELLE BARTH

My mother is Jewish, my father Catholic. I was brought up Catholic . . . with a Jewish mind. When we'd go to confession, I'd bring a lawyer with me. . . . "Bless me, Father, for I have sinned. I think you know Mr. Cohen?"

—BILL MAHER

A rabbi and a priest were seated together on a plane. After a while, they started talking and the priest said, "Rabbi, I hope you don't mind my asking, but I'm curious, have you ever eaten pork?"

"Actually, yes, once I got drunk and temptation overcame me. I had a ham sandwich and, I hate to admit it, I enjoyed it," replied the rabbi. "Now let me ask you, have you ever been with a woman?"

"Well," responded the priest, "I once got drunk and went to a whorehouse and purchased the services of a prostitute. I, too, quite enjoyed the experience."

"It's a lot better than a ham sandwich, isn't it?"

I do benefits for all religions—I'd hate to blow the hereafter on a technicality.

—BOB HOPE

There was once a nobleman who died at the age of sixty-five and then proceeded to heaven. At the pearly gates, he was met by St. Peter, who asked him whether he wanted to go to heaven or to hell. He could take a tour of both and decide for himself.

First, he was taken to heaven. There he was shown people praying and, in general, leading an austere kind of existence.

Then he was taken on a grand tour of hell, where he saw people were drinking and having a good time, lots of good-looking women and a lot of merrymaking.

When he was taken back to St. Peter, he asked to be put in hell. Suddenly, a huge servant from hell pulled him gruffly by the arm and took him to hell. But he was shocked to see that everywhere people were being tortured. There were vats of boiling oil and lots of strange-looking devilish creatures. He exclaimed to the attendant, "This is not what I was shown a little while ago."

To this the attendant laughed and replied, "Oh, that was our demo model!"

A Catholic, a Jew, and an Episcopalian are lined up at the pearly gates.

The Catholic asks to get in and St. Peter says, "Nope, sorry."

"Why not?" says the Catholic. "I've been good."

"Well, you ate meat on a Friday in Lent, so I can't let you in."

The Jew walks up and again St. Peter says no. The Jew wants an explanation, so St. Peter replies, "There was that time you ate pork . . . sorry, you have to go to the other place."

Then the Episcopalian goes up and asks to be let in and St. Peter again says no.

"Why not?" asks the Episcopalian. "What did I do wrong?"

"Well," says St. Peter, "you once ate your entrée with the salad fork."

Two Irishmen were digging a ditch across the street from a brothel, and one noticed a rabbi walk into the place. He said to the other, "It's a sad day when men of the cloth walk into a place like that."

After a little while, the other man saw a minister walk into the brothel. He stood up and said to his partner, "Did ya see that? It's no wonder the children today are so confused, what with the example that the clergy are settin' for them."

After about another hour, the first man saw a Catholic priest walk in. He promptly stood up and proclaimed to his partner, "Aw, that is truly sad. One of the poor lassies must be dyin'."

A young Protestant couple wants to become Catholic.

"How long have you been Protestant?" asks the priest.

"All our lives."

The priest thinks a while, then replies, "We usually ask those who wish to join the faith to perform some kind of penance to prove their sincerity. Your penance is simple. You must not make love for thirty days."

Thirty days later, the husband returns.

"How did it go?" asks the priest.

"Well, for the first twenty-nine days, it was fine. We didn't even look at each other. And then, on the thirtieth day . . . I saw her standing over the freezer . . . and I just had to. I'm sorry, Father."

The priest frowns. "Well, I'm afraid that this means I won't be able to let you into the arms of the Church."

"That's okay," says the husband. "They won't let me into the supermarket anymore either."

One day a Catholic priest goes to a barber for a haircut. After the barber has finished, the priest asks him how much he owes.

The barber says, "For a man of the cloth, the haircut is free!"

The priest thinks, "What a nice man!" And the next day the barber finds a case of wine outside his shop.

Then, a minister comes in for a haircut. Again, the barber tells him that the haircut is free.

The minister thinks, "What a nice man!" And the next day, the barber finds a box of chocolates outside his shop.

Then, a rabbi comes in for a haircut. Again, the barber gives the haircut on the house.

The rabbi thinks, "What a nice man!" The next day, the barber finds a long line of rabbis outside his shop!

Rabbi Greenberg is sitting alone in the sanctuary of his synagogue—crying. He is clutching a prayer book in his hands and a written sheet of paper. Tears are streaming down his upturned face, and his chest heaves with sobs.

"Why, Lord?" he cries out. "Why did this have to happen? How could my son, my only son, destroy me like this? My—my only son—he converted to Christianity!"

And a great voice booms down from the heavens: "Yours, too?"

Responsibility

The recent recruit was on guard at the main gate of a key naval base, and was given strict orders to admit absolutely no cars that had not been issued a special new permit. Finally, the inevitable happened. The recruit stopped a car in which a high-ranking officer was the passenger.

"Drive on," ordered the admiral to his driver, dismissing the guard with a wave.

"I'm sorry, sir, but I'm new at this," admitted the recruit, drawing a deep breath. "Who do I shoot, you or your driver?"

Two weeks after Paisley's transfer into the promotion department, his old boss got a phone call. "You told me Paisley was a responsible worker!" yelled the furious head of promotion.

"Oh, he is," she confirmed. "In the year he worked in my department, the computer went down five times and had to be completely reprogrammed, the petty cash got misplaced six times, and I developed an ulcer. And each time, Paisley was responsible."

I hate to advocate drugs, alcohol, violence, or insanity to anyone, but they've always worked for me.

—HUNTER S. THOMPSON

The farmer's son was returning from the market with the crate of chickens his father had entrusted to him, when all of a sudden the box fell and broke open. Chickens scurried off in different directions, but the determined boy walked all over the neighborhood scooping up the wayward birds and returning them to the repaired crate. Hoping he had found them all, the boy reluctantly returned home, anticipating the worst.

"Pa, the chickens got loose," the boy confessed sadly, "but I managed to find all twelve of them."

"Well, you did real good, son," the farmer beamed. "You left with seven."

Restaurants

The holdup guy walks into a Chinese restaurant and says, "Give me all your money."

The man behind the counter says, "To take out?"

—Henny Youngman

Never eat anyplace where they mark the restroom doors in any fashion but "Men" and "Women" or "Ladies" and "Gentlemen." Especially do not eat in a restaurant that specializes in seafood and marks its restroom doors "Buoys" and "Gulls," because they have been too busy thinking up cutesy names for the restroom doors to really pay attention to the food.

—Louis Grizzard

Waiters and waitresses are becoming nicer and much more caring. I used to pay my check, they'd say, "Thank you." That graduated into "Have a nice day." That's now escalated into "You take care of yourself, now." The other day I paid my check and the waiter said, "Don't put off that mammogram."

—Rita Rudner

The restaurant we ate at was so dirty, it looked like a Roman bath with all the water drained.

—DAVID BRINKLEY

I ordered a hot chocolate and the waiter brought me a Hershey bar and a match.

Have you ever been in a restaurant and there's a couple in the next booth being overly affectionate? They're necking and groping and you're trying to eat your eggs. I always want to go up to them and say, "Excuse me . . . would you mind if I join you?" How do these people think? Do they wake up in the morning: "Do you want to have sex, honey?" "No, let's wait until we get to Denny's!"

—BOBBY KELTON

We finally got a McDonald's in Bangladesh. They serve McNothings.

—GERRY BEDNOB

I went to a restaurant with a sign that said they served breakfast at any time. So I ordered French toast during the Renaissance.

—STEVEN WRIGHT

Can't we just get rid of wine lists? Do we really have to be reminded every time we go out to a nice restaurant that we have no idea what we are doing? Why don't they just give us a trigonometry quiz with the menu?

—JERRY SEINFELD

I went into an authentic Mexican restaurant. The waiter poured the water and warned me not to drink it.

—BRAD GARRETT

I started a grease fire at McDonald's. Threw a match in the cook's hair.

—STEVE MARTIN

If you want to have fun some time, go into a restaurant's kitchen and yell, "Immigration!"

—MILTON BERLE

After a delicious lunch in an Italian restaurant, the well-traveled businesswoman called the chef over to compliment him on the meal. "Frankly, your eggplant parmesan was better than the one I ate in Milan last Tuesday," she told him.

"It's not surprising," said the chef proudly. "They use domestic cheese. Here we use imported!"

Actor Lou Jacobi happened into a rundown restaurant and spotted a fellow actor sweeping the floor. "I can't understand it," said Lou, "someone with your talents, working in a joint like this?"
"At least I don't eat here," snapped the guy.

—JOEY ADAMS

Did you hear about the new restaurant that just opened up on the moon? Good food, but *no* atmosphere.

I went into a Polish-Cajun restaurant. They served blackened toast.

—RICH CEISLER

Guy walks into a restaurant. Orders eggs.
The waitress asks, "How would you like those eggs cooked?"
The guy says, "Hey, that would be great."

A waiter brings the customer the steak he ordered with his thumb over the meat.

"Are you crazy?" yelled the customer. "You have your hand on my steak!"

"What?" answers the waiter. "You want it to fall on the floor again?"

A guy goes into a luncheonette and orders a hamburger and a hot dog. A few minutes later, the waitress puts a plate in front of him with an open bun on it, pulls a hamburger out of her armpit, and tosses it on the bun.

The guy says, "What the hell was that all about?"

She says, "I was just keeping it warm for you."

He says, "Cancel my hot dog."

A man goes into a greasy spoon restaurant and orders a bowl of chicken soup. "What's this?" he screams after he's served. "There's a pussy hair in my soup! I'm not payin' for it!" And he storms out.

The waitress gets very upset, follows him outside, and sees him go to the whorehouse across the street. He pays the madam and retires to a room with a lovely blond and goes down on her with gusto.

The waitress bursts in and says, "You complain about a hair in your soup and then come over here and do *this*!" the waitress yells.

He lifts his head, turns to her, and says, "Yeah! And if I find a noodle in here, I ain't payin' for it *either*!"

S

Sales and Selling

Young man: I want to buy a diamond ring.

Salesman: Yes, sir. How would you like to buy one of our combination sets? Three pieces— engagement, wedding, and teething.

—JOEY ADAMS

When the legendary salesman was asked his secrets of success, he gave a humble shrug. "I'm sure you all know the cardinal rules: know your product; make lots of calls; never take no for an answer. But frankly, I owe my success to consistently missing a three-foot putt by two inches."

"I do happen to need somebody," admitted the owner of the variety store to the unimpressive-looking man who was interested in a job. "But tell me, can you sell?"

"Of course," was the confident reply.

"I mean really *sell*," reiterated the shopkeeper.

"You bet," said the young man.

"I'll show you what I mean," said the owner, going over to a customer who had just walked in and asked for grass seed. "We're having a very special sale on lawn mowers," he told the customer. "Could I interest you in one?"

"What do I need a lawn mower for?" protested the customer. "I don't even have any grass yet."

"Maybe not," said the owner agreeably, "but all that seed's going to grow like crazy very quickly and then you'll need a lawn mower in the worst way. And you won't find them on sale in midsummer, that's for sure.

"I guess you've got a point," admitted the fellow. "Okay, I'll take a lawn mower, too."

"Think you can do that?" asked the storekeeper of his prospective employee after the customer had left. The man nodded. "Okay, good. Now I have to run to the bank. I'll only be gone for a few minutes, but while I'm gone I want you to sell, sell, sell."

The new guy's first customer was a woman who came over and asked where the tampons were.

"Third aisle over, middle of the second shelf."

When she came to the counter to pay, he leaned over and said, "Hey, you wanna buy a lawn mower? They're on sale."

"Why on earth would I want a lawn mower?" she asked, eyeing him suspiciously.

"Well, you aren't going to be fucking for a few days," he blurted, "so you might as well mow the lawn."

A woman walked into an expensive dress store and announced to the owner, "I'm the greatest salesperson ever. And I want a job."

"That's quite a claim," the owner responded, "but unfortunately I don't have any openings."

Undaunted, the woman asked, "How many dresses does your best employee sell in a day?"

"Five or six," the owner answered.

Without blinking an eye, the woman claimed, "I'll sell twelve without pay or commission, just to show you how good I am."

The owner, knowing she couldn't lose, agreed. And, indeed, just an hour before closing, the new salesperson had sold eighteen dresses. "Do I get the job now?" she asked.

"I've got one more test for you," the owner declared. She went back into the storeroom and returned with the most hideous dress imaginable. "Sell this dress by the time the store closes tonight and you've got a job."

Forty-five minutes later, the woman marched into her office and threw down the sales receipt. "I'm impressed," the owner admitted in amazement. "You've got the job. How on earth did you convince somebody to buy that dress?"

"Getting the woman to buy it wasn't a problem. The hard part was strangling her Seeing Eye dog."

Customer: I'd like some rat poison.
> Clerk: Will you take it with you?
> Customer: No, I'll send the rats over to get it.

—Joey Bishop

The manager of a ladies' dress shop realized it was time to give one of her salesclerks a little talking-to. "Tina, your figures are well below any of our other salespeople's. In fact, unless you can improve your record by the end of the month, I'm going to have to let you go."

"I'm sorry, Mrs. Garcia," said a chastened Tina. "Can you give me any advice on how to do better?"

"Well, there is an old trick I can tell you about. It sounds silly, but it's worked for me in the past. Get hold of a dictionary and go through it page by page until you come to a word that has particular power for you. Memorize it, work it into your sales pitch whenever it seems appropriate, and you'll be amazed at the results."

Sure enough, Tina's figures went way up, and at the end of the month Mrs. Garcia called her in again and congratulated her. "Did you try my little trick?" she asked.

Tina nodded. "It took me the whole weekend to find the right word, but I did: 'fantastic' "

" 'Fantastic.' What a good word," said Mrs. Garcia encouragingly. "How've you been using it?"

"Well, my first customer on Monday was a woman who told me her little girl had just been accepted into the most exclusive prep school in the city. I said, 'Fantastic.' She went on to tell me how her daughter always got straight As, was captain of the swim team, and was the most popular girl in her class, but was always home in bed by eleven o'clock. I said, 'Fantastic.' And she bought three dresses, two blouses, a skirt, and a sweater set. My next customer told me she needed a formal dress for the spring ball at the Ardsley Country Club, which she was in charge of. I said, 'Fantastic.' She went on to say that ten other women had wanted to head the dance committee, but she had won because her tennis game was the best, she had the best figure, and her husband made the most money. I said, 'Fantastic.' And she not only bought a designer gown but also three pairs of shorts, two hats, and a raincoat. And it's been like that all the week: the customers keep boasting, I keep saying 'fantastic,' and they keep buying."

"Excellent work, Tina," complimented her boss. "Just as a point of interest, what did you used to say to customers before you discovered your power word?"

Tina shrugged. "I used to say, 'Who gives a shit?' "

Marveling at a certain employee's ability to sell toothbrushes, the head of the sales department decided to follow him around one day. He soon observed this particular salesman choose a busy street corner on which to set up an array of toothbrushes and a small bowl of brownish stuff surrounded by chips. The salesman would then select a likely customer and announce, "Good morning! We're introducing Nifty Chip Dip— would you like a free sample?"

Tasting the dip, the bystander would invariably spit it out in disgust and howl, "It tastes like mud!"

"It is," the salesman would inform them calmly. "Care to buy a toothbrush?"

George was killed in a hit-and-run accident just outside his jewelry store, and he arrived at the pearly gates at the same time as a flashy dude in a cheap suit.

"Welcome to heaven," said St. Peter warmly. "I'm in such a good mood today that I'm going to offer both of you whatever your heart desires. What would you like, sir?" he asked, turning to the man in the cheap suit.

The fellow considered for a moment, then said, "I'd like a million bucks."

In an instant his arms were filled with cash, and he walked through the gates with a smile a mile wide.

"And you, sir?" asked St. Peter, turning to George.

"I'd like twenty bucks' worth of fake gold jewelry," he responded instantly, "and ten minutes alone with the guy in the cheap suit."

Hersch was a salesman. One day, as he was driving across the Negev desert, he spotted what looked like a body by the side of the road. Hersch slammed on the brakes, ran over, and discovered an Arab on the brink of death. Hersch took the poor man into his arms and bent close so he could make out his parched whisper.

"Water, *effendi* . . . water."

"Are you in luck!" cried Hersch exultantly. "Why, in my carrying case, which I happen to have right here beside me, I have the finest collection of one hundred percent silk neckties to be found this side of the King David Hotel. Normally thirty-five dollars, but for you, twenty-two dollars and fifty cents."

"Water, *effendi*, water," gasped the Arab, plucking feebly at Hersch's sleeve.

"I tell you what. Since you seem like such a nice guy, I'll make it two for thirty-five dollars—that's for a polysilk blend, though, I gotta tell you."

"Water, *effendi*, water."

"You drive a hard bargain." Hersch shook his head regretfully. "Okay, any tie you want for sixteen dollars and fifty cents—but I can't go any lower."

"Water, *effendi*, water." The dying Arab's words were barely audible.

"Oh, it's water you want. Why didn't you say so?" Hersch's voice was filled with reproach. "Well, you're in luck again. Just over that sand dune's a lovely resort, I used to vacation there myself. They'll have all the water you can drink." And Hersch got back in his car and drove away.

The Arab managed to stagger to the top of the sand dune, and, sure enough, a neon-lit sign announcing Le Club Gaza was visible from the top. The Arab summoned the last of his strength, crawled across the burning sand to the entrance, and collapsed. "Water, *effendi*, water," he croaked.

"Ah, you want water," said the doorman sympathetically. "We have all kinds: mineral water, well water, club soda, Perrier, seltzer. Only thing is, you have to have a tie to get in."

The door-to-door vacuum salesman goes to the first house in his new territory. He knocks, a lady opens the door, and before she has a chance to say anything, he runs inside and dumps horseshit all over the carpet. He says, "Lady, if this vacuum cleaner don't do wonders cleaning up that horseshit, I'll eat every chunk of it."

She says, "You want tomato sauce on that? We just moved in and we haven't got the electricity turned on yet."

School

The third-grade teacher was shocked to find a number of foul words scrawled on the blackboard when she walked into the classroom. "Children," she said sternly, "you are much too young to use such vile language. Now we're all going to close our eyes and count to fifty, and while we're counting, I want the little boy or girl who wrote those words to tiptoe up and erase them."

At the signal, the teacher and her students closed their eyes and the teacher counted out loud, very slowly. When she reached fifty, she said, "All right, class, everybody open their eyes."

All eyes went to the blackboard.

None of the words had been erased, and below them was the message: "The Phantom strikes again."

Kids today think the Trojan War was fought over contraceptives.

—Norm Crosby

I'm enjoying summer school. I believe it's been good for me. It saves a lot on sunscreen.

—Charles M. Schulz

I had the worst study habits, the lowest grades . . . then I found out what I was doing wrong. I was highlighting with a black Magic Marker.

—Jeff Altman

I knew comedy was for me when I was the only Asian in high school who failed math. But you know, when I failed, eight other students around me failed, too.

—Dat Phan

In my day, girls used to get pinned in high school. That was the big thing. Now they're getting nailed.

—Bill Maher

My school was so tough, the school newspaper had an obituary column.

—Norm Crosby

I went to correspondence school. They threw me out from there. I played hooky . . . I sent them an empty envelope.

—Baron Munchausen (Jack Pearl)

My school was so tough, when the kids had their school pictures taken, there was one taken from the front and one from the side.

—Norm Crosby

A grade-school teacher gives the assignment to her class that each student should think of a story and then a moral for that story to share with the class the next day. The following day the teacher asks for the first volunteer to tell their story, and little Amy raises her hand.

"My dad owns a farm and every Sunday we load the chicken eggs on the truck and drive into town to sell them at the market. Well, one Sunday we hit a big bump and all the eggs flew out of the basket and onto the road." The teacher asks for the moral of the story and Amy replies, "Don't keep all your eggs in one basket."

Next, little Sandy offers to tell her story, and she says, "Well, my dad owns a farm, too, and every weekend we take the chicken eggs and put them in the incubator. Last weekend only eight of the twelve eggs hatched." The teacher asks for the moral of the story and Sandy replies, "Don't count your eggs before they're hatched."

Finally it's little Andy's turn and he says, "My uncle John fought in the war, and his plane was shot down over enemy territory. He jumped out before it crashed with only a machine gun, a machete, and case of beer. On the way down he drank the case of beer.

"Unfortunately, he landed right in the middle of one hundred enemy soldiers. He shot seventy with his machine gun, but ran out of bullets, so he pulled out his machete and killed twenty more. The blade on his machete broke, so he killed the last ten with his bare hands."

The teacher looks in shock at Andy and asks if there is possibly any moral to his story and Andy replies, "Don't mess with uncle John after he's been drinking."

I was terrible at history. I could never see the point of learning what people thought back when people were a lot stupider. For instance, the ancient Phoenicians believed that the sun was carried across the sky on the back of an enormous snake. So what? So they were idiots.

—DAVE BARRY

One day the teacher tells the class they're going to play a thinking game, and asks for a volunteer. "Pick me, pick me," begs Bobby.

"Okay, Bobby," says the teacher. "Now, I'm going to describe objects to you and you tell me what they are. Here we go. What's red, shiny, and you eat it?"

"A cherry," says Bobby.

"No, it's an apple, but it shows you're thinking," said the teacher gently. "Ready for the next one? What's yellow and you eat it?"

"A lemon," says Bobby.

"No," says the teacher, "it's a banana, but it shows you're thinking.

Before the teacher can continue, Bobby interrupts. "Okay, teacher, I've got one for you." He reaches into his pocket, looks down, pulls his hand out, and asks, "What's long, pink, and has a little red head on the end of it?"

"Oooh, Bobby!" squeals the teacher.

"No, it's a match—but it shows you're thinking."

Sex

I'm really concerned about my wife since we moved to California. She's gotten kind of kinky. She likes to tie me up and then go out with someone else.

—TOM DREESEN

A young man goes into a drugstore to buy condoms. The pharmacist says the condoms come in packs of three or six and asks which the young man wants. "Well," he said, "I've been seeing this beautiful girl for a while and she's really hot. I think tonight's 'the' night. We're having dinner with her parents, and then we're going out. And I've got a feeling I'm gonna get lucky after that." The young man makes his purchase and leaves. Later that evening, at the dinner table with his girlfriend and her parents, he asks if he might give the blessing. He begins the prayer, but continues praying for ten minutes. The girl leans over and whispers to him, "You never told me that you were such a religious person." He leans to her and whispers, "You never told me that your father is a pharmacist."

Several hard-core *Star Wars* fans who had tickets for the first showing actually said that when the movie finally began, they started crying. Mainly because they realized that it's twenty-two years later, and they still haven't lost their virginity.

—CONAN O'BRIEN

You don't get married to get sex. Getting married to get sex is like buying a 747 to get free peanuts.

—JEFF FOXWORTHY

This girl asked me out one time. She told me she was an actress in porno movies. I'm like, "All right, when do you want to go out?" She goes, "I'm working Tuesday and Wednesday. How about Thursday?" "Uh, how about Monday?"

—JEFFREY ROSS

There have been times when I have actually had sex indoors. And then you kind of sober up a little when it's over. I become like a bartender at 2 A.M. "Okay, people, let's move it out! Yeah, you don't have to go home but you can't stay here."

—JANEANE GAROFALO

I was walking through Central Park the other day, and I came upon the most beautiful woman sunbather, and she wiped it off and called the cops.

—TOM COTTER

One guy says to the other, "Do you and your wife have mutual climax?"

The other said, "I think we have Prudential."

—MILTON BERLE

My sex life is very bad. If it weren't for pickpockets, I'd have no sex life at all.

—HENNY YOUNGMAN

What's a Jewish porno film?

Ten minutes of sex, fifty minutes of guilt.

If God had intended that the genitals were more important than the brain, he would've put a skull over the genitals. What the hell do you care if someone comes over and fools around with your genitals? . . . But you don't want anybody coming over and stroking your brains. They'll scramble your brains, you'll write the wrong check, you'll lose money.

—MEL BROOKS

Did you hear about the poll conducted during National Orgasm Week?

Unfortunately, nine out of ten responders only pretended to celebrate.

Sex therapists think the whole problem is we don't communicate enough. Dr. Ruth says, as women, we should *tell* our lovers how to make love to us. My boyfriend goes nuts if I tell him how to *drive*!

—PAM STONE

Sex is one of the most beautiful, wholesome, and natural things that money can buy.

Italian woman: Oh, Gino, you are the world's greatest lover!

French woman: Ah, Jacques, you are marvelous. More, more!

Jewish woman: Oy, Jake, the ceiling needs painting.

—GENE BAYLOS

He knows why a Beverly Hills princess walks down the aisle with a great big smile. Because she knows she's given her last blow job.

—NORM CROSBY, ABOUT BILLY CRYSTAL

Girls who put out are tramps. Girls who don't are ladies. This is, however, a rather archaic use of the word. Should one of you boys happen upon a girl who doesn't put out, do not jump to the conclusion that you have found a lady. What you have probably found is a lesbian.

—FRAN LEBOWITZ

The butcher was eager to marry off his only daughter, but to his dismay she showed no interest whatsoever in any of her possible suitors. In fact, she seemed utterly disinterested in sex, and her father would lie awake at night wondering what would become of her.

Late one sleepless night, as the butcher headed down to the kitchen for a glass of warm milk, he heard strange sounds coming from his daughter's room. Peering into her room, he saw her masturbating energetically with a hunk of salami.

The next day a customer came into the shop, pointed at the display case, and asked for a half a pound of salami.

"I'm afraid that's not for sale," the butcher told him with a sigh. "That's my son-in-law."

The last woman I was in was the Statue of Liberty.

—WOODY ALLEN

One morning a milkman called on one of his regular customers and was surprised to see a white bedsheet with a hole in the middle hanging up in her living room. The housewife explained that she'd had a party the night before. They had played a game called "Who's Who" in which each of the men had put his equipment through the hole and the women tried to guess their identity.

"Gee, that sounds like fun," said the milkman. "Sure wish I'd been there."

"You should have been," said the housewife. "Your name came up three times."

Is sex dirty? Only if it's done right.

—Woody Allen

When I was growing up, all my friends wanted to have sex with anything that moved. "Why limit yourself?" I told them.

—Emo Phillips

Two Italians are walking down the street when one turns to the other and says, "Nunzio, you know, there's one time I really like to have sex."

"When is-a that, Mario?" asked his friend.

"Just before I have a cigarette."

I worry about kids today. Because of the sexual revolution, they're going to grow up and never know what "dirty" means.

—Lily Tomlin

Everybody has sex now. When I was a kid, only women had sex and you had to get it from them.

—Tony Stone

Is it wrong to have sex before you're married?
Only if it makes you late for the ceremony!

The salesgirl at the Pink Pussycat boutique didn't bat an eye when the customer purchased an artificial vagina. "What're you going to use it for?" she asked.

"None of your business," answered the customer, thoroughly offended.

"Calm down, buddy," soothed the salesgirl. "The only reason I'm asking is that if it's food, we don't have to charge you sales tax."

I don't want to see any faces at this party I haven't sat on.

—Bonnie Raitt

You know what those little bumps are on a girl's nipples? It's Braille for "lick here."

A young country girl came to town for a day. She was window shopping when a beautiful pair of red shoes caught her eye, and as she stood admiring them, the clerk came out and asked if he could help her. The girl admitted that she'd spent all her money, but that she'd do anything to get her hands on those red shoes.

The clerk thought it over for a moment. "I think we can work out a deal," he told her. "Go lie down on the couch in the back room." Soon he came in and closed the door. "So do you want those shoes bad enough to put out for them?" he asked. When she nodded, he pulled down his pants, exposing a hard-on about nine-inches long.

"Honey, I'll screw you with this big cock of mine until you squirm with pleasure and scream in ecstasy and go wild with desire."

"I don't get much of a kick out of sex, but go right ahead," said the girl, spreading her legs and lying back. Sure she couldn't last long, the salesman started pumping away, but she lay there like a dishrag. Pretty soon he'd come twice and began to worry about getting soft, so he started going at it for all he was worth. Sure enough he felt her arms go around his neck and her legs tighten

around his waist. "Best you've ever had, right?" chortled the man. "In a couple of seconds you'll be coming like crazy."

"Oh, no, it's not that," said the girl. "I'm just trying on my new shoes."

Little Billy was getting old enough to be curious about the birds and bees, so when he and his father encountered two dogs going at it in an empty lot, his dad explained that they were making puppies. It was only a week later that Billy stumbled into his parents' room in the middle of the night, catching them in the act. "What are you and Mommy doing?" he asked.

"Well, Billy," the red-faced parent explained, "Mommy and I are making babies."

"Roll her over, Dad, roll her over!" yelled the little boy. "I'd rather have puppies."

My wife insists on turning off the lights when we make love. That doesn't bother me. It's the hiding that seems so cruel.

—JONATHAN KATZ

Anybody who calls it "sexual intercourse" can't possibly be interested in actually doing it. You might as well announce you're ready for lunch by proclaiming, "I'd like to do some masticating and enzyme secreting."

—ALAN SHERMAN

Awakening the morning after the orgy, the god of war was stretching sleepily when he noticed a lovely Valkyrie standing in the doorway. "Good morning," he said. "I'm Thor."

She replied, "You're thor? I'm tho thor I can hardly pith."

Why do so many women fake orgasms?

Because so many men fake foreplay.

Three guys and a girl are marooned on a desert island.

After one week, the girl is so ashamed of what she's doing, she kills herself.

After another week, the guys are so ashamed of what they're doing, they bury her.

After another week, they're so ashamed of what they're doing, they dig her up again.

Mrs. Chester's husband has lost interest in her sexually, so she goes to the local lingerie boutique and buys some crotchless panties. That night, when her husband comes home from work, she yells down from the bedroom, "Honey, come upstairs. I have a surprise for you."

When he opens the bedroom door, she's lying on the bed wearing just a bra and the panties. She spreads her legs and says, "See anything you want?"

He says, "Why would I want that? Look what it did to your underwear."

What is the definition of "indecent"?

If it's long enough, hard enough, and in far enough, it's indecent!

Oral Sex

The patient had been in a coma for some time when one of the nurses happened to notice a distinct response on the monitor when her "private area" was touched during a sponge bath.

"Crazy as this sounds," said the nurse to the patient's husband on his next visit, "but maybe a little oral sex will do the trick and bring her out of the coma." He's quite skeptical, but the staff assures him that they'll close the curtains for privacy and points out that they don't have much to lose. Finally the husband agrees to give it a shot, and goes into his wife's room.

After a few minutes the woman's monitor flatlines. No pulse . . . no heart rate. Running into the room, they find the husband standing there, zipping up his fly. "I think she choked," he said.

After several years of marriage, Debbie's husband Mike died suddenly. According to his wishes, Debbie had his body cremated, and placed the remains in a small urn.

Several weeks later, Debbie came home wearing a full-length mink coat and an eight-carat diamond ring. She went into the living room, removed the urn from the mantel, and carefully tapped Mike's ashes into a small dish on the coffee table.

"Mike, my beloved Mike," she began, "I wish to talk to you. Mike, do you remember, for several years you promised me a mink coat? Well, here it is, Mike. Do you like it?

"And, Mike," she continued, "do you remember, for several years you promised me a diamond ring? Yes? You remember? Here it is, Mike. Do you like it?

"Well," Debbie exclaimed, puffing Mike's ashes into the air, "there's that blow job I was promising you."

What do yuppies call mutual oral sex?
Sixty-something.

What's LXIX?
Sixty-nine the hard way.

A fellow sitting in a bar noticed that the bartender was staring at him. Each time he'd look away, and finally he came over, a bit embarrassed.

"I'm sorry, sir, let me buy you a drink."

He accepted and accepted the subsequent two apologies and drinks.

"Really, sir, surely you know this, you must be the ugliest man I've ever seen and I can't keep from staring at you."

"You think I'm pretty ugly? That ugly? Are you a betting man?"

"Well, it depends on what I'm betting on, but I do bet from time to time."

"Do you see that cute little blond sitting over there with that young man? I've got fifty dollars that says I'll go over there and pick her up."

The bartender accepted immediately, plopping his fifty dollars on the bar next to the customer, who had started to approach the table, but wheeled around and came back.

"I've got another fifty dollars that says I'll pat her on the fanny as we walk by you and she'll give you a wink."

The bartender quickly added another fifty dollars and shortly after that, the guy walked out with the blond on his arm and as they went by, he patted her on the fanny, she winked at the bartender, and the guy collected the win.

Astonished, the bartender went over to the table where she had been sitting to quiz the young man she had been with. He was sitting there with a stunned look on his face.

"My gosh, fellow, I'm amazed! What did he do? What did he say?"

"Nothing! Nothing at all! He just stood there, licking his eyebrows. . . ."

What's the problem with oral sex?
The view.

Why are cowgirls all bowlegged?
   Because cowboys like to eat with their hats on.

What's the best thing about a blow job?
Five minutes of peace and quiet.

Why do men like blow jobs?
   It's the only time they get something into a woman's head straight.

A flea had oiled up his little flea legs and his little flea arms, had spread out his blanket, and was proceeding to soak up the Miami sun when who should stumble by on the beach but an old flea friend of his.

"Oscar, what happened to you?" asked the flea, because Oscar looked terrible, wrapped up in a blanket, his nose running, his eyes red, and his teeth chattering.

"I got a ride down here in some guy's mustache and he came by motorcycle. I nearly froze my nuts off," wheezed Oscar.

"Let me give you a tip, old pal," said the first flea, spreading some more suntan oil on his shoulders. "You go to the stewardess lounge at the airport, see, and you get up on the toilet seat, and when an Air Florida stewardess comes in to take a leak, you hop on for a nice warm ride. Got it?"

So you can imagine the flea's surprise when, a month or so later, while stretched out all warm and comfortable on the beach, he sees Oscar looking more chilled and miserable than before.

"Listen," said Oscar, "I did everything you said. I made it to the stewardess lounge and waited until a really cute one came in, and made a perfect landing and got so warm and cozy that I dozed right off."

"And so?" asked the first flea.

"And so, the next thing I know, I'm on this guy's mustache again!"

What do lobster thermidor and oral sex have in common?

You can't get either of them at home.

A young man is on a date with a young woman and they are sitting in his car on Lovers Lane. After some heavy petting the young man asks the young woman for oral sex.

"No," says the young woman, "you won't respect me."

So the young man is content to wait. After they had been dating a few months, the young man again asks the young woman for oral sex. Again the reply, "No, you won't respect me."

Eventually the two get married and the husband asks his bride "Honey, please, we're married now. You know I love you and respect you. Can we please have oral sex?"

"No," she says, "I just know that if I do that, you won't respect me." So the man waits, and waits, and waits. . . .

After twenty years of marriage, the man says, "Honey, we've been together twenty wonderful years now. We've raised three beautiful kids. You know that I love you and respect you completely. How about oral sex, just once? Please!"

The wife finally gives in to her husband's wish and performs oral sex on him. After she's finished, they're lying in bed relaxing, and the telephone rings.

The husband turns to his wife and says, "Answer that, you cocksucker."

Safe Sex

You have to be very careful these days. If you get involved with somebody, you have to know their health history. The best way to find out is to look through their medicine cabinet. It tells you what they don't have. . . . With this girl, I opened up the medicine cabinet, it was empty. I said, "Jeez, I don't know what she's got, but whatever it is, there ain't no cure for it!"

—JACK SIMMONS

In 1962 all the expression "safe sex" meant was that you move the bed away from the wall so you wouldn't bang your head.

—DAVID LETTERMAN

I used to go out every night and try and get laid, and fail, and I'd call that sexual frustration. Now I go out every night and try and get laid, and fail, but I can call it a "healthy lifestyle."

—SIMON FANSHAWE

One day a gentleman goes into a new grocery shop on the out-skirts of town. Just inside he sees a sign which says: "Condoms: Sold & Fitted."

He looks around and calls for service. An exceptionally attractive young lady emerges from the back.

"Do you work here?" he asks.

"Yes," she replies.

"And is the statement on the sign over there true?" The lady leans over the counter and says seductively, "Yes."

"Tell me," he asks, "who fits them?"

"I do," said the lady.

"Well," said the man, "would you please wash your hands and give me a pound of tomatoes?"

Sex Toys

Eager to keep his wife out of trouble while he was away on a long business trip, a businessman went to a store that sold sex toys and started looking around. After browsing through the dildos for something special, he decided to consult the old guy behind the counter.

The old man said, "We have vibrating dildos, special attachments, and so on, but I don't know of anything that will keep her occupied for weeks, except. . . ." and he stopped.

"Except what?" the man asked.

"Nothing, nothing."

"C'mon, tell me! I need something!"

"Well, sir, I don't usually mention this, but there is the 'voodoo dick.' " The old man reached under the counter, pulled out an old wooden box carved with strange symbols, and opened it. There lay a very ordinary-looking dildo.

The businessman laughed, and commented that it looked like every other dildo in this shop.

"But you haven't seen what it'll do," said the proprietor. He pointed to a door and said, "Voodoo dick, the door." The voodoo dick rose out of its box, darted over to the door, and started screwing the keyhole. The whole door shook, then started to split down the middle, at which point the old man commanded, "Voodoo dick, back in your box!"

The voodoo dick stopped, floated back to the box and lay there, quiescent once more.

"I'll take it!" said the businessman.

The old man said it wasn't for sale, but finally surrendered it for seven hundred dollars in cash. Pleased as punch, the businessman gave his wife the gift, explained that all she had to do was say "Voodoo dick, my pussy" if she got lonely, and set off on his business trip.

After a few days, the wife grew unbearably horny. Feeling a little foolish, she opened the box and said tentatively, "Voodoo dick, my pussy!" The voodoo dick shot out of the box, made a beeline for her crotch, and started pumping away. It was fabulous, like nothing she'd ever experienced before, and she lay back and enjoyed the rush of pleasure. After three orgasms, she decided she'd had enough and reached to pull out the dildo. It wouldn't budge. Nothing worked. The voodoo dick was stuck, thrusting away. Her husband had forgotten to tell her how to shut it off.

Desperate, she pulled on a skirt, got in the car, and headed for the hospital, nearly fainting with excitement and exhaustion. On the way, another orgasm nearly made her swerve off the road, and to her horror, a squad car pulled her over. First the policeman asked for her license. Then, observing her disheveled state, he asked how much she'd had to drink.

Twitching and sweating, she gasped, "I haven't been drinking, officer. A voodoo dick is stuck in my pussy, and it won't stop screwing!"

"Sure, lady," said the officer after another long look at her. "Voodoo dick, my ass!"

Why don't dumb girls use vibrators?
They are afraid they'll chip their teeth.

Why did the gay guy strip naked and tie a string to his dick?

He was going to a costume party as a pull toy.

Shopping

It makes no difference what it is, a woman will buy anything she thinks the store is losing money on.

—KIN HUBBARD

When I walk into the supermarket, the manager goes for a grocery cart for me. I said, "Why do you always give me a cart with a squeaky wheel?"

He said, "We've only got one store detective, we can't watch everybody."

—BOB HOPE

A blind man came into a big department store and headed for the center of the floor. Stopping, he picked up his Seeing Eye dog by the hind legs and proceeded to whirl him around in a circle.

Astonished, the department manager rushed over as the dog landed back on the ground. "Uh, can I help you with anything, sir?" asked the flustered salesman.

"No thanks," replied the blind man. "Just looking."

I went into a general store. They wouldn't let me buy anything specifically.

—STEVEN WRIGHT

My father was having a lot of security problems in his lingerie store because women were stealing underwear in the dressing rooms. He installed cameras in there. He's still getting ripped off, but he makes it all back on the video sales.

—DANNY KOCH

I went down the street to the twenty-four-hour grocery. When I got there the guy was locking the front door.

I said, "Hey, the sign says you're open twenty-four hours."

He said, "Yes, but not in a row."

I used to eat while I was in the supermarket. I guess I didn't consider it stealing 'cause I took it out inside my body.

—ARSENIO HALL

Silence

I have noticed that nothing I have never said ever did me any harm.

—CALVIN COOLIDGE

Women like silent men. They think they're listening.

—MARCEL ACHARD

If nobody ever said anything unless he knew what he was talking about, a ghastly hush would descend upon the earth.

—ALAN HERBERT

The only pay phone in sight was in use, so the woman stood off to the side politely, to wait until it was free. Minutes went by, however, and she couldn't help noticing that the man in the phone booth was just standing there silently, not saying a word. Finally she tapped him on the shoulder and asked if she could use the phone.

"Hold your horses," responded the fellow, covering the receiver. "I'm talking to my wife."

It's better to keep one's mouth shut and be thought a fool than to open it and resolve all doubt.

—ABRAHAM LINCOLN

Sleep

"Doc, I had the strangest dream last night. I dreamed I was the only man in a nudist colony."

"My, my," responded the doctor. "Did you sleep well?"

"I tried," answered the patient, "but it was hard."

The amount of sleep required by the average person is about five minutes more.

—Max Kauffmann

Hear about the guy who had such a bad case of insomnia, the sheep fell asleep?

Smoking

The FCC came along and it said no more cigarette commercials on television. . . .

I'd much rather watch a pretty girl offer me a cigarette than an old lady ask if I'm constipated.

—Mark Russell

Anybody got a cigarette? Thanks very much, sir—I left mine in the machine.

—London Lee

The only thing that bothers me is if I'm in a restaurant and I'm eating and someone says, "Hey, mind if I smoke?"

I always say, "No. Mind if I fart?"

A rebel leader was finally apprehended by the military police and summarily sentenced to death. The generallissimo watched as

the blindfolded man was led before the firing squad, then magnanimously came over to offer him a last cigarette.

"No thanks," was the condemned man's answer. "I'm trying to quit."

They used to have a smoking section at the airport. No more. They now have these glass-encased rooms. You're not just a smoker; you're an example to other people. You're an exhibit at a futuristic zoo. You're in a nicotine terrarium. There ought to be a sign that says, "The addict in his natural environment."

—Marc Maron

You know what bugs me? People who smoke cigars in restaurants. That's why I always carry a water pistol filled with gasoline.

—Paula Provenza

I quit smoking and it was a very disappointing experience. I found out my teeth are really brown.

—Bill Dana

What kind of cigarettes do Jewish mothers smoke?
    Gefiltered.

Space Travel

How about the dumb guy who was sent up into space with a monkey? The first day a red light went on and the monkey took down all the instrument readings. The second day a red light went on and the monkey took out his slide rule and made all the appropriate calculations. On the third day a green light went on.

"What do I do now?" asked the dumb guy. "Feed the monkey," said a little voice from earth.

Why don't they let teenagers become astronauts?

Because they'd honk the horn, squeal the tires, and play the radio too loud all the way to the moon.

The first astronaut to land on Mars was delighted to come across a beautiful Martian woman stirring a huge pot over a campfire.

"Hi there," he said casually. "What're you doing?"

"Making babies," she explained, looking up with a winsome smile.

Horny after the long space voyage, the astronaut decided to give it a shot. "That's not the way we do it on earth," he informed her.

"Oh, really?" The Martian woman looked up from her pot with interest. "How do your people do it?"

"Well, it's hard to describe," he conceded, "but I'd be glad to show you."

"Fine," agreed the lovely Martian maiden, and the two proceeded to make love in the glow of the fire. When they were finished, she asked, "So where are the babies?"

"Oh, they don't show up for another nine months," explained the astronaut patiently.

"So why'd you stop stirring?"

These astronauts land on a strange planet. They approach a funny-looking building near their ship. Inside they see hundreds of old men with beards and yarmulkes making suits. They're there stitching and sewing, stitching and sewing. One of them looks up and asks, "Who are you guys?"

"We're astronauts," was the reply.

The old man turned to the next table and said, "Astronauts. They send us astronauts. We need pressers."

—Norm Crosby

Sports and Recreation

Generally speaking, I look upon [sports] as dangerous and tiring activities performed by people with whom I share nothing except the right to trial by jury.

—FRAN LEBOWITZ

The women's uneven parallel bar event. I think I'm gonna be a little bit skeptical the next time a woman tells me I'm being too rough in bed. I'm watching these girls bang their cervix off a frozen theater rope at eighty miles per hour. You don't see men in that event, okay?

—DENNIS MILLER

We have fun—that's what I like about bowling. You can have fun even if you stink, unlike in, say, tennis. Every decade or so I attempt to play tennis, and it always consists of thirty-seven seconds of actually hitting the ball and two hours of yelling, "Where did the ball go?" "Over that condominium." Etc. With bowling, once you let go of the ball, it's no longer your legal responsibility. They have these wonderful machines that find it for you and send it right back.

—DAVE BARRY

Weight lifters are now taking steroids and the male hormone testosterone. One guy had so much testosterone in him, he had to be classified as an East German woman!

—CARL WOLFSON

Harvey's topics of conversation had always been limited to work and sports, and once he retired, he spent every waking minute attending games, glued to the sports channel, or reading *Sports Illustrated*. At first his wife, Shirley, was glad he had a hobby to keep him busy, but his obsession grew irritating, and eventually infuriating.

One night as they lay in bed together, Harvey raptly watching a

448

Rumanian soccer match, Shirley decided she'd had enough. She got up, walked across the room, and unplugged the television.

"Hey, what do you think you're doing?" he protested.

"Listen to me, Harvey," she screeched. "I'm sick of sports. You've barely talked to me in weeks, not to mention actually touching me. It's time to talk about sex."

"Uh . . . okay," agreed her startled mate. "So how often do you think Michael Jordan gets laid?"

There's an old, seedy, rundown gymnasium on the lower West Side catering to young and old boxers. Amid the yelling, the smell of fighters sweating, punching bags and each other, one of the boxers comes over to his corner after three rounds of heavy hitting and says to his manager, "I really want a shot at the Kid, Kid Jackson. I know I'm getting old and a little punchy, but before I retire I just want one chance in the ring with him!"

And the manager, wiping his fighter's face with a towel, says, "Look, if I've told you once I've told you a hundred times: you're Kid Jackson!"

—SOUPY SALES

The Olympics is really my favorite sporting event. Although I think I have a problem with that silver medal. 'Cause when you think about it, you win the gold, you feel good; you win the bronze, you think, "Well, at least I got something." But when you win that silver, it's like, "Congratulations, you 'almost' won. Of all the losers, you came in first of that group. You're the number one 'loser.' No one lost ahead of you!"

—JERRY SEINFELD

I wrestled in college . . . of course now they call it "date rape."

—TOM COTTER

Three old women are at an exclusive health club in Miami. They are debating how much to tip the towel boy. Edith says, "I'll give him five bucks." Esther says, "I'll give him ten."

"What about you, Rose, what are you going to tip him?" asked Edith.

"I'm going to give him sex," she said.

"Huh? Are you crazy?" asked Esther.

"No. In fact, I was wondering about this yesterday. So I called my husband, and I says, Benny, how much should I tip the towel boy?"

"Fuck 'em," he said.

A cowboy just won first place in a rodeo in a small western town. So proud of his horse was he that he rode him to the neighborhood saloon. After tieing the horse to a post, he went inside for a couple of brews. When he came out of the bar a few hours later, he noticed that someone had painted the horse's balls red. Furious, he barged back into the bar like a madman. At the top of his lungs, he asked who painted his horse's balls red. Suddenly, towards the rear of the bar, a tall, shirtless muscular man stands up. He's a good six feet six with nineteen-inch biceps. Tattoos cover his upper body. Scars are all over his face and chest. Two long Bowie knives are strapped to his waist. "I did," said the tough guy. "And what about it?"

"Just wanted to let you know," said the cowboy, "the first coat is dry."

There's this magician working on a small cruise ship. He's been doing his routines every night for two years now. The audiences appreciate him, and they change over often enough that he doesn't have to worry too much about new tricks. However, there is a parrot who sits in the back row and watches him night after night. Finally, the parrot figures out how all the tricks work and starts giving it away for the audience. For example, when the magician makes a bouquet of flowers disappear, the parrot squawks, "Behind his back! It's behind his back!" Well, the magician finally gets really annoyed, but doesn't know what to do. The parrot belongs to the captain, so he can't just kill it.

One day, the ship springs a leak and sinks. The magician manages to swim to a plank of wood floating by and grabs on. Low and behold, the parrot is sitting on the other end. They just stare at each other as they drift and drift. They drift for three days and still don't speak. On the morning of the fourth day, the parrot looks over at the magician and says: "Okay, I give up. Where did you hide the ship?"

It was a boring Sunday afternoon in the jungle, so the elephants decided to challenge the ants to a game of soccer. The game was going well with the elephants beating the ants ten goals to nil, when the ants gained possession.

The ants' star player was dribbling the ball toward the elephants' goal when the elephants' left back came lumbering toward him. The elephant trods on the little ant, killing him instantly.

The referee stops the game. "What the hell do you think you're doing? Do you call that sportsmanship, killing another player?"

The elephant replied, "Well, I didn't mean to kill him—I was just trying to trip him up."

At a posh Las Vegas casino, a blackjack dealer and a player with a thirteen count in his hand were arguing about whether or not it was appropriate to tip the dealer. The player said, "When I get bad cards, it's not the dealers fault. Accordingly, when I get good cards, the dealer obviously had nothing to do with that either, so why should I tip him?"

The dealer said, "When you eat at a restaurant do you tip the waiter?"

"Yes."

"Well then, he serves you food. I'm serving you cards so you should tip me."

"Okay, but the waiter gives me what I ask for . . . I'll take an eight."

Jim and George are in a bar, talking about horseracing. Jim is going on and on about how he understands the sport and always wins at the track. When he finally gets around to asking George what happens to the horses he follows, George says, "The horses I follow usually end up following the other horses."

Baseball

An American takes a foreigner to a baseball game. The foreigner is just beginning to get into cheering batters as they run to first, when a batter draws a walk.

The foreigner starts to yell, "Run, boy, run!"

His host, with a bemused smile explains, "He doesn't have to run; he has four balls."

The foreigner stands up and shouts, "Walk proudly, boy, walk proudly."

It was only her second date with the diehard baseball fan, and Helene was a little nervous. It was her fault that they arrived at the stadium a full hour after the game had begun. Taking her seat, Helene glanced up at the scoreboard. It was a tight pitcher's battle, bottom of the fifth, o-o.

"Look, Charlie," she exclaimed in relief, "we haven't missed a thing!"

Baseball's been called the national pastime. It's just the kind of game someone deserves who has nothing better to do than to try to pass his time.

—ANDY ROONEY

A Boston woman, unable to bear the indifference of her baseball-crazy husband any longer, yelled at him, "You love the Red Sox more than you love me!"

He turned around and replied, "I love the Yankees more than I love you!"

Men know that if a woman had to choose between catching a fly ball and saving an infant's life, she would probably save the infant's life without even considering whether there were men on base.

—DAVE BARRY

A couple of Yogi Berra's waggish teammates on the New York Yankees swear that one night the legendary catcher was horrified to see a baby toppling off the roof of a cottage across the way from him. He dashed over and made a miraculous catch, but then force of habit proved too strong for him. He straightened up and threw the baby to second base.

—JOEY ADAMS

I saw this guy at the baseball game all year, holding up a sign: "John-13." I looked it up. It said, "Go, Mookie!"

—ALAN HARVEY

Baseball's very big with my people. It figures. It's the only time we can shake a bat at a white man without starting a riot.

—DICK GREGORY

Football

I give the same halftime speech over and over. It works best when my players are better than the other coach's players.

—CHUCK MILLS

The exercise during history class one day was for each of the students to list whom they considered to be the eleven greatest Americans. After half an hour, everyone had turned in their papers except Irwin, who was still scratching his head and thinking furiously. "What's up?" asked the teacher. "Can't you come up with eleven great Americans?"

"I've got all but one," the student explained hastily. "It's the quarterback I can't decide on."

A football fan is a guy who'll yell at the quarterback for not spotting an open receiver forty-five yards away, then head for the parking lot and not be able to find his own car.

A man died and went to heaven. After reaching the gates to heaven, the man was talking with St. Peter and he asked, "I know I was good during my life, and I really appreciate being brought to heaven, but I'm really curious—what does hell look like?"

So St. Peter thought about it a moment and finally said, "I'll tell you what, I'll let you see what hell looks like before you are officially entered into heaven. Come with me."

And so St. Peter lead the man to an elevator and said, "Take this elevator to the very bottom floor. When the door opens, you will see what hell looks like, but whatever you do, do not get out of the elevator."

"Thank you," replied the man, who climbed into the elevator and hit the button for the lowest floor.

After nearly an hour waiting in the elevator, the doors opened and the man peered out. Before him was a lifeless frozen waste-land. All the man could see were huge mountains of ice through blankets of snow. Remembering what St. Peter said, the man quickly pushed the button for the top floor, the doors closed and he traveled back up to heaven.

After returning to heaven, the man approached St. Peter and said, "I'm ready to enter into heaven now, but before I do, I have just one more question."

"Go ahead," replied St. Peter, and so the man asked, "I thought hell would be fire and brimstone, but instead all I saw was snow and ice. Is that what it's really like?"

St. Peter thought about this for a second and finally answered, "Snow and ice, huh? I guess the Buffalo Bills finally won a Super Bowl."

If a man watches three football games in a row, he should be declared legally dead.

—ERMA BOMBECK

Football is not a contact sport. It's a collision sport. Dancing is a good example of a contact sport.

—DUFFY DAUGHERTY

Golf

Jesus and Moses went golfing, and were about even until they reached the fifteenth hole, a par five. Both balls landed about twenty feet from the edge of a little pond that stood between them and the hole. Moses took out a five-wood and landed his ball in excellent position. Jesus took out a five-iron.

"Hang on, hang on," cautioned Moses. "Use a wood—you'll never make it."

"If Arnold Palmer can make that shot with a five-iron, so can I," said Jesus. His ball landed in the middle of the lake. Moses parted the waters, retrieved the ball, and sighed when he saw Jesus still holding the five-iron.

"If Arnold Palmer can make that shot with a five-iron, so can I," maintained Jesus. Again Moses had to part the waters to retrieve the ball. By this time there were a number of people waiting to play through, and Moses said firmly, "Listen, Jesus, I'm not fetching the ball another time. Use a wood."

Jesus, however, still insisted, "If Arnold Palmer can make that shot with a five-iron, so can I." Splash!

Moses shook his head. "I told you, I'm not budging. Get it yourself."

So Jesus walked off across the water toward where the ball had landed.

At this, the onlookers gaped in astonishment. One came over to Moses and stammered, "I can't believe my eyes—that guy must think he's Jesus Christ!"

In response, Moses shook his head gloomily. "He *is* Jesus Christ. He *thinks* he's Arnold Palmer."

What's the difference between a golf ball and a woman's G-spot? A man will spend half an hour looking for a golf ball.

Jason, looking depressed, says to his business partner, "My doctor tells me I can't play golf."

"So he's played with you, too," the partner responds.

Golf is a lot like business. You drive hard to get in the green, and then wind up in the hole.

The avid golfer was out on the course with his wife one day. He played a shot on the fifth that sliced so badly, it ended up in the gardener's equipment shed. Looking in the door, the couple saw the ball sitting right in the middle of the room. "Look," volunteered the golfer's wife, "if I hold the door open, you can play a shot from here to the green."

This struck the golfer as an interesting challenge, but, alas, the ball missed the open door and struck his wife on the temple, killing her instantly.

Many years later, the widower was playing with a friend when he hit the exact same slice. The two of them walked into the shed, and, sure enough, there sat the ball in the center of the room. "I tell you what," said the friend. "If I hold the door open, I bet you can get the ball back onto the green."

"Oh, no," said the golfer, shaking his head. "I tried that once before and it took me seven shots to get out."

The club grouch was unhappy about everything: the food, the assessments, the parking, the other members. The first time he hit a hole-in-one, he complained, "Damn it, just when I needed the putting practice!"

—JOEY ADAMS

Give me my golf clubs, fresh air, and a beautiful partner, and you can keep my golf clubs and the fresh air.

—JACK BENNY

If you watch a game, it's fun. If you play it, it's recreation. If you work at it, it's golf.

—BOB HOPE

I play in the low eighties. If it's any hotter than that, I won't play.

—JOE E. LEWIS

One of the nicest things about golf is that you can play it for years and years. There were these two old friends who'd been playing together since they were kids, every Saturday morning and Sunday afternoon. Lester was eighty-two and his friend Ralph was eighty-one.

One day, on the eighth tee, Lester suddenly gave up. He turned to his pal and said, "Ralphie, old boy, I'm afraid I'm gonna have to quit. I just can't see anymore. I hit the ball, but I don't know where it goes."

Ralph said to him, "You can't quit. We've been playing together all these years. It wouldn't be the same without you."

"But what can I do?" asked Lester.

"You just leave it up to me. You go ahead and hit, and I'll keep my eye on it," said Ralph.

So Lester teed up and let fly. They stood silently for a few seconds. Then Lester said, "Well, Ralph, that sounded pretty good. Did you see where it went?"

"Of course I did!" said Ralph.

Lester said, "Well, where did it go?"

Ralph thought for a few seconds and said, "I forgot."

—Bob Kaliban

Mrs. Jones began to get nervous when dark fell and her husband hadn't returned from his regular Saturday golf game. Dinnertime came and went and she became more and more anxious, so when she heard his car pull in, she rushed out to the driveway. "Where've you been? I've been worried sick!" she exclaimed.

"Harry had a heart attack on the third hole," her husband explained.

"Oh, no! That's terrible."

"You're telling me," moaned her husband. "All day long it was hit the ball, drag Harry, hit the ball, drag Harry. . . ."

My neighbor was crying because her husband had left her for the sixth time. I consoled her, "Don't be unhappy, he'll be back."

"Not this time," she sobbed. "He's taken his golf clubs."

—Joey Adams

What do you call a woman who can suck a golf ball through fifty feet of garden hose?

Darling.

A shipwrecked man had spent ten years alone on a desert island, so he was overjoyed when a woman washed ashore one day. Tattered and clutching only a small watertight bag, she was the sole survivor of a pleasure boat that wrecked on the island's coral reef. The man could hardly wait to tell her of his survival by his wits alone for all that time.

"You mean you've been marooned for ten years?" asked the woman, awestruck.

"That's right," said the man, hanging his head modestly.

"Say, did you used to smoke?"

"You bet. Why?"

"I'd be delighted to offer you your first cigarette in ten years." With a smile, the woman pulled one out of her bag.

"Wow! Thanks a lot," said the man, taking a grateful puff.

"You didn't happen to be a drinking man, did you?" asked the woman shyly.

"I've been known to enjoy a glass or two," the man confessed, happily blowing smoke rings.

"Well, here you go," she said, pulling a flask out of her bag. As the man was gratefully taking a swig, the woman blushed. "Gee, I just realized it's been ten years since you, uh, played around, right?"

"Don't tell me," said the guy, a look of ecstasy coming over his face. "Have you got a set of *golf clubs* in that bag?"

One of the quickest ways to meet new people is to pick up the wrong ball on a golf course.

"You must be the worst caddie in the world," said the dejected golfer after a disastrous afternoon on the links.

"I doubt it, sir," replied the caddie. "That would be too much of a coincidence."

Eric: You know what your main trouble is?

Ernie: What?

Eric: You stand too close to the ball after you've hit it.

—Eric Morecambe and Ernie Wise

Three men went out on Sunday to play some golf. On the fourth hole, Fred chipped a shot into the rough. "You all play on ahead," he insisted. "I'll catch up with you."

Off they went, but after half an hour had gone by with no sign of their friend, Charlie said, "I'll go check on him."

The last guy played on for a while, but couldn't help wondering what on earth had happened to his companions. So, he too, finally turned back to check matters out.

An astonishing sight greeted him when he returned to the fourth hole: poor Fred was bent over the backseat of his golf cart, with his buddy energetically screwing him up the ass.

"Charlie, Charlie, what the hell are you doing!" he yelled, breaking into a run.

"It was horrible," gasped a red-faced Charlie. "When I got here, Fred had a massive heart attack."

"You're supposed to give him a heart massage, you idiot," cried the third guy, "and mouth-to-mouth resuscitation."

"I know *that*," retorted Charlie indignantly. "How do you think this got started?"

While playing golf today, I hit two good balls. I stepped on a rake.

—Henny Youngman

Hear about the naive golf widow who wanted to surprise her husband on his birthday?

She went into a sporting-goods store and asked the salesperson if she could see a low handicap.

I don't play golf. Personally, I think there's something psychologically wrong with any game in which the person who gets to hit the ball the most is the loser.

Some golfers are just natural cheaters. My brother-in-law cheats so much that the other day he had a hole-in-one and he marked a zero on his score card.

—Joey Adams

Why do businessmen play golf?

So they can dress up like pimps.

A guy is standing in front of his locker at the country club, admiring a golf ball in his hand. One of his golfing buddies says to him, "New ball?"

The guy says, "Would you believe this is the greatest golf ball ever made? You can't lose it. You hit it into the rough and it whistles. You hit it into the woods and a bell goes off. You drive it into the lake and a big burst of steam goes off six feet in the air for two whole minutes."

"That's amazing," says his friend. "Where'd you get it?"

And the guy says, "I found it."

—Soupy Sales

The prime minister of Israel invited the Pope to play a game of golf, and since the Pope had no idea how to play, he convened the College of Cardinals to ask their advice. "Call Jack Nicklaus," they suggested, "and let him play in your place. Tell the prime minister you're sick or something."

Honored by His Holiness's request, Nicklaus agreed to represent him on the links. The Pope, again on the advice of his staff, appointed him a cardinal to make the arrangement seem more legitimate. "So how'd you do?" he asked eagerly when Nicklaus returned to the Vatican.

"I came in second," was the reply.

"Second! You mean to tell me the prime minister of Israel beat you?" howled the Pope.

"No, Your Holiness," said Nicklaus. "Rabbi Palmer did."

A guy wakes up in the hospital with severe head injuries and the nurse says, "What happened to you?"

"Well," he says, "I was playing golf yesterday with my wife and we teed off at the second hole. I hit a beautiful drive two hundred and eighty yards down the middle of the fairway. My wife teed off and she sliced the ball into a field full of cows. We searched for several minutes and then I lifted up the tail of one of the cows

and spotted the ball lodged up it's ass. All I said was 'this looks like yours, dear' and that's the last thing I remember."

There was a foursome of doctors golfing. One was a guest. One by one the other three were "beeped" to their respective offices so the guest was left alone to finish out his round. When he finished, he went to the locker room.

Upon leaving the shower, he heard female voices and he realized he was in the wrong locker room. He decided to put a towel over his head so no one would see his face.

But as he was running out of the locker room, three women golfers saw him.

The first one said, "He's not my husband!"

The second said, "He's certainly not my husband!"

The third one chimes in, "Hell, he isn't even a member of this club!"

Hunting and Fishing

If God didn't want man to hunt, he wouldn't have given us plaid shirts.

—JOHNNY CARSON

What really happened to the buffaloes is just what you might expect if you've ever seen one in a suit—the moths got into them.

—WILL CUPPY

Stuffed deer heads on walls are bad enough, but it's worse when you see them wearing dark glasses and having streamers around their neck and a hat on their antlers, because then you know they were enjoying themselves at a party when they were shot.

—ELLEN DEGENERES

The fishing party was hopelessly lost in the deep woods. The sun was going down and the mosquitoes were starting to bite when one of the fishermen growled, "I thought you said you were the best damn guide in Minnesota."

"Oh, I am," replied the guide firmly, "but I'm pretty sure we're in Manitoba by now."

A fishing pal said to his buddy, "It seems that when you start talking about the fish you caught, the size changes depending on who you are talking to. How come?"

"Well," said the friend, "I never like to tell someone more than I think they'll ever believe."

While sports fishing off the Florida coast in Key West, a tourist capsized his boat. He could swim, but his fear of alligators kept him clinging to the overturned craft. Spotting an old beachcomber walking on the shore, the tourist shouted, "There wouldn't by chance be any alligators in these waters?!"

"No," the old man hollered back, "haven't been any for years!" Feeling relieved, the tourist started swimming leisurely toward the shore. About halfway toward shore he asked the old man, "Say, how'd you get rid of the gators, anyway?"

"We didn't do anything," the old man said. "The sharks got 'em."

I fish, therefore I lie.

Then there was Jake and Sal's fishing expedition. Sal went ahead to set up camp, only to realize that the rocky shores around Jackson Hole would make it impossible to maneuver their big boat to the water. Hiking into the nearest town, he sent his buddy a telegram instructing him to bring punts and a canoe instead.

Two days later, right on schedule, Jake arrived with two girls in tow. "I didn't know what a panoe was," he explained cheerfully, "but I got the girls."

The determined angler staggered up to the counter with an arm-load of the latest gear. As the cashier was ringing up the total, which came to several hundred dollars, the angler commented, "You know, you could save me an awful lot of money if you'd just start selling fish here."

Stinginess

Hear about the Scotsman who quit golf, then took it up again twelve years later?

He found his ball.

An engineer with a small construction company was in the field when a tremendous storm front caught up with him and all out-bound flights were canceled. He cabled the home office: "Marooned by floods. Send instructions."

Ms. Lowenstein, the owner of the firm and a woman of leg-endary tightfistedness, wired back: "Begin annual vacation im-mediately."

A chronic borrower begged an old friend to lend him a hundred dollars. "I'll pay it back the minute I return from Chicago," he promised.

"Exactly what day are you returning?" the friend asked.

The man shrugged. "Who's going?"

—Myron Cohen

Did you hear about the Scotsman who was so cheap that he went out into the yard on Christmas Eve and fired a shotgun?

So he could tell his kids that Santa had killed himself.

He likes to watch porno movies in reverse because he likes the part where the hooker gives the money back to the guy.

—Jim Belushi, about Billy Crystal

A tightwad owed a wedding present, and everything in the store seemed way overpriced—until he spotted a lovely porcelain vase which had, unfortunately, been broken. The storekeeper was delighted to part with the damaged item for a low price, and agreed to ship it to the newlyweds.

The next week the cheapskate received a note thanking him politely for the vase. It concluded, "Thank you, too, for taking care to wrap each piece separately."

He read in the paper that it takes ten dollars a year to support a kid in India, so he sent his kid there.

—RED BUTTONS

He had an awful dizzy spell. He dropped a dime in a revolving door and it took him five minutes to find it.

—BOB HOPE

Stress

Nervous? I feel like a pizza on the way to Jabba the Hut!

My husband was made president at the agency, and of course, it affected our lives. There are a lot of pressures. It made him very nervous. He became a nail-biter. Now, this doesn't sound like much, but it's my nails that he's biting.

My grandfather says, "You just write a few jokes and you're riding the gravy train?"

First of all, it's hard to write jokes. Second of all, what is a gravy train? I didn't know they were actually hauling gravy by rail. People gather around big mounds of mashed potatoes waiting for the five-fifteen gravy train to show up?

—RICH HALL

One has two duties—to be worried and not to be worried.

—E. M. FORSTER

What's the difference between anxiety and panic?

Anxiety is the first time you can't do it a second time, and panic is the second time you can't do it the first time.

When you don't have any money, the problem is food. When you have money, it's sex. When you have both, it's health. If everything is simply jake, then you're frightened of death.

—J. P. DONLEAVY

I have a new philosophy. I'm only going to dread one day at a time.

—CHARLES M. SCHULZ

The psychiatrist pointed out that most of the things his patient was anxious about never actually came to pass.

"I know," admitted the patient unhappily, "but then I worry about why they didn't happen."

The reason why worry kills more people than work is that more people worry than work.

—ROBERT FROST

Listening to the radio on the way to work doesn't help either. The other morning the disc jockey asked, "Hey, what makes you so sure you locked the front door?"

Stupidity

Mr. Weinberg came home unexpectedly and found his wife in bed with another man. Furious, he cried, "What are you doing?"

"See," said Mrs. Weinberg, turning to her lover, "I told you he was stupid."

When I was a kid, I was disappointed when I learned what an idiot Adam was. God gave him a woman and an apple and he ate the apple.

—Norm Crosby

Why did the Mafia have Einstein killed?

Because he knew too much.

Did you hear about the dumb guy who got his dick stuck in the battery?

He was told he had to jump it in order to get his car started.

Comic Stanley Myron Handelman says, "My house was burglarized about ten times. Finally I figured I'm really going to get this guy. So I made believe I went out, turned off all the lights, and hid in the closet. This guy thought I was out, came in, and stole two candlesticks, my silverware, and a portable television set. He thinks he's gonna get away. But this time I got a complete description of him. He was average height and build and he was wearing a rubber mask of Charles de Gaulle."

—Joey Adams

He would come in and say he changed his mind—which was a gilded figure of speech, because he didn't have any.

—Mark Twain

How about the kid whose teacher told him to write a hundred-word essay on what he did during summer vacation?

He wrote, "Not much," fifty times.

A carload of morons approached the scene of an accident. "Oh my God," gasped the driver, pulling over for a closer look at the crumpled sedan, "that looks like Joe's car." So they all piled out and walked closer.

467

"Look," said the second, "that's Joe's arm—I'd know that watch anywhere."

"I'm sure that's Joe's leg," said the third, pointing out where it lay against the curb.

"And look—that's definitely Joe's head," shouted the fourth, running after an object rolling slowly down the street. "Joe, Joe," he cried, picking it up. "Are you all right?"

Just before dawn, an Indian chief walked into his daughter's tent unannounced, only to find her in an embrace with one of the village's handsome young braves. Irate, he said to the brave, "Now that you've had relations with my daughter, you must marry her. But first you must pass an endurance test to prove your worth."

"I love your daughter," the young tribesman avowed, "and will be happy to submit to any test."

The chief and the brave walked down to the lake by the village, wrapped in their bearskins because it was mid-February and the temperature was five degrees below zero. They stopped on the edge of the frozen lake and the chief said, "You must chop a hole in the ice, swim the three miles to the other side, then swim back. Upon your return, we shall have a great feast and you shall wed my daughter."

"Love shall sustain me through this trial of my manhood," the brave vowed. And when he had finished chopping through the ice, he plunged into the icy waters. Three hours later there was no sign of the young brave. And though the vigil was kept until the wee hours of the evening, by then everyone in the village knew the worst—the young brave had not survived.

In his memory, the chief's daughter decided to name the lake after her lover. And to this day, it's referred to as Lake Stupid.

He's so stupid, he once studied five days for a urine test.

—Norm Crosby

The basketball coach stormed into the university president's office and demanded a raise right then and there.

"Jesus Christ, man," protested President Kubritski, "you already make more than the entire English department."

"Yeah, maybe so, but you don't know what I have to put up with," the coach blustered. "Look." He went out into the hall and grabbed a jock who was jogging down the hallway. "Run over to my office and see if I'm there," he ordered.

Twenty minutes later the jock returned, sweaty and out of breath. "You're not there, sir," he reported.

"Oh, I see what you mean," conceded President Kubritski, scratching his head. "I would have phoned."

A fellow walked into a nice-looking bar, sat down, and ordered a drink. As he sat there, he noticed people walking in and out of a back room but he didn't really think twice about it. Ordering another drink, he asked the bartender casually, "So, what do people around here do for excitement?"

"See that number on the back of your seat?" answered the bartender. "If your number's called, you get a free piece of ass."

"Wow, that sounds great," said the guy, deciding to stick around. When it came time to order another drink, he turned to the guy next to him and griped, "Hell, I've been here over an hour—how do you win at this thing?"

The man gave him a conspiratorial wink and said, "Don't give up, buddy. Hell, my wife has already won five times!"

"Look at my new watch," said one Aggie to another. "This here shows what time it is now. And when you push this little button, you can see what time it was at this exact time yesterday."

When the son of a wealthy Italian industrialist was kidnapped, his parents waited impatiently for word from his abductors. The first contact was a box that arrived on the doorstep containing the boy's left ear.

"Magnifico!" exclaimed the magnate. "As soon as we get alla his parts, we can put him back together again."

A stranger walks into a bar and announces loudly, "Hey, guys, have I got some great longshoremen jokes for you!"

The bartender leans over and says in an ominous tone, "Listen, if I were you, I'd watch my tongue. The two three-hundred-pound bouncers are longshoremen; I'm no midget, and I'm a longshoreman; and so is every other guy in here."

"Oh, no problem," counters the stranger cheerfully. "I'll talk v-e-r-y s-l-o-w-l-y."

Remember, even a head of iceberg lettuce knows more than you do. It knows whether or not that light really does go out when the refrigerator door shuts.

Three men were sitting at a bar. Ordering a drink, the first said, "I hate this place. I know a place on State Street where I can get every third drink free."

"That's nothing," spoke up the second. "I know a joint over on the west side where every other drink is free."

"Oh yeah?" chipped in the third guy. "Well I know a place on the south side where every drink is free and at the end of the night you can get laid in the parking lot!"

"No kidding?" asked his companions. "That sounds great— where'd you hear about it?"

"From my wife," he told them proudly.

If ignorance is bliss, why aren't more people happy?

A guy walks into work, and both of his ears are all bandaged up. The boss says, "What happened to your ears?"

He says, "Yesterday I was ironing a shirt when the phone rang and shhh! I accidentally answered the iron."

The boss says, "Well, that explains one ear, but what happened to your other ear?"

He says, "Well, jeez, I had to call the doctor!"

Chester walks into Marshall Dillon's office with a huge boner. The marshall says, "For Christ's sakes, Chester, go out in the barn and stick that thing in a shovelful of horseshit."

Chester walks into the barn with this huge hard-on, and there's Miss Kitty, lying in the hay playing with herself. She takes one look at Chester, spreads her legs, and says, "Put it in there, Chester."

Chester says, "The whole shovelful?"

Stupid Steven is walking home loaded late one night and smacks into a tree. He backs up, and then walks into the tree again. Twice more the same thing happens.

He says, "This is just terrific. I should have been home two hours ago, and here I am lost in the forest."

Why'd the dimwitted girl stop wearing her training bra?
The wheels were irritating her armpits.

Two friends rented a boat and fished in a lake every day. One day they caught thirty fish. One man said to the other, "Mark this spot so we can come here tomorrow."

The next day when they were driving to rent the boat, the same one said, "Did you mark that spot?"

His friend replied, "Yeah, I put a big X on the bottom of the boat."

The first one said, "You fool! What if we don't get that same boat today!"

Two guys, Tom and Jack, were sitting in a bar one day, when two fishermen walked in with two huge trout. Jack asked where they got the fish, and the fishermen told them that they go down to the bridge, and one guy holds the other by the ankles until a fish is caught.

Tom and Jack figured they could do that.

After holding Tom for about twenty minutes, Jack asked him if he had anything, and the reply was "No." About twenty more

minutes passed, Jack asked again, and again the reply was "No."
Finally, Tom yelled, "Pull me up!! Pull me up!"

Jack said, "Ya got one?"

Tom said, "No! A train is coming!!"

Lifeguard: I've been watching you, Mr. Jones, and you'll have to stop
urinating in the pool.

Mr. Jones: But everybody urinates in the pool.

Lifeguard: From the diving board?

A prominent Russian scientist conducted a very important experiment. He trained a flea to jump upon giving her a verbal
command ("Jump!").

In the first stage of the experiment, he removed the flea's leg,
told her to jump, and the flea jumped. So he wrote in his scien-
tific notebook: "Upon removing one leg, all flea organs function
properly."

So, he removed the second leg, asked the flea to jump, she
obeyed, so he wrote again: "Upon removing the second leg, all
flea organs function properly."

Thereafter he removed all the legs but one, the flea jumped
when ordered, so he wrote again: "Upon removing the next leg,
all flea organs function properly."

Then he removed the last leg, told the flea to jump, and nothing happened.

He did not want to take a chance, so he repeated the experiment several times, and the legless flea never jumped. So he
wrote the conclusion: "Upon removing the last leg, the flea loses
sense of hearing."

A man is walking past a travel agent's office when he notices a bill-
board announcing "Four-Day Cruise Down the Murray River—$40 all
inclusive." Impressed by the low price, he races into the shop, slaps
forty dollars on the counter and announces, "I'm here for the Murray
cruise."

Quick as a wink, the travel agent whips out a baseball bat and knocks him unconscious.

When the man wakes, he finds himself tied to a floating log and drifting down the river. After a time, he notices another man in the same predicament on the other side of the river. "Forty-dollar Murray cruise?" he calls out.

"Yep!" says the man on the other side. "I'll bet you we don't even get breakfast," he yells.

"Well," calls the other man, "we did last year."

Success

A friend of mine got a seat in his honor at a local college. He would have been more flattered had they taken off the strip that said "Sanitized for your protection."

When her formal education was over, a young woman went out into the world to start her own business. After a year, she reported that she was worth five thousand dollars, but her parents merely smiled. After a few more years her net worth had grown to some fifteen thousand dollars, and each year it increased by modest amounts, but her parents never had more than a smile or pat on the back for her.

Then one year she came home and announced that in order to keep the business going, she'd had to borrow a million dollars. At this her father bounded up from the sofa, clapped her on the back, and crowed, "Now that's an achievement!"

There's no secret about success. Did you ever know a successful man that didn't tell you all about it?

—KIN HUBBARD

Behind every successful man stands an amazed woman.

I bought a cassette tape on how to be successful. It was one of those subliminal tapes, a motivational cassette. It was twenty dollars and it kept saying, "Don't ask for your money back, don't ask for your money back." I exchanged it for one on how to be more assertive. Then I went back and threw it through the store window. The store owner came out. He had been listening to a motivational tape on how to commit murder. If he hadn't been listening at slow speed, I would never have been able to dodge the bullets.

—Ron Smith

Eighty percent of success is showing up.

—Woody Allen

When I was young, I used to think that wealth and power would bring me happiness. . . . I was right.

—Gahan Wilson

I've always gone along with the view that, first, the surest guarantee of sexual success is sexual success (you can't have one without the other and you can't have the other without the one), and, second, that the trappings of sexual success are only fleetingly distinguishable from sexual success itself.

—Martin Amis

All my life I said I wanted to be someone. . . . I can see now that I should have been more specific.

What does a little WASP girl want to be when she grows up?
  "The very best person I possibly can."

[Success] means that you have, as performers will call it, "fuck you" money. . . . All that means is that I don't have to do what I don't want to do.

474

In the Beginning was the Plan

And then came the Assumptions

And the Assumptions were without form

And the Plan was completely without substance

And the darkness was upon the face of the workers

And they spoke among themselves, saying,

"It is a crock of shit, and it stinketh to high heaven."

And the workers went unto their Supervisors and sayeth,

"It is a pail of dung and none may abide the odor thereof."

And the Supervisors went unto their Managers and sayeth unto them,

"It is a container of excrement and it is very strong, such that none may abide by it."

And the Managers went unto their Directors and sayeth,

"It is a vessel of fertilizer, and none may abide its strength."

And the Directors spoke amongst themselves, saying one to another,

"It contains that which aids plant growth, and it is very strong."

And the Directors went unto the Vice Presidents and sayeth unto them,

"It promotes growth and is very powerful."

And the Vice Presidents went unto the President and sayeth unto him,

"This new plan will actively promote the growth and efficiency of this Company, and these Areas in particular."

And the President looked upon the Plan,

And saw that it was good, and the Plan became Company Policy.

This Is How Shit Happens.

T

Talent

After my screen test, the director clapped his hands gleefully and yelled, "She can't talk! She can't act! She's sensational!"

—AVA GARDNER

Some people think a juggler is talented. Could be a schizophrenic playing catch.

—BOB DUBAC

I know this guy who's a gift to humanity, but so is Kaopectate.

—JAN MURRAY

A TV producer was pitching his idea for a holiday special to a room full of jaded network executives. "It's gonna get fabulous ratings," he raved. "I've gotten Spielberg to direct it."

"Steven?"

"No, Bernie. Bright kid right out of UCLA film school, does great work. And for the composer, I've got Sondheim all lined up."

"Stephen?"

"No, Maxie. She's written some great jingles, very talented, you'll eat her work right up. And for the singer, I've got Goulet."

"Robert?"

"Yes!"

"Shit."

"Please, Mr. Grossman, my act is really something special. Just give me a minute." Before the talent scout could object, the desperate actor climbed up on the desk, flapped his arms, and proceeded to fly around the room twice.

"Okay," said the agent, "so you can imitate birds. What else?"

We've all been blessed with God-given talents. Mine just happens to be beating people up.

—Sugar Ray Leonard

I know a guy who plays a pretty good piano. It's a Steinway.

If it wasn't for my faults, I'd be perfect.

This woman is sitting in a bar, wearing some sort of tube top. She has never shaved her armpits in her entire life, so, as a result, she has a thick black bush under each arm. Every twenty minutes, she raises her arm up and flags the bartender for another drink.

This goes on all night. The other people in the bar see her hairy armpits every time she raises her arm.

Near the end of the evening, this drunk at the end of the bar says to the bartender, "Hey, I'd like to buy the ballerina a drink."

The bartender replies, "She's not a ballerina. What makes you think she's a ballerina?"

The drunk says, "Any girl who can lift her leg that high *has* to be a ballerina!"

Taxes

When Mr. Fine was audited, the IRS took exception to certain deductions, among them one for the birth of a child. "She was born in January," the auditor pointed out.

"So?" he protested. "It was last year's business."

Somehow the IRS auditor knew it was my first audit. "How could you tell?" I asked.

"For this kind of examination you don't have to undress," she explained.

What gets me is that estimated tax return. You have to guess how much money you're going to make. You have to fill it out, sign it, send it in. I sent mine in last week. I didn't sign it. If I have to guess how much money I'm gonna make, let them guess who sent it.

—JIMMY EDMONTON (PROFESSOR BACKWARDS)

"Where's my paycheck?" asked the clerk of the paymaster in the big plant. The cashier explained, "Well, after deducting withholding tax, state income tax, city tax, Social Security, retirement fund, unemployment insurance, hospitalization, dental insurance, group life insurance, and your donation to the company welfare fund, you owe us fourteen dollars and twenty-five cents."

—JOEY ADAMS

"Now, class, who can tell me what caused the American Revolution to break out?" asked Mrs. Humphries of her freshman economics class.

"Taxation," replied a student in the front row.

"Very good, Sherry," The teacher turned to a boy whose hand was waving. "Yes, Andrew?"

"I have a question, Mrs. Humphries. How come they teach that we won?"

You know what they're doing with your taxes? They're spending your money, hundreds of billions of dollars, on defense. To defend us from the Russians, the Nicaraguans, the Libyans, the Iranians. When was the last time a Russian broke into your car? I'm not worried about Russians, I'm worried about Americans! You're going to defend me, defend me from Americans! Get my butt back from Burger King alive!

—BLAKE CLARK

When Joe Louis was asked who had hit him the hardest during his boxing career, he replied, "That's easy—Uncle Sam!"

I just saw a modern-day version of *Faust*. In the first act he sells his soul to the devil. Then he spends the rest of the opera trying to convince the Internal Revenue Service it was a long-term capital gain.

The income tax has made more liars out of the American people than golf has.

—WILL ROGERS (ATTRIBUTED)

I don't know why they couple death and taxes. You only die once.

Of the two basic certainties, death and taxes, death is preferable. At least you're not called in six months later for an audit.

—BILL VAUGHAN

You've got to admire the IRS. Any organization that makes that much money without advertising deserves respect.

One young man applied for the job of bookkeeper. "Can you do double-entry?" he was asked.
    "No problem," he replied, "and I can do triple-entry, too."
    "Triple-entry?"
    "Sure. One for the working partner, showing the true profits, another for the sleeping partner showing small profits, and a third for the tax authorities showing a loss."

—JOEY ADAMS

I wouldn't mind paying taxes, if I knew they were going to a friendly country.

—DICK GREGORY

Technology

Cordless phones are great. If you can find them.

—Glenn Foster

Now they've got a stereo that gives real concert hall sound. Every two minutes it coughs and rattles a program.

A guy is walking down the street and passes a hardware store advertising a sale on a chain saw that is capable of cutting seven hundred trees in seven hours. The guy thinks that's a great deal and decides to buy one.

The next day, he comes back with the saw and complains to the salesman that the thing didn't come close to chopping down the seven hundred trees the ad said it would.

"Well," said the salesman, "let's test it out back."

Finding a log, the salesman pulls the starter cord and the saw makes a great roaring sound.

"What's that noise?" asks the guy.

Smith was a man of cold facts, a scientist, a computer jock, and a confirmed atheist. He became somewhat obsessed with the desire to prove the truth. So he mortgaged his house and sold his car in order to put a down payment on the most powerful computer commercially available.

Then Smith plugged it into every data bank in the world, accessed every library in the United States and Europe, and had the machine scan every book published since the invention of the printing press.

Finally, Smith sat down at the console, took a deep breath, and typed, "Is there a God?"

The monitor flickered, the hard drives clicked, and up on the screen came the words, "There is now."

"I hate this darn machine," complained an office worker about his newly automated work station. "It never does what I want it to do, only what I tell it."

I don't see why religion and science can't cooperate. What's wrong with using a computer to count our blessings?

—Robert Orben

I'm addicted to the Internet. I check into the hotel. Try to go online on my laptop. Doesn't work. Call the front desk. Lady's like, "Sorry, sir, we don't have Internet service in all our hotel rooms. But don't worry, we have free wireless in the lobby."
 "You're saying I have to whack off in the lobby?"

—Jeffrey Ross

It is amazing how email has changed our lives. You ever get a handwritten letter in the mail today? "What the . . . ? Has someone been kidnapped?"

—Jim Gaffigan

At mail call, Ensign Smith was delighted to be handed a big envelope from his wife, but was rather puzzled by the intricate drawing it contained. At the bottom he found his wife had scrawled a brief note. "This is how our dashboard looks," it read. "Do we need oil?"

Did you hear about the inventor who worked for years on a cross between a toaster and an electric blanket?
 He was going to sell it to people who wanted to pop out of bed.
 He's also developing a new smoke detector—it comes with a snooze alarm.

How do they know computers existed in biblical times?
 Because Eve had an Apple, and Adam had a Wang.

What do you call a genetic engineering company in Italy?

Genitalia.

What's dumb?

Directions on toilet paper.

What's dumber than that?

Reading them.

Even dumber?

Reading them and learning something.

Dumbest of all?

Reading them and having to correct something you've been doing wrong.

Did you hear about the new calculator for dumb people?

It's a giant hand with ten thousand fingers.

How can you spot a secretary who's a slow learner?

He's the one with White-Out all over his screen, and the one who puts his floppies in the Xerox machine to copy files.

What's the difference between a JAP and a computer?

A computer sometimes goes down.

Teenagers

Remember that as a teenager you are at the last stage in your life when you will be happy to hear that the phone is for you.

—Fran Lebowitz

When I was a boy of fourteen, my father was so ignorant, I could hardly stand to have the old man around. But when I got to be twenty-one, I was astonished at how much he had learned in seven years.

—Mark Twain

She has her own apartment, in mine.

—JEAN CARROLL, ABOUT HER TEENAGE DAUGHTER'S LIFESTYLE

Somewhat skeptical of his son's newfound determination to become Charles Atlas, the father nevertheless followed the teenager over to the weight-lifting department. "Please, Dad," wheedled the boy, "I promise I'll use 'em every day. . . ."

"I dunno, Michael. It's really a commitment on your part," the father pointed out.

"Please, Dad?"

"They're not cheap either."

"I'll use 'em Dad, I promise. You'll see."

Finally won over, the father paid for the equipment and headed for the door. From the corner of the store he heard his son yelp, "What! You mean I have to carry them to the car?"

Many a man wishes he were strong enough to tear a telephone book in half—especially if he has a teenage daughter.

—GUY LOMBARDO

Television

I was watching the Discovery channel the other day and I discovered something. I need a girlfriend.

—DAVE ATTELL

Who else but a television executive would refer to a salad as a "lead in?"

—BOB HOPE

Let me get this straight: The networks won't give gavel-to-gavel coverage of political conventions because they're dull, but fight for the privilege of broadcasting all the laps of the Indianapolis 500?

—ROGER SIMON

Imitation is the sincerest form of television.

—FRED ALLEN

A television producer is someone who spends your money, picks up your laundry, books your guests, and when your show is canceled, lends you his car for you to go to the unemployment office.

—BOB HOPE

Ninety-eight percent of American homes have TV sets—which means the people in the other two percent of the households have to generate their own sex and violence.

—FRANKLIN P. JONES

Some sports I can't watch on TV. I don't mind the games—I don't like the interview after the game. Because the winning players always give credit to God while the losing players blame themselves. Just once I'd like to hear a player say, "Yeah, we were in the game—until Jesus made me fumble!"

—JEFF STILSON

You can always tell when television executives are in a restaurant: they keep ordering and canceling, ordering and canceling.

—BOB HOPE

Thought and Thinking

If I look confused, it's because I'm thinking.

—SAMUEL GOLDWYN

If you make people think they're thinking, they'll love you. If you really make them think, they'll hate you.

—DON MARQUIS

The rich are nothing but poor people with yachts.

When you open a new bag of cotton balls, is the top one meant to be thrown away?

Help stamp out and abolish redundancy!

There's times when I just have to quit thinking . . . and the only way I can quit thinking is by shopping.

—TAMMY FAYE BAKKER

It's not an optical illusion, it just looks like one.

The father was very proud when his son went off to college. He came to tour the school on Parents' Day, and observed his son hard at work in the chemistry lab. "What are you working on?" he asked.

"A universal solvent," explained the son, "a solvent that'll dissolve anything."

The father whistled, clearly impressed, then wondered aloud, "What'll you keep it in?"

—GILBERT GOTTFRIED

Einstein explained his theory to me every day, and on my arrival, I was fully convinced that he understood it.

—CHAIM WEIZMANN, PRESIDENT OF ISRAEL,
ABOUT A TRANSATLANTIC CROSSING WITH ALBERT EINSTEIN

What's the difference between apathy and ignorance?
 I don't know, and I don't care!

Time

Everywhere is walking distance if you have the time.

—STEVE WRIGHT

A man was trying to understand the nature of God, and asked him: "God, how long is a million years to you?" God answered: "A million years is like a minute." Then the man asked: "God, how much is a million dollars to you?" And God replied: "A million dollars is like a penny." Finally the man asked: "God, could you give me a penny?" And God said, "In a minute."

Backwards thinking. I plan dates backwards. The movie's at ten, that means I pick her up at nine, that means I'm in the shower at eight, that means I'm running at seven, that means I leave work at six, that means I get to work at nine, that means I'm asleep the night before at midnight, that means . . . I'm late now. I can't make it.

—Larry Miller

We prefer the old-fashioned alarm clock to the kind that awakens you with soft music or a gentle whisper. If there's one thing we can't stand early in the morning, it's hypocrisy.

—Bill Vaughan

Tourists

There was a hijacking of a tourist bus. Luckily, it was filled with Japanese tourists—they got more than two thousand photographs of the hijackers.

—Jan Murray

I was walking around Taiwan and bought some flip-flops for my feet. I said, "I wonder where these were made." I looked under the bottom, it said, "Just around the corner."

—George Wallace

A timid tourist stopped a New York City cop. "Can you tell me how to get to Carnegie Hall," she asked, clearing her throat nervously, "or should I just go fuck myself?"

Transportation

I'm astounded by people who want to know the universe when it's hard enough to find your way around Chinatown.

—WOODY ALLEN

Love the questions at the airport because, they make you feel real intelligent. "Sir, do you know what's in your luggage?"
     "No. I tied a sock around my eyes and packed with my feet. I'm thinking hot dogs and gunpowder."

—KEVIN JAMES

Two tour groups visited England. They happened to rent a double-decker bus, with one group downstairs and the others upstairs. The downstairs group was singing and dancing and the group upstairs just sat there. Finally, one of the downstairs people went upstairs and asked why they weren't having as much fun. "That's easy for you to say," said one of the upstairs guys, "You have a driver."

—FREDDIE ROMAN

If the 'black box' flight recorder is never damaged during a plane crash, why isn't the whole damn plane made out of that shit?

—GEORGE CARLIN

Travel

What do *National Geographic* and *Penthouse* have in common?
     Both have great places you'll probably never visit.

To give you an idea of how fast we traveled: we left Spokane with two rabbits and when we got to Topeka, we still had only two.

—Bob Hope

The wealthy Iranian tourist was outraged at being searched by customs upon his arrival at JFK Airport. "New York is the asshole of the world!" he screamed.

"Yessir," said the customs official. "Are you just passing through?"

A naive fellow boarded an ocean liner for a fancy cruise and was amazed at the grand scale of shipboard life. The ballroom was the size of a ball field, the couches seated ten couples, the banquet tables stretched for what seemed like miles. After a considerable amount to eat and drink, he asked the steward directions to the men's room, but got lost en route and fell into the Olympic-size pool. Splashing frantically toward the ladder, he screamed in a panic, "Don't flush! Don't flush!"

The project manager was stuck in a tiny town out in the middle of nowhere, waiting for materials to arrive. One week stretched to two, and by the end of the third week he couldn't take it anymore. He went into the local whorehouse, plunked down a hundred dollars, and requested the worst blow job in the joint.

Pocketing the cash, the madam said, "Sir, for a hundred dollars, you don't have to settle for the worst. Why, it'll buy you the very best we have to offer."

"Let me set you straight," explained the fellow. "I'm not horny, I'm homesick."

When does this place get to England?

—Bea Lillie, aboard the Queen Mary

You remember the story of the Ark, the ship that carried a male and female of every living creature on earth? I'm pretty sure it was the last cruise ship that was evenly matched.

Thanks to the miles of super highways under construction, America will soon be a wonderful place to drive—if you don't want to stop.

—FLETCHER KNEBEL

A tired traveler pulls into a hotel around midnight. Very tired after a long day's trip, he asks the clerk for a single room. As the clerk does the paperwork, the man looks around and sees a gorgeous blond sitting in the lobby. He tells the clerk to wait while he goes into the lobby. After a minute he comes back, with the girl on his arm.

"Fancy meeting my wife here," he says to the clerk. "Guess I'll need a double room for the night."

The next morning, he goes to the front desk to settle his bill, and finds the amount to be over three thousand dollars. "What's the meaning of this?" he yells at the clerk. "I've only been here one night!"

"Yes," says the clerk, "but your wife has been here for three weeks."

I wouldn't mind seeing China if I could come back the same day.

—PHILIP LARKIN

A man and a woman are driving along when they see a wounded skunk on the side of the road. They stop, the woman gets out, picks it up, and brings it into the car.

She says, "Look, it's shivering . . . it must be cold. What should I do?"

He says, "Put it between your legs."

She says, "What about the smell?"

He says, "Hold its nose."

A guy is on a trip on a small airline. The stewardess says, "Would you like dinner?"

He says, "What are my choices?"

She says, "Yes or no."

Trust

Never put anything on paper, my boy, and never trust a man with a small black mustache.

—P. G. WODEHOUSE

The louder he talked of his honor, the faster we counted our spoons.

—RALPH WALDO EMERSON

After almost twenty years of teaching kindergarten, Miss Groden had composed a note that she had each child carry home at the end of the first week of school. It read, "Dear Parents—if you promise not to believe everything your child says happens at school, I'll promise not to believe everything he or she says happens at home."

Why don't men trust women?

Would you trust anything that bled for three days and didn't die?

What's the definition of "trust"?

Two cannibals giving each other a blow job.

Truth

Of course, facts are only as useful as one permits them to be. Take the example of the fellow who was convinced he was dead. He visited his doctor with this complaint several times and the doctor was unable to change his mind. Finally, the exasperated doctor demanded whether his patient would believe otherwise in the face of physical evidence that he was alive. "Of course," said the man calmly. "I'm a reasonable fellow."

"Now would you agree that dead men don't bleed?"

"Of course."

"Fine. Give me your hand," ordered the physician. Taking a needle, he swiftly pricked a fingertip, then squeezed it until a drop of blood beaded up. He thrust it in front of the man's eyes. "Look! Is that not blood?"

"I'll be darned," said the patient after a moment's astonished reflection. "Dead men do bleed."

He uses statistics as a drunken man uses lampposts—for support rather than for illumination.

—Andrew Lang

The trouble with facts is that there are so many of them.

—Samuel McChord Crothers

"Private, where did you get that rifle?" asked the colonel when the young soldier returned from the battlefield.

"I stole it, sir!" barked the private.

"You see," said the colonel to his lieutenant, "they'll steal, but they sure as hell won't lie. That's a soldier!"

On a blind date, a man met his date at a very fancy restaurant. Unfortunately, she looked nothing like he was led to believe. When they received the menu, his date said, "Can I really order anything?"

"Of course you may," he responded.

"Well, then I guess I'll have the lobster."

Her date then responded, "Why don't you guess again?"

V

Vanity

Have you ever had one of those nights when you didn't want to go out . . . but your hair looked too good to stay home?

—Jack Simmons

The trendy dresser fancied himself quite a lady-killer, and was delighted to find a note pinned inside a new shirt. It contained a girl's name and address, and asked the recipient to send a photograph. How romantic, he thought to himself, very taken with the idea of this mystery woman so eager to meet him, and promptly mailed off a note and a photograph.

Heart aflutter, he opened her response. It read, "Thanks for writing. I was just curious to see what kind of guy would buy such a funny shirt."

To impress a girl, Harry Richman would tip the waiter fifty dollars just to get a menu. It is reliably reported that he said to the maitre d' at the Stork Club, "What's the biggest tip you ever received?"

The headwaiter replied, "A hundred dollars."

Harry gave him two hundred dollars, then asked, "Now tell me—who gave you the hundred?"

The man said, "You did, Mr. Richman."

—Joey Adams, about Harry Richman

I don't deserve this, but then, I have arthritis and I don't deserve that either.

—Jack Benny, accepting an award

The handsome actor had no qualms about pointing out that he was a perfect physical specimen. "In fact, I'm so perfect, I had my whole self insured. Why, my dick alone is insured with Lloyds of London for fifty thousand dollars."

"Smart," commented a lady friend, who was thoroughly fed up with his boasting. "What did you do with the money?"

Mort knew he was probably oversensitive about the problem, but the fact was that his eyes bulged. He went to doctor after doctor, but none seemed to know of any treatment. In desperation he looked up "Eye, Bulging" in the Yellow Pages. Sure enough a doctor was listed, and a few days later Mort found himself sitting on a vinyl couch in a seedy waiting room. A little nervous about being the only patient, he reminded himself how rare the condition was and that the doctor was a specialist.

At long last he was admitted to the doctor's office and was examined. The doctor leaned back and informed him that there was a remedy, but not an easy one. "I must cut your balls off," he said.

Mort's eyes bulged even more as he headed for the door. But after a few weeks of thinking it over, Mort acknowledged that his bulging eyes were what kept him from getting laid in the first place, so he decided to go ahead with the operation. So he returned for the operation, and sure enough, his eyeballs sunk back into their sockets most agreeably. In fact, he looked not only normal but actually rather handsome.

Delighted, he thanked the doctor profusely, and decided to treat himself to a new suit.

"Charcoal gray pinstripe," he instructed the tailor. "Medium lapel, no cuffs."

"Fine," said the tailor, nodding. "Come back on Tuesday."

"Aren't you going to measure me?" asked Mort.

"Nah. I've been at this over thirty years; I can tell your size just by looking," the tailor assured him.

"That's impossible," blurted Mort.

"Size forty-two jacket, right?"

"Yes," admitted Mort, amazed.

"Thirty-two-inch inseam, right?"

Mort nodded, dumbstruck.

"Thirty-six-inch waist?"

Again Mort nodded.

"And you wear size forty underwear, right?" concluded the tailor with a smile.

"Nope!" Mort told him. "Thirty-four."

"Listen, you can't fool me," said the tailor wearily. "Don't even try to put one over."

"I'm telling you, I wear size thirty-four underwear," Mort insisted.

"You can't wear size thirty-four underwear," protested the exasperated tailor. "Your eyes would bulge out of their sockets!"

I never loved a person the way I loved myself.

—MAE WEST

The man says to his hair stylist, "My hair is falling out. What can I use to keep it in?"

The stylist replies, "Might I suggest a shoe box?"

Weather

On cable TV they have a weather channel—twenty-four hours of weather. We had something like that where I grew up. We called it a window.

—Dan Spencer

"How did you find the weather in London?" asked a man's wife upon his return from a long trip. "You don't have to find the weather in London, it bumps into you at every corner.

Edith and Roberta were hanging out their laundry in their backyards when the talk came around to why Marcia's laundry never got rained on. So when Marcia came out with her laundry basket, Roberta asked her how come she always seemed to know in advance whether it was going to rain. "Your laundry's never hanging out on those days," she commented in an aggrieved tone.

Marcia leaned over her fence and winked at her two friends. "When I wake up in the morning, I look over at Buddy," she explained. "If his penis is hanging over his right leg, I know it's going to be fair weather and I come right out with my laundry. On the other hand, if it's hanging left, for sure it's going to rain, so I hang it up inside."

"Well, smarty-pants," said Edith, "what's the forecast if Buddy's got a hard-on?"

"Honey," replied Marcia with a smile, "on a day like *that* you don't do the *laundry*."

What did the flasher say to the woman in subzero weather?
"It's so cold—should I just describe myself?"

495

Three macho Eskimos were arguing about who had the coldest igloo, so they decided to check each in turn. Sure he'd clinched the argument, the first Eskimo pulled back his polar-bear-skin blanket and revealed that his bed was made of ice.

"Nah, mine's colder," claimed the second Eskimo. And when they reached his igloo, it was snowing inside.

"Pretty cold," conceded the third Eskimo, "but I've got you beat." He led the way to his igloo, where he pulled back the bedcovers to reveal a brown spot on the bed. Chipping it off with an ice pick, he tossed it into the fire, and after several minutes a noise came forth like someone passing gas. In response to the puzzled glances of the other two Eskimos, he explained with a smile, "Frozen fart."

Two farmers were boasting about the strongest wind they'd ever experienced. "Out here in California," said one, "I've seen the fiercest wind in my life. You know those giant redwood trees? Well the wind got so strong, it bent them right over."

"That's nothing," said the farmer from Iowa. "Back on my farm we had a wind one day that blew a hundred miles per hour. It was so bad that one of my hens had her back turned to the wind and she laid the same egg six times."

—JOE LAURIE, JR.

Wives

Wives are people who feel they don't dance enough.

—GROUCHO MARX

Basically my wife was immature. I'd be at home in the bath and she'd come in and sink my boats.

—WOODY ALLEN

**What's the difference between your paycheck and your wife?
You don't have to beg your wife to blow your paycheck.**

Definition of a diplomat: A man who can convince his wife that a fur coat will make her look fat.

A couple came upon a wishing well. The husband leaned over, made a wish, and threw in a penny. The wife decided to make a wish, too. But she leaned over too much, fell into the well, and was yelling and screaming because she was all wet. The husband was stunned for a while, but then smiled and said, "It really works!"

Some mornings I wake up Grouchy . . . and some mornings I just let her sleep.

For the first year of marriage, I had a basically bad attitude. I tended to place my wife underneath a pedestal.

—WOODY ALLEN

Explaining to his doctor that his sex life wasn't all it could be, Norm asked his doctor for a pill that would enable him to perform for his wife. It so happened that the doctor had just the right medication, so Norm popped a pill and drove home, but it also happened that his wife had to work late that night. So after waiting for a while in growing discomfort, Norm finally had to jerk off.

When the doctor called to check the next day, Norm explained what had happened. "Gee, Norm," the doctor explained, "there are other women in the building, you know."

"Doctor," Norm explained in an exasperated tone, "for other women I don't need a pill."

I made a big mistake when I put my wife on a pedestal. Now she can't reach the floor to clean.

Women

One day, three men are out having a relaxing day fishing, when suddenly they catch a mermaid. After they haul the mermaid up in a net, she promises that if the men set her free, she will grant each of them a wish in return. The first man doesn't believe it, so he says, "All right, if you can really grant wishes, then double my IQ." The mermaid says, "Done," and suddenly, the first man starts to flawlessly recite Shakespeare and analyze it with extreme insight.

The second man is so amazed, he looks at the mermaid and says, "Triple my IQ." The mermaid says, "Done," and the second man starts to recite solutions to mathematical problems that have been stumping all of the scientists in various fields from physics to chemistry.

The third man is so enthralled with the changes in his friends, he says to the mermaid: "Quintuple my IQ." The mermaid looks at him and says, "You know, I normally don't try to change people's minds when they make a wish, but I really wish you'd reconsider." The man responds, "Nope, I want you to increase my IQ times five, and if you don't do it, I won't set you free."

"Please," said the mermaid. "You don't know what you're asking, it'll change your entire view on the universe. Won't you ask for something else, a million dollars, anything?" But no matter what the mermaid said, the third man insisted on having his IQ increased by five times its usual power. So the mermaid finally relented and said, "Done." The third man became a woman.

Girls got balls. They're just a little higher up, that's all.

—JOAN JETT

I hate women because they always know where things are.

—JAMES THURBER

Women: You can't live with them, and you can't get them to dress up in a skimpy Nazi costume and beat you with a warm squash.

—EMO PHILLIPS

Men lie the most, women tell the biggest lies . . . a man lie is, "I was at Kevin's house!" A woman lie is like, "It's your baby!"

—CHRIS ROCK

Real women don't have hot flashes, they have power surges.

Why don't women have any brains?
   Because they don't have any testicles to put them in.

Rick: I mean, what am I supposed to call you? My girlfriend? My companion? My roommate? Nothing sounds quite right.
   Joanie: How about your "reason for living"?
   Rick: No, no, I need something I can use around the office.

—GARRY TRUDEAU

On one issue at least, men and women agree: They both distrust women.

—H. L. MENCKEN (ATTRIBUTED)

There are two ways to handle a woman, and nobody knows either of them.

—KIN HUBBARD

How can you tell which bottle contains the PMS medicine?
   It's the one with bite marks on the cap.

I used to walk into a party and scan the room for attractive women. Now I look for women to hold my baby so I can eat potato salad sitting down.

—PAUL REISER

Women today may not know how to cook, but they sure know what's cooking.

Never argue with a woman when she's tired . . . or when she's rested.

Women who think they are the equal of men lack ambition.

A good woman is like a good bar . . . liquor in the front and poker in the rear.

Why is it so hard for women to find men that are sensitive, caring, and good-looking?
Because they already have boyfriends.

What's the difference between a terrorist and a woman with PMS?
You can negotiate with a terrorist.

What is the difference between a pit bull and a woman with PMS?
Lip gloss.

Why did God create women?
Because after one look at Adam, He realized man was going to need some help.

Work

Phillips fancied himself quite the ladies man, so when his cruise ship went down in a storm and he found himself stranded on a desert island with six women, he couldn't believe his good fortune. They quickly agreed that each woman would have one night a week with the only man. Phillips threw himself into the arrangement with gusto, working even on his day off, but as the weeks stretched into months, he found himself looking forward to that day of rest more and more eagerly.

One afternoon he was sitting on the beach and wishing for some more men to share his duties when he caught sight of a man waving from a life raft that was bobbing on the waves. Phillips swam out, pulled the raft to shore, and did a little jig of happiness. "You can't believe how happy I am to see you," he cried.

The new fellow eyed him up and down and cooed, "You're a sight for sore eyes, too, you gorgeous thing."

"Shit," sighed Phillips, "there go my Sundays."

First employee: So, is your job secure?
Second employee: Oh, yes. It's me they can do without.

A conference is a gathering of important people who singly can do nothing but together can decide that nothing can be done.

—FRED ALLEN

Business meetings are important—because they're one way of demonstrating how many people the company can operate without.

The nearest customer was five stools away, but that didn't keep Josh from leaning over toward the bartender and commenting, "Geez, there's a lousy smell in here." A few minutes later he added, "It smells just like . . . shit." Puzzled by the origin of the stench, he moved closer to the other customer, and sure enough, the smell worsened. "Phew, you really stink," he pointed out.

"I know," said the man apologetically. "It's because of my job." Seeing that Josh was interested in a further explanation, he went on, "I'm with an elephant act, and before each show I have to give the elephant an enema so he doesn't take a dump during the performance. Frankly, it's a tricky business, because I have to administer it quickly and then jump back. And sometimes I just don't move fast enough."

"Jesus," commiserated Josh, shaking his head. "How much do they pay you for this lousy job?"

"Eighty-five bucks a week," said the man cheerfully.

"You've got to be kidding. Why don't you quit?"

"What?" retorted the man, "and get out of show business?!"

How can I retire? I still have three hundred glossy pictures and two hundred dollars worth of makeup left.

—MILTON BERLE

I got a job as a short-order cook. I was cooking a chicken on the rotisserie, I was turning the wheel, and I was singing "Arrivederci, Roma," and a drunk came by and said, "You've got a nice voice, but your monkey's on fire."

—LONDON LEE

He and I had an office so tiny that an inch smaller and it would have been adultery.

—DOROTHY PARKER

Guidelines for Bureaucrats:
1. **When in charge, ponder.**
2. **When in trouble, delegate.**
3. **When in doubt, mumble.**

"Working hard, Stan?"

"Nah, I'm fooling the boss," replied the laborer with a wink. "He thinks I'm working, but I'm carrying the same load of cement up and down all day."

Well, we can't stand around here doing nothing, people will think we're workmen.

—SPIKE MILLIGAN

The six phases of a project:
1. Enthusiasm
2. Disillusionment

3. Panic and hysteria

4. Search for the guilty

5. Punishment of the innocent

6. Praise and honor for the nonparticipants

"So tell me, Ms. Harris," asked the interviewer, "have you any other skills you think might be worth mentioning?"

"Actually, yes," said the applicant modestly. "Last year I had two short stories published in national magazines, and I finished a novel."

"Very impressive," he commented, "but I was thinking of skills you could apply during office hours."

The applicant explained brightly, "Oh, that *was* during office hours."

"All the other presidents did what I told them. This one thinks he's bigger than Winchell," complained Walter Winchell about Harry Truman one night at the Stork Club. "We had a lulu of an argument yesterday and he hasn't called me to at least say he's sorry."

"Walter, why don't you call *him*," suggested Joey Adams. "He's a pretty busy man, he's the president of the United States of America, he's got a big country to run."

"*He's* busy?" he screamed. "*He's* busy? Does he have six columns and a radio show to get out every week?"

—Joey Adams, about Walter Winchell

"Now tell me, Miss Gundell," asked the senior partner to the very junior employee, "what is the main purpose of a holiday?"

"To impress upon the employees that the company can get along without them," she responded promptly.

Work is the greatest thing in the world, so we should always save some of it for tomorrow.

—Don Herold

The boss looked over the efficiency report on the new employee and added a few words of his own. "Hedges is a definite asset to the firm. She is efficient, discreet, energetic, creative, and—best of all—she makes the other people in her department very nervous."

I used to have a job in the Kotex factory. I thought I was making mattresses for mice.

—Ray Scott

Two dimwitted ditch diggers got upset because they did all the hard work and received only one-tenth of the pay of the crew boss. Finally, deciding to confront his boss, one guy climbed out of the ditch and went over to the foreman, who was leaning against a tree, reading the racing form.

"How come we do all the hard work while you sit here and earn ten times as much?" he demanded.

"Intelligence," was the crew boss's answer. "Let me give you an example." He put his hand in front of the tree. "See my hand? Hit it as hard as you can." The ditch digger took a mighty swing, the boss moved his hand at the last minute, and commented to the worker, now clutching his bruised fist, "See what I mean?"

Back in the ditch, the second guy eagerly questioned his friend. "It's a matter of intelligence," was the reply. "Let me give you an example: hit my hand as hard as you can." And he held it up in front of his face.

Anyone can do any amount of work, provided it isn't the work he is supposed to be doing at that moment.

—Robert Benchley

According to the latest statistics, there are [current figure] million Americans who aren't working. And there are plenty more if you count the ones with jobs.

Sexual harassment at work—is it a problem for the self-employed?

—Victoria Wood

The worse job I ever had was working in a Fotomat booth. I was the only one at the Christmas party.

—Mark Dobrient

Index